Date Due

MAR 0 9 2017			
MAR 2 0 2017			

LONE STAR STALAG

LONE STAR STALAG

GERMAN PRISONERS OF WAR AT CAMP HEARNE

MICHAEL R. WATERS

with

Mark Long, William Dickens, Sam Sweitz, Anna Lee Presley, Ian Buvit,

Michelle Raisor, Bryan Mason, Hilary Standish, and Norbert Dannhaeuser

Foreword by Willi Nellessen

Texas A&M University Press
College Station

The paper used in this book meets the minimum requirements
of the American National Standard for Permanence
of Paper for Printed Library Materials, Z39.48-1984.
Binding materials have been chosen for durability.
⊗

Library of Congress Cataloging-in-Publication Data

Waters, Michael R.
   Lone Star Stalag : German prisoners of war at Camp Hearne / by Michael R. Waters with
Mark Long . . . [et al.].—1st ed.
       p. cm.
Includes bibliographical references and index.
   ISBN 1-58544-318-2 (alk. paper)
   1. Camp Hearne—History. 2. Camp Hearne—Management. 3. World War, 1939–1945—
Prisoners and prisons, American. 4. Prisoners of war—Germany 5. Prisoners of war—United
States. I. Title.
D805.5.C365W38 2004
940.54'72764239—dc22
                                                                                        2003023762

Contents

Tables

Foreword

WITHIN THE LAST DECADES I had the opportunity to talk with American tourists and visitors in Germany as well as American citizens when I visited the United States in 1980, 1995, and 1999. Some of these people were surprised when they heard that I had spent nearly three years as a prisoner of war (POW) in Texas. They did not know that nearly 380,000 German prisoners of war lived in American POW camps at the end of the World War II.

I thus think it was a very good idea that Michael R. Waters and his colleagues write a book about the history of Camp Hearne in order to preserve this part of American history for coming generations.

I am grateful both to God and the Americans who stood guard at Camp Hearne during those terrible last two years of the war. I am especially glad to see this book published because of the information about the camp's history it contains, including a number of things I did not know about before reading it.

Lone Star Stalag is based on a thorough study of documents found in archives, newspapers, and interviews with still-living former POWs, guards, citizens of Hearne, and local farmers. The combination of facts with the memories expressed by the many interviewed persons as well as the results of archeological excavations make the book exciting reading matter.

The Geneva Convention states that captured officers and noncommissioned officers are not obliged to work. Our captors minded the rules as long as the war lasted and we were impressed by the tolerance shown by the American officers, guards, and farmers. It all was somewhat unusual for us.

I took the opportunity to learn in the camp's school instead of working somewhere. This was very important for me because just six months after my repatriation in 1947 I started studying in a bank academy. Partly owing to the training I received at Camp Hearne I was successful at the academy and thus fulfilled one of the requirements needed to attain important positions. For more than twenty years I have been a member of the board and for the last ten years the chairman of a bank. The educational activities at Camp Hearne were one of the foundation stones of my long and successful professional life. This is one of the reasons why I never forget the time I spent there. Of course, it was hard for a young man to be a prisoner far from his mother country and divided from his dear ones at home. It seemed at times that our repatriation would not occur until far in the future. I spent four long years as a POW, three in the United States and another in the United Kingdom. Looking back, I am convinced that the time I spent at Camp Hearne was the best.

I am so glad that Michael Waters came to Germany to interview us. Despite the difference in our ages, he became a good friend to a number of former POWs. He took care of us when we came to a reunion and brought us together with some of our former guards. This reunion trip was the beginning of friendships which will last as long as I live. The grandchildren of one former guard became pen-pals with three of my grandchildren. Two grandsons flew to America without their parents and spent two weeks of their vacation as guests of the family of one guard's daughter. Now we are looking forward to the promised visit of the boys and their whole family.

All of this serves as proof of the lasting validity of the motto of the veterans of the German Afrika Korps: "Former enemies became friends." I am sure that we, our children, and our grandchildren will be friends forever.

I write this foreword as a representative for the comrades and former POWs who came to a reunion at Hearne in 1999: Werner Kritzler, Walter Fricke, Heino Erichsen, Alfred Jasper, and Erich Spix. All of them took advantage of the varied activities at the camp and all returned healthy and were successful in their professions.

Fritz Haus, one of the former POWs, wrote that his American friend, Chaplain G. A. Zoch was hopeful we prisoners would reject Hitler's tyrannical and oppressive rule by force and work for a new democratic Germany that will rise from the ashes after the war.

This hope has been realized and I am sure that the former POWs played an important part in the reconstruction of a democratic Germany as they built a dignified future for their families and themselves.

Willi Nellessen
Former POW, Camp Hearne
1943–45

Preface

I HAVE LONG HAD A STRONG INTEREST in twentieth century world history, especially the conflicts of World Wars I and II. My father, John D. Waters, served in the navy during the Second World War and told me many stories when I was young. One of the stories I remember is about the German prisoners of war my dad saw every day working around the naval base in New Orleans, where he was stationed in 1944–45. He told me that sometimes when he and his buddies were walking by the POW compound, they would hold up the newspaper and show the Germans the headlines, teasing them by shouting, "We're winning; you're losing!" The Germans would yell back, "Propaganda!" He also told me stories of several POW escapes. They were not dramatic and dangerous, like the one depicted in the movie *The Great Escape,* but instead were almost comical and benign incidents. He recalled that most escapees just wanted to get out and go to the French Quarter to have a good time. When they were done having fun, they would go to a barbershop and sit down for a haircut. The barber would then call the Military Police and they would come and pick up the prisoner—after his hair had been cut—and return him to camp.

The Camp Hearne project allowed me a chance to combine my personal interest in World War II history with my professional interest in archaeology. I usually pursue studies of the archaeology and geology of Paleolithic sites in Russia, Paleoamerican sites in North America, or late prehistoric Hohokam sites in Arizona. This project was something completely different.

The Camp Hearne project began after I read Arnold Krammer's book *Nazi Prisoners of War in America.* In his book, I noted, was information about a POW camp on the outskirts of Hearne, Texas, just twenty miles north of where I live. I visited the area several times, but was at first unsuccessful in locating the camp's grounds. I eventually discovered its remains after I received more detailed directions from Paul Russell. The foundations of the old buildings and grounds were completely covered by thick vegetation. One literally had to be standing on the cement foundations in order to see them. Paul Russell showed me a collection of artifacts that included buttons, coins, canteens, and other items he had recovered from the site. After seeing the site and Russell's collection, I thought that an investigation of Camp Hearne would make an interesting project.

Although there are many books on the general POW experience both at the national (Bailey 1981; Carlson 1997; Krammer 1996) and regional (Billinger 2000; Choate 1989; Cowley 2002; Geiger 1996; Hoza 1995; Koop 1998; May 1995; Powell 1989; Simmons 2000; Thompson 1993; Walker 2001) level, no single POW camp such as Camp Hearne has ever been intensively investigated. The study of Camp Hearne was undertaken to provide a comprehensive account of the POW experience at a typical POW camp, by recording as much as possible about its history before aspects of that story were forever lost. This was accomplished by studying historical documents in the archives and repositories of many organizations; interviewing former POWs, guards, and citizens who experienced the camp; and conducting archaeological investigations at the camp.

Each of these three data sets—the documents, personal accounts, and archaeological evidence—provides a different perspective on Camp Hearne. The archival research provides such basic information as how many prisoners were at the camp, when they arrived, when they left, what types of problems occurred at the camp, how many prisoners worked, and other factual data. The interviews are firsthand accounts that bring a human element to the research, providing information about daily life not documented in archival records or existing books. These oral histories offer insights into camp life, activities, and events. Finally, the archaeological excavations uncovered artifacts that were made and used by the POWs as well as features that were built by the POWs but not recorded in the archival documents and are only remembered by a very few. By melding these historical, archaeological, and ethnographic data together, a comprehensive and multidimensional account of the POW experience at a large camp in the United States emerged. This would not have been possible with just a single data set.

One other point is worth making: Although the abbreviation P.W. most often appears in World War II documents describing prisoners of war, this book uses POW, the more prevalent and widely recognized abbreviation employed today.

Lone Star Stalag would not have been possible without the support of many people at Texas A&M University and the dedication of a small group of graduate students (my coauthors). To conduct this research, I put together several graduate research seminars centered around the investigation of the old camp. Together, we conducted archeological excavations at the camp and involved undergraduate students in the field research. I collected information from many archives and Norbert Dannhaeuser, a friend and colleague, traveled to Germany to record the oral histories of many former POWs. In addition, my students and I collected additional oral histories from local citizens and former guards. We then went on to analyze these artifacts, documents, and oral histories. A final seminar resulted in the preparation of the first draft of this manuscript.

This study has been one of the most enjoyable and rewarding research projects I have ever undertaken. Along the way, I met many wonderful people who openly shared their stories with me. All were glad that I was asking about Camp Hearne. Many of the former prisoners I interviewed told me that this was the first time anyone had ever asked them about their experiences outside of their families, friends, and old comrades. It was a chance for them to let their stories be heard and remembered. As news of the project spread, I heard from many people: former guards, former POWs, citizens who visited the camp as children or worked there, and sons and daughters of former guards and POWs. All have graciously shared their stories, photographs, and other camp memorabilia. It is a project that never ended and probably never will. I continue to hear from people who were somehow involved with the camp. It is always exciting when I see a letter from someone I do not know in my mailbox and it turns out to be someone who wants to provide more information about the camp.

Sadly, as happened with my father in April, 2001, the World War II generation is quickly passing away. Now is the time to act if we are to preserve their history and stories for future generations. What follows is the story of Camp Hearne as told from archaeological evidence, historical documents, and the recollections of those who were there. This book is divided into seven chapters. The first four present the story of Camp Hearne through the analysis of historical documents and personal accounts. Chapters 5 and 6 describe the archaeological investigations, including a discussion of the artifacts, features, and structures found at the site combined with insights provided from the oral histories. The final chapter describes Camp Hearne's lasting legacy.

Every piece of ground has a story to tell. The cement slabs and decaying fountains obscured by vegetation at the site where Camp Hearne once stood echo a forgotten time and provide a portrait of a bustling city of nearly five thousand men brought together by world conflict. This is their story.

This book could not have been written without the help and support of numerous individuals and institutions.

Former POWs held at Camp Hearne who provided valuable insights about the camp include: Carl Bruns, Arno Einicke, Heino Erichsen, Walter Fricke, Ernst Froembsdorf, Hans Goebeler, Robert Goede, Fritz Haus, Peter Hermann, Alfred Jasper, Werner Kritzler, Walter Koch, Hans Lammersdorf, Hermann Leonhardt, Willi Nellessen, Fritz Pferdekämper-Geissel, Joseph Pohl, Otto Schulz, Erich Spix, Peter Spoden, Hugo Wannemacher, and Walter Werner. I want to thank all these men for taking the time to share with me their stories, experiences, photographs, and mementos from Camp Hearne. Arno Einicke, Heino Erichsen, Walter Fricke, Ernst Froembsdorf, Alfred Jasper, Werner Kritzler, Willi Nellessen, Fritz Pferdekämper-Geissel, Joseph Pohl, Peter Spoden, and Hugo Wannemacher kindly opened their homes to me and Norbert Dannhaeuser during our visit to Germany. Fritz Haus traveled all the way from South Africa to visit me in Texas and share his diaries and stories.

Former Camp Hearne guards who provided important information include: Francis Burdick, Tom Bussell, Tex Geyser, Pat Hughes, Ken Johns, Jack Kuttruff,

John Luparelli, Ben Mason, Ed Munson, Paul Reinhold, John Shugars, Bobby Sullivan, and Matt Ware. These individuals provided valuable insights about their time at Camp Hearne and shared their photographs and souvenirs of the camp.

Current and former Hearne and Brazos Valley residents who provided valuable information and stories included: Wanda Burdick, Doris Emshoff, Roy Henry, Inez Lawney, Virgie Lout, E. R. Mason, Johnoween Mathis, Pat Mathis, Norman McCarver, John Nigliazzo, Helen Palmos, Bill Palmos, Mildred Payne, Jim Stegall, Annie Sweat, Tommy Ryan, and Glenn Zoch. All kindly shared their stories and photographs of the camp.

The following individuals and organizations are acknowledged for their contributions: Jason Barrett, Amy Borgens, Mary Dorsey, Lorie Hanson, Steve Hoza, Arnold Krammer, Karl Kuttruff, Laverne Light, Tom Lincoln and Christine Kaiser, Jim Lyle, Arland Marlette, Scott Minchak, Don McGruder, Kathy Neal, Bruce Nightengale, James Nowak, Tony Painter, Bill Presnell, Kathryn Quackenbush, Eugene Sharick, Michael Luick-Thrams, Mark Valvo, and the Center for Ecological Archaeology at Texas A&M University. All kindly provided assistance, equipment, or other information about Camp Hearne. Special thanks goes to Norbert Dannhaeuser for his willingness to travel to Germany and to translate during the interviews conducted with former POWs. In addition, he was always willing to translate letters and documents whenever I needed them.

I want to thank all the Hearne, Texas, city officials and personnel for their assistance with the Camp Hearne project. Without their cooperation and assistance, none of this would have been possible. Floyd Hafley and Ken Pryor, former Hearne city managers, allowed me to investigate the site and encouraged my research. Robert Penney, the director of public works, arranged for the mowing and burning of the property, which allowed better access for the study. Robert Nelson, the supervisor of parks and recreation, and his crews were responsible for the mowing and assisted the project in many ways. I would especially like to thank Kathy Stracener, former president of the Hearne Heritage League, for her support during the entire project. I could always depend on Kathy for support and help whenever I asked. I also want to acknowledge Cathy Lazarus for her ongoing efforts to preserve the camp and establish a museum in Hearne to make Camp Hearne's story accessible to the public.

Finally, I thank Paul Russell. Paul spent many years investigating Camp Hearne and was the first person to show me the site and the artifacts he collected there. Paul freely shared his knowledge of the camp and allowed me to examine, borrow, and photograph his collections. Paul several times lent his expertise to the project in the field assisting with the survey. This study would be less complete without his insights and assistance.

Numerous students from Texas A&M University helped with the investigations at Camp Hearne. Members of the 1996 field class included: Steve Ahr, Carolyn Boyd, Damon Burden, Bill Dickens, Jeff Johnson, and Lee Presley. Members of the 1997 field class included: Amy Dase, Bill Dickens, Michelle Huebner, Mark Long, Bryan Mason, Lee Presley, Michelle Raisor, and Sam Sweitz. All of these students worked in the field conducting surveys and excavation, as well as archival research and interviews. Mark Long, Bill Dickens, Sam Sweitz, Lee Presley, Ian Buvit, Bryan Mason, Hilary Standish, and Michelle Raisor assisted in the organization of the archaeological data and with the synthesis of the archival documents and oral histories. Mark Long and Michelle Raisor were particularly helpful in the final stages of the preparation of this manuscript. In addition, Karisa Terry, Allen Bettis, John Dockall, and Lorie Gillmartin assisted with the fieldwork. Finally, we were assisted by more than three hundred undergraduate students from introductory anthropology classes at Texas A&M University. These students worked in the field clearing brush from foundations, excavating units and features, and in the sorting and cataloging of artifacts. Thanks are due to all of them for their efforts.

I thank the personnel at the following archives for their assistance: the National Archives, College Park, Maryland; the National Archives–Southwest Region, Fort Worth, Texas; the Texas A&M University Archives, College Station; the Institute for Oral History at Baylor University, Waco, Texas; the archives of the *Hearne Democrat*, Hearne, Texas; the archives of the International Committee of the Red Cross, Geneva, Switzerland; the archives of the World Alliance of the Young Men's Christian Associations (YMCA), Geneva, Switzerland; the U.S. Army Court of Criminal Appeals, Falls Church, Virginia; the Alexander Turnball Library, Wellington, New Zealand; the Imperial War Museum, London; and the Library of Congress, Washington, D.C.

Financial support was provided from numerous organizations, including: the Hearne Heritage League; White's Electronics; the Department of Anthropology, the College of Geosciences, and the Center for Teaching Excellence, Texas A&M University; the Texas A&M University Mini-Grant Program; the College of Liberal Arts Faculty Fellowship; and an Interdisciplinary Research Initiative Grant from the Office of the Vice President for Research, Texas A&M University. I also thank the College of Liberal Arts and Roll Call: Friends of Camp Hearne, a nonprofit organization dedicated to the preservation of Camp Hearne, for the generous assistance they provided to make this book more affordable.

Finally, I wish to thank my wife, Susan, and daughter, Kate, for their help with and support of this project.

LONE STAR STALAG

CHAPTER 1

The Prisoners Arrive at Camp Hearne

LARGE NUMBERS OF AXIS SOLDIERS surrendered to the Allies during the Second World War. The first combatants taken prisoner by the American army belonged to Field Marshal Erwin Rommel's Afrika Korps. German soldiers captured in North Africa in 1943 (fig. 1), as well as other prisoners captured by the American and British armies later in the war, were brought across the Atlantic Ocean and interned at prisoner of war (POW) camps throughout the United States. By June, 1945, more than 425,000 Axis POWs (approximately 371,000 Germans, 50,000 Italians, and 4,000 Japanese) were housed in more than 650 POW camps (some 125 main and 425 branch camps) across the United States. Of these, 22 main camps and 48 branch camps were located in Texas.

One of the first and largest POW camps in the United States was located on the outskirts of Hearne, Texas. Camp Hearne, as it was known, housed more than forty-eight hundred German soldiers from 1943 to 1945. This is Camp Hearne's story. It is a human story of survival and conflict as told from documents, the men who were there, and the artifacts they left behind.

PLANNING AND CONSTRUCTING THE CAMP

In 1942, the U.S. Army Provost Marshal General's Office (PMGO) was searching for suitable locations at which to build POW camps. The civic leaders of Hearne, Texas (a rural agricultural community of thirty-five hundred residents) knew they did not have the manpower and infrastructure to attract a war-related manufacturing plant, so they decided to lobby for the construction of a POW camp because they thought it would bring economic prosperity to their town. Representative Luther Johnson received a letter from Hearne Chamber of Commerce president Roy Henry, dated March 10, 1942, suggesting Hearne as a possible location for a camp (Bryan 1942a). The congressman in turn contacted Col. B. M. Bryan of the PMGO with this proposal (Johnson 1942). After receiving additional information from Hearne officials, Colonel Bryan dispatched engineers to Hearne to conduct a preliminary survey of the area (Office of the

Fig. 1. German soldiers surrender to a British tank crew in Tunisia, May, 1943. Photography courtesy of the Imperial War Museum, London.

Chief of Engineers 1942; Robins 1942). The inspection was completed by mid-April and in June a site one-half mile northwest of Hearne was selected as a suitable location for a POW camp. Hearne fit the criteria for an ideal camp location: it was located in a rural setting far from critical war industries, it was not within the coastal blackout zone (which extended 170 miles inland from the coast), and it was over 150 miles from the Mexican border (fig. 2; Krammer 1996).

On June 30, 1942, Colonel Bryan approved the plans for a three-thousand-man POW camp at Hearne (fig. 3) and in July, 1942, the U.S. government acquired 720 acres from five landowners at a cost of $27,500. On September 26, after several unsuccessful submissions, the PMGO approved the final camp layout and construction began almost immediately (Bryan 1942b).

Construction of the camp, the largest building project Robertson County had ever witnessed, progressed rapidly (*Hearne Democrat* 1942a). Heartened by the prospect of short- and long-term economic gain, Hearne's residents enthusiastically supported the camp's construction. Transient workers contributed to the local economy by quickly filling motels and renting rooms in private homes (*Hearne Democrat* 1942b, 1942c). Local farmers were eager to begin using POW labor in their fields because of the labor shortage created by the military draft.

As the town's residents watched the construction progress, some became concerned that the facility being built for the POWs was too nice and were suspicious that the U.S. government would coddle the prisoners. Local business-man Jack Morgan complained to his congressman, Rep. Tom Connally, when he discovered that an auditorium was being built at the camp:

> One of the things that makes me as well as most tax-payers a bit hot is the way money is being thrown away on things that are simply silly.
> The point in mind at this time is the Internment Camp being built at Hearne, Texas. I have just had a request for prices on lighting mate-rial for their auditorium.
> It strikes me that this kindness idea is being taken advantage of, when we have to furnish auditoriums for prisoners.
> I wonder how many stage shows etc., our boys in Japan and Ger-many enjoy (Morgan 1942).

Representative Connally assured Morgan that the auditorium (which was, in fact, a recreation room) was intended for use by American servicemen and not the foreign prisoners. The concerns voiced by Morgan and others regarding the

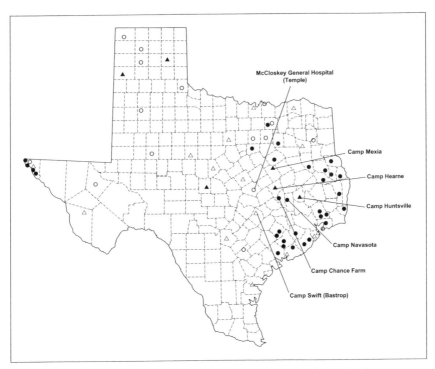

Fig. 2. Map showing the location of POW camps in Texas. Those camps discussed in the text are identified by name. Filled triangles are base camps that were not associated with military bases; open triangles are base camps that were associated with military bases; filled circles are agricultural branch camps; unfilled circles are branch camps associated with military bases (classification from Walker 2001). Camp Hearne Collection, Texas A&M University.

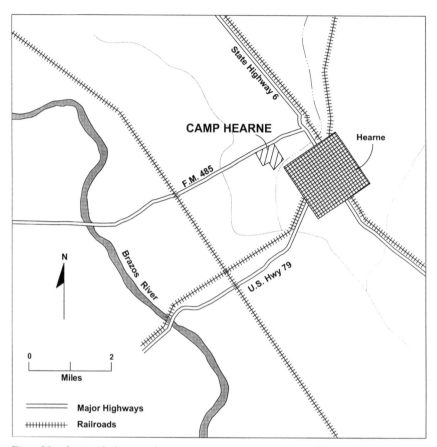

Fig. 3. Map showing the location of Camp Hearne, just to the northwest of the city of Hearne, Texas.

overindulgence of prisoners arose out of the fact that the POW compounds and barracks were built to the same specifications and quality as those in the American compound. This was because of America's strict adherence to the Geneva Convention concerning prisoners of war, which states that POWs must be fed and housed in the same manner as soldiers of the country holding the prisoners.

The camp's construction was largely completed by December, 1942, but detail work continued until February, 1943. The camp commander, Lt. Col. Albert Tucker, arrived in December and the camp was organized, supplied, and staffed. It was officially activated on December 15, 1942.

Originally designed to hold about three thousand prisoners, the camp's capacity was increased to forty-eight hundred when the army reduced its regulation space requirements from sixty to forty square feet per man. In January, 1943, someone suggested that a thousand-man compound be added at Camp Hearne to hold German officers. However, the army believed the electrical supply was insufficient and scrapped the plan, despite the efforts of local officials to assure the army that sufficient electrical power was available (Henry 1943).

Camp Layout

Camp Hearne's basic layout conformed to U.S. Army standards. Only about fifty-eight of the 720 acres acquired by the army were used for the buildings and grounds. A total of 250 buildings were constructed at the camp, which was divided into three main areas: the POW compounds, the hospital, and the American sector (fig. 4; U.S. Engineers Office 1943).

The majority of the camp consisted of three prisoner compounds, which were numbered 1, 2, and 3 from west to east. Each was approximately eight acres in size and contained fifty buildings. In addition, each compound was subdivided into four company areas. Each company area had eight barracks, a mess hall, a lavatory, a company office, and two open areas. At the north end of each compound were an administration building, infirmary, post exchange (PX), and two recreation buildings that serviced the entire compound (U.S. Engineers Office 1943).

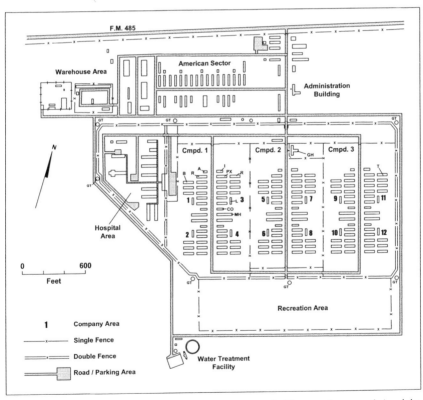

Fig. 4. Layout of Camp Hearne. Shown are the POW compounds (Compounds 1, 2, and 3) and the other sectors of the camp. Boldface numbers identify the German company areas. Specific buildings are identified on the map: A = administration building, I = infirmary, R = recreation building, PX = post exchange or canteen, L = lavatory, B = barrack, CO = company office, MH = mess hall, T = theater (Deutsche Bühne), GT = guard tower, GH = guardhouse.

The buildings within the compounds were not designed to be permanent structures. They were temporary "war mobilization" structures designed to last for twenty years. Each of the barracks had wooden floors supported by beams that rested on brick piers. The other buildings—latrines, mess halls, offices, and common buildings—had cement foundations. All of the buildings, regardless of foundation type, had walls composed of wooden beams covered by black tar paper and asphalt roofs (fig. 5; Garner 1993; Kriv 1993).

A gravel-lined road bisected each compound. Fire hydrants lined the street and a drainage ditch ran parallel to it. Gravel pathways connected the barrack areas and other buildings, and narrow cement bridges spanned the drainage ditches. Walkways were necessary because the ground became muddy when wet. Just outside the compounds, but still within the security zone, was a building where prisoners could meet with visitors and a guardhouse for disciplinary cases. South of the compounds was an eight-acre recreation area for the prisoners. Two side-by-side fences separated this open area from the rest of the camp (U.S. Engineers Office 1943).

To the west of the prison compounds was a seven-acre hospital complex with fourteen buildings. Within this complex stood a variety of facilities: a modern operating room, x-ray facility, medical laboratories, dental clinic, and seven fully staffed wards. In addition, there were storehouses, an administration building, and a mess hall within the hospital grounds. The hospital complex, which

Fig. 5. View of barracks in the American compound. Barracks in the German compounds were identical in construction. All of the buildings at Camp Hearne were "war mobilization" structures. Most had wooden floors and walls made of black tar paper over two-by-four studs. Camp Hearne Collection, Texas A&M University.

included a single barrack and lavatory for the use of German medical officers, was separated from the adjacent compound and the American sector to the north by two barbed-wire fences (U.S. Engineers Office 1943).

For security, two ten-foot-tall fences strung with barbed wire surrounded the compounds, recreation area, and hospital complex. The upper two feet of the fence was bent inward at an angle to discourage prisoners from trying to climb it. Lights suspended from poles were located every 150 feet along the fence line and seven guard towers were positioned outside the fences at strategic locations in order to provide total visibility of the camp. In addition, a road encircled the entire camp, thus allowing the guards to regularly patrol the camp's perimeter. A single barbed-wire fence separated the compounds (U.S. Engineers Office 1943). A line of poles strung with a low wire was set five feet from the inside of the perimeter fence and the fences separating the compounds. Prisoners were not allowed to enter the space between this low fence and the main fence.

The American sector was situated at the north end of the camp. In the center of this area were the facilities for the guard and service units. These included eighteen enlisted men's barracks, five lavatories, five mess halls, five company offices, and a recreation building. Wooden boardwalks connected these facilities. To the east were three barracks that housed the officers, lavatories, nurses' quarters, a mess hall, administration building, officers' club, and PX. The commanding officer had a small private residence at the entrance to the camp.

To the east of the American compound was the POW cemetery. To the west was a complex of warehouses, maintenance shops, and other facilities. Just outside the entrance to the prison compounds stood the guardhouse for soldiers on duty, the fire station, and two water towers (U.S. Engineers Office 1943). Gravel-lined roads provided access to all areas in the American compound and a single low fence encircled it.

The local power company supplied electricity, but the camp obtained water from its own well, which had been dug just outside the compounds (McCarver 1958). A modern waste treatment facility was constructed away from the camp to handle all of the waste it generated. Camp Hearne was clearly a city unto itself: when staffed with the American guard and service units and filled with POWs, it had a population greater than the city after which it was named.

THE AMERICANS

About five hundred personnel from the Eighth Service Command were assigned to guard the POWs and operate the camp. The 346th and the 420th Military Police Escort Guard Units were assigned the guard mission and also provided escorts for prisoners coming to Hearne from North Africa and Great Britain, and from Hearne to other camps in the United States. The 1805th Service Unit was responsible for camp administration as well as guarding prisoners.

Camp Hearne had six commanding officers during the course of its operation. The first, Lieutenant Colonel Tucker, was recalled to active duty from retirement and served from December, 1942, until about October, 1943. He was followed by Lt. Col. Robert Whitson (October, 1943, to February, 1944), Lt. Col. John Dunn (February to August, 1944), Lt. Col. Cecil Stiles (August, 1944, to January, 1945), Lt. Col. Napoleon Rainbolt (January to June, 1945), and Maj. Theodore Zaetsch (June, 1945, to closing. See Fischer 1944; Greuter 1944; *Hearne Democrat* 1942d, 1943, 1945a; Perret 1945).

The guards worked in groups, patrolling within the compounds and around the camp's perimeter. One noncommissioned officer (NCO) and two privates were stationed in each compound. They patrolled on foot inside the compounds at irregular intervals every day from 6:30 A.M. until 11 P.M. to ensure that POWs did not engage in "unauthorized meetings" and that the fences had no "defects in the wire that would facilitate easy escape." The external perimeter patrol consisted of three soldiers in a vehicle that monotonously drove in circles around the camp at a maximum speed of twelve miles per hour. A .30-caliber machine gun sat atop a swivel pedestal mount in the truck bed and each man also carried a rifle and sidearm. At least two guards were also stationed in each of the seven guard towers located around the camp's perimeter. These men were armed with rifles and automatic weapons. Sentries also walked between the guard towers in the corridor between the two exterior compound fences (Shaw 1944).

The GIs at Camp Hearne performed a wide variety of related tasks. For example, they searched the prisoners when they returned from work details, assisted with the morning and evening roll calls, conducted clerical work, repaired vehicles, and so on. In short, they did everything required to keep the camp operating smoothly (Shaw 1944; Dorwart 1944).

When they were off duty the guards attended to personal chores at the camp, but they preferred to spend the bulk of their free time in town. As a result, a relationship developed between the local civilians and the military personnel stationed at the camp. When asked whether the local people were worried about POWs escaping, former guard Tex Geyser recalled: "At first they were more worried about the GIs than the prisoners. In Hearne, you couldn't buy whiskey in that town but you could buy beer and there was lots of beer joints in that town. And the GIs would get wound up pretty good." The Blue Moon Dance Club was a favorite watering hole and many of the guards spent their free time in town on the weekends "looking for girls and drinking beer." Helen Palmos, who ran the City Cafe in Hearne, served a lot of GIs. She tried to save her allotment of beer for her local civilian customers, because she knew that the GIs had plenty available to them at camp. Nevertheless, some of the men preferred to drink in town. On one occasion, recalled Mrs. Palmos, "this sergeant decided when he was at the Dixie [Cafe that] he wanted a beer and he was going to get one and he tore the Dixie place up. I mean he whacked the chairs and everything." The sergeant then went to the City Cafe and asked the waitress there for a beer. According to Mrs. Palmos, the waitress said: "'We cannot sell you beer.' And he said, 'Yes, you're selling beer and I want a beer.' He said, 'If you don't serve it, I'll get it.' He walked over and lifted up the door to the beer case. I put my butcher knife in his belly and said 'Open it up and I'll open you up.' I mean, the GIs and everybody else left the cafe, and then came the MPs [military policemen]. And the MP asked me if I was having any trouble. I looked at him and said 'Sergeant, are we having any trouble?' And he said, 'No ma'am.' So he left on out." The following day the sergeant went back to the cafe and apologized to Mrs. Palmos. He was especially grateful to her for not filing a complaint against him, which would have resulted in his demotion. From that point on, the GIs did not give Mrs. Palmos any trouble.

Despite occasional problems, Hearne's residents generally felt that the camp was an asset to the town. Businesses profited from their presence and grew, and some of the GIs married local women. The general attitude was: since the camp had to be somewhere, why not Hearne? For the most part, the people in town treated the guards well. A large United Service Organization (USO) club was located downtown and dances and other activities were held there. In addition, soldiers frequented the movie theater. Many residents also "adopted" soldiers, knowing that they were far from home and family, and would invite them to their homes for Sunday dinner. Some rented rooms to married soldiers and their wives.

The Prisoners

The first prisoners, a contingent of four hundred German enlisted men and noncommissioned officers from the Afrika Korps, arrived at Camp Hearne on June 3, 1943 (fig. 6; Fischer 1943a; Schwieger and Shannahan 1945). It was an exciting time for the town's residents. Roy Henry, then a high school sophomore,

Fig. 6. A group of German soldiers in their Afrika Korps uniforms and caps, one sporting an Iron Cross, pose outside of one of the hospital buildings. Camp Hearne Collection, Texas A&M University.

Fig. 7. Guard Kenneth Johns at Camp Hearne in 1943. Johns was a sergeant in the 346th MPEG stationed at Camp Hearne from the summer of 1943 to the spring of 1944. Camp Hearne Collection, Texas A&M University.

saw the first trainload of POWs arrive. He recalls that their arrival was announced in school and that everyone ran to watch. The prisoners were unloaded from a Southern Pacific Railroad train at 10:40 A.M. near the intersection of State Highway 6 and F.M. 485, and were marched four-abreast to the camp (Woods 1943a). The military authorities blocked the roads and told the townspeople to remain in their homes, but the townspeople wandered into the fields to see their new "neighbors." Most were struck by how young the captives were. Roy Henry observed that they were "not much older than myself."

Former guard Tex Geyser recalled that "the first ones were in bad shape . . . straight off the battlefields." Kenneth Johns (fig. 7, 1996), another guard who was present that day, said: "We took them off the train right out there and marched them into camp. We had jeeps with machine guns on them because we didn't know if they were going to break and run or what. We had machine guns mounted up on the ridges above the road all the way back to camp. Some were

Table 1. German POW Population at Camp Hearne

Date	Enlisted Men	NCOs	EM+NCO	Officers	Total
July, 1943					2275
August			2280		2280
September			3251		3251
October			4702		4702
November			4575		4575
December			4465	2	4567
January, 1944			4467	2	4469
February			4456	2	4458
March			2799	2	2801
April			3434	4	3438
May			3166	3	3169
June			3054	3	3057
July			3050	3	3053
August			3069	3	3072
September			2945	3	2948
October			3310	2	3312
November	572	3225	3797	2	3799
December	709	3262	3971	11	3982
January, 1945	707	3262	3969	12	3981
February	696	3260	3956	3	3959
March	687	3220	3907	3	3910
April	675	3156	3831	3	3834
May	665	3186	3851	3	3854
June	2181	923	3104	4	3108
July	1438	1066	2504	3	2507
August	2226	921	3147	7	3154
September	1530	701	2231	11	2242
October	1483	660	2143	11	2154
November	1567	715	2282	12	2294
December	1468	630	2098	3	2101

Source: Census data 1943, 1944, 1945.

walking wounded, they were still wearing their bandages and uniforms . . . [the townspeople] thought that [watching the POWs arrive] was the greatest thing since popcorn. They crowded around there as close as the military would let them." Geyser believed that the army went too far in guarding the prisoners: "They had weapons carriers with .30-caliber machine guns mounted on them [and] a GI standing there with a rifle every few feet. Someone would have thought that they were a bunch of desperadoes." Within a few months, more prisoners arrived and all three POW compounds were full. On average, about thirty-five hundred POWs resided at Camp Hearne at any one time. However, the camp's POW population varied from a high of 4,702 to a low of 1,471, during its operation (Table 1; Census Data 1943, 1944, 1945).

As noted earlier, the first POWs to arrive at Camp Hearne, as at most camps in 1943, came from the battlefields of North Africa, where the majority had been members of the famed Afrika Korps. In addition, there were prisoners from other military units that had been sent from France and Italy to reinforce the German forces in Tunisia during the closing stages of the North African campaign in the summer of 1943 (McGuirk 1993). The prisoners at Camp Hearne were battled-hardened veterans who had served in the 10th, 15th, and 21st Panzer (tank) Divisions, the 5th Leichte Division, the 90th and 164th Leichte Afrika Divisions, the 334th Infanterie Division, the 999th Leichte Afrika Division, the Von Broich/Von Manteuffel Division, the "Hermann Göring" Division, the Luftwaffe Field Division Barenthin (Fallschirmjäger [paratrooper]), the 19th and 20th Luftwaffe Flak Divisions, and a number of other smaller units. The veterans of these units had seen many years of conflict in Europe and North Africa. Scattered within these divisions were a small number of prisoners with SA, SS, and Gestapo affiliations (Eighth Service Command 1945). Willi Nellessen confirms this by pointing out that the Afrika Korps was composed of soldiers, "not Nazis. Only a few were members of the National Socialist [Nazi] Party." McGuirk (1993, 7) similarly observed that the Afrika Korps "was not a 'Nazi' army of the ilk portrayed in war films and still written about in popular novels. Its members were soldiers, under military discipline and fighting in a war that they believed was necessary to protect the interests of their nation."

While Camp Hearne remained largely composed of Afrika Korps veterans, transfers and new arrivals caused the percentage of Afrika Korps members in the population to decline. Later arrivals came from the battlefields of Italy and Normandy and from various infantry, Panzer, Fallschirmjäger, Waffen SS (elite combat forces not to be confused with the Allgemeine SS), and Luftwaffe squadrons and flak units.

Not only were the German POWs from different military branches and units, they came from all over Germany—including the annexed territories of Austria and Czechoslovakia. The prisoners also came from diverse backgrounds and professions. Before the war they had been barbers, professional musicians, construction workers, foresters, university professors, professional military men, professional athletes, public school teachers, janitors, students, railroad conductors, shopkeepers, jewelers, and merchants. In short, Camp Hearne was a city composed of a mixed group of people with many diverse abilities.

Almost all of the prisoners at Camp Hearne were enlisted men, with privates and corporals accounting for approximately 15 percent of the population and noncommissioned officers about 85 percent. At first, the NCOs and junior enlisted men were mixed together. However, within a few months they were segregated by rank into different compounds. Junior enlisted men were placed in

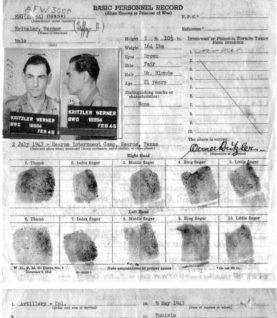

Fig. 8. The front and back of a prisoner's "Basic Personnel Record." A card such as this one was created and maintained for each POW. The front of the card displayed a frontal and profile view of the prisoner, his fingerprints, and other identifying information. The reverse of the card contained information on the camps where the prisoner had been interned, as well as personal information such as birth date, place and date of capture, rank, and education. This card is for Werner Kritzler, who was held at Camp Hearne from July 2, 1943, to July 7, 1945. The POWs were given these personnel records at the end of the war. Camp Hearne Collection, Texas A&M University.

Compound 1 and NCOs occupied Compounds 2 and 3. Although primarily from the army (Heer) and air force (Luftwaffe), a handful of navy (Kriegsmarine) personnel were also held at the camp. Only a few, generally two to four, officers were held at Camp Hearne at any one time. These were all medical personnel who were housed in a separate barrack in the hospital complex.

Heino Erichsen (2001) recalled how he and other prisoners were processed when they arrived at Camp Hearne in 1943. First they had their pictures taken and an identification file was created (fig. 8). They were then given a POW num-

Fig. 9. *Watercolor done by former POW Walter Werner in August, 1944. This is a view looking south along the main road through Compound 2. To the left is Company 8 and to the right is Company 6. Note the guard tower, barracks, and bridge over the drainage ditch. Camp Hearne Collection, Texas A&M University.*

ber and issued new uniforms and supplies. After that, recalled Erichsen: "The camp commander said to us through an interpreter, 'We must all make the best of the situation.' He explained the rules, medical and dental services, and how to write and send letters home. He ended by explaining the punishment that would be enforced for escapes or intended escapes: isolation in the stockade for a length of time that would be determined by the type of offense. Then he dismissed us to find our new homes" (2001, 58). Later in the war, most new arrivals at Camp Hearne had already been processed at various East Coast locations.

Most of the Germans were pleased with their new surroundings and the camp (fig. 9). Their first impressions focused on amenities they had lacked on the battlefield. According to Heino Erichsen: "The first thing we saw, were the fence and new barracks. I think I took three showers a day at first. Hot showers, cold showers, whatever you wanted! And they had a mess hall—we got a meal with everything: there was bread and potatoes and desert, and I thought, well this is great."

The men felt a great sense of relief at being out of the war. "We knew we were probably going to be here until the end of the war and that was tolerable to us," recalled Heino Erichsen, "especially after our experiences in Africa." Some, like Ernst Froembsdorf, felt "the deepest sense of peace when I was there, because you didn't notice anything of the war while being there. Everything was far removed." He said that after a while the men became quite comfortable and even felt at home. The camp was a welcome refuge for Arno Einicke after years of "always being on the move, at least this was some place where you could settle down. We had a real mattress, we had sheets and a comforter, and we had real pillows." Willi Nellessen felt the same way after years of "sleeping in tents on the ground near our guns" (fig. 10, 1997). Some of the men, like Hans Lammersdorf, were a bit uneasy when they first arrived at Camp Hearne because

they had no idea how they would be treated. These fears abated when it became clear that the Americans had no intention of mistreating them.

Even though the POWs found the accommodations appealing, they universally complained about the Central Texas climate. Most found the summer heat and humidity oppressive. According to Lammersdorf: "It was August. Texas was not my dream state by any means. It did not appeal to me, and I suppose [not] to many of the others, either. The climate was horrible, and it was humid and hot, and sometimes we couldn't even sleep at night." Walter Fricke agreed, saying, "Texas is so hot, that it is a place where the Devil would fight his own grandmother" (fig. 11). Despite this and other complaints, like many of his comrades, Lammersdorf was glad he no longer had to fight anymore. Nevertheless, he did worry about losing the war and his family in Germany. As Fritz Haus and most other former POWs later noted: "As German prisoners of war in the United States we were better off than most of our compatriots in enemy hands elsewhere. We knew that, and were grateful."

Camp Hearne was occupied almost exclusively by German POWs during its operation. However, the Germans in Compound 3 were transferred to other

Fig. 11. Walter Fricke (right) in a photograph taken at Camp Hearne. Fricke, an NCO, was a glider pilot who was captured in Tunisia in May, 1943. He was interned at Camp Hearne from August, 1943, until June, 1945, and lived in Compound 3. Fricke and Nellessen were good friends and occupied the same barrack. Note that Fricke and the two others are wearing German military uniforms. These were made at Camp Hearne by tailors who modified U.S. Army uniforms. Note the garden and sitting area between the barracks. Camp Hearne Collection, Texas A&M University.

camps in August, 1945, to create space for the arrival of Japanese POWs from the Pacific theater. Camp Hearne was one of only three camps in Texas to house Japanese POWs (Krammer 1983b). The first Japanese prisoners arrived in early September, 1945, and were gone by mid-December. The total number of Japanese prisoners ranged from 254 to 478. These were primarily enlisted men (about 79 percent on average), with fewer NCOs (about 18 percent), and an even smaller number of officers (about 3 percent).

The prisoners of war at Camp Hearne, as at all camps in the United States, were treated according to a strict interpretation of the Geneva Prisoner of War Convention of 1929 (the code adopted by many nations on the conduct of war and the treatment of POWs). To insure the well being of the prisoners, several humanitarian organizations—most notably the Swiss Legation, the International Committee of the Red Cross, and the Young Men's Christian Association (YMCA)—independently evaluated the camp, acted as a liaison between the American and German governments, and listened to and evaluated prisoner complaints. Observed former POW Peter Spoden: "During the war, I must say—it was the best thing. . . . It was nice. It was the best life I had ever had, so far. The Americans were acting in a way that was very 'according to' the Geneva Convention."

Indeed, the American government adhered to a strict interpretation of the Geneva Convention, often exceeding the agreed upon requirements (Krammer 1996). Former POW Fritz Haus (fig. 12) marveled about his good treatment at the hands of the Americans and asked his American friend, Chaplain Gustave Zoch (fig. 13), about it. Haus later wrote in his memoir:

> Right from the beginning, on my first day in the comfort and luxury of the Pullman car, the question had nagged me: Why are they treating us so well? Later I discussed this aspect of our prison life with my friend, the [American] Chaplain G. A. Zoch. He smiled and said he would give me three reasons which were obvious and entirely selfish: Firstly, well-fed prisoners were content and happy, and easier to control than hungry ones; they caused little trouble. The prison authorities were not keen to have constant riots and strikes on their hands.
>
> Secondly, they wanted to demonstrate that the American democratic way of life was superior to the dictatorships of Hitler and Mus-

Fig. 12. Fritz Haus in his wool continental Luftwaffe uniform and visor cap. Haus was an NCO and commanded a radarlike system used for detecting enemy planes while serving in an antiaircraft battery in North Africa. He was captured in Tunisia in May, 1943, and resided in Compound 3 from October, 1943, to May, 1945. Camp Hearne Collection, Texas A&M University.

Fig. 13. Chaplain Gustave Zoch. Zoch was a Lutheran minister in charge of all religious activities at Camp Hearne from 1943 to 1945. Camp Hearne Collection, Texas A&M University.

solini; Americans were proud of their liberties and freedom of speech, thought, and religion, without having to fear arrest or punishment. Hopefully, we prisoners would, after the war, reject Hitler's tyrannical and oppressive rule by force and work for a new democratic Germany, which will rise from the ashes [of a defeated Germany].

But thirdly, and most importantly, they were deeply afraid that many thousands of American prisoners in German hands might suffer retaliation and reprisals if America does violate the Geneva Convention on the treatment of prisoners of war. Atrocities and irregularities must not occur lest the Germans have an excuse to rough-handle American captives, as they do with Russian and Polish POWs.

"These are three very good and valid reasons why we look after you as we do," Zoch said to me. "And as any good sermon has three points, these three reasons are also honest and true." I thanked him for being so frank and judging me worthy of his confidence regarding the future prognosis and outcome of the war. His predictions frightened me. But they were realistic, I had to admit. I better keep my mouth shut and seal my lips! Now I understood their motivation and purpose, and why we had such a good time in American custody.

When the camp was first established, some of the citizens were apprehensive and concerned that the prisoners were dangerous and might escape. Mildred Payne, however, was not worried, "they had enough soldiers out there to corral them." Johnoween Mathis remarked that some of the locals thought she was taking a risk by working at the camp. They were afraid of the POWs, but she was not: "They used to ask me if I wasn't afraid and I'd said, 'Why would I be afraid?' They said, 'Well those prisoners could get loose over there and could hurt you.' They said, 'You live right over there next to the camp' and I said, 'Once you see how fortified the place is [you will see that] I don't have anything to worry about.'" Jim Stegall made deliveries to the camp and said of the Germans that as time wore on "we didn't look on them as being dangerous at all. We had an idea [that they] were very good people, and they weren't a danger to anyone."

CHAPTER 2

Life at Camp Hearne

EACH OF CAMP HEARNE'S three POW compounds held up to sixteen hundred prisoners. The compounds were further subdivided into four companies each, with about four hundred men per company (Fischer 1943a, 1944). Compound 1 housed Companies 1–4, Compound 2 Companies 5–8, and Compound 3 Companies 9–12 (fig. 4). There were forty to fifty men in each barracks.

One American officer (either a captain or lieutenant) and one American sergeant oversaw each company. These personnel were required to be in the company area every day from reveille to taps. An American captain handled the operation of each compound. The compound commanders reported directly to the camp executive officer, who in turn reported directly to the camp commander. A senior German NCO was chosen to command each company, and he and his assistant coordinated with the American personnel (Cardinaux 1943; Organizational Chart 1945; Shaw 1944). In addition, each company had an English-speaking POW who served as interpreter. These personnel were responsible for dealing with any problems that arose (such as personal disputes, complaints, requests, inspections, and chores). In some companies, barrack leaders were chosen to maintain order within individual barracks. The barrack leader was responsible for such mundane tasks as turning the lights on and off and ensuring cleanliness standards were observed.

The Germans had a spokesman for each compound and a single spokesman for all three compounds. These spokesmen were commonly the prisoners of highest rank, but sometimes a spokesman was elected on the basis of his personality and was someone the men respected. The camp spokesman acted as a liaison between the camp commander and the prisoners. He heard the complaints, concerns, and requests voiced by his comrades and communicated these to the Americans. In addition, his duties included attending meetings with members of the Swiss Legation and international humanitarian organizations such as the Red Cross and YMCA, which inspected the camp (Krammer 1996, 37–38). Based on the inspection reports submitted by representatives of the Committee of the International Red Cross and other organizations, Camp Hearne appears to have had at least seven spokesmen from 1943 to 1945 (Cardinaux 1943, 1944; Dawson and Schweiger 1944; Fischer 1943a, 1945; Greuter 1944; Metraux 1945).

THE POWs' ROUTINE

The prisoners' daily routine varied little (Metraux 1945). Most of the prisoners were awakened between 5:30 and 6 A.M., after which they were served breakfast. Those who worked got up earlier and returned to camp at about 6 P.M. The rest of the prisoners, however, remained at the camp, pursuing camp chores and leisure activities throughout the day. Lunch was provided around noon and dinner was usually served around 7 P.M. Barrack "lights out" was at 9:30 P.M. All POWs were required to be in their barracks by 11 P.M. and were not allowed outside after that hour. All other lights except those in the latrines, on the exterior of buildings, streetlights, and those on the fence were turned off at that time.

The Americans counted the POWs twice a day, once at reveille (6:30 A.M.) and again at retreat (5:10 P.M.), in an effort to discourage escape attempts. The American officer and NCO assigned to each company conducted the count, a duty they never delegated. The German companies stood in formation until the count was completed and verified (Shaw 1944). Once verified by the senior American officer in each compound, the Americans dismissed the POWs.

During the day, prisoners performed routine chores around the camp. One of the most important was keeping the barracks, grounds, and other buildings in the compound clean and tidy. Regular camp inspections were conducted to ensure a high standard of cleanliness was maintained. Each day at 9:30 A.M., an American officer and sergeant inspected the barracks and the washrooms. According to Willi Nellessen, "They looked for litter and we had to clean and wash the floor every morning." Nellessen recalled that the POWs disposed of the dirty water in the mop buckets by lifting a few of the floorboards in the barrack and sweeping it through the openings. The Americans insisted that the POW compounds be kept spotless; the guards even looked under the barracks. Joseph Pohl remarked that there were competitions to keep the barracks clean. More than one camp inspector commented on the tidiness of the prisoners' personal appearance and their barracks. "I was not the only civilian to visit the camp, only the most brazen," recalled Helen Palmos, who had occasion to see the barracks interiors. She commented that they were indeed kept very clean. Clothes were never left out—they were kept in footlockers—and she said she never saw a cigarette butt on the ground.

The POWs were responsible for washing their own clothes. Laundry was done in washtubs located in and outside of the lavatories (Cardinaux 1944; Fischer 1943b). Hugo Wannemacher recalled washing his clothes in large tubs located in the lavatory and then hanging them on a line outside the barracks or lavatory to dry. Arno Einicke and Heino Erichsen preferred to wash their clothes by putting them on the floor of the shower stall while they bathed.

The POWs' Diet

Every POW interviewed commented favorably on the food served at Camp Hearne. There is complete agreement that the food was both plentiful and of high quality. Hans Lammersdorf stated: "We had good food, we all admitted that the food was superb. We had better food than we ever had before, either as civilians or military men in Germany. You could offer us things which Germany could not. [In Germany] I had very meager rations sometimes . . . we here in America, we were so spoiled. You couldn't believe it the way they fed us. Just marvelous!" Fritz Haus remarked in his memoir: "We lacked nothing. If anything, they pampered us. Food was sufficient, regular, and much better than what our German soldiers and civilians had available at home."

Many of those interviewed recalled specific foods with remarkable clarity and even fondness. Ernst Froembsdorf said the POWs were allowed to bake their own bread and that for breakfast they "had butter, cheese, marmalade, all the condiments. Coffee with milk." Fritz Haus recalled that his favorite chocolate milk was available at almost any time of the day.

The prisoners looked forward to special occasions because they knew that the food would be even better than usual. Peter Spoden remembered getting oysters one Sunday and commented, "The food was so good we got fat." Ernst Froembsdorf recalled that each man was given a cake on his birthday. At Thanksgiving and Christmas, their captors prepared turkey dinners with all the trimmings. Fifty years later, Froembsdorf still has in his possession place cards used at those special meals.

The Americans also were willing to accommodate the prisoners' requests for more German-style foods. Initially, the bread served in the mess halls was white bread obtained from a commercial bakery. Later, after many complaints, the German cooks were given the supplies they needed to bake their own hearty bread in the camp kitchens. Robert Goede recalled that the men did not like beans and that at their request potatoes were often served instead. Fritz Pferdekämper-Geissel (fig. 14) said that the Germans working in the kitchens prepared such fine food that the Americans preferred it to their own and often ate lunch inside the compound.

The POWs also were allowed to receive care packages containing food from home. Hugo Wannemacher recollected receiving packages of donuts. Walter Fricke remembered getting Red Cross parcels with fruitcakes at Christmas and chocolates from the Pope. Willi Nellessen said that he received bread, sausages, and cakes, but would have preferred books instead because he always had plenty of food. Fritz Haus wrote to his parents that he had plenty of food in America and that they should save their food for themselves because they needed it more. Later, after being repatriated to Germany, Haus was surprised to find out that whoever censored the mail had deleted his references to the abundance of good food at the camp.

Word of the quality of Camp Hearne's cuisine reached the neighboring townsfolk. "The POWs ate everything," recalled Helen Palmos. "They had ham, they

had beef, they had pork, lamb, goat, chicken, turkey." Roy Henry, who made deliveries to the camp and often talked with the POWs commented: "They were tickled as could be. Man, they were eating good, they had good medical attention." According to Jim Potts, who headed the Agricultural Extension's Emergency War Service: "They fed those boys real good there. They gained weight; their appearance changed after they'd been over here for a while."

Some of the civilians, believing that the POWs were treated too well, referred to Camp Hearne as the "Fritz Ritz" (Krammer 1996). This feeling is understandable when one considers that civilians, because of rationing, had a hard time obtaining luxury items or even foods they thought of as staple items. For example, Helen Palmos, who ran the City Cafe in Hearne, was reluctant to submit to the camp commander's demand that she feed his men stationed in Hearne, because she simply did not have access to large quantities of food. Special arrangements had to be made in order for her to comply. Concerns over the pampering of German POWs came to a head in 1944. Jim Potts recalled that famous New York radio personality Walter Winchell complained that some of the POWs had it too good based on the fact that prisoners at Camp Hearne had a barbecue for the farmers and ranchers who employed them in order to express their gratitude. Potts clearly thought that Winchell was overreacting: "He made a big splash out of it and it never did amount to nothing. About how we catered to the POWs and so on." Many years later, Mrs. Hazel Chartain, the widow of J. D. Prewit, associate director of the Texas Extension Service, was still bothered by this incident. She recalled how she and her husband had been invited to the camp with other couples for a barbecue on the Fourth of July. "We had so much fun," she said. "We were served by POW waiters while a POW orchestra played German songs, American swing, and the favorite tune of German prisoners at almost every camp: *Don't Fence Me In*." She was shocked when she heard the Winchell broadcast charging the Texas Extension Service with "consorting with the enemy." Fifty years later she was still indignant: "Can you imagine, here we were supervising their agricultural program and were given [a] little thanks and that was consorting with the enemy?" (as quoted in Krammer 1994).

Local farmer John Nigliazzo also recalled hearing the New York City radio broadcaster's claim that the Camp Hearne POWs were being fed too well. "One time," he said, "it was in the evening, and this guy from New York was telling how we feed the prisoners real well. We heard it over the radio, and he was talking about Hearne, Texas, and how we were feeding our prisoners better than what our soldiers were getting in Germany. We were feeding them an apple a day, meat, and veggies. We were feeding them according to the League deal. We fed them like they were a soldier, regardless if they were a German or an American soldier."

Even though it seemed to some civilians that the POWs at Hearne were eating too well, the camp commander was simply complying with the rules of the Geneva Convention. German prisoners at Hearne, as at other POW camps across the country, were fed the same rations as their captors (Greuter 1944). In fact, the U.S. spent about sixty cents a day per prisoner at Camp Hearne (Fischer 1944). This was done in the hope that the German government holding American soldiers would reciprocate this act of kindness.

After the Germans surrendered in May, 1945, the quantity and quality of food given to prisoners in U.S. POW camps was reduced because officials saw no point in continuing to rigorously follow the Geneva Convention concerning the rations provided to prisoners of war. Furthermore, there was a public outcry about the overindulgence of POWs held at U.S. camps after news of German mistreatment of American prisoners reached the United States (Zoch 1946). "I remember after they liberated the concentration camps over in Germany, they had these atrocity pictures," Wanda Burdick recalled. "Our government cut their rations when they found out what terrible things they had done to our boys. And they [the German POWs] were just eating something like cabbage soup and they got that about three times a day. You could see the weight falling off of them." Peter Spoden, who said he had gotten fat while at Camp Hearne, recalled losing twenty pounds at the end of the war because the POWs were given only water, bread, and a minnow for breakfast, and soup for lunch. This prompted some complaints from the prisoners. A common gripe was a lack of fats, proteins, and sugars in their diet, which caused them to feel so weak and tired that it "prevented the men from working normally" (Metraux 1945). During this time, some of the women working in the camp offices felt sorry for the hungry prisoners with whom they worked. One former secretary recalled that a nice fellow, a POW named Otto, worked in her office and everyone liked him. When the rations were cut, people in the office brought him a plate of food every day. It was typically left in the restroom, where he could eat the food without being observed. Although the POWs' rations had been reduced and were of lesser quality than before, each prisoner still received thirty-four hundred calories per day (Metraux 1945).

ATHLETIC AND RECREATIONAL ACTIVITIES

Article 17 of the Geneva Convention states: "So far as possible, belligerents shall encourage intellectual diversions and sports organizations by prisoners of war." Athletic and recreational activities were important at Camp Hearne because the majority of prisoners were NCOs and thus, under the Geneva Convention, not required to perform manual labor. As a result, most of the camp's prisoners had a great deal of free time to fill after the morning headcount was completed.

On June 24–25, 1943, just twenty-one days after the camp opened, Dr. Rudolph Fischer of the YMCA inspected Camp Hearne and found that it lacked a library, education program, theater, and other facilities for prisoner diversion (Fischer 1943a). However, this situation did not last long. Thanks to donations from the International Red Cross, German Red Cross, YMCA, and other organizations, as well as POW canteen fund purchases, the prisoners soon had a wide variety of activities to occupy their time.

Motion pictures became one of the first diversions available at Camp Hearne because the War Department believed movies were an excellent source of amusement for POWs. In the summer of 1943, Dr. Fischer purchased a reconditioned sixteen-millimeter projector and screen for the camp with the understanding that the YMCA would eventually be reimbursed from the profits of the compound canteens. While some films were supplied free of charge, most were rented and paid for with canteen funds (Fischer 1943a). Each compound eventually purchased its own projector. Movies were initially shown outdoors. Later, after the recreation halls in each compound opened, the prisoners were able to watch movies inside the halls once a week (Lakes 1945). The former POWs recalled seeing some German movies, but said that most of the films were American westerns, newsreels, and short subjects. Heino Erichsen recalled seeing newsreels about American victories over the Japanese at Midway. Hans Goebeler reacted negatively when asked about the films: "we didn't like the pictures which were showed to us because they were kind of propaganda films. You saw Hermann Göring standing there full of decorations, then all of a sudden a rabbit showed up and took all the decorations off, and stuff like that. And we didn't care for that." Goebeler said the prisoners were forced to watch films that depicted the Germans losing the war and Allied bombing raids over Germany.

This was particularly upsetting to men who had received word that their home-towns had been destroyed. He assumed the films were lies. Heino Erichsen re-called seeing a movie about the 1814 battle at New Orleans between the Amer-icans and the British. He said there was a scene in which "the British flag falls and we all broke out in applause." Because most of the prisoners did not speak English, Carl Bruns would watch films in the American compound before the other prisoners saw them. Afterward he would prepare a summary of the movie in German and post it at several locations in the camp.

Before long, the POWs' entertainment options expanded. Requests to build a theater and produce plays were submitted almost immediately after the first Germans arrived in June, 1943. The prisoners in each compound quickly or-ganized theater troupes and began to produce well-organized theatrical perfor-mances with makeup, wigs, and other supplies provided by the Americans or purchased with canteen funds (Fischer 1943a). By mid-August, prisoners were performing plays in the recreation halls and an outdoor theater for the entire camp was being planned (Cardinaux 1943). Erich Spix, a prisoner in Com-pound 2, recalled: "As we all were not required to work in the first month, some former actors and singers started to build a theater group and organized and practiced the roles for the actors of the opera *Maske in Blau*." Theaters were op-erating in each compound by 1944, the most elaborate of which was in Com-pound 3. The theaters in Compounds 1 and 2 occupied modified barracks and each had a stage and bench seats capable of holding an audience of two hundred (Inventory, Compound 1, Company 3 1944; Inventory, Compound 2). Walter Koch said that the theater in Compound 2 was named "Das Kleine Theater für Klassiker" (The Small Theater for Classics). Compound 3's theater was an elab-orately modified barrack in which the wooden floor was removed and a stage, orchestra pit, and tiered seating for over two hundred were constructed. Ac-cording to former POW Otto Schulz: "The theater was built together with my comrades after our arrival in Camp Hearne around September, 1943. Camp leaders provided construction materials upon specific request. Special craftsmen from the POW ranks built the stage, the orchestra floor, and the spectator room. Two separate rooms were established in order to facilitate dress-up, hair-dressing, and make-up for the actors." The theater took about a year to construct and Schulz, who became its deputy director, said it was officially christened the "Deutsche Bühne" (German Stage).

An average of four productions were performed at the "Deutsche Bühne" each year. Performances were given regularly so that everyone who wanted to see the plays could attend. Even the prisoners in Compounds 1 and 2 were al-lowed to attend productions at the "Deutsche Bühne." Hans Goebeler, who lived in Compound 1, remembered that the prisoners had to line up and march into the theater under guard because it was located in another compound.

Performances were held at least once a week on Sunday. Colorful cards and posters were prepared and posted to advertise the performances. Admission was free. "We had a blackboard and on it was a listing of the plays that we could at-tend," Schulz said. "You would say, 'Yes, I want to go to this,' and other people would say, 'I want to go to that,' so that the people in charge of the theater would know how many would attend."

Fritz Haus recalled seeing performances of *The Merry Widow, The Flying Dutchman, The Student Prince, The Czar and Carpenter,* and a western–theme play (possibly *Oklahoma!*). "Ambitious plays were produced on this stage," Haus remarked, "among them the classical and moving drama *Die Brücke* (*The Bridge*) by Erwin Kolbenheyer." In February, 1944, POWs produced a musical comedy written by prisoner Bernhard Redetzki (Cardinaux 1944). An entry from Fritz Pferdekämper-Geissel's diary reads: "Wonderful theater stage. There was a production [that was] very good. I was surprised, astounded about the professional ability and the costumes and decor."

Producing these plays required much energy and the talent of many POWs. The prisoners had to write and make everything for each performance: scripts, dialogues, costumes, and scenery. "Most of the theater productions were of the German popular type," Schulz recalled. "There were no ready scripts or books available to study the parts. The dialogues were written down from the memory of a POW whose profession was director of the Koenigsberg Theater in the former German province of East Prussia. Scripts, songs, and melodies of other plays, i.e., the musical-type piece (Operetta) called *Maske in Blau (Mask in Blue)* were also reproduced from memory by POWs who were stage actors and members of orchestras and opera singers in civilian life. The same is true for the music of any kind that was played. The parts and sets for the different instruments were reproduced from memory."

Each play had new scenery and costumes (fig. 15). According to Schulz:

> The material for the costumes came from some of those guard people who had sympathy towards the Germans. Other clothes and makeup material were provided by American citizens who came to see the open-air concerts. They secretly handed those things over to the band members. Costumes or parts of it which were not on hand by means of gifts from U.S. citizens had to be handcrafted by professional tailors found among the POWs. The raw materials were bed linens, blankets, et cetera of the camp's stock. The sewing machine to tailor the costumes was a "gift" from a grateful U.S. visitor of the camp concerts. When the sewing machine was brought inside the camp by the POWs, the U.S. guards did not intervene. To produce the wigs for the actors, hairdressers among the POWs used untwisted manila ropes as the raw material.

Peter Spoden said some of the women's clothes used as costumes were provided by an American captain whose wife had left him. He showed up one day and said, "You can have these." Walter Fricke mentioned that some German women in Argentina had sent clothing for costumes to the camp. The American authorities gave the POWs some of the stage props, because they were interested in the theater themselves. The Germans, however, made most of the elaborate sets and props themselves. Some twenty-five to thirty men from each compound participated in the productions. Robert Goede learned to tap dance for a role in a play. The POWs worked hard to make each performance a success. Otto Schulz said "the theater group rehearsed for about twenty-five times on each of the productions (on average)." Because there were no women at the camp, prisoners had to play the female roles. The POWs playing women sometimes looked so convincingly female in their costumes that the guards would inspect them to make sure that women had not been smuggled into camp (fig. 16). "The Colonel, the guy who headed the whole camp, was fooled occasionally by the guys dressing up so well and even sitting among the soldiers in the audience. He would walk in and see these people, they were perfect. He would ask, 'Where did those females come from?'" Willi Nellessen said men with nice legs would play female roles wearing short dresses and that men with fat legs wore longer dresses.

"The guards were frequently invited to the plays," Schulz observed. "Although they did not catch many of the German dialogues, they always enjoyed it very much and had a lot of fun." American officers and their wives would sometimes attend the theatrical productions. They sat in the front rows and were provided an English translation of the script (Cardinaux 1944). By 1944 there was concern that the plays being produced at Camp Hearne were not being monitored closely enough for inappropriate material. To remedy this, the drama troupes in each compound were given greater access to American plays (Lakes 1945). Furthermore, a German-speaking American guard attended all performances (Neuland 1945a). Theatrical productions were a big hit and continued at Camp Hearne until its closure in December, 1945.

Fig. 15. A scene from the Czar and the Carpenter. Note the elaborate and professional sets, props, and costumes. These were all made by the POWs from scraps of lumber and other materials. Camp Hearne Collection, Texas A&M University.

Fig. 16. German POWs apply makeup and help with costumes in the dressing room for the production of the Czar and the Carpenter. *The female roles were played by men. The man seated to the right applying makeup is Walter Koch, the associate director of the "Deutsche Bühne." Note the stenciled "PW" on the shorts worn by the prisoners. Camp Hearne Collection, Texas A&M University.*

As Fritz Haus summarized in his memoir: "These performances were quite popular. Franz Lehar's operetta, *The Merry Widow,* for example, ran before capacity crowds for many weeks. How the 'female' characters kept up their falsetto 'soprano' pitch surprised us tremendously—but these 'ladies' managed without getting laryngitis! The cast and their performances were the talk of the town. Our American officers and 'keepers' always occupied the reserved front seats, often with their wives, families, and guests. They applauded the artists enthusiastically."

Musical entertainment was also important at Camp Hearne. "I have not met a German group yet which was not very fond of music," said YMCA inspector Dr. Rudolph Fischer (1943a). "The same holds true of this camp." The YMCA immediately began to supply or make arrangements for the arrival of musical instruments, sheet music, choir song sheets, radio-gramophones, and records. Commenting on the YMCA's pivotal role, Fritz Haus said: "[We] received much more than we ever asked for. Gramophone records arrived by the hundreds, with the necessary turntables and speakers. Our friends from the 'Y' were simply marvelous and supplied luxuries we had [not] known before. It was not long until we had all the instruments for our orchestra, including kettledrums and trombones. We paid for these expensive quality instruments with our own funds, generated by levies and profits from the canteens and tuck [British term for eatables, especially candy and pastry] shops."

Each compound eventually had its own orchestra. By 1944, Compound 1 had a ten-piece orchestra, Compound 2 had a thirteen-piece orchestra, and Compound 3 had a fifteen-piece orchestra. Each orchestra had a piano, violins, a bass fiddle, a clarinet, saxophones, cornets, a tuba, a drum set, an accordion, and a guitar, as well as ample sheet music. By 1945, the separate compound orchestras were combined into a campwide orchestra dubbed the "Philharmonic Orchestra of Hearne" that consisted of about twenty-five musicians (Karg 1945b). The musicians in the camp also organized a "brass orchestra" and a "dance music band." According to Haus: "Everything was professional in Hearne. Even the theaters and the operas, and the music there, it was professional stuff. This was not amateurish. They knew what they were doing." It turns out that the core of the main camp orchestra consisted of a German military band captured in North Africa along with most of its instruments. The band had spent two years traveling from one German military unit to another, putting on musical programs for the troops. One of its musicians had been a church organist in civilian life, another a composer, and still another a concert pianist. Others had played with such orchestras as the Berlin Philharmonic, the Frankfurt and Saarbrücken Symphony Orchestras, and other professional groups. The conductors of the Camp Hearne orchestra were also professional musicians who had studied at such renowned places as the University of Leipzig (*Hearne Democrat* 1943).

For a while, Walter Pohlmann, a well-known German conductor, conducted the orchestra in Compound 3. Later, Willi Mets, who had conducted the world-renowned Leipzig Symphony Orchestra, conducted the Compound 3 orchestra. As a result of this collective talent, Camp Hearne was considered to have one of the finest POW orchestras in the nation (*Hearne Democrat* 1943).

Orchestra members were constantly practicing and rehearsing—so much that the noise distracted many of their fellow POWs. Walter Fricke recalled that one man was constantly playing the flute: "He'd practice and practice, and it got on our nerves."

Because prisoners were periodically transferred to other camps, the orchestra conductor was always searching for new talent. Fritz Haus, relating his experience of trying out for a position in the orchestra, said: "When the leader of the orchestra saw me playing the recorder behind our barracks, he gave me some music by Gluck (*Orpheus*), Mozart (*Eine Kleine Nachtmuzik*) and Handel (*Water Music*) and begged me to join the orchestra. I tried hard to come to terms with the score for woodwinds (flute, clarinet, et cetera), but got quite bamboozled. When our leader, himself a principal flute player with the Berlin State Symphony Orchestra under Wilhelm Furtwängler, returned one week later and asked me to play for him, he listened and said after a short while, 'Thank you, Fritz, just continue to practice hard in the meantime. You have plenty of time to improve your runs, scales, and tempo.' He never asked me again to join his elite band; and I did not have the nerve to offer myself."

On Sundays, all POWs were able to attend a musical concert in their com-

Fig. 17. Prisoners enjoying an outdoor concert. Note the fence separating two compounds in the background. Also note the flowers planted around the band shell. Camp Hearne Collection, Texas A&M University.

pound if they wished (fig. 17; Axberg 1945). The most popular pieces played by the orchestra at Camp Hearne in 1944 were German music, polkas, and classical pieces. The POWs also enjoyed playing and listening to American jazz and "hillbilly" music (Lakes 1945). Carl Bruns recalled, "They offered everything from classic to jazz, from German folk songs to American western songs. The jazz music was very popular with us. Harry James, Tom Dorsey, Frank Sinatra, Louis Armstrong, and we loved the Andrew Sisters and Bing Crosby." Whenever there was a large prisoner transfer, one of the orchestras would play a farewell concert for their departing comrades (Karg 1945b).

In addition to the orchestras, Camp Hearne also had a number of choral groups. For example, a fifty-man choir was organized in Compound 3 (Inventory, Compound 3 1944). "We sang everything from simple folk songs to the level of Beethoven and Mozart," recalled Arno Einicke, a member of this choir. Fritz Haus organized a choir for his church services, and also felt that the men were very talented singers. "That was such a 'spine-shivering' experience," he said. "Men singing, you know. Then I thought: this is the thing. You make your men sing together and that is the way of overcoming barbed wire." Otto Schulz added: "A number of professional opera singers also gave concerts. One prominent artist was a tenor singer named Josef Traxel who was engaged at the 'Staatsoper' of Dresden."

The orchestra and choir performances provided a welcome distraction not only for the POWs, but also for the Americans stationed at Hearne and even for some of the civilians. The orchestra played for the Americans every weekend and was frequently called upon to entertain the guests of the camp commander or of other officers. At Mrs. Redwine's invitation, Mrs. Palmos attended various social events at the camp, such as parties and concerts, including one given at the officers' mess. She reminisced that Olin Teague, who held a position in Washington D.C., at the time, and Lyndon B. Johnson, who was at the time a state representative, frequented the camp and enjoyed the performances. "A number of these [civilians] were of German offspring and asked the bands for special songs of their old German home," recalled Otto Schulz. "The bands were ambitious to fulfill all those requests and there were many sentimental moments with tears on the cheeks of the people in the audience. On many occasions the 'tip' to the POW artists for fulfilling special music requests was a Coke bottle filled with liquor." Weekly performances for American personnel earned each musician eighty cents (Fischer 1944). In 1945, the camp orchestra was allowed to travel and provide concerts for POWs in the branch camp at Chance Farm (Karg 1945b).

Prisoners could also hear music on radios, which were allowed in each barrack. Froembsdorf said that he could hear music all day long in his barrack. The POWs received local stations and a Dallas station that played American folk music. Alfred Jasper remembered hearing a classical music radio program sponsored by Texaco. Arno Einicke remembered hearing "Oh Susanna" and "Home on the Range," but he was surprised at the amount of advertising that was done on the radio. "I sat for long periods of time and listened to operas," Schulz recalled. "A new musical world was also opened up for us. I heard *Rhapsody in Blue* of George Gershwin, *Symphony for the New World* of Anton Dvorak, music of Hindemith, Bartok, and much more. I heard Wagner opera in New York from the Metropolitan. Despite the war, these works were played in this world famous opera house. . . . On every Sunday noon, there was a Czech hour on the radio." In 1945, the guards seized all of the radios in the camp after it was discovered that some had been "skillfully transformed by the prisoners to pick up shortwave broadcasts" (Perret 1945).

Phonographs were also available at the camp, usually in the canteen. Each month four hundred records circulated throughout the camp. In addition to this, two concerts, one consisting light music and the other classical, were broadcast each week over the camp's public address system (Axberg 1945).

The POWs at Camp Hearne also enjoyed sporting activities. In June, 1943, there were no sports facilities available at Hearne, but within a year 85 percent of the prisoners were participating in outdoor sporting activities (Lakes 1945). Some of the prisoner's early plans for sports facilities included construction of a four-hundred-meter track, a regulation-size soccer field, and a swimming pool. The POWs also hoped to build sets of parallel and horizontal bars for gymnastics (Fischer 1943a).

Each compound had ample room for physical recreation and athletic fields. Facilities were quickly established in these areas. Space devoted to sports in

Compound 3, for instance, included four soccer fields, four fist-ball fields, two jumping pits, a ring swing, and a stage for boxing, gymnastics, and acrobatics (Inventory, Compound 3 1944). Each compound had ample sports equipment provided by the YMCA, International Red Cross, and the Americans. Additional equipment was purchased with profits from the camp canteens (Greuter 1944). An inventory dated October 10, 1944, listed the sporting equipment available to Company 3 in Compound 1 as follows: four soccer balls, three fist-balls, three handballs, four table-tennis outfits, six javelins, eight pairs of horseshoes, six cricket outfits, and a discus (Inventory, Compound 1, Company 3 1944). There was also a larger eight-acre area south of the POW compounds that was sometimes used by the entire camp for sports and recreation.

Soccer was the most popular sport at Camp Hearne (figs. 18 and 19). Guard Tex Geyser was at the camp when the first POWs were processed and he remembered that the Germans were playing soccer within days of their arrival. "On any given Sunday morning," Fritz Haus recalled, "prisoners would watch the soccer games of our prison teams and cheer every move—a very noisy affair. We had some professional footballers in the camp. It was fascinating to watch how they seemed to cast a spell on the ball which then performed as they wished—most of the time." Even the guards enjoyed watching the soccer matches. Betting on the winner of a match was a common affair amongst the guards and

Fig. 18. Germans playing soccer in one of the compounds. Note the crowd in the background. Camp Hearne Collection, Texas A&M University.

Fig. 19. Prisoners are shown here enjoying a soccer match. Soccer was a major source of recreation and entertainment at Camp Hearne. Camp Hearne Collection, Texas A&M University.

POWs. Each company had one or two teams that competed against each other to become the compound champion. Certificates and awards were always presented to members of the winning team.

The individual compound champs would also engage in intercompound soccer matches (Der Spiegel 1945a, 15–16). This competition was typically held near Christmas in the large recreation field at the south end of the camp. Spectators watched from the southern fence of each compound because the prisoners were not allowed in the recreation area unless they were members of one of the teams. This restriction was imposed to prevent fraternization. Near the end of the war, Camp Hearne's champion soccer team was allowed to play teams from other POW camps (Der Spiegel 1945b, 16).

Former POW Hugo Wannemacher recalled that when the prisoners ran out of chalk to mark the soccer field they used flour, which proved to be quite messy. Then one day, before an important game, they discovered they "didn't even have any flour for marking the field, but we did have sugar. So we marked the field with sugar." No one noticed the substitution until a dog brought by one of the Americans "began to lick up the sugar and when the guard investigated he found out what we had done. We got a lecture from the Americans about that, but not much else." Sugar was an extremely scarce commodity and rationed for American civilians during the war.

LONE STAR STALAG

"Fistball" was another favorite sport. As with soccer, there were intercompany and intercompound fistball competitions. In addition to soccer and fistball, prisoners at Camp Hearne regularly played volleyball and basketball (Cardinaux 1943). By August, 1945, three tennis courts were available for the prisoners' use (Axberg 1945). They also enjoyed handball, bowling, cricket, horseshoes, croquet, ping-pong, and various track and field events. One sport that did not go over well with the German prisoners was American baseball. Heino Erichsen commented that "none of us knew how to play baseball, I mean that was an unknown thing that we had never heard of. Up to this day I don't even know how that game works."

Twice a year there was a special sporting event, a "sportsfest," held at the camp. This included individual track and field competitions. Erichsen emphatically stated that sports activities were "big all over the camp because the activity kept your body in shape and kept you occupied."

Early on, the establishment of libraries was a high priority for the prisoners at Camp Hearne (Fischer 1943a). Reading was a good way for the prisoners to pass time and alleviate boredom. It made the men feel that they were at least doing something productive. Reading was especially important when cold or wet weather made it impossible to partake in sports. However, by August, 1943, Hearne still had not received any books to set up the much-desired libraries and reading rooms (Cardinaux 1943). Through the efforts of the German Red Cross, YMCA, and Swiss organizations, books started pouring in by the hundreds. By 1944, the library and reading facilities the prisoners had envisioned a year earlier had been realized (Cardinaux 1944; Greuter 1944). There eventually were separate libraries in the day rooms of each compound and a supply of books rotated throughout the entire camp. Most of the material was in German, but there were also books in English, Italian, and French for prisoners interested in learning a foreign language (Fischer 1943a). The camp also received the *Houston Post, New York Times,* and several German-language newspapers printed in the United States. Magazines such as *Time, Life, Newsweek, Reader's Digest,* and *Colliers* were also stocked in the libraries. Most of the POWs at Camp Hearne thought that much of the information in both the English and German newspapers was American propaganda (Fischer 1943b). Nonetheless, some prisoners were impressed by the open nature of the American news media, especially the *New York Times,* which published official German, Japanese, Italian, American, Russian, and English military communiqués. According to Fritz Haus, "We were liberally supplied with American newspapers and magazines, books on the American way of life and pamphlets on the ideals of democracy."

The library in Compound 1 was open daily from 8 A.M. to 11 P.M. Its 687 books included 232 romance novels, 330 other works of fiction, 31 history books, 16 textbooks, and 78 American books (Inventory, Compound 1, Company 3 1944). Compound 3 had 1,350 German and 100 American books (Inventory, Compound 3 1944). The prisoners requested some types of books more than others. English dictionaries, Spanish language, U.S. history, and geography books were so popular with the POWs that they were sold in the canteens (Lakes

1945). Much to the prisoners' dismay, German-language books were detained for censorship in New York. However, this three- to four-week delay did not discourage the YMCA and International Red Cross from supplying an enormous amount of reading material to the camp. When the POW camps in Huntsville and Mexia closed in 1945, the material from their libraries was transferred to Hearne and by August of that year there were approximately 7,000 German and 500 English books available in Camp Hearne's libraries (Axberg 1945; Metraux 1945). There was one controversial episode involving censored books: "Under the previous commanding officer 260 disapproved books by Nazi authors had been removed in such a manner that was not in accordance with U.S. Army regulations. Instead of discreetly removing the books by means of routine rotation, it was announced to the prisoners that the books were undesirable and all were removed at once. This resulted in a protest by the camp spokesman and the books were returned" (Neuland 1945b). The books were later removed piecemeal through regular rotation.

Many of the POWs enjoyed the diversion that reading provided as it filled the many idle hours. Fritz Pferdekämper-Geissel wrote in his diary: "There are many books in the library and I have time to devote myself to them." Fritz Haus commented: "I read the whole Shakespeare in the original. The religious section gave us Latin, Greek, and Hebrew standard works, with concordances, encyclopedias, and commentaries. The World Council of Churches donated stuff of a different kind to us pastors and spiritual leaders than we had seen during the Hitler regime, because it was of an explosive and controversial nature. The writings, sermons, lectures and articles by Karl Barth, Martin Niemoller, and Dietrich Bonhoeffer, we saw them in printed form for the first time in Camp Hearne and I devoured them."

Religious activities were also important to some of the POWs. About 45 percent of the prisoners were Protestant, 45 percent Catholic, and 10 percent had no membership in any church (Axberg 1945). During the first year, thirty-five-minute services were held outside or in the recreation hall of each compound depending on the number of POWs in attendance. A joint service for the POWs in all compounds was not allowed. Religious literature in German could almost always be found in the hospital, libraries, and reading rooms (Zoch 1946, 17).

From June 8, 1943, until January 27, 1946, Chaplain Gustave A. Zoch, a U.S. Army captain, presided over all of Camp Hearne's religious services. Chaplain Zoch was an enthusiastic Lutheran who spoke fluent German. He performed almost all of the camp's religious duties, including burials and weddings, through 1944. During that time, Father Peter Villani and Father B. Bravi of Saint Anthony's Catholic Church in Bryan assisted Chaplain Zoch. They celebrated mass at the camp each Tuesday and heard confessions and distributed communion on the last Saturday of each month (*Hearne Democrat* 1943). In 1944, at Chaplain Zoch's request, two captured German clergymen—one Catholic, the other Protestant—were transferred to Hearne. From then on, Zoch supervised the two German chaplains while continuing to perform services for the American personnel. The two German clergymen, with whom the POWs undoubtedly felt more comfortable, conducted all direct religious services for the prisoners. By that time joint services were being held in "a large building right at the entrance of the gate leading to the different compounds which was converted into a beautiful little chapel." The new chapel included an altar, pulpit, pews, organ, and offices (Zoch 1946, 18–19).

Church attendance was highest in 1943, when the camp first opened, and declined over time. About fifteen hundred POWs attended the first services held by Zoch. For the next few months, attendance averaged about a thousand men at each service, then decreased dramatically. Within a week, attendance fell from about a thousand prisoners to only twenty. Zoch attributed the decline to the transfer of a number of what he called "Nazis" to Camp Hearne. They were men he considered to be "enemies of Christianity" (Zoch 1946, 21). Fritz Haus, a minister in training, reported that the church services were not without their detractors. A small number of devout men, twenty or thirty in all, would attend the services instead of participating in sports. As they marched by the sports field en route to the services, the sports fans would jeer them. When the camp chapel was built some time later, it was deliberately built away from the athletic fields and services were held earlier in the day, enabling the men to participate in both activities. The chapel was completed on April 4, 1944, on the POW side and near the entrance to the camp. Scenes of Calvary were painted on its walls and a "huge wooden cross" hung above the altar. The day after the first service was held in the new building, someone vandalized it. Haus suspected that Nazis were responsible because they were known to intimidate people in an effort to prevent them from attending services. "The next morning," he recalled, "when Erich Muller and I went back to the chapel, the walls were defaced and some windows had been smashed. Broken glass lay all over the place. We never found out who the culprits were, but the Americans gave us fine wire mesh to cover the windows and protect them from further damage. It worked, we never had trouble from vandals again." The devout men were undeterred. By the end of the first year of operation, about thirty-five prisoners regularly attended services. Attendance at sermons "improved slightly" when the two German chaplains were transferred to Hearne and took over most religious activities. However, after Germany's surrender on May 8, 1945, attendance "improved greatly" (Zoch 1946, 22). According to an inspector, Zoch reported that attendance in August, 1945, was generally about 120 Catholics and forty Protestants (Axberg 1945). Zoch believed that Hitler's defeat prompted many Christian POWs to become less fearful of reprisals and former Nazis to regain their religious roots. Haus revealed in his memoir that he had prayed for Hitler's defeat: "In Germany our parents and the Christians prayed that Hitler would lose the war. But this was a private thing. Not openly in the service, (I could not do this) from the pulpit. So we did the same thing, but (it was done) very privately in the camp."

As an interesting footnote, there was one Muslim in the camp. Otto Schulz remembers that his barrack housed an Arab named Mohammed Bouheddu who had "fought with the Germans in Africa in an Arabic unit [the Deutsche-Arabische Lehr Abteilung, also known as the Freies Arabien Legion or Free

Arab Corps] with us. Every day, he extended his clean towel as a prayer carpet on the ground and bowed eastward to the city of Mecca."

Educational activities were also popular at Camp Hearne. The Germans were eager to learn, but in the summer of 1943 a lack of books and supplies limited the scope and depth of courses offered to the POWs (Cardinaux 1943). Day rooms and theaters were initially used as classrooms. Later, said Arno Einicke, "for those hungry to learn, we had a school barrack." A permanent classroom building was established in each compound by taking a barrack and subdividing it into four smaller rooms for classes. The walls dividing the rooms were made of paper obtained from the kitchen. Initially, each student had to bring his own chair. Later, POW carpenters made tables and chairs for the classrooms. The school was equipped with chalkboards and the men had textbooks and took exams. Attendance in most classes was high, but it waned somewhat during the summer months (Fischer 1944). A wide variety of courses were available to the prisoners. A report on a 1944 inspection indicates that courses included "mathematics, trigonometry, building, building materials, physics, chemistry, machine construction, . . . English, French, Latin, Spanish, Italian, agriculture, gardening, biology, book binding, [and] stenography" (Greuter 1944). Another inspection report, this one dated October 10, 1944, provides specific information about the courses offered and enrollments in them at Camp Hearne (Table 2). Sometimes, special lectures would be given in the theaters so that more prisoners could attend. Courses at the camp were very thorough. Notes from courses taken by Willi Nellessen on art history, mathematics, and grammar illustrate that the courses were very detailed. Arno Einicke recalled that an "Agricultural School" taught men how to grow cotton. He said they would take field trips to cotton fields on the edge of the Brazos River to inspect crops.

Prisoners who had been university professors, public school teachers, accountants, engineers, or other professionals prior to being conscripted taught the classes. As Fritz Haus put it, "they knew their stuff." All of the POW instructors were paid for their work.

The reasons offered for taking courses varied from a way to combat boredom to a desire to learn. Peter Spoden took English classes in the hopes that he would obtain a position as a camp interpreter, which he thought was a good job. Many of the prisoners were eager to learn new skills while they were interned, in the hopes that it would help them find work when they returned home after the war. As Fritz Haus said, "Even though you weren't sure what you would do when you got back, you wouldn't know the circumstances, at least you would have something."

Baylor University in Waco, Texas, sponsored educational programs at Camp Hearne. Given its proximity, camp officials solicited Texas A&M University (then known as the Agricultural and Mechanical College of Texas) to sponsor various classes (Neuland 1945b), but no such educational program was established. Fritz Haus took religion correspondence courses offered by Concordia Theological Seminary of St. Louis, Missouri. The camp chaplain, Captain Zoch, acted as Haus's mentor and administered his exams. The courses were in German

Table 2. Courses Offered and Enrollments in Compound 2 at Camp Hearne on October 10, 1944

Courses	Enrollment
Preparation for school graduation examination	35
Business	58
Technical training	25
Handicrafts course	48
Professional soldiering	126
History	50
German	25
Mathematics	15
Physics	15
Chemistry	8
Short-hand writing	80
Bookkeeping	70
Political economy	40
English	80
French	30
Spanish	12
History of Art	45
Jurisprudence	7
Technical drawing	15
Total Enrollment	764

Source: Inventory, Compound 2, 1944

and met full university standards. Credits were transferred to Germany after the war and helped Haus earn his seminary degree more quickly than otherwise might have been the case. Some prisoners were even able to take correspondence courses from Germany through the International Red Cross (Lakes 1945).

By 1945, participation in educational activities was so widespread at Hearne that the camp's commanding officer, Lieutenant Colonel Rainbolt, assigned Captain Ingles, a former schoolteacher, to oversee all educational activities. The education program at Camp Hearne clearly was a success from start to finish.

A canteen and post exchange (PX) occupied a single building at the north end of each compound (fig. 20). One also was located in the hospital complex. These canteens were entirely operated by the prisoners. A variety of products were available in the canteens. Each POW, whether an enlisted man or an NCO, was given three dollars per month in coupons (which came in one- and five-cent denominations) to purchase personal items such as soap, toothpaste, and additional clothing (fig. 21). Luxury goods were also available. A list of items that

Fig. 20. The counter where goods could be purchased inside the camp canteen. Camp Hearne Collection, Texas A&M University.

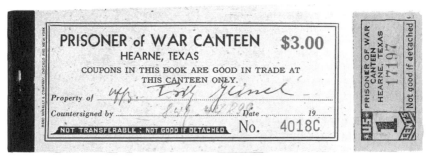

Fig. 21. Shown here are a booklet containing coupons used to purchase items at the camp canteen and a one-cent coupon (right). Camp Hearne Collection, Texas A&M University.

prisoners could buy in the canteens is provided in Table 3. In addition to these items, books selected from a list could be special ordered and prisoners could purchase items from the Sears catalog with their canteen coupons. Postcards featuring a photograph of the camp could also be purchased. Prisoners could make arrangements for a photographer to take their portrait or take a photograph of anything else in the camp. The POWs who worked had more to spend because they earned eighty cents per day. Ernst Froembsdorf recalled that he could buy quite a lot at the PX with the nineteen dollars a month worth of coupons that

Table 3. List of Items for Sale at the POW Canteen in July, 1945, and Their Prices

Item	Price ($)	Item	Price ($)
Speedball pen sets	1.10, 0.66, 0.63	Nox Shave	0.20
Penholders	0.05	Burma Shave	0.30
Venus Eraser	0.05	G.P. Coldcream	0.10
Thin leads	0.05	Woodbury Handcream	0.18
Pencils Velvet	0.03	Noxema skin cream	0.23
Pencils Eagle color	0.06, 0.10	Fitch shaving cream	0.16, 0.31
Pencils Eagle	0.06, 0.10	Getro Jelly	0.10
Carter's Drawing Ink	0.15	Lucky combination	0.47
Higgins Drawing Ink	0.20	Kreml shampoo	0.41
Zippo Flints	0.05	Fitch DR	0.18
Buttons	0.05	Fitch coconut oil	0.33
Thread	0.05	Jerris combination	0.37
Bull Durham Tobacco	0.05	Royal Paper	0.26
Mennen Quins	0.35	Drawing Paper	0.04, 0.05, 0.18
Mennen Talcum	0.13	Water color sets	3.36
Ammen Powder	0.17	Oil color sets	3.55, 5.75, 7.35, 15.20
Marvel Shaving Cream	0.10	Chapstick	0.14
Colgate Shaving Cream	0.35	Vaseline	0.30
Mennen Shaving Cream	0.23	Owens Tooth Brush	0.13
Sheets Ring Book	0.28	Shaving Brush	0.65
Combination Books	0.07	Brillantine	0.08
Linen Tablets	0.08	Mennen skin balm	0.35
Steno Books	0.04, 0.05	Gaby. Lotion	0.30

continued

Table 3. *continued*

Item	Price ($)	Item	Price ($)
Notebook Paper	0.05	Cigarette Papers	0.05
Colgate Shaving Sticks	0.08	Listerine foot powder	0.18
Lucky Non-Alcohol	0.28	Wilder cream oil	0.35
Carter's Writing ink	0.08	Famos blades	0.05
Bon ton	0.15	Sewing kits	0.35
Pocket Games	0.70	Fixative pots	0.63
Cornet Model	0.20	Animals	0.26
Chess Books	0.30	English–French Dictionary	0.75
Ash trays	0.10	Fixative	0.20
Metro games	2.20	Pepco Toothpaste	0.85, 1.65
Pepsodent toothpaste	0.18	Jergens lotion	0.18
Green shampoo	0.10	Book of matches	0.05
Pauline Lotion	0.10	Sandpaper	0.01
Wildroot White Oil	0.35	Listerine antiseptic	0.33
London Lotion	0.22	Mirrors	0.18
Cramers lotion	0.20	Gem razor blades	0.08
Gem double-edge razors	0.09	Wovel Soap	0.09
Glue	0.60	English Books	0.21
Billfolds	4.00, 3.75	Styptic Pencil	0.07
Embassy aftershave	0.40, 0.33	Fitch Hair Tonic	0.33
Huga Dictionary	0.50	Paper	5.00
Star Razors	0.17		

Source: Weiss 1945a.

he earned picking cotton. Arno Einicke observed "that the common soldiers had more money than the NCOs," and Willi Nellessen said: "These were the rich men, they were able to buy a radio and books and to drink a bottle of beer on Sunday morning. They got, I think, 24 dollars a month and we got only three dollars. And from the three dollars we had to buy soap and razor blades."

There were refrigerators and counters in the canteens so that prisoners could enjoy cool beverages on hot summer afternoons and even ice cream at times (Fischer 1943a). On September 27, 1943, it was impossible for POWs to buy beer at the canteens (Fischer 1943b), but less than six months later prisoners were able to purchase a pint each day (Cardinaux 1944). Fritz Pferdekämper-Geissel recalled that 2.5-proof versions of Schlitz and Budweiser brands were available, and that they cost ten cents a bottle. The Americans figured that if the prisoners were limited to purchasing only one bottle of beer a day, it would not be possible for them to get drunk. However, Hugo Wannemacher recalled that with a little creative planning and bartering it was possible to get tipsy: "The people who didn't want their beer would give it to others who did want it and then something was taken in exchange . . . then you'd have a number of bottles of beer to drink." Robert Goede said the trick was to "get together with six other people and then you could have six beers once a week."

The canteen was also a place for the prisoners to meet and relax. Tables and chairs were available for the prisoners to sit, drink, smoke, and talk (fig. 22). A barbershop was also located in a room at the east end of each canteen (fig. 23; Shaw 1944). A haircut cost ten cents (Inventory, Compound 2 1944).

Fig. 22. German prisoners relax and enjoy a cold drink in the sitting area of the camp canteen. Camp Hearne Collection, Texas A&M University.

Fig. 23. Shown here is the barbershop where the POWS got their hair cut. Camp Hearne Collection, Texas A&M University.

Each compound's canteen made a profit from the sale of products and from the barbershop. Within a few months after opening, the canteens were realizing significant profits (Cardinaux 1944) that went back to the POWs. A committee made up of representatives from each company decided how the profits from the canteens were to be used. Arno Einicke remembered that while he was at Camp Hearne in 1943, some of the money went toward buying tables for the school. Fritz Haus said that the committee funded the cost of sporting equipment and musical instruments. In August, 1944, canteen funds were used to buy watermelons for the entire camp (Fischer 1944).

Other buildings at Camp Hearne were also used to accommodate the POWs' recreational and pastime needs. One barrack in each company was converted for use as a day room in which prisoners could write letters, read books, play cards and board games, or simply relax (Inventory, Compound 3 1944). Werner Kritzler said that prisoners were always playing cards, especially the card game of Skat. Skat tournaments were played and an announcement indicated how much money one needed in order to enter the competitions.

Other recreational activities included construction projects and gardening. The prisoners made concrete fountains and statues in the compounds and outside the barracks were mosaics of unit insignia and coats of arms created with colored pebbles and glass (Fischer 1943a, 1943b). The POWs also engaged in large-scale construction projects. By October, 1944, between the canteen and dispensary in Compound 1, prisoners had built an outdoor beer garden with tables, benches, a petting zoo, and a turtle pond (Inventory, Compound 1, Company 3 1944). Flower gardens were also created at Camp Hearne and irises and lilies planted by POWs over fifty years ago still bloom on the grounds today. According to Willi Nellessen, "Between the barracks there were lawn and flowers, planted and tended by POWs." The prisoners also planted and maintained a twenty-five-acre vegetable garden for the POW kitchen, grew smaller gardens of peanuts and beans around the compounds, constructed bowling alleys, and built the theater in Compound 3 (Fischer 1943a, 1943b).

Many of the POWs were skilled craftsman and artists, so arts and crafts proved to be very popular with them. A special building on the north end of each compound was designated as a recreation building. There, prisoners pursued oil and watercolor painting (figs. 24, 25), drawing, sculpting, model building, woodcarving (fig. 26), leather working, and wood burning (Fischer 1943a). Some of the most common artistic themes included castles, landscapes, and villages.

Walter Fricke made suitcases and also liked to carve portraits of Native Americans on wood salvaged from crates. Fricke said the men had nothing to do with their time, so they built things. He remembered that some made toys for children. As a five-year-old girl, Doris Emshoff was allowed to visit with some of

Fig. 24. A self-portrait of Werner Kritzler done on March 21, 1944, at Camp Hearne. Kritzler was an NCO in a Luftwaffe flak unit captured in May, 1943. He resided in Compound 2 at Camp Hearne from July, 1943 to July, 1945. Camp Hearne Collection, Texas A&M University.

Fig. 25. A German artist named Fenderi poses with some of his artwork in the recreation room in 1944. Note the large wooden ship model perched on the ledge behind him. Camp Hearne Collection, Texas A&M University.

the POWs on Sundays while her aunt shopped at the Post Exchange in the American compound. In addition to cookies, these men gave her toys they had made. She remarked that a prisoner named Fritz gave her a dancing wooden doll (a limber jack) and later an articulated paper doll, both of which she retains to this day. Mrs. Emshoff felt that the POWs looked forward to these visits as much as she did. Willi Nellessen made knives for woodcarving, and Fritz Pferdekämper-Geissel made furniture and carved little wooden boxes that he sold to the guards. Nellessen still has a wooden box, richly carved, that he received in Camp Hearne as a birthday gift. Civilian Helen Palmos, who employed several POWs in her cafe in Hearne, recalled that one of the men was a gifted carver. He made beautiful little picture frames and gave one to her for her daughter's photograph and also gave her little wooden boxes. The POWs made dishtowels from bleached sugar sacks for her restaurant. Some of the Germans interviewed recalled that their comrades entertained themselves by sketching and painting. American guards and civilians bought artworks, paying primarily in cigarettes, but on occasion in cash. Guard Tom Bussell said, "They'd ask you, 'Do you want me to paint a picture of your wife?' Then they would ask for shoe strings or something like that." Civilian E. R. Mason said, "I was just amazed whenever I looked at the buildings, at some of the artwork those prisoners had done." He recalled paintings with war themes and beautiful scenes of mountains, streams, and castles that the men created in tribute to their homeland. These murals adorned the walls of the theater and the mess halls. When Mason visited Germany later in life, he was stunned to see how accurately the German landscape had been rendered.

Murals also adorned the walls of the camp chapel, which was completed in April, 1944. "It was a beautiful place, with appropriate oil and water paintings on the walls," said Fritz Haus. "A Calvary scene and 'The Stilling of the Storm,' all done by our own men and artists, were put on each side, and above the altar in front. Three tremendous artistic and exquisite flower arrangements enhanced and emphasized the altar scene with the huge wooden Protestant cross and the smaller Catholic crucifix. The flowers came from our own gardens. Several of the vases and flower pots were handmade and hand painted in our own camp pottery."

The prisoners were sometimes allowed to send their artwork to relatives and friends in Germany. In 1945, the International Red Cross sent five hundred boxes of arts and crafts made by Camp Hearne POWs to Germany (Axberg 1945).

Also present at the north end of each compound was a workshop building equipped with carpentry tools and some power tools. Prisoners using the facility constructed furniture for use around the camp in the barracks, classrooms, and theater (Fischer 1943a). Hugo Wannemacher recalled that some prisoners

Fig. 26. German POWs receive instruction on the art of wood carving in the recreation room. Camp Hearne Collection, Texas A&M University.

made items such as clocks and violins in the carpentry workshop. The orchestra used some of the instruments and others were sold. "One of our comrades built a harmonium (an American organ) from empty fruit tins from the kitchen (for the reed pipes), cartons, surplus wooden boxes, strings, wires, robes, and other throw-away items, many of them rescued from the refuse dumps," said Haus. "The wooden keyboard was neatly varnished. He made the bellows from discarded army canvas material we salvaged for him from the warehouse. He made them water and air proof." The organ performed reliably in the chapel every Sunday and was used until the camp closed.

The animals around Hearne were always of interest to the POWs. Fritz Haus and Ernst Froembsdorf both recalled not being allowed to have pets for hygienic reasons. However, Hugo Wannemacher said some of the men secretly kept cats as pets. Walter Fricke remembered some men who used to capture snakes and skin them. Fritz Pferdekämper-Geissel also caught snakes and made bags from their skins. Peter Spoden caught possums when he was working and brought them back to camp. He also had a collection of turtles. Walter Werner recalled that one fellow kept a tamed possum in his barrack. "Because of its wonderfully soft fur, many liked to pet the animal," said Werner. "When its owner wanted to go for a walk with the possum, he put a wooden stick under its tail. With the animal's tail solidly curled around the rod, the man would lift the stick and carry it around." Fritz Pferdekämper-Geissel was something of a naturalist. He told his interviewer that he kept a variety of animals as pets or specimens. He built a little zoo, complete with barbed wire, to house turtles, lizards, and rabbits.

Bug collecting was another popular pastime among the POWs (Lakes 1945). Pferdekämper-Geissel's collection included insects and butterflies, stuffed hawks, buzzards, possums, and the skins of various snakes including copperheads, water moccasins, rattlesnakes, and king snakes. Fifty years later, back in Germany, he still has a stuffed possum and some of the snakeskins he gathered while in Texas. "One comrade collected snakes which he kept in gallon jars," said Arno Einicke. "At one point, he did not close the jars properly so the reptiles escaped into the barracks which caused a lot of excitement. There was a snake alarm and Gerhardt—that was his first name—tried to collect as many of those little animals as he could before they escaped. He continued to collect all those specimens again."

Animals they had never previously seen fascinated many of the POWs. Fritz Haus related this story:

> During the first week at Hearne a strange thing happened to us fifty men from our barracks. Two small black and white animals with a bushy tail were sitting on the front steps of our main entrance. We rather liked them and thought they were the American version of our cute squirrels under a German oak tree. We ventured nearer and were amazed how tame and totally unconcerned they were about our presence. "Let's try and catch them to cuddle in our arms" some said. When we were just about to make physical contact, two or three

squirts of foul smelling fluid, like jets from a water pistol, hit three of us, wetting them all over (fortunately it wasn't me!). After this, the infamous animals disappeared under the barrack floor. When the Americans noticed our commotion and understood the cause of it, they came with a canister and sprayed some chemical stuff around the foundations to drive them away. We never saw these particular two skunks again. But the smell remained for weeks. Our three comrades were ordered to report to the quartermaster's stores outside the gates without delay, where they were issued a complete new outfit of clothing. Because all the soap or detergents in America would not eradicate or neutralize the despicable secretion from the skunks, the old clothes were burned. I saw some others of these ill-smelling creatures some two years later, but made a hasty retreat, without hesitation or delay.

Leisure and recreation activities were an important part of the day-to-day lives of the prisoners at Hearne. The company commander and recreation officer were very open and responsive to their needs. When prisoners requested something for education, entertainment, or sports it was usually only a matter of weeks before camp officials supplied it. Clearly, there was a variety of activities for prisoners to pursue. Almost every interest was covered. This usually kept the nonworking POWs busy and out of trouble.

POW Labor

According to the Geneva Convention, captured officers are not required to work, NCOs are required to provide only supervisory labor, and enlisted men are required to work. The convention also states that prisoners are to labor no more than six days each week and are to be paid for their labor. This pay was to be equal to that earned by civilians doing the same work. The U.S. government determined that all prisoners would be paid eighty cents a day. The Geneva Convention further requires that the work performed by POWs cannot be directly related to the war effort and that prisoners cannot be forced to perform dangerous tasks. This meant that most of the prisoners at Camp Hearne were involved in either chores around the camp (such as cutting grass, building repairs, and painting) or in agricultural work on nearby farms. Many POW camps in the United States were located in rural settings to provide an inexpensive source of agricultural labor. The government recognized that with so many young men being drafted into the military, a labor shortage had developed in agricultural areas—a shortage that government planners believed could be made up by POWs.

Although privates and corporals accounted for only about 15 percent of Camp Hearne's population, they performed most of the labor both inside and outside the camp.

Initially there was some hesitation and ethical concerns voiced by the prisoners about working. Some thought that their work helped the American war effort, but this feeling did not last long. Robert Goede recalled that when the camp first opened he wanted to work and was one of the first to volunteer because he would receive eighty cents a day to spend at the PX. He claims that there was some conflict between himself and the other POWs about his working, "They said I was abetting the enemy. So I went to the front office and I said I don't want to go out anymore, but I'd like to work. So I said, 'Can I work in the kitchen?' But then, about a month later, it seemed like everybody wanted to go out to work in the camp. So, after telling me that they thought I was abetting the enemy, those that told me so, they went out to work, too." Many of the POWs liked having the opportunity to learn new skills. Fritz Haus learned how to drive jeeps and delivery vans in the mechanical workshops in the hopes that this work would make it easier for him to get a license when he returned to Germany.

Prisoners worked within the camp as clerks, janitors, cooks, bakers, gardeners, quartermaster aides, truck drivers, tailors, cobblers, canteen attendants, interpreters, general maintenance workers (such as painters and carpenters), warehouse personnel, mechanics, cemetery attendants, as well as performing many other functions (War Department 1944a, 1945). In addition, 381 POWs worked in a shop that repaired blankets and raincoats for POW use in camps operated by the Eighth Military Service Command (Perret 1945). Many of the prisoners preferred this labor to agricultural work outside the camp. Ernst Froembsdorf, who was a POW waiter in the American officers' club, enjoyed his job because he was secretly able to drink whiskey left over in glasses and sneek a few shots from the bottles.

Neighboring farmers employed a number of prisoners (fig. 27). Farmers needing labor submitted formal written requests to the War Manpower Commission (WMC) describing the type of labor required and certifying that no other source of labor was available. When the WMC approved such a request, the employer was issued a Certificate of Need. The certificate was then submitted to the nearest WMC employment office. It contained a detailed description of the work that was to be performed along with assurances that other labor was not available and that the hiring of POW labor would not lead to the lowering of wages or working conditions for civilian workers. Once the certificate was approved, the request was forwarded to local military officials, who in turn gave it to the Department of Agriculture Extension Service to determine the number of prisoners needed to complete the job. At that point, the employer entered into a contract with the War Department for the use of POW workers. In response to the frustrations of the farmers requiring the labor and recognizing the need for a quicker turn around time, the system was streamlined in March, 1944. The War Department allowed the Agricultural Extension Service of Texas' land-grant college, in this case the Agricultural and Mechanical College of Texas (now Texas A&M University), to act as the official liaison between farmers and POW camp officials. This new system greatly reduced the paperwork and shortened the lag time between the farmers' initial requests for labor and their getting it. By the end of the war, farmers were able to obtain German workers by directly contacting the camp commander (Krammer 1996, 87).

Fig. 27. German POWs at work in an agricultural field. Camp Hearne Collection, Texas A&M University.

Contracts for POW labor in the area around Camp Hearne were issued to Chance Farm, Elmwood Ranch, Goodland Farm, Mooring Farm, M. F. Smith Farm, and other nearby farms such as Cotropia, Scarmardo, and Reistino (War Department 1945).

Typically, the POWs and an appropriate number of guards would leave the camp early in the morning and return between 5:30 and 6 P.M. (War Department 1945). The prisoners worked for fifty-minute intervals followed by a ten-minute rest period during each eight-hour shift. Swiss representatives inspected the POW work sites every few months to ensure that the prisoners were not being overworked.

Generally, the prisoners had a good rapport with the farmers and the farmers were satisfied with the work completed. Jim Potts, who headed the Agricultural Extension Emergency War Service, said that 90 percent of the labor demand at Camp Hearne was for cotton harvesting. The other 10 percent was for clearing fields of Johnson grass, preparing soil, planting onions, or harvesting other crops. In the winter, POWs baled hay, cleared land, and built fences. Potts recalled one farmer who complained that local laborers he had hired were clearing twice as much land as the POWs. Potts and a state labor supervisor made a field inspection to see if the POWs were goofing off. They arrived at the farm at sunup and found the POWs already there working. Potts and the supervisor joined in the work and found it to be hard. Potts also noted that the local laborers were doing sloppy work. Although they covered more ground, they did not efficiently get all the weeds out the way the Germans did. He concluded that the prisoners were doing an excellent job: "Everything we had them on they did a good job with and this complaint the old boy made, we just laughed at him after that. There was no comparison between what those POWs did and what his local staff did."

Potts said that, in general, the POWs did a better job picking cotton because they would pick out all the trash and have no rocks or clods in their sacks when they weighed them. According to Potts there was a difference of nearly two cents per pound between the cotton harvested by the POWs compared with that harvested by the local labor force. He noted that the same thing occurred when the POWs harvested potatoes: the local laborers left the small ones, whereas the Germans harvested all of them. In general, the farmers had a good relationship with the POWs and vise versa. "They were real good boys," recalled local farmer John Nigliazzo, "well-mannered, and they did exactly what we told them to do . . . good, good workers. We were planting onions, and we tell them to plant them four inches apart, and they were very precise. They couldn't be any better and they were real nice." Fritz Pferdekämper-Geissel had only positive things to say about his experiences working for American farmers: "You get a connection with the farmer. I never heard of any trouble with a farmer. It just was that way. Therefore, I can't say anything but good things [for] the whole time [I was there]." In the mid-1960s, back in Germany, Pferdekämper-Geissel received a package of pecans from a Texas farmer. In it was a note that read: "I found your name and address in my book. I remember that you were a friendly boy. I send you some pecans." This act of kindness is reflective of Pferdekämper-Geissel's general experiences in America. He made many American friends during the war and he said they never referred to each other as enemies. Some of these Americans visited him in Germany after the war, and he visited them (including several farmers) when he traveled in the United States.

Occasionally, however, there were problems between the POWs and the farmers. Prisoners working at Elmwood Farm, for example, claimed they were threatened with confinement if they did not work harder. The farmer allegedly encouraged the prisoners to work slowly and do a thorough job, and then later complained that they were not working hard enough. The farmer threatened to have them picked up by prison officials and put in the guardhouse if they did not work harder. The following day, the same farmer left his sixteen-year-old son in charge. The prisoners said the boy used abusive language and ordered them about "in an unbecoming tone" and that the drinking water they were given came from a dirty barrel and lacked ice (Metraux 1945).

Some farmers complained that the POWs were cheating on their cotton quotas. There was some truth to this complaint, according to Peter Spoden and Hugo Wannemacher. Spoden recalled that they were required to fill long white sacks two or three times a day with cotton, each weighing approximately eighty pounds. He claimed that it was impossible to meet this daily quota. To get around this problem, he explained, they secretly added earth to some of the sacks to increase the weight and then pretended that it was full. Willi Nellessen admitted that he, too, added stones to his cotton bags to increase their weight. Workers who were not clever enough to adopt this strategy and who failed to meet the quota were often punished at the end of the day.

Former POW Arno Einicke recalled that one afternoon, after their lunch break, the prisoners on his work crew decided to "strike" because of a disagreement with the farmer. Two jeeps showed up with a reinforcement of guards carrying machine guns. The Germans were proud that they had made the Americans uncomfortable, but the Americans just laughed—the prisoners had just made more trouble for themselves. No other work stoppages took place after that.

Hans Goebeler also worked in the fields. He clearly remembered how the relationship between himself and a farmer he worked for was built:

> The farmer at first was very nasty, he was mean. After a certain time, he had about fifty and eighty POWs in his different fields. He came riding on his horse at noontime and waited until the first two or three [POWs] were close to the end [of a row of cotton and] gave each one a cigarette. So the rest [of the POWs] didn't get anything and my roommate and others told me "Tell that asshole that he should give a cigarette to each of us or none of us or he can keep them." So I had to tell him. He said, "Listen, I give cigarettes to whom I want." So, we tried a different way. As soon as we were getting close to the end, we watched those fellows who were trying to race to the end, and when they got close to the end we threw stones at them and they stopped. They knew it was better staying in line. So we ended up in one line. Then the farmer came over to me. "Shorty"—he called me Shorty— "What happened?" he said. "I can tell you what exactly happened. If you want to give a cigarette to one, that's not our way. You give us cigarettes, all or none." He said, "That's none of your business, that's my business." I said, "Yes, okay it's your business. But we end up all in one line on the end and then you can choose one or two to whom you give a cigarette or not." But I told him, "It would be more in your favor if you would come at lunch time with perhaps two or three loaves of bread and some peanut butter." We don't care about cigarettes because we smoke rose leaves. We picked leaves of roses and we made our cigarettes from that. A few days later at noon he called me, "Shorty, come over here." And he had a big basket; it had bread in there; it had peanut butter in it, and on the bottom three packs of cigarettes. So, then he realized that we guys were working better for him. And that's what I told him. "I think that's more in your favor, you spent some money but you have more success."

The farmer eventually became so comfortable with the POWs working for him that he did not bother to follow them out to the fields and he even let Goebeler drive his truck.

Despite the occasional minor controversy, the POW labor provided much needed manpower to farmers around Hearne. One local farmer remarked to a Swiss inspector in 1945 that although he could not brag about the work that the POWs did, they had nonetheless saved his crop the year before (Metraux 1945b).

Initially, POWs working away from the camp were closely guarded. Over time, security became lax as the farmers and guards came to know and trust the prisoners. Farmer John Nigliazzo said he never worried about the POWs running off. Ernst Froembsdorf recalled that some men tried to escape, but they were always caught, "Besides, where would you run away to?" According to Hugo Wannemacher: "Within a week, the guards knew the prisoners and so they trusted us. The guards assigned to our work detail sometimes went to sleep and then as a favor when the prisoners noticed someone, like a roving guard coming up the road, they woke the guard. The prisoners would say, 'Hey, watch it' or 'Watch out.' So there was a lot of give and take." Kathleen Stegall recalled that her husband sometimes had to awaken the American guard who had given his unloaded rifle to one of the POWs to guard the other prisoners (*Bryan-College Station Eagle* 1994). Heino Erichsen remembered one work detail during which the American assigned to guard duty began drinking whiskey immediately after the POWs got busy in the fields. Erichsen said the guard was so drunk that he passed out: "We carried the guard and his rifle and we put him on the truck and drove back to camp. We then got him off the truck and marched down the road into the camp. We were going to march him in as our prisoner, but then we thought we better not overdo this. Somebody might not have a sense of humor. So we shouldered his weapon and carried him into camp. I'm sure he spent a few days in the stockade for that."

Sometimes the Germans negotiated with the guards and farmers for favors. One time, Hugo Wannemacher recalled, "we asked the guard to put the amount that we were supposed to pluck at a very low level. Then in actuality, we plucked more and the difference the farmer gave to the guard, who in cooperation with the farmer could get money for that and make a profit and the guard shared the profit with the workers. So everybody got something good." What the POWs wanted—and got—was "a block of ice cream, ten centimeters long and very wide."

Many of the prisoners enjoyed the agricultural work outside the camp. Ernst Froembsdorf picked cotton while at Camp Hearne and claimed it was "good for his muscles." For others it was a relief to get out of the confines of the camp and to see the countryside. Sometimes POWs working on farms near the Brazos River were allowed to fish and swim during breaks and before they returned to camp (*Hearne Democrat* 1993). However, some of the men found agricultural work undesirable after a few days and sought alternative employment at the camp.

While performing agricultural work, such as picking cotton, many of the POWs developed relationships with local African Americans, who likened themselves to the Germans because they both were prisoners in America. They thus bonded in a special way. Peter Spoden said he stole clothing and shoes from the camp warehouses to give to African-American field hands he knew because the clothing these coworkers owned was worn out and tattered.

Hugo Wannemacher related an incident that occurred when he was work-ing in an onion field: "It turned out that the black people worked much faster than the Germans. And they helped the Germans." He said one African Amer-ican told him, "We're both the same." Arno Einicke, who had hardly ever in-teracted with black people in Germany, could not understand why Americans talked of equality for all human beings and yet seemed to treat African Ameri-cans as underlings: "I said, this is a weird country, when you treat your prison-ers better than your own people."

War Department officials realized that transporting prisoners to and from work sites every day was time consuming and expensive. As a solution, the War Department began to establish small branch camps for laboring prisoners (Kram-mer 1996, 88). In March, 1945, Lt. Col. Napoleon Rainbolt, Camp Hearne's com-mander, recommended that a branch camp capable of housing four hundred POWs be established at Chance Farm, some forty miles southwest of Hearne near Bryan (Schwieger and Shannahan 1945). The Chance Farm branch camp was activated April 1. Later that summer, the two large POW base camps at Huntsville and Mexia, which had largely been depopulated as prisoners were transferred to other camps in the United States or returned to Europe, became agricultural branch camps administered by Camp Hearne. In addition, a branch camp at Navasota, previously under the jurisdiction of Camp Huntsville, came under Camp Hearne's jurisdiction in July (Metraux 1945). Thus, Camp Hearne administered four branch camps in 1945. Table 4 lists the population of each of the branch camps from April, 1945, to January, 1946 (Census Data 1945).

Prisoners also engaged in other employment. They cleared brush from land and ditches, worked in gravel pits, and built fences. Peter Spoden stated that he

Table 4. German POW Population at Branch Camps Administered by Camp Hearne

Date	Chance Farm	Navasota	Huntsville	Mexia
April, 1945	65			
May	171			
June	179			
July	229			
August	247	164	577	545
September	187	214	343	358
October	230	271	0	370
November	230	264	0	414
December	230	0	0	0
January, 1946	231	0	0	0

Source: Census data 1945.

and other POWs helped build a house for a local farmer doing brickwork and carpentry. This house still stands next to the Brazos River, directly off Highway 21. Helen Palmos, who ran the City Cafe in downtown Hearne, remembered that she had a booming business during the war and employed three POWs who "cooked, washed dishes, made pies, and baked." When asked if the POWs were good workers, Palmos answered, "Oh yes, yes, yes. Goodness they worked."

As previously noted, most of the prisoners at Camp Hearne were NCOs and thus not required to work. According to Article 27 of the Geneva Convention, unless they volunteered to perform other duties, NCOs could only be required to engage in supervisory jobs. Very few of the NCOs at Camp Hearne volunteered to work. "No one worked at Camp Hearne because of principle," Willi Nellessen recalled. "Plus they had other things to do. They did not want to work." However, a small number of the NCOs did work. These prisoners took positions that they thought would benefit their comrades without helping the enemy. This included such positions as spokesman, interpreter, company leader, work crew leader, or as clerks around the camp.

Most employed NCOs worked in the mail distribution center established at Camp Hearne in March, 1944. The facility was set up to sort all incoming mail from Germany and to distribute it to other POW camps across the entire United States. About three hundred NCOs worked eight-hour shifts in the German Postal Unit. It operated around the clock and handled almost a hundred thousand pieces of mail per day (Fischer 1945).

At Hearne and elsewhere, NCOs refused to participate in other types of labor. The War Department believed this was a waste of potential labor and, as the European war drew to a close and Germany's defeat was assured, the War Department initiated "a vigorous, carefully planned campaign to sign up non-commissioned officers for three months voluntary work" (Adair 1945). A memorandum sent to the Camp Hearne commander in February, 1945, described some of the recommended tactics to recruit NCOs for work. For example, the memorandum suggested gathering NCOs together in small groups and asking them:

(1) If they do not feel that the privates who have been working in U.S. agriculture, industry, and military shops have gained valuable experience.

(2) If the privates have learned interesting things about America and gained interesting experiences from their many trips away from the stockade that will be good to talk about back in Germany.

(3) If they do not feel that the non-commissioned officers have become stagnant, learned little of American ways and work, improved very little their opportunity to make a living in Germany after the war, and seen little of interest in America from inside the compound.

(4) If they do not realize that there will soon be no war. That all able bodied men must go to work in the fields, or in the shops or in the building of homes to replace lost crops, food, machinery, and buildings.

(5) If they do not feel that they will be at a disadvantage in getting good jobs [in Germany] at such work when they have to compete with privates who have had more experience at this in America, and that it will be dangerous to them to be unable to do useful work skillfully in Germany (Adair 1945).

Furthermore, the document continued: "Inform them that there will be no member of the Nazi party in any position to cause retaliation on their family after the war if they sign to work here. It appears many such members of the Nazi party will be taken charge of by the allied Governments." The memo adds that one suggested method was not approved: "To have anyone pose as a Russian, or give any false publicity as to Russian representatives in the community or make any threats that they will be sent to Russia" (Adair 1945).

The NCO recruitment program at Camp Hearne was not completely successful, so on April 11, 1945, Lieutenant Colonel Rainbolt, the camp commander, acting on orders from Eighth Service Command, required that all German NCOs prove they held the rank they claimed. The commanding officer's position was resolute: "If these non-commissioned officers have documents of the German Army which prove their rank without any shadow of a doubt, they will be recognized as such. If the documents are lacking, they are considered as privates until proof of the contrary" (Metraux 1945). At first, the POWs had only to show something such as a letter addressed to them with the title "Unteroffizier" (the German rank designation for NCO). Later, when this was deemed insufficient, the NCOs had to produce an official document. Acceptable documentation included a "Soldbuch" (military record and pay book with identification carried by each soldier), "Luftwaffe special certificates, promotion certificates, certificates for granted medals of honor, [and] drivers licenses" (Weiss 1945b). However, many POWs did not have these documents because they had been confiscated when they were captured and not returned to them (Metraux 1945). Heino Erichsen recalled that two British soldiers took his "Soldbuch" in North Africa as a souvenir. According to Arno Einicke, some entrepreneurial noncoms began producing forged documents. "With the help of potatoes," he explained, "a stamp was made to fake the required documents." Regardless, the requirement led to a major reclassification of POWs at Hearne. The sudden drop in the number of NCOs and the corresponding dramatic increase in the number of junior enlisted men at Camp Hearne at this time are clearly attributed to this reclassification effort (Table 1).

Documentation of NCO status at Hearne, as well as at other internment camps across the country, was part of a campaign to increase the number of POW laborers. It proved quite successful. It also prompted outcries, complaints, and incorrigible actions by the POWs. On April 17, 1945, for instance, a group of prisoners from Compound 2 who had lost their NCO status were escorted outside the camp on a work detail. In the field, however, they refused to perform any labor. This led to disciplinary action by the guards: the prisoners were made to stand outside the camp gates in the sun all day and then were put in the guardhouse for supervision (Weiss 1945b).

All of the NCOs able to prove their rank status were placed in Compound 3. Additional pressures were placed on these prisoners in an effort to force them to work. Walter Fricke recalled that POWs who were working continued to have a regular diet because they needed to keep up their strength. Working prisoners were also given chocolate and encouraged to eat it in the open near the fence and thus "irritate those prisoners who were not working," said Fricke. However, the camp commander's plan backfired: the working prisoners shared their food with the nonworking prisoners through the fence. Fricke said the Americans quickly put a stop to this practice, but the Germans in Compound 2 continued to deliver food to those in Compound 3 at night. According to Fricke, several men would take a plank of wood and set it up like a seesaw near the fence. A bag of food was then placed on one end and two men jumped on the other, sending the food over the fence to the hungry prisoners on the far side.

The NCOs in Compound 3 did not yield to their captors' pressures. On April 5, 1945, to punish the prisoners for not working, the War Department revoked the privilege of NCOs interned in POW camps across the country to purchase "luxury goods" such as beer, candy, and cigarettes. This edict did not affect the junior enlisted men, which meant they had a larger selection of items to choose from at the canteens than did the NCOs. In addition, the camp's education programs were suspended for nonworking NCOs (Perret 1945). Some men eventually relented. "At the end of the war we didn't see the point anymore to refuse work," observed Willi Nellessen. "Additionally, we heard that if you continued to refuse work you were transferred out of Hearne to another camp, the reputation of which wasn't very good." After Germany surrendered in May, 1945, all NCOs were forced to work when the U.S. government decided to no longer adhere to the Geneva Convention on this matter.

Camp Hearne also employed a contingent of "protected personnel." These were prisoners who upon capture served as medical personnel, chaplains, or were members of voluntary aid societies, such as the German Red Cross (War Department 1944b). At Camp Hearne, protected personnel worked in the hospital and chapel. Officers, according to the Geneva Convention, were not required to work at all. However, the few German officers at the camp were all physicians and dentists and so worked at the camp hospital.

A few of the POWs were disabled and therefore unable to work. The others devised a way to pay them. The disabled POWs would maintain the barracks, cleaning them while the others were out on work details. In turn, the working POWs would give them scrip so that they could purchase items at the canteen.

In summary, the POWs at Camp Hearne performed most of the jobs needed to keep the camp running smoothly as well as much of the needed labor on area farms. This freed up hundreds of Americans who would otherwise have been required to do the jobs the prisoners performed. Every position that a POW filled meant one more American soldier was available for the war effort at home or overseas.

POW Morale

As time wore on, the POWs suffered from what Heino Erichsen calls "barbed wire sickness." According to Erichsen (2001, 58): "They [the prisoners] knew they were lucky to have survived the Africa Campaign, yet they did not feel completely relieved. All of their physical and mental energy had been spent fighting. Now that they were idle, they were worried, homesick, anxious, depressed, and angry by turns. Many had left wives and children behind in Germany and despaired over their fate." In his memoir, Fritz Haus commented: "Worse than the lack of privacy was our lack of freedom. The fenced-in feeling and a barbed wire mentality took hold of us."

The U.S. military authorities were aware of these problems and did everything they could to maintain the POWs' morale. Prisoners were allowed to write letters and cards to Germany so that they could stay in contact with loved ones back home. Camp authorities facilitated transfers in some cases to reunite fathers and sons, as well as brothers. Prisoners were also allowed to celebrate holidays and marry their fiancées in Germany via long-distance ceremonies. The importance of maintaining morale among the prisoners was not lost on their captors. They believed it would be easier to control the prisoners and that they would work harder if the men's morale was high.

Communication Home

Mail from home was eagerly anticipated by all the prisoners and usually provided a welcome emotional uplift. Pferdekämper-Geissel described how happy he was to receive fifteen birthday cards during the month of January. However, because of the long time between the posting of mail in Germany and the receipt of it at Camp Hearne, the news was always old. Fritz Haus said that the lag time seemed even longer after the bombing of a German city in which a prisoner had family and friends. Near the end of October, 1943, Haus read in the American newspapers that Kassel, his fiancée's hometown, had been destroyed. The paper included an aerial photo of the city taken after the raid that looked "as if a tornado had swept the city clean of every house and [all] permanent structures." Unfortunately, this destruction included the street on which his fiancée lived. "Was my Lisa among the estimated 25,000 dead victims?" Haus wondered. "Was she blown to pieces, burned to death or squashed and suffocated under the rubble of her four-story house? There was no way of finding out . . . I could do nothing but pray, wait, and trust." Haus did not receive a letter from his fiancée until five months after the bombing.

According to regulations created on April 22, 1942, each prisoner was allowed to write two letters and one postcard per week. Letters could be no more than twenty-four lines and a specific kind of ink was to be used when writing them. All correspondence had to be written in clear language and could not contain information about the POW camp or the treatment they received (Walker 2001, 65–66). Any letter violating these rules was confiscated. All correspondence was routed through the Office of Censorship, which resulted in a significant delay in sending the mail on to Germany. This caused many complaints and led to the issuance of new regulations in the summer of 1943. Enlisted men and NCOs were allowed to send only one letter and one postcard per week, whereas officers were allowed five of each per week. Eventually, to further streamline the process, which had developed a considerable backlog, the Office of Censorship randomly chose one out of every twenty pieces of prisoner mail for examination. In February, 1944, the POWs' allotment was reduced to two letters and four post cards per month for enlisted men and NCOs. There was no change for officers. These efforts never completely ended the problems or delays that engendered complaints. When POW mail arrived in Germany, government officials read and censored it before forwarding it to the addressee. Mail to the prisoners was also examined, analyzed, and censored by both countries. "Both sides censored the mail," said Heino Erichsen. "One side blacked out the words and the other side cut them out." He said sometimes the POWs were left with only greetings and the smallest bits of news.

Haus described how he was able to write more letters than he was allowed:

> I established a flourishing letter writing business from my Hearne vestry and exceeded the monthly allowance many times over by using the wasted forms and postcards of those who did not want to or could not write. Some had lost their immediate loved ones through bombs and air raids. Others had no knowledge of their people's whereabouts in Poland and other eastern countries, now in Russian hands. This enabled me to write to many friends and churches, under many names and guises. [Friends and family in] Hamburg, Pinneberg, Greifswald, Hersfeld, Kassel, and Hohnstedt/Einbeck received regular reports, greetings, and encouragement [from me]. More than ever before, Hearne gave me the perfect opportunity to continue my involvement with the German Baptists which had so fruitfully began during the Thirties . . . Most of my letters were copied by friends at home and sent on to Lisa [my fiancée]; she had quite a collection of letters from "behind the barbed wire church" in her file. . . . It was fun to write so much every week. It was still greater to receive so many replies.

Prisoners were also permitted to correspond with relatives in the United States. However, these had to be close relatives: grandparents, parents, siblings, aunts, or uncles. Carl Bruns corresponded with Lanah H. Newcomer, one of his father's first cousins, who lived in Mount Morris, Illinois. She had visited Carl and his family in 1935 in Germany. In order to correspond with her, he referred to her as Aunt Newcomer. Bruns believes the Americans were aware of the charade and that they chose to allow it to continue.

Visitors and Fraternization

The POWs also were authorized visits from relatives living in the United States. Many of the prisoners had brothers, sisters, uncles, aunts, and even parents who had become naturalized citizens before the war. In the spring of 1944, for example, Chris Smoellner of Lawrence, Kansas, a naturalized U.S. citizen, visited his brother, Hans, who was a prisoner held at Camp Hearne. Smoellner, who had not seen his brother in twenty-five years, took advantage of the opportunity for a reunion when he learned that he was in a POW camp in Texas (*Hearne Democrat* 1944a). Similarly, the parents and sister of Cpl. Hugo Krauss visited often (Erichsen 2001). These visits took place in a special building outside the prison compounds.

The German POWs also looked forward to interacting with the guards and local residents they encountered, especially women. Helen Palmos, who brought magazines to the German prisoners, said she would chitchat with the POWs, but was ordered not to discuss the war. Some of the men would discuss the fashions depicted in magazine ads, commenting that their wives would look good in a particular style. Some showed her photographs of their families. Civilian Roy Henry, a classmate of the camp commander's son, spent time at the American officers' club where all the waiters were POWs. Henry said that he talked with the POWs quite a bit, mostly "about women, the movies, [and] the war."

Haus recalled a pleasant incident that occurred when he was working in a warehouse. He said he heard someone on the other side of a wall whistling the tune, "What a Friend We Have in Jesus." Curious as to whom it might be, he walked to the divider and began to whistle the song's alto part. The melody stopped, but Haus continued on his own, switching to the melody. After about five minutes of solo whistling, the other whistler joined back in the song, so Haus again took the accompanying alto part. Finally, Haus opened the divider and asked who was whistling. A black man with a huge smile on his face admitted that it was he and asked, "Do you know Jesus?" Haus replied, "Of course I do!" The two men shook hands and chatted. From that day forward, whenever Haus had an occasion to visit the warehouse he would try to find his friend and strike up a conversation.

"We were friendly to them [the Germans] and all that," said former guard Matt Ware. "The longer we stayed the more lax it got." Besides, he reasoned, "The POWs had it made. Why would they run?" John Luparelli said the prisoners would joke with him, sometimes calling him "Mussolini" because of his Italian heritage and large size. Peter Spoden said the prisoners often played cards with the guards when the officer was gone and wagered with cigarettes, a practice that was clearly against regulations.

The POWs working around the camp, especially in the PX, looked forward to visits with children. Doris Emshoff, who was five or six years old at the time, recalled visiting the camp with her uncle and aunt. They usually visited on Sundays and, while the adults visited and shopped in the PX, the POWs entertained the children, often giving them cookies and toys. Glenn Zoch, Chaplain Gustave Zoch's son, recalled that on his birthday the POWs "baked a cake for me. It was the richest cake I guess I've ever eaten. It was my tenth birthday—that would have been in '43. They made a ten-layer cake and each layer was about an inch thick, and it was made with butter, because it was a yellow cake. The layers in between were different kinds of jellies, like grape jelly, raspberry jelly, and this kind of thing. And the frosting on the cake was made with butter and sugar. What a combination. And it was so rich. Man, I can still taste it. One of those things that you just don't forget."

Peter Spoden suggested that some of the POWs may have fraternized with civilian women: "There were farmer's daughters who were very concerned or were willing to show the farm and chickens and so on, you know." Former guard Jack Kuttruff said he heard a rumor that one of the POWs was sneaking out at night to meet a local woman: "He was getting out and meeting this old girl out there in the pasture. I always thought it wasn't true, but it could have been."

Transfers

To help boost prisoner morale, POWs were sometimes allowed to transfer to another camp to be reunited with a relative. According to this policy, the United States would allow immediate family members (fathers and sons or brothers) to transfer if camp officials approved of the transfers, if the prisoners themselves covered the expenses, and if the prisoners were considered cooperative. Noncooperative prisoners were automatically denied this privilege. The army received negative coverage from various newspapers across the country because of this policy. Judged by the number of transfer requests, the practice became so commonplace that it sometimes hindered the efficient use of POW labor. Still, the practice continued until the end of the war (Walker 2001, 69–70).

Camp Hearne was no exception to this policy. Prisoners there filed numerous transfer requests and the desire to reunite family members was just one of the reasons cited. Camp Hearne provides several examples that illustrate the variety of reasons transfers were sought. When Rudolf Kleinmichel, who was incarcerated at Camp McCoy, Wisconsin, learned that his brother Helmut was being held at Camp Hearne, he requested that his brother be transferred to join him in Wisconsin. His request received favorable consideration in the summer of 1944 (Edwards 1944a). That autumn, Rudi Traue requested transfer to Camp Clarinda, Iowa, to be reunited with his brother Heinz. Lieutenant Colonel Cecil Stiles, the commanding officer, considered Traue to be noncooperative and rejected his request. However, Stiles suggested that Traue's transfer request would be favorably reconsidered at a later date if he would become more cooperative (Adair 1944; Smith 1944a; Stiles 1944a; Traue 1944). In January, 1945, Hans Mueller, interned at Camp Perry, Ohio, sought the transfer of his father, Karl, who was a prisoner at Hearne. American officials granted this request (Smith 1945a). Likewise, Josef Victoris of Camp Crowder, Missouri, requested that his brother Hans be transferred to his camp in Missouri and at least one U.S. official agreed to the transfer (Smith 1944b). In June, 1945, two prisoners approached the visitor from the Swiss Legation to put forward their requests. Max Remsheid wished to be reunited with his brother Rudi at Fort Sam Houston, Texas, and Alfred Sellin wanted to be with his son Lothar, who was being held in Louisiana (he was uncertain as to which camp). Both expressed their willingness to cover the expenses and the Swiss inspector endorsed both transfer requests (Metraux 1945).

Some transfers occurred for political reasons rather than at the request of a POW. Ardent Nazis were sent to camps designed specifically for them, particularly Camp Alva, Oklahoma. This practice began on October 19, 1943, when Lt. Col. Robert Whitson, the Camp Hearne commander, requested the transfer of six prisoners to Camp Alva. Whitson described Cpl. Klaus Eberhard Bork as "deceitful" in that he was "quiet and polite in the presence of American officers, but when with other prisoners of war he is arrogant and boisterous." Further, Bork had been reprimanded for "making agitating speeches to other prisoners of war." Herman Waschk was also seen as "an active agitator" who constantly praised the Nazi regime. Willi Steder, Siegfried Kalkbrenner, and Ewald Nieswand were described as "arrogant and persistent Nazi agitators" who used their higher ranks to demoralize the other prisoners and had a negative influence on productivity by "hindering the work" of the others, by themselves being "reluctant to work," and by causing "a similar reluctance in their companies." Max Jettkowski was reported to have been a "trouble-maker" previously, and was suspected of continuing in this habit. While none of these allegations were established conclusively, the camp commander obviously thought them sufficient to justify a transfer (Whitson 1943). At least one other officer agreed with him in this judgment (Edwards 1943a). Inspection reports note that other prisoners also were transferred to the "Nazi" camp in Alva, Oklahoma. In February, 1945, it was noted that fifteen were transferred to Camp Alva "for subversive activity," meaning that they were Nazis (Lakes 1945).

Anti-Nazi POWs were also sent to camps specifically designed for them for their own protection. For example, in July, 1943, army officials in Washington ordered the transfer of three prisoners from Hearne to Camp McCain, Mississippi, which had been designated in June as a permanent anti-Nazi camp. These prisoners—Gerhard Krueger, Ernst Beck, and one named Doberenz—were to be treated with care. All necessary arrangements were to be made for their medical needs and, "in accordance with a recent directive from the Secretary of War, none of these prisoners should be handcuffed for any reason whatsoever" (Summers 1943a). The Office of the Assistant Chief of Staff issued a similar order in October, directing that Mathias Steffes be sent to Camp McCain (Edwards 1943b). In both cases, no specific reason was given for the transfers. It should also be noted that the inspection reports occasionally mentioned that prisoners were being held under protective custody in the guardhouse pending their transfer to another camp (Fischer 1945). Presumably this meant that they were anti-Nazis or at least felt threatened by the Nazis in the camp.

In February, 1944, two prisoners—Peter Fey and Fritz Emil Tschofen—both of whom claimed to be anti-Nazi, expressed anxiety about being transferred from the hospital in Temple, where they were then residing, to Camp Hearne. Lieutenant Colonel John Dunn, Hearne's commanding officer, requested their transfer elsewhere because he thought the prisoners' lives would be in danger at Camp Hearne. Higher authorities agreed. They had "shown themselves to be anti-Nazi" and so were sent to Camp McCain (Dunn 1944a; Edwards 1944b; Guerre 1944; Jones 1944; Venable 1944). Later that month, arrangements were made for Walter Goetze to be sent to Camp McCain as well (Edwards 1944c).

As the case of Fey and Tschofen illustrates, officers at Camp Hearne sometimes made the arrangements for these transfers on the POWs' behalf. Another example of this took place in December, 1943, when Lieutenant Colonel Stiles forwarded the names of ten men who claimed to be anti-Nazi and to have been threatened by the Nazis in the camp. Stiles noted that three of them had been attacked already, had been saved "by prompt action" by the Americans, and were being held in protective custody. This request successfully navigated the bureaucratic channels so that the prisoners in question could be transferred to Camp McCain. (Byrd 1943; Edwards 1944d; Shaw 1943; Stiles 1943a).

In early 1944, Gottfried Günther, who claimed to be a Protestant minister, requested transfer to an anti-Nazi camp. He was accepted as an anti-Nazi and his request was approved. Although scheduled to be sent to Camp McCain like the others, his orders were changed to Fort Devens, Massachusetts. For some unspecified reason, his move was delayed until after March 15, 1944 (Edwards 1944e; Guerre 1944; Stiles 1944b). In the spring of 1944 Hugo Klapper, Johannes Preuss, and Gustel Schartz sought transfer for their own protection. This example has another angle to it: "these men have requested that they be transferred to a camp where they can work in the woods. They claim to be lumbermen." They claimed that they were not "Democrats" (anti-Nazi) but feared that they could become the victims of violence and bodily harm. Arrangements were made to send them to Camp Campbell, Kentucky (Byrd 1944a; Dunn 1944b). Perhaps they posed as lumberjacks in an effort to fool their fellow Germans concerning their reasons for seeking a transfer.

One of the more curious examples of a political transfer involves the only known Italian POW to be held at Camp Hearne. However, the case is actually more complex. On December 11, 1943, a POW at Camp Hulen named Hans Palmieri was attacked by five fellow prisoners and sustained injuries. He was treated at the infirmary and remained there for eight days. He was then transferred to Camp Hearne and later to Camp Maxey. On December 20, 1943, Lieutenant Colonel Stiles requested that Palmieri be transferred from Hearne to a camp "more suitable to prisoners of his kind" because he was "a moral pervert who does not have a place among other prisoners. He is a Swiss-Italian and claims he is not a Nazi" (Carnahan 1944; Jaffe 1943; Stiles 1943b). Although Stiles did not explain what he meant by the term "moral pervert," it may be an oblique accusation that he displayed homosexual tendencies.

An officer at Eighth Service Command's headquarters suggested that Palmieri be disciplined for conduct prejudicial to "good order and discipline, and that this prisoner be required to keep his person and personal equipment and clothing in a clean and orderly condition." Furthermore, the officer recommended that Palmieri be hospitalized so that a medical diagnosis could determine if he was truly a "moral pervert." A medical report was made at Camp Hulen, but it concerned only the wounds Palmieri had sustained in the December attack. After further inquiries into his case, Stiles explained that Palmieri had been transferred from the Italian army to the German army prior to being captured and concluded that his "demeanor is not so good." A night patrol had apprehended him at Camp Maxey for being outside his barracks. His excuse was that he was afraid to sleep inside, so he was taken into protective custody. According to a later report, Germans at Camp Hearne told the Americans that Palmieri was a "moral pervert" but "careful observation does not indicate anything of this character. The Germans are believed to have made this charge in the usual Nazi manner so that suspicion would be thrown upon him." Apparently, Stiles fell for the deception. In any event, it was no longer safe for Palmieri to be incarcerated with the German POWs at Hearne. Palmieri was transferred to Camp Campbell, Kentucky—another anti-Nazi camp (Byrd 1944a, 1944b; Carnahan 1944; Holmes 1943; Jaffe 1943; Stiles 1943b).

On at least one occasion, a prisoner was less concerned about where he was interned in the United States than he was with the destination of his eventual repatriation after the war. Robert Weller sent a letter to the commanding officer on August 10, 1945, after the war was over, requesting repatriation to Guatemala. His father was German and his mother was Guatemalan, he claimed, and he had been an architectural engineering student in Germany. While in Germany, he had been required to participate in the labor service and was later conscripted into the German army when the war began in 1939. He was sent to North Africa in August, 1942, and captured by the British in November. He said he had to be cautious during his military service because "on account of my native place and of my unpolitical attitude I often met distrust and reserve in the German service unit. Therefore in war-captivity I always concealed my real native place. This was the result of a pure instinct of self-preservation." He feared being labeled a spy or traitor and claimed to have witnessed a prisoner from South Africa being beaten to death while in a POW camp in Egypt. He also claimed that a prisoner had been beaten to death in the United States. His request for a discharge based on his extenuating circumstances was rejected. American authorities stated that because Weller's father was a German citizen, he was considered to be one as well (Weller 1945).

Major Theodore Zaetsch, Camp Hearne's last commander, sent a memorandum to his commanding general that mentioned additional information from the censorship office that already had been sent to headquarters and which cast doubt on Weller's claims. These included information about his South American contacts who were deemed "suspicious"; his denials of correspondence with U.S. residents with whom the censors claimed he had corresponded; and the fact that these individuals, along with his mother, were on a list of contacts for a POW named Maximilian Schubart, who had attempted an escape. Finally, Zaetsch noted that although Weller claimed to be an anti-Nazi, he knew nothing about the activities of the camp's Nazi POWs (Zaetsch 1945a). The end result of this correspondence was a memorandum from the commanding general in Washington, D.C., stating that Weller would "be repatriated to the country in whose army he was serving at the time of capture." As it turns out, this was standard procedure; no prisoners were repatriated elsewhere or allowed to remain in the United States. However, many did later return to live in the United States (Walker 2001, 84).

Finally, several transfers stand out because of the unusual circumstances surrounding them. On December 10, 1943, secret orders were transmitted for the transfer of three prisoners being held at Camp Mexia and Sgt. August Sevenheck at Camp Hearne. The prisoners were to be transported to Love Field in Dallas, where, on December 11, they would board a military aircraft and fly to Halifax, Novia Scotia, and be turned over to British control. No explanation was offered for the urgency, the unusual nature of the transportation arranged for the transfers, their transfer to British authority, or the secrecy (Ulio 1943; Summers 1943b). Several months later, in August, 1944, arrangements were made to transfer 125 German prisoners of Polish origin from Hearne to the United Kingdom (Coyne 1945a; Smith 1944c). Finally, in October of that year, twenty-five German prisoners claiming to be Czechs were transferred to various camps in Texas and other states—most of them to Florence, Arizona. American officials decided that these prisoners would be screened at their destination camps (Zaetsch 1945b). Although the documents do not offer any explanation for the transfer of either group, their nationalities may have been the reason. Once U.S. officials realized that they were holding citizens of Allied nations as POWs, arrangements were made to return them to their respective embassies so that they could be restored to active duty (Krammer 1996, 299). Since Poland was considered an ally in the struggle against Nazi Germany, it is very likely that those POWs were repatriated in this manner.

Holidays

Separated from their loved ones by a great distance and knowing that their families were in a war zone, it is understandable that holidays were of particular significance to the prisoners. Several recalled that they were allowed to celebrate holidays such as Christmas, New Year's Eve, and Easter. The extent of these celebrations is illustrated by the 1943 Christmas celebration, as recounted in a story that appeared in the *Hearne Democrat* on December 31. On the twenty-third, several hundred prisoners made extensive preparations to observe their first Christmas in America. They decorated Christmas trees, one for each company mess hall, with homemade decorations and items bought by the compound leaders, who had been taken shopping in town under guard. The prisoners received gift packages from families and friends in Germany, planned for a Christmas meal, and posed for photographs to be sent home. Each POW was allowed to send one photograph and one Christmas greeting, in addition to his normal postal quota. The men primped and preened themselves, pinching their cheeks to give them a glow, so they would look their best for the photographer; some even went to the camp barbershop for a trim.

Religious services were held on Christmas Eve and Christmas Day, one each for Catholics and Lutherans. The Lutheran services were conducted by Chaplain Zoch, himself a Lutheran, aided by an unnamed prisoner who had studied theology (probably Fritz Haus). Fathers Peter Villani and B. Bravi of Saint Anthony's Catholic Church and Father J. B. Gleissner of Saint Joseph Catholic Church, both in nearby Bryan, performed the Catholic services. Despite Nazism's antireligious nature, Chaplain Zoch said, Christians and non-Christians alike generally observed Christmas. The Americans even bent the rules for the Christmas service in that they permitted the prisoners to mingle between compounds, a practice usually not allowed. As an additional preparation for the festivities, one of the mess halls baked thousands of bell-shaped cookies. A prisoner using metal from a tin can handcrafted the bell-shaped cookie cutter. The prisoners grew, shelled, and roasted peanuts for their Christmas feast. Finally, the holiday festivities included a concert by the prisoner orchestra (*Hearne Democrat* 1943).

Arno Einicke recalled that he and his comrades also brewed homemade "spirits" to enliven the celebration. He mentioned that on Christmas Day, he and another comrade from Compound 2 visited a friend in the hospital. His partner brought a present in a Coca Cola bottle, which Einicke was able to sample: schnapps made from oranges, grapefruit, and other fruits.

Long-Distance Marriages

Long-distance marriages between prisoners and their fiancées in Germany were sometimes conducted at Camp Hearne. The American camp chaplain, Gustave Zoch, performed many marriages, once conducting twelve such ceremonies in a single day. Reverend Zoch said that the highest-ranking prisoner in the camp officiated at these proceedings. The marriages were not religious ceremonies and thus no prayers were involved. Typically, the German bride had legal papers drawn up in Germany, signed them in front of witnesses, and then mailed them to her intended husband. Zoch explained that after the soldier signed the documents in front of witnesses, the two were considered husband and wife "in the name of Hitler and the Third Reich."

Arno Einicke related a story about the marriage of a prisoner named Heinz. This prisoner decided to marry his girl when "he learned that he had become a father. This was a bad situation because there was another girl whom he loved even more." He discussed the situation with his friends and was "convinced that he should marry the mother of the child, even though he was in love with someone else." Apparently it was a German tradition that friends pay a surprise visit to the bride and groom the evening after the ceremony. Because the POW was separated from his bride, his comrades performed the ritual on him alone. According to Einicke:

> In Germany it was customary to make all kinds of noise and place garbage and other things in front of the doorway of the bride and groom. In Hearne, this happened in front of the groom's bunk. Heinz was sleeping in his bed at the barrack entrance. Nobody, not even Heinz or his neighbors, was moving. It was after ten o'clock. When we

burst in, Heinz and his neighbors got a little scared as we threw all this stuff down. He got up, turned on the lamp and looked at the pile of garbage and shook his head. Everybody laughed. At this point, the groom had to remove the garbage. Now, in Germany both the groom and the bride are supposed to do that. But in this case he had to do it himself and he did that with all kinds of other people around giving him all sorts of good advice, which he probably loved. And this took practically the entire night . . . and the rest of the people were very happy to do without sleep because they had fun seeing what he had to go through.

Fritz Haus, a prisoner and assistant to Chaplain Zoch, was also married by proxy. After he learned in late February, 1944, that his fiancée, Lisa Paukstadt, had survived the air raids on Kassel the preceding October, he resolved to marry her. This took place on the morning of March 4, 1944. The procedure, as described earlier, was quite simple: he signed the official papers (which were in German, English, French, Swedish, and Spanish) in the presence of the camp commander, Chaplain Zoch, and a representative from the International Red Cross. The papers were then sent to a German magistrate in Hohnstedt by way of Geneva, Switzerland, for his bride's signature. Once that was accomplished, said Haus, the marriage contract "was legal and binding, in other words, we then were officially and truly married." As part of the ceremony at Camp Hearne, Zoch administered a wedding vow to Haus and said a prayer. "It was such a solemn occasion when I took the ring from my left hand and put it onto the right ring finger," Haus recalled. Afterward, everyone shook his hand and congratulated him. His bride went through a similar ceremony in Hohnstedt on July 25. Haus noted that about twenty fellow prisoners had been married in the same way during the previous three months. When he returned to Germany, the couple had a church wedding in Oberzwehren/Kassel. Haus later boasted with a touch of humor: "Lisa and I can claim the rare distinction of having been married three times to the same man and to the same woman. We have three wedding dates!"

Deaths and Funerals

About a dozen prisoners died at Camp Hearne of natural causes (heart disease, tuberculosis, cancer, and pneumonia), in accidents, or as the result wounds. In addition, two POWs committed suicide, one was murdered, and another was shot and killed by American guards while trying to escape.

Burials were in the camp cemetery, which was located northeast of the camp on a small hill within a cluster of trees. The POWs voluntarily worked to construct and maintain the cemetery. A small fountain was constructed at the site and each grave was marked by a wooden cross. The POWs planted flowers on the graves and kept the cemetery immaculate.

According to Arno Einicke:

When a death occurred, the German leadership decided who among the Germans would be in the honor guard and who would carry the casket. Normally these people came from the company of the dead person and then it was decided whether the army or air force uniform should be worn. In any case, the clothing had to be of the first order. Only a few comrades entered into Camp Hearne with their uniforms intact. We had to borrow our uniforms from them. A priest gave the final talk at the grave and he prayed. This took place with every person being buried in an honorary fashion. At one point when the casket was being carried by the POWs at the ceremony, two comrades covered it in a V-shaped manner with a German battle flag [that] was as large as a U-boat flag. None of the American guards interfered with this because the ceremony was holy and was not allowed to be disrupted. When the casket was lowered into the grave, somebody, a comrade, pulled the flag away and hid it on his person.

Einicke and the others then marched back to camp and into their compound. The flag was contraband and the Americans would search for it as soon as the service over. However, they never recovered it. Einicke said he thought the flag was hidden in one of the lavatories or under a barrack.

The Americans assisted with the funerals by providing a military coffin and an honor guard to fire a twenty-one-gun salute. Matt Ware recalled that the Germans "had their own funeral, just like they would if they were in Germany and we gave them full military honors. They were given the same honors as if they were American soldiers. It was a regular military coffin." Some recalled that an American honor guard fired a twenty-one-gun salute. Mildred Payne, who lived on Milam Street overlooking the camp, could see the camp cemetery from her back porch. On one occasion, she heard shots and assumed that one of the Germans in attendance had been fired at, but what she actually heard was the military salute being given at the gravesite. Typically, ten to forty POWs attended a funeral.

Civilians were not allowed to watch the POW funerals. Helen Palmos said that Lt. Col. Albert Tucker, then serving as camp commander, denied her request to attend a funeral. Not one to be told what to do, Palmos replied: "'Well, I can stop on the highway and watch them.' In reply he said, 'You cannot stop on the highway.' I said, 'What if my car goes dead?' Colonel Tucker replied that he couldn't help that." On the day of the funeral, Palmos drove to a high point on the nearby highway and pretended that her car had stalled. She said a chaplain performed the funeral rites and that the POWs participating in the funeral service wore their German uniforms and clicked their heels and said, "Heil Hitler."

Former POW Walter Fricke said that none of the Germans wanted to attend the funeral of Hugo Krauss, a German corporal murdered by his fellow POWs, in uniform because they thought Krauss was a traitor. Usually, those who attended funerals would go out of their way to borrow a German uniform if they did not have one of their own. Hugo Wannemacher recalled that some were suspicious that Krauss was a planted spy because he frequently conversed with the guards and was accorded special privileges, such as being able to go outside the camp. The POWs wore their regular POW clothing at Krauss's funeral as a form of protest. Krauss's parents and sister drove from New York to attend the funeral. He was buried with American military honors.

After the war, the bodies in the Camp Hearne cemetery were disinterred before the camp was deactivated and the property sold back to civilians. Most of the remains were returned to relatives in Germany or other countries such as Austria or Czechoslovakia. Those that were not claimed by relatives were relocated to an American military cemetery. Hugo Krauss and a number of other former German POWs from various camps in Texas are now buried in a separate part of the National Cemetery at Fort Sam Houston in San Antonio.

CHAPTER 3

Problems at the Camp

DURING THE COURSE OF ITS OPERATION, Camp Hearne experienced a variety of political and nonpolitical problems. These occurrences often amounted to little more than harmless pranks or various other efforts by the prisoners to relieve the stress and tedium of their incarceration. For the Americans and for some of the prisoners, however, these events were disturbing because they involved breaking the rules. Some of the more violent events were sources of consternation for the Americans. The various infractions include the use of secret shortwave radios, a hidden room, alcohol distillation, attempted escapes, shootings, suicides, Nazi propaganda activities, subversion of the Postal Unit, and even the murder of one of the prisoners. Moreover, the ways in which the officials running the camp dealt with these issues is revealing. These are some of the most intriguing aspects of the history of Camp Hearne.

ALCOHOL DISTILLATION

Nearly all of the POWs, even those who did not drink, knew that alcoholic beverages were being illegally produced inside the compounds. "Alcohol was prohibited in the camp," Otto Schulz recalled. "This caused the POWs to produce it secretly. Experts constructed distilling devices out of parts such as tubes from the heating system. Fruits were collected, squeezed, and the juice was heated in the kitchen stove and distilled to liquor." Some of the POWs had worked in distilleries before the war and were knowledgeable about the craft of brewing and fermenting alcohol. They had everything they needed to make contraband beverages right at their fingertips: fruit, fruit juice, vegetables, water, yeast, and sugar. Many of the POWs remember their comrades getting drunk at night on homemade spirits. Robert Goede remembered making wine in the kitchen: "We used to get a lot of pineapple in cans and we would save the juice and we would put a little yeast in it. Put it up in the attic and let it ferment and it turned into alcohol alright, but it gave you a terrible headache!" Walter Fricke recalled that some of the men in his barrack fermented grapefruit juice to produce schnapps. This form of alcohol was fermented in one-gallon glass jars obtained from the kitchen and hidden in a hole in the ground under his barrack. He said only small amounts of schnapps were produced, not gallons. "There was a period during which we made a type of wine from grapefruit," said Alfred Jasper, "but unfortunately there was so much alcohol in it we all got headaches. So I did that only once." Willi Nellessen recalled that some of the prisoners even made alcohol from watermelons. Jasper said that one of his comrades who had served in Russia apparently learned how to make vodka while there. "One day," recounted Jasper, "he said, 'Bring me some potatoes from the kitchen. Smaller ones . . . and put sugar on them and put them in gallon glass jars with water.' [When someone asked,] 'What are you going to do?' [he answered,] 'Don't worry about it.' Eight days, fourteen days . . . we all waited. . . . We produced vodka!"

Guard Bobby Sullivan said the POWs made alcohol in pots and pans or whatever other containers they could find. Because each company had its own mess hall and kitchen, it was not difficult for the prisoners to obtain the necessary supplies. "I remember we would raid the compounds because they would take the potatoes and orange peels and they would make booze. They would hide it in different places," recalled Sullivan. He estimated that the guards discovered a stash of alcohol about once a month. The most common hiding places were under the barracks or up in the rafters.

Peter Spoden revealed another method by which the prisoners obtained alcohol: "Some people tried to clean up aftershave lotion in such a way that you could drink the alcohol." Spoden did not know how this was accomplished, but guard Matt Ware recalled how "they took shaving lotion, shaving tonic, and purified it through bread [as a filter] and drank it, and got drunk. They could buy the stuff. If I remember correctly, I was on guard duty one day and a pick-up [truck] came out there and it had cases of that old green shaving tonic which was about sixty or seventy percent alcohol and that old colonel said, 'Them prisoners are clean prisoners.' [But] they were making alcohol out of that stuff, taking the other stuff out and drinking the alcohol. Now I don't know what they cut it with to drink, [but I imagine] they were probably coughing and everything else." Werner Kritzler confirms Ware's description. He said he watched some of his comrades clean up the shaving tonic by taking a loaf of bread, cutting off the ends of the loaf, and then pouring the shaving lotion through the bread. What came out was pure alcohol.

Arno Einicke recalled that on New Year's Eve, 1944, the members of the camp orchestra and the choir celebrated with music and drink. After consuming much homemade alcohol, the men became quite boisterous in their enthusiasm and organized a parade. Members of the band, the choir, and other prisoners began to march down the main road in the compound. The Americans mobilized to stop the celebration before it got out of hand. "The searchlights went on," said Einicke, "and the Americans entered the compound with clubs. The streamlined marchers disappeared into the barracks as well as the musicians with their instruments. There was one exception, the fellow with the big drum tried to get across the drainage ditch, fell, and got stuck." The drum and its owner were apprehended by the guards and placed in the guardhouse, then released the next day because the band was scheduled for a New Year's Day performance for the camp commander.

THEFT AND OTHER CRIMES

Criminal behavior was occasionally a problem at Camp Hearne. In the beginning, prisoners did not steal from other prisoners. Arno Einicke said a special camaraderie existed between prisoners who had served together in the Afrika Korps, "which was such that you could put your laundry on the laundry line and nobody would steal it. Now, when the Normandy and other troops came in, that is, prisoners of war, say, from France, then you couldn't do that anymore." Clearly, the same level of trust did not exist between the prisoners who had fought on different battlefields later in the war. The prisoners themselves punished comrades who stole from their fellow POWs. "They would steal [things] from each other like cigarettes," said guard John Luparelli, "but they handled it between themselves. They had their own way of correcting that."

On the other hand, the prisoners had no qualms about taking things that were useful to them from the Americans. Spoden recalled that sometimes the prisoners would get a guard involved in a conversation to distract him so that their cohorts could steal something. Robert Goede, who worked in the camp kitchen, recalled that men sometimes stole utensils, even though the utensils had to be accounted for every evening. Theft was not limited to the POWs. Clerk-typist Annie Sweat said that a guard from Oklahoma who worked in the hospital supply office "stole silverware, sheets, and everything that he could get [his hands on]. I think that they slapped him on the wrist and took the things back and let him continue to work."

Other forms of theft took place as well. A common complaint of prisoners all over the country was that their captors stole from them. The POWs at Camp Hearne were no exception. Seven prisoners complained to representatives of the Swiss Legation that Americans had confiscated various personal articles from them before they arrived at Camp Hearne. Gustav Fischer, Hans Wellhafer, and Richard Rangsdorf claimed that suitcases were taken from them at Camp Huntsville prior to their being sent to Hearne. A POW named Mannheim added that the receipts of twenty-four German POWs were altered at Huntsville and that listings of cameras, pocketknives, and other personal effects had been erased and the amounts altered. Herman Schauble and Joachim Marker both said personal belongings were taken from them when they arrived in Norfolk, Virginia. Specifically, receipts from Casablanca totaling twenty-four thousand francs were taken from Schauble and a leather case with personal items from Marker. Lastly, Georg Prestel said American officials took twenty-three thousand French francs from him at Camp Chancy in North Africa and that upon arrival at Ellis Island in New York an American soldier placed all of his personal belongings—about forty items in all, including a pocket watch, a wallet containing the receipt for the French francs, a fountain pen, and a travel kit—in a bag. Then, according to Prestel, the bag and its contents "disappeared while he was taking a shower. He explains that he placed the bag near the shower, but a soldier ordered him to another shower. When he returned, the bag was allegedly gone and he was unable to locate the soldier" (Swiss Legation 1943).

The State Department referred the matter to the War Department, which pursued a two-month investigation, the results of which undoubtedly disappointed the Germans. No information was available concerning the personal items allegedly taken from the three POWs at Camp Huntsville. With regard to Mannheim's complaint, the report flatly stated that the personal belongings of POWs were forwarded to them. The report was more specific for Schauble and Marker: their personal belongings were forwarded to the Property Pool of the Prisoner of War Information Bureau. Prestel's case received much attention. The initial report concluded that his property had not been found and expressed doubts as to the authenticity of his story, but a subsequent detailed report expanded upon those findings. According to the later report, an "exhaustive and thorough search of the records of the Internal Security Office and other agencies" connected to the movements of POWs in the Staten Island Terminal "failed to reveal any information whatsoever pertaining either to the subject, or to his personal property." Finally, a memorandum concluded that there was no record of personal property taken from Prestel "or that he made complaint of the theft at the time he was processed" and that his initial complaint erroneously referred to Ellis Island when prisoners were processed at Staten Island, hence the investigation at that office (Bryan 1944a; Department of State 1944; Elfenbein 1944; Rogers 1944a; Tollefson 1944a; Tyler 1944). The reports repeatedly emphasized the procedures for handling POW property and assumed that all of the American personnel involved faithfully followed them. It is possible that Prestel's complaint, as well as the others, were merely attempts to make life difficult for the Americans (Walker 1980, 182–83). However, it is also possible that their stories were truthful and that unscrupulous GIs robbed them.

Another problem concerned homosexuality. In the 1930s and 1940s, having homosexual relations was a serious crime in Nazi Germany and a court-martial offense in the German military. Although rare, several prisoners remembered hearing stories about prisoners trying to engage in homosexual acts. According to Fritz Haus, there were "some weak characters who were trying to do that. You can't really do this without being found out. They deviated from the Nazi line, so the Nazis in the camp resorted to the 'kangaroo court.' This is especially [true] with homosexuality. The Nazi group, they said, 'Look here, this is forbidden. German party members and Hitler's people don't do this.' And then the homosexuals got a real beating. There were official warnings given from time to time in the barracks. I remember one or two cases in which men were caught underneath the barracks [engaging in homosexual activities]. If you wanted to slip in there, two fellows they could easily try and hide away in there and do their thing. But they would be found out." Hugo Wannemacher recalled: "The good-looking boys had an inclination to play the female roles in the theater productions. There was a law in Germany against homosexual relationships. Some of the prisoners who took the female roles on the stage began to act like women off the stage. Things happened and they were beaten up. After that, [they stopped doing it and] nothing happened again. Then it was okay."

INTERCOMPOUND COMMUNICATION

The prisoners at Camp Hearne were always allowed to mingle and converse with other POWs in their own compound. However, camp authorities discouraged communication and fraternization between compounds in an effort to effectively control and manage the POWs and to diminish the possibility of a coordinated subversive event between the compounds.

Arno Einicke, who arrived in September, 1943, recalled that at the beginning of his internment prisoners were allowed to hang out and talk to one another at the fence line, meaning that the men could congregate and communicate with each other at the fences that divided the camp into compounds. After some POWs hung a Nazi flag on the water tower one night in January, 1944, the Americans got much tougher. A new commander, Lt. Col. John Dunn, was assigned and one of his first acts was to stop prisoners from lingering near the fences. A double fence with bright lights replaced the single fence separating the compounds and a tall, white wall was installed at one end of the double fence. At the other end stood an armed guard. Anyone near the fence would stand out against the white wall. In addition, the area in front of the fence was raked so that footprints could be readily detected in the dirt. A warning line was placed about three feet from the double fences separating the compounds and the POWs were instructed not to cross it. If a prisoner went too close to the fence lines separating the compounds, guards would shout at him and make threatening gestures with their machine guns. Any POWs going too close to the fence line during sporting events risked being shot without warning.

"I had friends who resided in a different compound, so sometimes I would visit them, which was not allowed," said Hans Lammersdorf. "We were supposed to stay where we belonged. One night I made a hole through the fence that separated our compounds. The next evening, I and a few others went through and visited my friends. I came back much later when it was dark. The problem was this: the Americans had counted and found out who was missing in that particular area. The next morning I lined up with the rest of the prisoners and they called my name along with a few others. They told us to follow them to the stockade, where we ended up for ten days with bread and water, literally, [and] with nothing else. No activity whatsoever. It was very, very boring, to put it mildly. They finally let us go back to our compound. It was a great relief. I never tried to do that again."

Ernst Froembsdorf said there was minimal communication between the compounds except during big events, when all the men congregated in one place. Men living in the various compounds were temporarily united when they attended theatrical productions at the "Deutsche Bühne" in Compound 3 and during major sporting events in the recreational area. Thus, the large recreation area south of the compounds became a prime location for the exchange of information. Illegal fraternization also occurred at work sites. Fritz Pferdekämper-Geissel said men sometimes would sneak into assigned work groups in order to be able to communicate with men in other compounds. This was accomplished by pretending to be someone else during the morning headcount. Once in the field, the men could talk during the day.

SHOOTINGS AND SUICIDES

At least two POWs committed suicide during the two and one-half years that Camp Hearne was in operation, and several prisoners were shot, one fatally, while apparently trying to escape.

The most serious case, which resulted in the shooting death of POW Hans Lukowski, occurred on June 19, 1944. A few minutes after 6 A.M. the guards in Towers 5 and 6, Pvts. Joseph Kidney and John A. Klescik, saw a prisoner climbing the south fence of Compound 2 near the recreation area (see fig. 4 in chapter 1). Kidney ran inside the guard tower to pull the siren and then ran outside again. He told the prisoner to halt and when this failed to stop him, opened fire. Klescik did the same thing. At first the guards aimed ahead of the man, hoping to deter him, but that did not work. They finally fired several rounds directly at the POW, after he had already climbed the second fence into the recreation area. The prisoner ran to a ditch where he was out of the line of fire and the guards fired several rounds at a culvert that went under the fence in an effort to prevent him from trying to escape through it. Additional help was sought and soon a weapons carrier, driven by Pvt. George F. Klinger, who had been in the guardhouse, arrived with several other soldiers. They found Lukowski wounded and bleeding in the ditch. He seemed to be in considerable pain and repeatedly said in English, "Shoot me dead." They took him to the hospital where the doctors treated the gunshot wound he had received in the abdomen. According to their report, the doctors considered Lukowski to be seriously wounded, but anticipated a recovery barring unforeseen complications. Lukowski admitted that he was attempting to escape, but refused to explain why. They did not question him any further. As soon as he was able, Lukowski was transferred to a civilian hospital in Temple, where he could be given more comprehensive care (Dunn 1944c; Langford 1944; C. Rogers 1944).

Many of the former POWs remembered this incident. "There was a prisoner who climbed the fence," recalled Peter Spoden. "While he was climbing he called out, 'Gun me down! Gun me down!' The Americans did not do anything. Then, when he climbed over the second fence and fell, they shot him. It was a form of suicide. That happened during the daylight hours. He knew what he was doing, and so, obviously it was the case, other people kill[ed] him, which is a form of self-destruction."

Walter Fricke also remembered the shooting:

A guy came out of his barracks [acting] a little bit crazy. He had bundled shoe cartons together with a cord. He ran around the barracks saying, "Entrance, entrance" . . . "Step in, step in," as if [he were] on a train. Yes, in the morning about four, five o'clock. About five o'clock, I think. He climbed over one of the fences. The tower guard sounded the alarm. The other prisoners got out of their beds when they heard the gunshots. We saw him between the two fences. He didn't have a chance, because the guard man was shooting. He [the guard] could have gone down and said, "Come fellow. Come, go on." It was not necessary, that they [the guards] shot him dead . . . and he stops the fire, I think, ten or fifteen [shots]. They [the POWs] were standing there right at the edge [of the fence] and they were complaining, whistling and boo[ing] and stuff like that, because obviously the guy couldn't escape. So why gun him down? This fellow was crazy. He wanted to go home. He was crying, "I want to go home, I want to go home." But this wasn't possible.

Einicke vividly remembered Lukowski being shot, even recalling his name and the fact that it occurred shortly after the Allied invasion of Normandy: "a dense fog covered the large recreation area south of the camp. One morning, it was sometime between 6:00 and 6:30, we were awakened by machine-gun fire. We rushed outside and screamed without knowing anything, without seeing anything. Then suddenly the fog lifted and we were standing in the bright sun. We looked into the ditch [and saw] a comrade who was apparently dead lying there. Our excitement cooled at that point." An officer arrived on the scene and ordered the prisoners to go back to their barracks. An ambulance followed him. Apparently, the escape attempt was a suicide. Einicke suggested that during his interrogation in Tunis, Lukowski had admitted "more than he was allowed to do according to German directions or German rules. As a result, his conscience was troubling him. Now, at this time with the invasion [of France] he believed that the final victory of the Germans was moved closer and that he would be subject to court-martial. He had observed exactly the fog that covered the fences which he climbed. He also knew that the ditch could be observed from the towers. In a sense, he certainly knew [what] the consequences of his actions would be. However, most of us did not realize yet that the war for us was lost."

Captain Clarence B. Rogers began an investigation that very day and 2d Lt. Thomas B. Langford conducted another, slightly more thorough, investigation a month later, beginning on July 24. Both officers took statements from the guards in the towers and the soldiers who had been in the weapons carrier. Only Rogers took statements from the chief surgeon, who had treated Lukowski's wounds, and from two prisoners who had seen Lukowski's attempted escape. The prisoners' and medical officer's statements included in the second report were copies of the statements Rogers included with the first report. The two investigation reports and their conclusions are virtually identical, as would be expected, but Langford's included a few more minor details (Howard 1944a; Langford 1944; C. Rogers 1944).

The investigations revealed that the guards in the towers fired a large amount of ammunition in trying to prevent Lukowski's escape, so much so that it is quite remarkable that he was not more seriously injured. Klescik admitted to firing a total of nineteen rounds and Kidney admitted to twenty-five. Although not all of these were fired directly at Lukowski, Kidney estimated that five or six were; a total of forty-four rounds of live ammunition might be considered excessive. Klescik did not offer an estimate on the number of rounds he shot directly at Lukowski. Two prisoners, Walter Kopf and Andreas Heiliger, were questioned. Both claimed that they heard the sirens, saw a POW climbing the fence, and described the shooting by the guards in the towers. Their accounts do not differ substantially from that of the Americans except that Heiliger said Lukowski fell twice: the first time after several shots had been fired and the second time after he had gotten up again and continued running toward the ditch. Both Rogers and Langford concluded that Lukowski "must have been temporarily mentally unbalanced to make such a desperate attempt to escape. This also seems to be the consensus of opinion among the prisoners" (both used the exact same words in their statements). Additionally, the reports concluded that Lukowski's wounds were not likely to have been fatal. Finally, they placed no blame on the GIs who fired the shots; they concluded the men had performed their duties properly (Langford 1944; C. Rogers 1944).

The case, however, was not yet closed. A few weeks after the shooting, on July 16, Lukowski died of peritonitis. He was buried at Camp Hearne two days later in a casket covered with a full-size Nazi flag and with full military honors. As a result, the Swiss Legation, acting for German interests, became involved, thus making it a much more complicated issue. This time Lt. Col. Cecil Stiles, then serving as camp commander, submitted an investigation report stating that although additional U.S. personnel were questioned about the shooting, "no reason has been found for this rash attempt to escape in daylight by this POW" (Lukowski 1944; Stiles 1944d).

Meanwhile, when German authorities learned of the shooting, they requested, through the Swiss Legation, "that the incident leading to the shooting of Lukowski be investigated by a court-martial." Specifically, they objected to the American guards firing their weapons after the alarm had been sounded and it was discovered the prisoner was still within the fences (Swiss Legation 1945). Responding to a State Department request regarding these issues, the provost marshal general's office rejected the German demand on the grounds that the investigations that had already been conducted were sufficiently thorough that another investigation would be unlikely to "throw additional light upon the subject" and that a court-martial proceeding is only used when someone was accused of having violated an Article of War, which clearly was not the case. The conclusion was that "since Lukowski was shot while attempting to escape, no grounds existed for preferring charges against the guards who fired upon him" (Department of State 1945; Tollefson 1945a). With that, the case was closed.

Another shooting occurred because an American guard thought a POW was attempting to escape, although that may not have been his intent. The circumstances were actually somewhat humorous and the outcome far less serious.

There were, however, discrepancies between the accounts given by the guard and POW involved. A detailed investigation of this shooting was conducted immediately after the incident.

On the morning of July 17, 1945, prisoner Heinrich Waltering was part of a four-man grass-cutting detail in Compound 3 working without a supervising guard. At about 9:15 A.M., a guard in Tower 5, Pvt. Pedro Reynosa, noticed that one of the POWs was missing. He said he looked around and saw Waltering about 250 to three hundred yards away, walking away from the fence. Reynosa claimed he shouted three times for the man to halt, but was ignored each time. Finally, he fired a single shot at the prisoner, striking him in the left heel. The prisoner was then taken to the infirmary and treated for his wound. Waltering, however, said he was walking toward the fence, not away from it, and that Reynosa never called out a warning. Moreover, Waltering said, he had simply gone to relieve himself. The investigator accepted Reynosa's account and said he believed Waltering did not hear the guard's shouted warnings because of the distance involved. The investigator recommended that no charges be filed against Private Reynosa (Haddock 1945).

Adding to the tension between the guards and prisoners, Waltering's statement implied that Reynosa had deliberately shot at him. "Two shots hit the ground about three feet in front and beside me," Waltering said. "I stopped immediately; then I saw the guard moving again without giving any further signals. When I saw that, I continued to move. The guard must have seen that I was attached to a work-detail, because I carried my grass-cutter. But in spite of this the guard took another shot at me." According to Reynosa's statement, however, he only fired his weapon twice. The statements of various witnesses corroborated parts of each story, but this only added to the confusion. Sergeant John Webber at the guardhouse and William J. Alsup, the officer of the day, confirmed the messages originating from Reynosa that they had received about the incident, but did not corroborate the disputed details (Haddock 1945, Exhibits A–D).

Three POW witnesses interviewed during the investigation—Joseph Kappes, George Niemann, and Bruno Gersitz—all claimed that there were three shots fired, but Kappes and Gersitz said they heard one shot followed by two more, whereas only Niemann agreed with Waltering that it was the other way around. All three witnesses claimed they had heard no warning, but they added that they were too far away. In addition, Kappes said Waltering had told them what had happened, whereas Gersitz insisted he had said nothing. Finally, George Papkin's medical report confirmed that the bullet had entered Waltering's foot from the rear (Haddock 1945, Exhibits E–H). Thus, the conclusions reached by the investigator seem fairly sound because of the contradictions of the POWs' testimony and the physical evidence derived from the medical report. Nothing in the reports indicates Reynosa's weapon was ever examined to determine how many rounds he fired.

Most of the Americans interviewed for this project did not mention any shootings. The guards recalled that they would occasionally shoot off a round to scare the prisoners away from the fence or if they thought someone was trying to escape, but none claimed they ever saw any prisoners hit by gunfire. Bobby Sullivan, however, did recall "one incident where a prisoner received word that his family was killed, I guess in a bomb raid, and he went berserk and ran out and they shot him." This is likely the Lukowski shooting.

There are only two recorded incidents of prisoners committing suicide at Camp Hearne. The best-documented case is that of POW Karl Erler. On June 27, 1944, Erler was working in the fields on the Astin Estate Plantation, located about fifteen miles south of Hearne. According to the *Bryan Daily Eagle* (1944a) and a later army report (Howard 1944b), Erler jumped in front of a Missouri Pacific train and was decapitated. It was Erler's second suicide attempt that day. The first occurred while the prisoners in his work detail were getting something to drink. He attempted "to throw himself in front of the train" but was "knocked aside" by one of his comrades. Erler made his second suicide attempt at 2:35 in the afternoon. He "dropped down on his hands and knees and laid his neck on the rail after the engine and several cars of a freight train had passed. The wheels of the fifth car cut his head off." This plain language barely conveys the horror that civilian Albert Garcia, the only witness, must have felt.

Ben Mason, who was guarding the prisoners that day at the Astin farm, offered an explanation for this tragedy: "We had a few things happen while we were there, the guys were getting sad letters from their families in Germany. Some of them would harm themselves and some would take their own life. There was one time when a guy [Karl Erler] got a message that his family had been killed in Germany. We were working next to the railroad on a big cotton field that day, and he ran over to the train and put his head under the train." Erler, distraught over the loss of his family, decided to commit suicide that summer afternoon. His body was taken to the Camp Hearne hospital for official identification and examination. He was buried at the camp cemetery two days later (Howard 1944b).

Erler, who had arrived at Camp Hearne in October, 1943, was usually quiet and reserved, but his fellow prisoners told the investigating officer they thought he was in good spirits. He regularly attended school through the camp's education program. The investigating officer concluded that his death was clearly a suicide because there was "no evidence of foul play" and that Erler was "mentally unsound at the time he committed suicide" (Howard 1944b). This certainly ranks as one of the more bizarre and horrific events in the history of Camp Hearne.

The second such incident occurred on February 9, 1944, when August Saleyka attempted suicide by self-strangulation. He was nearly dead when found and taken to McClosky Hospital, where he died on February 11. Little else is known about this case.

ESCAPES

One problem common to all POW camps during the war was the desire of prisoners to escape from captivity and return to their homeland. This was a nearly impossible task for German POWs in the United States. Even if they managed to escape from their camp and initially elude capture, they were still thousands of miles from home and surrounded by enemy territory in all directions. Furthermore, civilians were not likely to be sympathetic nor would they aid a prisoner attempting to escape. The Mexican border perhaps offered an inviting opportunity to POWs incarcerated near it, but it was not one that could be capitalized upon easily. Escapees would first have to find their way to a friendly country and then find passage across the Atlantic to Germany. Nevertheless, although a number of prisoners held in the United States made the attempt, only a few of them were able to elude their captors for even short periods of time.

American military authorities had an excellent record of apprehending escaped POWs. By February 5, 1945, although there had been a total of 1,288 escapes from all of the prison camps operated in the United States, only sixteen prisoners were still at large. Furthermore, only about half of the escapees were able to remain free for up to a day and there was no record of sabotage attempts by escaped POWs. The few criminal acts committed by escaped prisoners occurred in their efforts to evade capture. In twelve cases, escaped prisoners stole vehicles "for use in furthering their escapes." Escapees committed no violent crimes and city, county, or state law enforcement personnel captured most of those who broke out. Significantly, the FBI apprehended only thirty-seven escaped prisoners. In comparative terms, the rate of escape by German POWs was only slightly greater from POW camps than that of criminals incarcerated in federal penal institutions (Smith 1945b). Camp Hearne was no exception. On several occasions prisoners sought to escape, either singly or in groups.

The first documented escape occurred in March, 1944. Without identifying their names, the local newspaper reported that two men had been taken into custody. Texas highway patrolman James A. Mason apprehended them at 8:15 on the morning of March 15 as they headed south on Highway 6. A railroad man who directed Mason to their location had seen them near the rail yards, casually walking along the highway. When he caught up with them, one of the men told the officer in good English that they had been captured in North Africa. Mason returned them to Camp Hearne (*Hearne Democrat* 1944b).

However, the Americans did not discover all of the escape attempts. Willi Nellessen and Walter Fricke recalled an aborted escape attempt from Camp Hearne involving two men, one of them a friend of theirs named Otto Holduck. They said the duo hid under a small bridge in the recreation area while the prisoners were engaged in the day's physical activities. The men were well prepared for the escape, having equipped themselves with a backpack, food, and a compass. Their plan was to break out that night, but the moon was shining too brightly so they could not get away. The next morning, when roll call was taken, two kitchen workers ran back and got into the line to be included in the head count again so that their comrades would not be missed. Later, the two snuck back into camp. They never tried to escape again.

A few months later, at nine in the evening on July 13, Helmut Hellwig and Gottfried Rastetter individually escaped from Compounds 2 and 3 by going through fences to the recreation area and then crawling through the wire. Three hours later they surrendered to a farmer, Louis Fachorn, on his farm located fifteen miles to the southeast. He and two neighbors returned the two men to camp. The two POWs were confined to the stockade guardhouse for thirty days as punishment (Stiles 1944e).

A month after these failed attempts, four more prisoners escaped. Otto Franke escaped on the afternoon of August 9, 1944, while part of a work detail "clearing brush in a thickly wooded area" a few miles northwest of Franklin, a nearby community. A local farmer notified the authorities and he was captured at about ten that evening by highway patrolman Jimmie Mason and Capt. Hilton B. McQuarrie from Camp Hearne. Franke was wearing civilian clothes over his POW uniform and marching along the road "heartily singing German army marching songs" at the time of his apprehension. He was surprised that the farmer had seen through his disguise. Franke was briefly placed in confinement on a restricted diet (Stiles 1944f).

That same night, three other prisoners attempted to escape. Heinz Watermeier, Gerhard Becker, and Hugo Schwarzmeier fled sometime between 11 P.M. and seven the next morning. The three were sighted fifteen miles downstream two days later by an African-American civilian. The man was fishing as they floated down the Brazos River in crude boats they had constructed from wood, canvas, and raincoats. The man alerted the authorities and an army pilot flying a training mission from Bryan Airfield confirmed his story. The three escaped prisoners were captured and returned to Camp Hearne on August 12 (*Cameron Herald* 1944a; *Hearne Democrat* 1944c; Stiles 1944f; Richardson 1944; Krammer 1996, 130; Walker 2001, 124–25). The *Cameron Herald* (1944a) reported that the "prisoners were well supplied with money, clothing, and food" and that they were hoping to make their way to Argentina.

Walter Werner recalled the Brazos River escape well and provided many details of this story. According to Werner:

> Three comrades constructed folding kayak-type boats constructed out of raincoats and large tins (four-gallon size) that held butter and powdered milk for the kitchen. Their plan was to go to the Gulf. They hid in trash drums at night and were transported out of the camp and then they went by foot to the river. The kayaks had already been stashed during a previous work detail outside the camp. Since it was late summer, however, the water level of the Brazos River had receded. In order to gain time and to give the impression that the escapees were present in the camp, three big [paper mâché] dolls were made and we put the typical blue sunhats that we wore on them. When the Americans were counting us, we stood in three lines by company. These dummies were put in the third row and counted. We all had on the same blue caps. Three days the escapees were overlooked. Then the deception was discovered. The Americans took it with good humor, because almost simultaneously they had caught the escapees. They received twenty-eight days for the escape in the guardhouse. These penalties were not feared very much.

Former guard Tom Bussell was part of the American team sent to apprehend the escapees after they were sighted. "There was a fellow by the name of Davenport," he recalled. "He was from Brooklyn, and he had that Brooklyn drawl. And we got word that a couple of prisoners were coming down the Brazos River in a canoe. So I had a couple of men on one side and he had a couple of men on the other side [of the river] and sure enough here come the canoes. So we ordered them on over to the bank and they shook their heads [from side to side] and laughed at us. And so Davenport, he got mad and disgusted. He liked to cut that one canoe in two with that machine gun. They both come over to the bank without any problems."

The river escape looms large in the memories of former POWs interviewed for this project, although they did not always agree on the details. Many rumors apparently circulated about what happened in the course of this escape attempt. One common feature of their stories is that a prisoner named Stauffenberg—a nephew of Claus von Stauffenberg, who was part of the plot to assassinate Hitler in July, 1944—was among those who attempted to escape via the river. Walter Fricke, one of those who thought Stauffenberg was involved in an escape with a folding boat, described him as "a creative and active man." Peter Spoden repeated a rumor that Stauffenberg had escaped through a sewer system that drained into the Brazos River. Unfortunately, the prisoners' accounts do not correlate with official sources. The official documents show that Stauffenberg was a prisoner at Camp Hearne, but there is no record of him attempting to escape from the camp. The U.S. Army records also fail to mention any other escape by way of the river. The one documented case of a river escape clearly did not involve Stauffenberg. Regardless of the veracity of individual versions of the story, these personal recollections help to illuminate the incident.

Some prisoners tried to escape by digging a tunnel under the fence. Joseph Pohl said he heard that there was an attempt to escape by tunneling. Since there was a question about what to do with dirt taken from the tunnel, the POWs decided to wait until construction began on the theater in Compound 3 so that they could mix earth excavated from the tunnel with earth removed during the theater construction.

Tom Bussell remembered still other escapes: "Yeah, they [the POWs] would get out to work every so often. One of them would wander off, but they had real good security; we didn't have too much trouble finding them. See, we didn't have any portable cans [latrines], so they'd have to go in the weeds and if you didn't watch them real close, they'd back up into the brush farther out. And you do know, they had brush down there, don't you? We found them pretty quick."

Guard Ben Mason recalled a few escape attempts made while he was at Camp Hearne. "Some tried to paint their way out of prison," he said. "They were painting the stripes on the road and they would almost wander off too far and we would almost forget about them. But we eventually got them back. Some would try to run, but we would fire a shot over their head and they usually would stop. We had to guard the compound at night. There were about six to eight towers with two hundred yards between them and we would have to guard them at night and all day long. Occasionally they would try to jump the fences. We had a double fence and sometimes they would get between the two fences before we could see them." Mason said there were about two or three escape attempts a month while he was there. "Usually we had a Tommy gun up there and we would fire at first two shots and they would stop . . . some way or another they would try to dig tunnels and it was amazing at what they would try to do," he said. "One or two of them got outside. I don't think that we lost any of them. When the war got bad and they realized that they were losing, they attempted even more [often] to escape. They seemed to do it more as time went on. I heard after we left to go to Germany that a few realized that they weren't going to win the war and that they resigned [themselves] from [the idea of] escaping."

Tommy Ryan, a resident of the Brazos Valley, related an interesting incident that occurred on Christmas night, 1945, when he was about five years old. Some prisoners were being transferred from Camp Hearne to Camp Swift in Bastrop, Texas. The transport vehicle experienced mechanical failure on the way there, so the POWs were temporarily housed in the Burleson County jail in the small town of Caldwell. Because of the jail's poor condition, three prisoners were able to escape. Unfortunately for them, a cold front came in that night resulting in freezing rain. The weather was miserable, recalled Ryan,

> and my dogs woke us all up barking. My grandfather went out on the front porch, and of course he had his light and his shotgun. We'd heard about these three escaped prisoners, but we never thought about them being in our area. And, sure enough, it was the three prisoners standing in our front yard. And of course, they were cold and wet and hungry and were just ready to give up. My grandfather had been in World War I and had fought in Germany. [He] told them to come on in the house and of course we had lots of leftovers from Christmas dinner: turkey and ham and all the trimmings. And so my grandmother brought them in by the fire and she spread the table with all the food and they ate.

The Ryans's house was located in the country and did not have a telephone, so they were unable to notify authorities they had found the escaped prisoners until the next day. Tommy Ryan's grandparents were not very alarmed by the presence of the escapees. Instead, they treated the Germans as guests. In the morning, Tommy's mother took a bus to work in town. She stopped at the sheriff's office and informed him that the prisoners were at the family farm. Meanwhile, young Tommy tried to converse with the Germans, but it was difficult because only one of the Germans spoke English to any degree. He showed the POWs his Christmas presents and the men spoke about their families in Germany.

The sheriff arrived at about 9 A.M. with two carloads of policemen. All of them had their guns drawn. Tommy said his grandfather tried to put the officers at ease:

[He] walked out on the porch and he said, "Cleve, come at ease. Put those guns up. These boys [are] not gonna hurt anybody." [Somebody said], "Come on, they're ready to go get some dry clothes on." So, they [the police] came in, or came up to the porch and the two of them [POWs] went on out. And they handcuffed them and put them in the car, and the other one kind of stayed back a little bit and my grandmother was standing [alone]. [She] was the only one in the house there at the time. And so he [the remaining German] went over to her and he hugged her and told her how grateful he was and how nice we'd been to them. And he put something in her hand, he opened her hand and put something in it. And then he walked off. And they cuffed him and took him away, too. And when we got back in the house and my grandmother was there, she had a military issue German knife that he'd given her. And I don't know how he concealed it, all that time, you know, and all the check stations that he went through, but he had that knife. It was his only possession. And he told her, "You know you've been so nice and all, I don't have anything to give you but this." Needless to say, that was a very special Christmas for us.

Prisoner escapes were not limited to the main Hearne camp itself. On at least two occasions, prisoners attempted to escape from the Chance Farm branch camp. On December 24, 1944, three POWs—Karl Blabl, Peter Kleifges, and Ludwig Gisberger—escaped from a work detail at about 3:30 in the afternoon and were picked up the next day. The other recorded example of an escape from Chance Farm occurred a year later. Wolfgang Radzie escaped while working on one of the local farms early on a Friday morning in December, 1945. According to a local news report, an unnamed and unarmed resident of neighboring Bryan picked Radzie up the following Sunday morning and turned him over to the authorities. The city police and county sheriffs knew nothing about the escape until they heard a radio report from the Houston FBI headquarters after the capture. Radzie himself said the civilian had captured him (*Bryan Daily Eagle* 1944d, 1945; Fischer 1945). These two incidents reflect the fact that prisoners on work details could not be guarded as well as those confined within the POW compound. The possibility of escape was the price for using POW labor and apparently it was considered worth the risk (Walker 2001, 125).

A common feature of these accounts is a certain degree of laxity on the part of U.S. Army personnel. Apparently, attempting an escape was quite easy. Fritz Haus said he acquired an atlas of the United States while working in a warehouse. The atlas was being thrown away and the guards showed no concern when he asked if he might have it. He remembered that POWs were supposedly not allowed to have access to detailed maps. Haus's interest was clearly more educational than anything else, but if the guards were careless on this point, they may have been careless in other instances. It is quite likely the guards were not overly concerned because they knew the prisoners had no place to go and that they generally saw escape attempts as more of a game than anything else. Of course, as soon as prisoners tried to escape, the guards and everyone else diligently set out to apprehend the escapees.

"The thing is," observed Joseph Pohl, "we were told in the military that we were supposed to make at least one serious attempt to flee." He said "escaping was crazy in a place like Texas, where the distances were so great." In Europe, where distances were not nearly so vast, "it would have been more sensible. Normal people would not have thought about that. Mostly people did it for sport anyway."

German Patriotism

Some of the more curious incidents at Camp Hearne were little more than harmless pranks. But because they involved German patriotism, which included raising the German flag or other displays of the swastika, they were troubling to the Americans.

One such incident occurred on July 4, 1944. While it was not quite as dangerous or threatening as some of the other Nazi activities in the camp, it was disturbing and resulted in a public relations disaster (Walker 2001, 134–35). The camp commander, Lieutenant Colonel Dunn, was hosting an Independence Day celebration, hoping to gain positive publicity for the camp. The camp officers, their wives, and civilian notables from the town were invited. The entertainment scheduled for the day included a concert by the POW orchestra and a dance in the officers' club. A special stand had been constructed for the outdoor concert. According to the *Cameron Herald,* the "stand was decorated with bunting . . . and Old Glory was gently waving in the wind under a soft Texas sky [in] back of the stand on a shaft which had been placed there for that purpose." As the orchestra was preparing to perform for the four hundred guests in the late afternoon, the conductor said that the men would not begin until the large American flag on the pole behind the stage was removed. This came as a surprise to Lieutenant Colonel Dunn, who had already met with the orchestra leader "to ascertain if the Germans would play while the flag was displayed" and secured the German leader's agreement that the orchestra would play with the flag in place (*Cameron Herald* 1944b). Apparently not wanting to create a stir, Colonel Dunn ordered a sergeant to remove the flag. The Germans then took their places and began the concert. Some of the people present protested this action and immediately left. However, many of the guests remained to enjoy the day's activities. The celebration continued uneventfully into the night. Meanwhile, noted radio commentator Walter Winchell found out about the Fourth of July incident at Camp Hearne and criticized the camp commander during his Sunday evening broadcast from New York (*Cameron Herald* 1944c). This broadcast, complaints from local residents (especially World War I veterans), and sharp editorial criticism in the local newspapers led to an inquiry by the War Department and Sen. Tom Connally. Connally was later informed that "appropriate action" had been taken to prevent a repeat of this incident.

American soldiers on the front lines eventually heard about the Fourth of

July incident at Camp Hearne. Corporal Leo Krenek of nearby Cameron was in France and received copies of his hometown newspaper, the *Cameron Herald*. He wrote a letter of complaint to his father and excerpts from this letter subsequently appeared in the *Cameron Herald* (1944d) and *Hearne Democrat* (1944d). Corporal Krenek expressed the sentiment that POW camps would not be necessary if some of the American soldiers were sent home from the front. "It really burned me up when I read about that incident at Hearne prison camp," he wrote. "Boy that was the worst. Take down the American flag because some damn Nazi didn't like it and on the Fourth of July, too. Something should be done. So many good men have given their lives to capture those rats and then they have their way, with luxuries to go with it." He also mentioned the English-language German propaganda he and other soldiers were being subjected to, emphasizing that they were not being fooled (*Cameron Herald* 1944d; *Hearne Democrat* 1944d). The *Cameron Herald* (1944e) also published the comments of Pfc. Alfred Dusek, who was fighting in the Pacific. "Yes," he wrote, "it really knocked me for a loop when I read about an Army officer ordering the stars and stripes down because they looked distasteful to a bunch of German prisoners, and on the 4th of July, too. Well I'm glad I can say the stars and stripes look good to us over here."

This incident caused quite a stir in Hearne. As one Great War veteran commented in the *Cameron Herald* (1944b), "things got pretty hot around Hearne." Switchboard operator Johnoween Mathis said she did not attend the Fourth of July celebration, but heard about the event through the rumor mill. Mathis said that while the incident was kept under wraps because the Camp Hearne personnel did not want the folks in town to know about it, those who did were angry: "I was dumbfounded. I could not believe that the elite here, who were so patriotic, and well, that's for the birds."

Several of the guards and POWs remembered instances in which the POWs secretly hung German flags in the camp. Guard Edwin Munson recalled an incident on January 30, 1945, the day of the anniversary of Hitler's rise to power (Hitler was appointed chancellor of Germany on January 30, 1933). Munson came out to play reveille early in the morning, "and when you looked over at the water tower in the center of the compound there was a great big German swastika flag. I don't know how they got it up there but we think that it was some of the cooks who went in to cook on the outside of the fence."

Munson said the flag was mounted during the night and not discovered until daylight: "It was up on top, on the very top, on a pole up there! It was pretty ingenious what they did to get it up there and keep it flying; there was no flagpole up there originally to hold it up. I would say it [the flag] was a four by six [feet] or a four by ten [feet] or something like that. You could see it all over the compound." The Americans were unsure how the prisoners obtained the flag, but surmised that it must have been smuggled into the camp somehow or made there. Otto Schulz said he believed the sewing machine used for tailoring costumes for the theater was used to make the flag. The main part of the flag was a bed sheet that had been dyed red, with the white circle and black swastika added. The POWs were quite proud of their comrades who had pulled off this stunt without being caught. Werner Kritzler said the prisoners who put up the flag were mountain climbers from a mountain troop unit: "The fellows who raised the flag were with the garbage detail. The garbage was removed during the night, so they took advantage of that. Nobody could remove it [the flag]." According to Schulz: "When the guard ordered us [the POWs] to take the flag down, no POW would be found to do it. Finally, a local U.S. chimney sweep was brought in to climb up on the tower to loosen the flag. It fell down [blew into one of the compounds] and was immediately hidden by the POWs. The guards never found the flag since it was buried under a building." The flag flew over the water tower for at least half a day. Willi Nellessen said the Americans "were impressed, but not pleased." The camp commander was naturally quite upset that the POWs were able to carry out such a scheme. In order to teach them a lesson, the movement of all the prisoners was restricted for some time after this stunt.

Arno Einicke reported a second flag incident that occurred on Hitler's birthday, April 20, 1945. Just eighteen days before the war ended, someone snuck out of the camp and placed a Nazi flag on the water tower at the Hearne train station. Einicke thought this action was "bull-headed and fanatical," since the end of the war was clearly impending.

Another way the swastika was displayed around the camp was on the sides of hot air balloons made by the POWs. The balloons were made in the camp out of paper, shaped like octagons, and a candle supplied the hot air needed to make them rise. A big swastika was usually painted on the side of the balloon.

Fritz Pferdekämper-Geissel, assisted by a Brazilian POW, created one of these balloons. He and his cohort constructed the balloon by gluing together numerous small sheets of paper that had been wrapped around grapefruits. He gathered these wrappers while he was working in the kitchen. The guards had eyed him suspiciously and asked, "What do you want them for?" He claimed that he wanted to use the papers as stationery and the guards believed him. "We kept the balloon in our barrack. It was lying flat so if a guard came in, they would think nothing of it. Then in the early evening we sent it off. A friend and I went between the barracks where the guards could not see us inflate and release the balloon." Pferdekämper-Geissel said they did this on the evening of April 20, 1945, in celebration of Hitler's birthday.

Both Peter Spoden and Arno Einicke recalled seeing several such balloons while they were at Camp Hearne. Spoden remembered the balloons being set aloft at night and hovering for hours, "They went up and up and up until the candle burned down. They just floated up and disappeared. They [the guards] did not know if they should shoot at them or not." Otto Schulz said that a rumor went around "that the balloon floated into an ammunition store in the vicinity of the camp and caused an explosion there. But this rumor was never verified."

Walter Werner told another interesting story:

> A hobby group at one time made gliders (fig. 28) that were used to
> distribute leaflets via the air. On the recreation field a glider went in
> big circles around and around. Because the glider was so effective as a

Fig. 28. German POWs wearing Afrika Korps uniforms pose behind the band shell in Compound 2 with gliders that they constructed in the camp. Gliders similar to these were used to distribute German propaganda. Camp Hearne Collection, Texas A&M University.

flying machine, someone suggested using it for propaganda purposes and it worked. Pieces of paper, the size of post cards, were written on with "Germany wins the war" and worse. In the corners of each of the pieces of paper, a hole was punched and the papers were strung along a straw and attached to the airplane. Before the plane took off, the straw was set on fire so that the pieces of paper dispersed during flight. What the reaction was to the propaganda is unknown. Only two flights were made before the Americans discovered our propaganda efforts and the third plane was confiscated.

An old-timer who remembered an interesting German prank involving a swastika of a different sort passed the following story on to Mary Dorsey. She was told that some of the German prisoners at Camp Hearne had been instructed to plant flowers and bulbs in the area around the flagpole at the entrance to the camp. Apparently, some of them were skilled in landscaping. "When the flowers came up in the spring, they were in the shape of a swastika. And so they had a good time with that."

Secret Shortwave Radios and Transmitters

At Camp Hearne, as at most POW camps in the United States, prisoners secretly modified or constructed radios to receive shortwave broadcasts from Germany. They said this allowed them to hear accurate reports on the progress of the war as well as any special messages that might be intended for them. Prisoners were not allowed to have shortwave radios and the American authorities were always searching for this illegal contraband.

Fritz Pferdekämper-Geissel said the POWs were allowed to have regular radios in their barracks and that they secretly modified some of them to receive shortwave broadcasts. Radios were obtained from local farmers, the YMCA, or from other organizations. On occasion, discarded radios were salvaged from the dump and adapted with parts into a shortwave set. Ironically, the prisoners could order radios and the parts they needed to modify them for shortwave use from the Sears catalog.

Shortwave radios were also easily constructed from scratch. There were many signal troops (radiomen) in the camp with the knowledge and skill to build radios. Parts were obtained from friendly people, such as some of the African-American men who the POWs worked with in the fields outside the camp. If a part could not be obtained, the prisoners made it.

These radios were skillfully hidden from the Americans. Former POW Erich Spix recalled that a radio was hidden under his barrack, beneath the floorboards. There was a space of approximately eighty centimeters between the barracks and the ground, and the radio was placed in a hole and covered up with clumps of vegetation. The American officers suspected that there was a radio in the area, but never found it because POWs would alert others that a guard was on the way to the barrack. "When the inspector was gone," said Walter Fricke, "the radio came out again." He added that the antenna of one shortwave radio was a wire hidden in a ceiling lamp: "You couldn't see it unless you really looked for it. In one place they hid the radio within a large wooden table and you could pull the top of the table piece off and the radio was positioned in the center of it. They never found that." When the guards came in for inspection, the specialized knobs were simply removed from the modified radios and the antenna covered up.

Most of the POWs did not know precisely where the shortwave radios were hidden. "It was very, very secret. Even among us," said Willi Nellessen. The fewer people who knew of a radio's existence and location, the less chance the Americans would discover it. Fritz Haus accidentally discovered a radio in his barrack one evening: "They challenged me and said, 'Well, what are we going to do with you?' And I said, 'Well, I give you my word. I won't give you away. Not the location, nor the fact or nothing to the Americans." It was probably fortunate for Haus that he was a man of the cloth or else he might not have been trusted to keep his promise. In his memoir he commented that he was given a stern lecture about what would happen to him if he ever betrayed this confidence. Haus had many opportunities to do so, since he was often alone with American chaplains and educators, but he saw no reason to intervene: "I was a pastor and not a politician."

According to Haus, the radio was hidden in a hole under his barrack. The hole was cut into the wooden floor under the furnace and concealed with a tin plate. The POWs were quite adept at quickly stashing the radio when guards approached: "The whole operation of getting in or out—in cases of emergency—took less than a minute. The team to assist was well trained." Apparently the guards interviewed rarely discovered radios during their periodic searches, because none of them mentioned finding any of the contraband shortwave devices.

Fritz Haus said that news from Germany was received late at night in Texas, which was convenient because this was when the POWs were left unguarded. The news was then dispersed the following day. Haus remembered that a word-of-mouth network was used to spread information about the German war effort as reported by the broadcasts: "There was a man, not always the same man, but there was somebody coming to the barracks who would say, 'Here, listen chaps. This is the news,' or 'This is what we would like you to know.'" Joseph Pohl said, "those who were particularly Nazi-oriented would announce things from the radio such as [the invasion of] Normandy, [and that] the Americans were pushed back." The German news broadcasts that the POWs heard reported on German victories, which contradicted what the American newspapers were reporting. While some of the POWs believed the German broadcasts, including their talk of secret Nazi weapons, Hugo Wannemacher and others found it hard to believe they were really winning the war when the Allies continued to advance toward German territory. Arno Einicke recalled a second way the news was dispersed. He said some of the POWs allowed access to typewriters during the day would temporarily steal one and use it to make secret reports at night. "They would put bricks into one of the containers," explained Einicke, "so the Americans thought there was a typewriter inside. But actually they kept the typewriter for their own use. The Americans did not suspect anything was wrong." The news would then be summarized and typed onto pieces of paper to be dispersed the next day. This secret "newspaper" was most likely the underground paper referred to as *Die Mahnung* (Bachmayer 1945; Hombeck 1945). Einicke said that sometimes during the theatrical productions some POWs made verbal announcements regarding the war effort in an attempt to keep the prisoners' spirits elevated and to instill a sense of nationalistic pride. During these announcements someone would be posted outside the theater, keeping watch for approaching Americans. When the Americans entered, the prisoners would pretend to be discussing religion or some other topic.

In April, 1944, the POWs built a radio transmitter capable of broadcasting. Every day for two weeks, this station broadcast ten to fifteen minutes of music, news, and commentary. Fritz Pferdekämper-Geissel recalled that German marching music was played at the beginning of the broadcast, followed by the POWs announcing: "Now we are calling! Germany calling! Germany calling!" Peter Spoden heard that this secret transmitter was hidden in the theater building between the ceiling and the roof. He recalled that it did not take long for the Americans to become aware of these illegal broadcasts. "The Americans dispatched trucks that would try to triangulate on the signal," he explained. "The Americans would wait all day by the trucks and when they were standing around we did not broadcast anything. So the Americans could not triangulate [our location]." At one point, the guards entered the compound with metal detectors because they figured the station was hidden underground. According to Pferdekämper-Geissel, in order to throw off the metal detectors, "We all collected nails, steel pieces, and tin. In the evening we dug holes with a spade, buried the tin and iron pieces, and then the Americans came with mine detectors. Bing!" Pferdekämper-Geissel laughed as he remembered the guards' initial excitement when they thought they had discovered a secret radio, and how they cussed the Germans when they realized they had been fooled. Arno Einicke also recalled that the POWs enjoyed thwarting the guards' search efforts: "Just to increase the anger and frustration among the Americans, we Germans buried tins and metal objects so that the Americans would think that they found something when they did not. They found the decoys, but they did not find the radio. For two days we laughed about it." As a joke, one German made a replica of a pistol and buried it where it would deliberately set off the metal detectors. "So one fellow made a pistol out of metal and it looked real. He buried it, not too deep, and the next morning the Americans came with their metal detectors. They found it and there was a big alarm when it was found." After a long series of false hits, the Americans became frustrated and gave up the search. After about a month of this cat-and-mouse game, the Germans stopped broadcasting because it became too risky for both themselves and the rest of their comrades at Camp Hearne. The radio was dismantled so the Americans could never find it. The POWs considered this a victory.

Evidence of a second broadcasting station, or perhaps the same one, is provided by a memo written by 2d Lt. Martin Klughaupt on May 30, 1945. The memo mentions that on February 15, 1945, eighteen miles south of Camp Hearne at Bryan Air Base, a radio technician monitored a coded radio voice message that ended with the letters "SYROIC." Using triangulation and special equipment, the radio operator was able to trace the signal back to Camp Hearne. In addition, a prisoner informant at the camp had reported the existence of a radio transmitter. The American officials initiated an investigation and "a shakedown inspection of the compound" that failed to find the transmitter, but exposed much more. The Americans found "technical equipment, transmitter tubes, intricate electrical parts, meters, transformers, condensers, large quantities of cable and wire, units of the type used in radio transmitters, [and] tools necessary to assemble a transmitter." In addition to the communications equipment, the guards made related discoveries of such items as "a buried telephone cable running from Compound #1 underneath a double barbed-wire fence to Compound #2, underground caves dug out underneath barracks to a cleverly camouflaged room below the ground" which was eight feet by ten feet by ten feet in size. The room had a cement floor that was "padded with Army comforters and blankets and thoroughly insulated against noise." The Americans concluded that the hidden room "could have been used to house a radio transmitter." But, of course, it could have been used for much more (Klughaupt 1945). The American chaplain, Gustave Zoch, remembers learning about a subterranean room that "was quite large" with a "huge portrait of Adolf Hitler." The POWs used this room for secret meetings, including "their so-called trials pertaining to what they thought was maybe getting too close to their enemy and so forth . . . sort of a . . . kangaroo court" (Zoch 1946).

As part of the investigation, the Americans asked a radio technician from Bryan Air Base to use the confiscated materials from the shakedown inspection to construct a radio transmitter. In just two hours time, using only those materials, he was able to assemble a transmitter capable of sending a signal at the precise frequency of the original intercepted signal. Moreover, there were enough spare parts left over to assemble two more transmitters like the first one. The Americans knew the POWs were supposed to have thirteen regular and unmodified radios, including one that had been donated by the Red Cross, but none were found in the shakedown inspection. The obvious conclusion is that the miscellaneous parts that were found came from units that the prisoners had disassembled in order to make their illicit transmitter (Klughaupt 1945).

THE POSTAL UNIT

The one feature that distinguished Camp Hearne from all of the other POW camps in the United States was that it became the headquarters of the German Postal Unit. This meant that all mail from Germany to German prisoners of war in the U.S. was sent to Camp Hearne for processing and dispatch. Previously, all incoming POW mail had been handled by the Office of Censorship in the New York District Postal Center, but the volume overwhelmed the staff there, resulting in a huge backlog of undelivered mail. The backlog was eliminated within a matter of weeks following the transfer of this responsibility to Camp Hearne in early March, 1944. The Postal Unit continued to operate at Hearne until mid-July, 1945, at which time it was moved elsewhere for security reasons (Farrand 1945; Lerch 1945; Record of Mail Received 1945).

Operation of the Postal Unit

The Postal Unit operated in a manner that proved efficient in managing the high volume of letters and parcels arriving from Germany. Former POW Fritz Haus was surprised at the amount of mail that came through the camp. He recalled seeing "bags and bags of post . . . such a lot . . . even the Berlin post office couldn't cope with this."

As one can see in table 5, the volume of mail handled by the unit fluctuated from month to month (Record of Mail Received 1945). As noted above, the initial high volume of mail and large number of Germans employed in the Postal Unit was due to the backlog that had built up in New York. After a few months, the number of incoming letters and parcels declined to a stable level. There is no apparent explanation for the surge of mail in September, 1944. The January, 1945, increase might be attributed to the delay in receiving Christmas mail from Europe caused by the war (the Battle of the Bulge in particular may have disrupted communications). It is also noteworthy that the volume of mail began to decrease in early 1945 so that by the time the Postal Unit was transferred from Hearne in July, the lightest loads were being recorded. This might be explained

Table 5. Volume of Mail Dispatched by the German Postal Unit

Date	Number of Letters Processed[1]	Parcel Bags Processed[2]	Average Number of Parcels and Letters Processed Daily[1]	Average Daily Number of German Postal Workers[1]
March–April, 1944	1,839,700	20,276		
May	570,980	1,600		
June	693,069	5,107	27,560	382
July	540,391	2,401	21,707	334
August	795,687	2,505	32,829	330
September	1,007,982	3,176	39,990	371
October	468,860	2,851	19,129	286
November	202,683	2,930	8,922	223
December	568,001	1,642	23,380	269
January, 1945	1,113,560	5,003	43,092	308
February	889,335	1,419	37,650	270
March	832,395	2,783	31,860	225
April	451,160	1,619	14,694	136
May	113,745	1,119	4,875	125
June	97,340	949		
July 1–19, 1945	82,456	371		

[1]Mail Dispatch and Strength Report 1945; Record of Mail Received 1945.
[2]Outgoing parcel bags had an average of eleven parcels each (Farrand 1945; Record of Mail Received 1945).

by the problems brought on as Germany began to collapse at the end of the war, with the German postal authorities being unable to transport mail for distribution to the United States when its citizens were struggling to survive perpetual bombings.

The Postal Unit was located in the southern half of Compound 1. The occupants of company areas 2 and 4 were relocated and the buildings converted for use by the Postal Unit. A fence was erected to separate it from the occupants at the north end of the compound. The area occupied by the Postal Unit was about five hundred feet by seven hundred feet and contained twenty-two buildings, fourteen of which were used for processing mail. A core of "permanent personnel" staffed the Postal Unit. Additional help, when needed, was drawn from the other compounds. The mail was sorted six days a week and the Germans worked three eight-hour shifts. The prisoners were supervised by U.S.

Army personnel, generally two officers and ten enlisted men, but this number varied over time. The German labor force, for the period when figures are available, averaged 290 men per day (Klughaupt 1945; Lerch 1945; Turner 1944, 1945). Initially, no POWs lived in the Postal Unit area; however, in 1945, 152 Germans—the "permanent personnel" assigned to the Postal Unit—were moved into a few of the barracks in the Postal Unit sector.

Five color-coded sets of locator cards were used to sort the mail for distribution to the various camps around the country: one set for use by the Americans, one numerically organized by the serial number of each POW, one set for the directory service of letter mail, another set for parcel post directory service, and a final set for the "Dead Letter" and "Returned Letter" files. In addition, copies of prisoner rosters for each POW camp were kept and regularly updated to keep track of transfers and to correct inevitable errors (Carpenter 1945; Irlenborn 1944; Klughaupt 1945; Turner 1944, 1945). When one inspector described this system as "very wasteful" in March, 1945, the system was simplified by reducing the number of card sets to three: the American set was eliminated and the parcel and Dead Letter sets were combined.

The German Postal Unit used trucks to pick up the mail at the Hearne railroad station every day except Sundays. Each day, the mail pouches were registered and weighed. The number of letters in each was estimated by first subtracting the weight of the pouch and lock, if it had one, and then dividing seventy into the remainder (assuming a total of seventy letters to the pound). Letters that did not have a censorship stamp were returned to the district postal censor in New York City. Letters were first taken to the "initial break-down" room to be alphabetized with at least four subdivisions for each letter of the alphabet (fig. 29). After this initial sorting, the letters were taken to the "Letter Dispatch" room to be sorted by camp. Each camp had a number and this was written on the outside of each envelope. Letters going to the same camp were tied into bundles with a label for the destination camp, which included the date of dispatch and the initials of the POW who tied the bundle. Dispatches were made daily, except Sundays, at 3:15 P.M. using mail pouches—unless a camp had three bundles or less, in which case manila envelopes were placed in the pouches. All pouches were weighed before leaving the dispatch room and a daily record was kept of the pouches that were dispatched (Turner 1944).

The goal of the German Postal Unit was to process each letter within twenty-four hours of receipt. This was not a problem in most cases. If the address on a letter was in error or could not be found, it was sent to the Dead Letter section for further directory service. If this effort did not succeed, then the letter was forwarded to Fort Meade, Maryland, where letters sent to POWs who had died, escaped, or been repatriated were held. All returned mail was to be given additional directory service by personnel who had been selected and trained for such activity (Turner 1944).

Parcels were handled in a similar manner. The sacks with the parcels were taken to the "Dumping and Sorting" room to be sorted alphabetically. Those packages that were damaged or torn were rewrapped. Parcels were then taken

Fig. 29. Shown here is the view inside the post office. Mail from Germany to prisoners in the United States was sorted alphabetically and placed into boxes before receiving directory services. Camp Hearne Collection, Texas A&M University.

to the "Parcel Post Directory" room and given directory service according to the alphabetical sorting that had been done. Each parcel was labeled with a code for the camp of destination and then taken to the "Parcel Post Dispatch" room to be sacked for the appropriate camps. Each sack was locked and labeled as "P.W. Mail." As with the letters, parcel sacks were dispatched by 3:15 P.M. daily except Sundays and a daily record was kept of incoming and outgoing sacks. Undeliverable packages were turned over to the camp commander to be distributed amongst the POWs or sent to other camps in the area. Walter Fricke recalled that a misdirected parcel addressed to a person living in Herne, Germany, once arrived at Camp Hearne. Finally, a report to the Office of the Provost Marshal General in Washington, D.C., was submitted twice each month, on the first and sixteenth, listing the numbers of pouches, letters, and bags of parcels received, dispatched, and remaining on hand for the preceding period including cumulative totals (Turner 1944).

Abuses at the German Postal Unit

Although the German Postal Unit proved to be quite efficient in handling the large volume of POW mail, problems occasionally arose. According to an inspection report, this efficiency "was maintained at the price of a complete lack of security and numerous violations of mail regulation" (Neuland 1945c). The POWs working in the Postal Unit had a golden opportunity to use the system for their own advantage, and they did. They used their positions to communicate covertly with prisoners of war in other camps across the country. "Suddenly we found ourselves in a very key position," Fritz Haus recalled, "enjoying the importance of it all. We had access to files and the whereabouts of all the German prisoners in the American hands. Everything was now possible from Camp Hearne. I took full advantage of the Hearne postal center and had no qualms or conscience about it. I know my exercise was harmless and did not hurt anyone."

To communicate with their friends in other camps, former POW Arno Einicke revealed that some postal workers wrote messages on the bottoms of letters to acquaintances whose names they recognized. For example, Willi Nellessen sometimes sent greetings to friends by writing on the back of the envelopes. Sometimes, letters returned to Hearne from other POW camps as undeliverable had notes inside for the Postal Unit personnel. Fritz Pferdekämper-Geissel, who worked in the Postal Unit for a short time sorting the mail, happened to see a letter addressed to a friend in another POW camp and figured out how to send a secret message to him by writing the message in Latinized German (which the censors could not read), "I wrote, 'Fritz, if you get this letter, open it and write me a message, put it back into the letter and say that this is not your letter, it must be a mistake. Give it back. And they will send it back [to Hearne].' I told my comrade [working in the Post Office], 'if this letter is returned to you, that's a letter for me.' Eventually the letter came back [to Hearne] and I heard from him. That was a correspondence between the two of us. This was not allowed." Pferdekämper-Geissel said that he only did this a few times because he was afraid he would eventually be caught. Fritz Haus also used the misdirected mail scheme to get messages to friends: "In my case this was harmless. There was no political reason or underground schemes. They were letters of encouragement and good news and said, 'Well, hang on. And I can tell you that our friend so and so he is safe and they were bombed out but they are now there and there.' And things like that." Carl Bruns said this form of illegal mail was called "Texas Post." While these notes were "mostly innocuous," there was a great possibility of far more serious abuses (Carpenter 1945). This proved to be a legitimate security concern.

The American authorities at first viewed the German prisoners performance in the Postal Unit with an optimism and trust bordering on naiveté, testing the limits of credulity. For instance, an early report focused on the language barrier between the German and American staff without considering security issues. Neither Capt. H. M. Turner, the officer in charge of the Postal Unit when it first opened, nor his assistant, Capt. Freelan J. Short, knew any German. It seems that they tried to get by with the little English that some of the prisoners knew. The two American enlisted personnel assigned to the unit had neither clerical nor interpreting experience. On the other hand, the Americans were pleased with the speed with which the Germans were able to process the mail. They worked at their tasks with diligence. The Americans cited a German NCO with postal experience who volunteered to remain on duty for twenty-one continuous hours. This letter also boasted that one prisoner told the Americans, "to bring on some American mail for distribution besides, so as to fill out their spare time"

(Irlenborn 1944). Within a few months, however, it had become clear that the operation needed a larger number of experienced postal workers. The request of a prisoner at Camp Fannin, Texas, Sgt. Antonios Hertwig, to be transferred to the Postal Unit was given enthusiastic endorsement: "Being a professional mail employee I like to ask you, if you would test the possibility, that I can be transferred to the German Mail Unit for Prisoners of War within the United States of America. I should like to get some more improvements of education and should be very pleased, if you can give me your final instructions" (Hertwig 1944; Matthews 1944; Smith 1944d). There is no record the transfer actually took place or whether, for security reasons, an inquiry was made as to possible ulterior motives behind this request.

When abuses were detected after only a few weeks of operation, Lt. Col. John Dunn, then the Camp Hearne commander, concluded the charge was most likely incorrect. He noted that letters often arrived that were open or partly open and he admitted the temptation this presented to the German POWs to insert a note. However, he expressed with perhaps undue confidence the belief that "all such attempts to write to other prisoners have been unsuccessful, due to the vigilance of the personnel at the camp of destination." He conjectured that the mail was of such "vital importance" to all prisoners in general that they would be angry with any prisoners who were "discovered tampering with personal mail" and would themselves "take severe action resulting in serious bodily harm to the offender." For this reason, prisoners caught performing such acts were not publicly accused but were instead quietly removed from the Postal Unit (Dunn 1944d). As it turned out, Lieutenant Colonel Dunn trusted the POWs' intentions to a greater degree than perhaps was merited.

A more specific and apparently harmless example of such an abuse was found in an envelope addressed to Obergefreiter Albert Sieger in another camp. A small piece of paper was slipped into the envelope with the following message:

> Master Sergeant:
> Greetings of comradeship went to you from Obergefreiter Rudolf Hambuch, also regards from von Naufenberg, Herdt, Karsten, Hillebrand and Seemann. I am employed at Box 20 here. I feel well, except my wounds on my head, which bother me terribly. At the present time, I obtain real good medical treatment. I hope that you also feel well, and that you still are the old humoristic Saettler, whom I knew so long ago. Again regards from everybody and the best for the future.
> Goodbye,
>
> Hambuch, Obergefr.
>
> Also best regards,
> Obergefr. Herdt

The Americans noted on the English translation of this letter that a POW Hauptfeldwebel Saettler was interned at Camp Shelby, Mississippi (Hambuch 1944;

Miley 1944). This little note, though seemingly harmless, caused some concern amongst the Americans, for if this form of unauthorized communication could take place between prisoners, then so could other forms that might be much more serious.

Another innocent abuse documented by the American authorities took place in February, 1945, on the day that Capt. Alexander Lakes visited the camp with Maj. Paul A. Neuland on an inspection tour of the camp. A German employee in the Postal Unit intercepted a letter from Germany to his brother who was being held at Ashford General Hospital in West Virginia. He slipped a note to his brother into the letter, urging him to believe in German unity and the new V-2 weapon, and then dispatched it. However, he was caught in the act. Captain Lakes assisted in the interrogation that resulted in a signed confession. Unfortunately, the inspectors noted, "a great number of similar violations have gone undiscovered" (Neuland 1945a).

This suspicion was true, according to Peter Spoden. "I would watch for letters when we were sorting the letters," recalled Spoden. "If a letter was going to a friend, say like in Huntsville, I would get cigarette paper. I would put a message on it, fold it very small, and stick it inside the letter. I would then send it off." Fritz Haus also recalled corresponding with other prisoners in this fashion: "in our barracks there were three or four people who worked at the post office and I gave them a list of names, five or ten names and I told them 'Look out if for Rusher or Kleirbein or for Schmidt, if there is a letter, then open it and put my note into it.' And so they opened that letter. It was no problem. Just carefully open it, and put my note in and close it again. And it had been through the censors already."

More serious were the political abuses, often using the same methods to secretly pass notes, but with more serious potential consequences. These abuses proved more troublesome and ultimately were one of the main reasons for the Postal Unit's transfer from Camp Hearne. One pertinent illustration of this was in the form of a surreptitious note being sent to a POW in another camp in the spring of 1944. A prisoner interned at Fort Devens, Massachusetts, Heinz Lebender, found the following hidden message in his mail:

Dear Heinz,
      You'll probably be surprised when you get this little slip of paper in your letter. We have the job here in Hearne of sorting and distributing mail. Besides myself there is Steiner, Schuster and Naurer as well as Falk and Schmied. I hope you are doing as well as we. My sister sends you her regards; she got married in the summer. With the best wishes I am your old friend and leader of the radio-detachment.
                              Berthold Richter. (Worked at CH)

Regards also to the others.

Although the note seems innocent enough, Lebender reported it to the American commander at Fort Devens because it alarmed him. The note was originally addressed to Camp Opelika, Tennessee, where Lebender previously had been held. But Fort Devens was an anti-Nazi camp, meaning, of course, that Lebender himself was an anti-Nazi. Moreover, Lebender identified Richter and the other individuals mentioned as dedicated Nazis. Richter, in particular, was a person he did not trust and with whom he previously had a political argument. The Americans noted, after a closer look at the original German text, that the note was not as benign as it appeared. The word translated "friend" was "Rumpel," which could be translated as "tease" or "nuisance," and the dictionary translation is "rumble" or "jolt." Thus, a letter that "reads as though written in a very friendly vein" could be reinterpreted in an entirely different manner by hinting "at possible disturbance or a jolt." In this light, the note could be interpreted as a threat. Richter was a POW who worked in the Mail Distribution Section of the German Postal Unit at Camp Hearne and used his position to insert the note into Lebender's mail (Glaser 1944; Osmond 1944; Richter 1944; Tulatz 1944).

Fritz Haus saw such activity as a real problem: "The same system lent itself to sinister plots and dangerous adventures. It didn't take me long to become aware of several underground schemes." Haus stated that through the master list of all the POWs in the United States, it was possible to track the location of Nazi and anti-Nazi individuals. The master list was used by the Nazis to notify their cohorts "in charge" at other camps who the anti-Nazis were so that they could be harassed or beaten.

Postal Unit Investigations

The frequency and nature of these abuses led American officials to conduct several investigations of the German Postal Unit at Camp Hearne. These in turn uncovered a greater variety of abuses. It apparently was quite common for POWs in other camps to use Camp Hearne as a return address, knowing that the Postal Unit was located there. They could thus send messages to POWs at Camp Hearne. One such example was a card sent by Herbert Lemke, a POW interned at Camp Florence, Arizona, but never at Camp Hearne. In fact, this problem was so common that Camp Hearne's commanding officer at the time, Lt. Col. Cecil Stiles, alerted his commanding general on September 20, 1944, after intercepting this letter. The result was a memo sent three days later by Lt. Col. Harold H. Richardson advising Stiles to continue to forward the mail to the correct camps. Stiles countered on October 9 that the volume was too great for such a solution and suggested that other POW camps were negligent in not detecting such abuses. Moreover, he complained about other irregularities that hindered the Postal Unit's efficient operation, such as delays in receiving reports of transfers, the forwarding of mail for transferred POWs to Hearne instead of to the new camp, and uncensored outgoing and incoming mail being sent to Hearne. He concluded with a recommendation that every camp in the country be instructed to stamp outgoing mail with its own stamp so as to clearly identify its place of origin (Stiles 1944; Szilagyi 1944).

By the end of 1944 it was becoming more obvious that the situation was deteriorating as the Germans "displayed ingenuity and cunning in devising schemes to circumvent censorship and security regulations" (Klughaupt 1945). The Americans knew of at least five such methods:

1. Uncensored mail was arriving at Hearne and then sent to various POW camps without the knowledge of American officials (Szilagyi 1944).
2. The German postal employees made marks, such as greetings, on the outside of envelopes bound for POWs at other camps (Szilagyi 1944).
3. The POWs could leave old envelopes, stamped to indicate they had been censored, with friends in the Postal Unit when they were transferred to another camp. This enabled the prisoners who remained at Hearne to communicate covertly with their transferred friend by labeling the envelope as an incorrect address and then mailing a new note with whatever message they desired to send him. After the letter was opened and read and a reply inserted, it was returned to the local camp post office as unclaimed and thus sent back to Camp Hearne to the person who had originally sent it. As a matter of routine, American authorities usually did not examine miss-sent mail (Neuland 1945a; Szilagyi 1944; Ulio 1945). Thus, letters were returned to Hearne as undeliverable with notes that were "mostly innocuous," addressed to Postal Unit employees or to the initially intended recipient (Carpenter 1945).
4. Selected letters were opened so that information could be inserted for the addressee or with orders for the addressee to forward it to someone else in the same camp (Neuland 1945a).
5. Forged censor and postmark stamps were produced to use with faked letter covers (Ulio 1945). Former POW Hugo Wannemacher recalled that sometimes he would send secret letters, using a fictitious German address and by stamping the envelope with a postmark carved into a cut potato. He used this method to write to his friend in Arizona. "There was nothing secret in those letters," said Wannemacher. "It was just transfer of news. This was the height of enjoyment . . . they [the forged letters] looked official. All kinds of stamps, all kinds of signatures" to make the letters look authentic. Wannemacher still had one of these letters that spoke about a friend in the hospital, about all the people still in the camp, about transfers, and penned with greetings from other friends. In April, 1944, Wannemacher wrote: "and next year we will certainly come home and there all the girls will be waiting for us. And then we will have the time of our lives." The return address read Hugo Wannemacher, Hintertupfingen, Germany. He also included an envelope inside for his friend's reply and instructed him to return it to Hearne as incorrectly delivered. Wannemacher noted in his letter, "there are many letters which come back because they are wrongly addressed, but they really are not."

The German POWs working in the Postal Unit clearly had ample opportunity to open mail, insert notes, or make notations on envelopes (Szilagyi 1944). Using such strategies, Hearne POWs were able to "maintain continual correspondence" with POWs interned in other camps. Furthermore, having access to the Postal Unit records allowed them to keep track of all German POWs in the United States (Neuland 1945a; Ulio 1945).

Although not discovered until later, a secret code apparently was developed for use in communication between Camp Hearne and Camp Mexia, Texas (a camp for German officers), and Camp Alva, Oklahoma (a camp for Nazi trouble-makers). An excerpt from an American report illustrates the elaborate nature of this code: "If the day of the year is 50 or less, the proper cell for inscription of the basic number 20 may be determined by direct count. If the day of the year is greater than 50, the largest multiple of 50 contained within the number is first subtracted. The remainder indicates the proper cell for inscription of the basic number. In this instance the day of the year is 135 and the largest multiple of 50 to be subtracted therefrom is 100, resulting in a remainder of 35. The basic number 20 is thereupon inscribed into the 35th cell of the 10 x 5 grid." This information came from a German soldier who was captured in France in August, 1944, but the information was not obtained in the United States until May, 1945. Nevertheless, American authorities believed it to be reliable (Peabody 1945). Using a code such as this, it was possible for Camp Hearne prisoners to communicate an infinite variety of covert messages to prisoners between these camps and in other camps and apparently, considering the source of this information, even with Europe.

By early 1945, American officials had concluded that the Postal Unit was "the center of the German Intelligence Service" between POWs where the prisoners engaged in the "organized misuse of prisoner of war mail facilities and circumvention of United States Censorship." The situation was seen as serious enough to require the attention of the secretary of war, who ordered that the problems be rectified (Neuland 1945a; Ulio 1945). The abuse was quite severe. According to Fritz Haus: "within the first two weeks copies were made of all prisoner lists. Then the German spokesmen in all camps were instructed to mark on their particular list the pro-Nazi, anti-Nazi, and apolitical or indifferent prisoners of the camp and return the annotated copy to the Hearne hierarchy. The secret committee at Hearne, consisting of SS men, Gestapo agents, and party functionaries, then went into operation and sent regular directives and requests to their counterparts for action and information. The official Hearne envelopes ensured a safe traffic between the camps."

The result, said Haus, was that "an elaborate but highly secret and efficient Nazi network had come into being, with strings being pulled by headquarters in Hearne, as if it were a glorious puppet show. Intimidations, blackmailing, beatings, work stoppages, go-slow strikes, and demands for more food and pay, or easier working conditions were largely coordinated from, or initiated by, the Hearne committee." Because Hearne was the postal center for all German POW mail, all this was possible for innovative Nazis. This explains many of the difficulties the Americans had. Nevertheless, Haus was convinced they took too long to recognize this fact: "at first they did not connect the two as a possible clue and solution to their problems." He described the whole operation as "cunningly devised and cleverly operated." It was "a powerful tool in the hands of the Nazi bosses." For some time, the Americans could not understand why "negative actions and reactions with bold demands should occur with military clockwork precision on the same day and time in many camps, some of them hundreds of miles apart. How could that be?!"

Haus recalled that when the Americans realized what was happening—"almost by accident," the result of a guard overhearing a heated argument between two German leaders of the Postal Unit—"they almost panicked and didn't know what to do." Actually, as stated above, the Americans had several ideas as to what they could or should do about the situation; it just took too long for the military bureaucracy to act. On one hand, they had to stop the Nazi infiltration of the postal system. On the other hand, the Red Cross insisted on the quick delivery of mail "which had run so smoothly from Hearne." Further complicating the situation was the fact that, according to the Geneva Convention, the American authorities had no right to interfere with the political beliefs of the prisoners; if some POWs chose to be diehard Nazis, the United States had to accept it—at least until the end of the war.

Because of the plethora of problems, higher authorities agreed to assign an additional six American enlisted men to maintain constant supervision over the POWs who actually handled the mail. But the memo announcing this decision also admitted that this would allow only one American enlisted man for every two buildings (Szilagyi 1944). The incongruity inherent in such statements seems to have been lost in the bureaucratic shuffle.

The real problem with the Postal Unit seems to have been the German personnel who operated it, the "non-cooperative" NCOs who were later described as "tough and hard-boiled" Nazis. The logical conclusion was that having such prisoners operate the Postal Unit was most "undesirable" (Lakes 1945; Lerch 1945). One observer described the very appearance of these POWs as "more ruthless and overbearing than" most German sergeants. Perhaps more significant, one report stated: "a considerable number of these sergeants wear the skull-designed ring on their fingers indicating SS membership." Captain Short, the intelligence officer at Camp Hearne, observed, "these men were never screened before they were assigned to duty in the Postal Unit" (Neuland 1945c). Most disturbing, though, is the fact that because of poor oversight by the Americans, the German NCOs actually supervised and operated the Postal Unit at Camp Hearne, "A so-called German Office, having at its head a Chief Clerk, [who] decides daily how many men from each company in the compound will work the next day in the unit. These men rotate at the discretion of the German Chief Clerk. The number of days each man may work in the unit is decided by the German Office." In the margins of the memo describing this situation, someone had written the comment, "Rotten" (Carpenter 1945). The operation of the German Postal Unit seems to have been comparable to the proverbial inmates running the asylum.

During a routine visit in early October, 1944, by two field liaison officers, other serious problems were discovered that were broader in scope and in their implications. The two officers noted that "a general lack of efficiency" characterized the Postal Unit. Captain Turner, who had previously worked for the U.S. Postal Service, admitted that twice as many men worked in the unit as were needed. He stated that 150 men could manage the load "if they worked with ordinary diligence" yet the two officers noted on one day that 289 men were working. This confirms the view of another memo that "at least twice as many Germans are employed as is necessary." The memo concluded that too much time was spent trying to trace "Dead Letters" with a special file kept only for that purpose, "More complete directory service is being given to this mail at the present time than is being given to the civilian mail at the local post office." When the two officers questioned him about the situation, Lieutenant Colonel Stiles explained that the German NCOs merely wanted to pad their paychecks. He explained that work in the Postal Unit was the only work they were willing to engage in and thus was their only source of revenue. Moreover, cutting the staff might have resulted in a strike and a backlog with no other labor source available to take over. The field liaison officers' report quoted Stiles as saying, "They have me over a barrel and I think they know it" (Carpenter 1945; Dawson and Schwieger 1944). This is quite a remarkable statement, coming as it does from the camp commander. Stiles never seems to have questioned why this was the only work the NCOs were willing to perform.

The Dead Letter Office appears to have been the heart of the German inter-camp communication system. A large number of POWs would be needed to handle the volume of covert messages being sent to and from Hearne, thus the large number of Germans who worked there. Oddly, the American authorities realized this fact only belatedly.

Captain Lakes's inspection of the camp with Major Neuland in February, 1945, resulted in damning reports on the Postal Unit. Neuland's follow-up report was a more extensive memo that focused on the Postal Unit itself. He reported that Lakes had observed "certain marked deficiencies in the operation of the German Postal Unit." For one thing, he noticed the POWs tampering with the mail and cited the earlier investigation that indicated the German POWs handling the mail had committed "extremely serious violations of mail privacy." Neuland added that Captain Lakes had observed that the two to three hundred NCOs working in the Postal Unit were "non-cooperative sergeants who were transferred to Hearne for segregation." Furthermore, while these men were unwilling to do maintenance or farm labor they "readily welcome[d] the opportunity to handle the mail and thus get all the vital information necessary to maintain their own intelligence records on prisoners of war in this country." As a result, these POWs knew that Fort Devens, Massachusetts; Camp Campbell, Kentucky; and Camp Livingston, Louisiana, were anti-Nazi camps and they had access "to the rosters of names of prisoners of war transferred to these camps." Captain Short knew that the "strong-arm" men of the unit kept a blacklist of anti-Nazis (Neuland 1945c). If the report of the two field liaison officers had not alerted higher authorities to the unreliability of those employed in the Postal Unit, this memo certainly should have.

Neuland was critical of Capt. Henry M. Turner, the Camp Hearne Postal Unit officer. He deemed Turner "to be unable to cope with the situation" because his only qualification for the position was his previous experience as a postal clerk in Lincoln, Nebraska, and because he did not "have the personality and discerning nature that an important assignment like this one calls for." Specifically, Turner was "too prone to give the German prisoners of war the benefit of any doubt." Turner had acknowledged that the four Americans assigned to supervise the Postal Unit were unable to prevent Germans from tampering with the mail. Moreover, he noted that an increase in American personnel would not solve the problem because they could not read "what the Germans write on the envelopes or letters." In addition, their duties were interrupted by other obligations so that their attention was not focused. On the day of Lakes's visit, four American soldiers were assigned to supervise 250 prisoners in fifteen barracks and two of them stood "in the corner of a barracks chatting about their personal affairs, completely ignoring" their charges (Neuland 1945c).

The lack of American control was quite apparent. According to one report, "prisoners are permitted to stroll through the area of the Postal Unit on their way to recreation areas, and on Sunday to attend chapel." The chapel was removed from the Postal Unit area after December 16, 1944 but "on April 19, 1945, *152 prisoners of war were actually moved from Compound #1 into the Postal Unit Compound.*" While these POWs resided in the same compound as the Postal Unit, there were no Americans within the compounds between midnight and 7 A.M. This means that the POWs who resided within the Postal Unit compound were "left entirely up to their own devices *without American supervision*" during this time. Moreover, the gates separating the Postal Unit compound from Compound #1 were unattended and unlocked during the day (Klughaupt 1945, emphasis in original).

Finally, the effectiveness of the Postal Unit became reduced over time. Less and less mail was arriving from Germany, yet the German workforce was not proportionally reduced. As a result, the Postal Unit's efficiency declined sharply. American officials noticed that there was "very little relation between the monthly production and the number of prisoners employed." In fact, the average number of items processed, both letters and parcels, per man per day fluctuated greatly with no real pattern. Part of the overstaffing can be explained by the existence of extraneous full-time employees, including two carpenters, three gardeners, a painter, an electrician, and a bookbinder. None of these positions was necessary for the operation of the Postal Unit. This, in itself, was an object of criticism. In fact, the large size of Camp Hearne's Postal Unit was part of the problem because it was spread out over several buildings, thus increasing the security risks. Noncooperative prisoners required close supervision at all times, but there were inadequate numbers of American personnel for the task, especially because they had a much larger area to control and some of them had other duties that prevented them from adequately performing this particular one. This meant that two Americans were "expected to supervise operations conducted in 13 buildings." Thus, according to one report, the prisoners were "at liberty to do precisely as they please to the extent virtually of German operational autonomy." As another report summarized the situation: "It is difficult to understand the decision to move the Prisoner of War personnel into the German Postal Unit compound itself. The manner in which they now are deployed and virtually occupy the Postal Unit compound almost takes on some of the finer aspects of the Von Schlieffen Plan" (Klughaupt 1945; Lerch 1945). The Schlieffen Plan was Germany's war plan in 1914 and one of the main reasons a small Balkan war became World War I. By analogy, the organization and operation of the German Postal Unit was a plan for disaster from the very start. It is no small wonder that American officials became dissatisfied with the operation of Camp Hearne's Postal Unit.

Recommendations and Closure

From the various reports and memos that came out of the inspections and investigations of the Postal Unit, several possible solutions were offered. A 1944 memo by Col. N. Szilagyi offered suggestions that applied to all POW camps in the United States. These included assigning "competent American personnel . . . to supervise the opening of all mail pouches and to collect and return to the District Postal Censor all uncensored mail" and to "carefully scrutinize incoming mail" before releasing it to prisoners in order to curtail abuses. In addition, Lieutenant Colonel Stiles's recommendation that each camp cancel every incoming letter "with a large, conspicuous stamp" was endorsed. Finally, Szilagyi advised that all camps should check outgoing mail to insure the correct return address was used.

Unfortunately, the suggested reforms did not address the problems that existed at Camp Hearne. Although they might have reduced the abuses if implemented fully, this did not happen. The abuses continued. One possible solution to the problem was to replace the Postal Unit's staff with "trustworthy" personnel, specifically anti-Nazi POWs (Neuland 1945a). A more thorough recommendation was that the unit be moved from Hearne to another camp where reliable anti-Nazi prisoners could operate it. Fort Campbell, Kentucky, and Fort Devens, Massachusetts, were cited as possible locations (Lakes 1945). During the visit by Captain Lakes, Captain Short, and the new Camp Hearne commander, Lt. Col. Napoleon Rainbolt, all three men agreed that the Postal Unit should be transferred to another camp (Neuland 1945c).

An alternative suggestion to using anti-Nazi POWs was that American personnel take over the operation of the German Postal Unit. In 1945, Maj. John Dvorovy expressed the strong belief that POW mail "should in no case be handled by prisoners of war themselves." Using anti-Nazis, including those in an anti-Nazi camp, would not alleviate the problems because anti-Nazis were divided into different political groups who likewise might abuse the system for their own advantages. Dvorovy argued that the volume of mail was no longer prohibitively high and thus Americans would be able to handle the load. Captain Turner made this same recommendation to Major Neuland, but his newly arrived commanding officer, Lieutenant Colonel Rainbolt, wanted to make his own investigation and suggested in the meantime that the best solution was to transfer the Postal Unit "to another unit where trustworthy prisoners of war could be used." In fact, the problem with the Postal Unit was "one of the foremost reasons for a change of Commanding Officers at Hearne by the Service Command." It seems that Stiles had lost the favor of his superiors. Neuland's own recommendation differed slightly, but he used a similar argument that the volume of mail had declined, while security was of great importance. Therefore, he concluded, the Postal Unit should be transferred to an anti-Nazi camp and only American personnel should handle mail at Camp Hearne (Dvorovy 1945; Neuland 1945c).

The final suggestion made is the one that was finally chosen: moving the Postal Unit to the U.S. East Coast. Several possible locales were considered, including at least two camps in Virginia, but the decision was finally made to collocate the unit with the Italian mail distribution center at Fort Meade, Maryland. This was one of the more popular choices among those making such recommendations. Another common theme of the various recommendations was the idea of using Italian Service Unit officers to handle German mail and increasing the number of American personnel supervising its operation (Carpenter 1945). For one thing, the Italian POWs had been screened already and were available for that purpose. In theory, this would reduce or eliminate the major security concerns such as those at Camp Hearne. The argument was also convincing from a practical standpoint: because most mail from Germany came into the United States through East Coast ports (especially New York and Philadelphia), transferring the Postal Unit to a nearby locale would reduce transportation costs and the time delay in distributing the mail (Klughaupt 1945; Lerch 1945). Fort Meade initially was rejected because of insufficient space even though report noted, "the disadvantage of limited space is far outweighed by the innumerable disadvantages in the operation at Camp Hearne." However, by June, 1945, new space had become available at Fort Meade for use by the Postal Unit. While awaiting final authorization, two measures were ordered to alleviate the worst problems: American personnel were to be used "exclusively" in dealing with returned mail and strict supervision was to be maintained over all German POWs still working in the unit. The transfer was finally completed in July and the Postal Unit ceased operation at Camp Hearne on July 19 (Bryan 1945; Klughaupt 1945; Neuland 1945a).

Considering all of the problems encountered by the German Postal Unit, it seems surprising that a solution was not reached more quickly. The Americans seem to have made several crucial errors that resulted in the problems described above. From the beginning, they apparently failed to anticipate the potential for abuse by using POWs to handle the mail. Their only concern seems to have been the speed with which the mail could be processed and the backlog eliminated. The Germans thus had many opportunities to abuse the system and were often able to do so because of the lack of American supervision. Moreover, the Americans did not take politics into consideration. If they had, they would have screened the Germans assigned to the Postal Unit. When the problems eventually became more obvious, some American officials seemed unwilling to accept its seriousness until it was staring them in the face. Finally, by the time the U.S. Army began to respond, the negative reports were multiplying. The response to what was clearly a critical situation was slow and inefficient. Considering the potential seriousness of the problem, perhaps this was the greatest mistake of all.

NAZI CONTROL AND INTIMIDATION

The prisoners at Camp Hearne and other camps in the United States ranged from fanatical Nazis to equally dedicated anti-Nazis (Krammer 1996, 154, 161; Pluth 1970, 303; Walker 2001, 88). The U.S. Army was aware of the different political philosophies among the POWs and realized that confinement of a large number of men with such strong and divergent political viewpoints in small POW camps would created a tense situation. As a result, the army tried to defuse these potentially explosive situations by identifying and segregating prisoners who held strong Nazi beliefs from the rest of the prisoner population. However, the segregation policies developed in February, 1943, were vague and provided camp commanders with no guidelines on how to identify ardent Nazis. The policies were clarified six months later and again in October, 1943, but they were still of little help in the difficult task of identifying Nazi POWs (Krammer 1996, 188; Pluth 1980, 298–99; Walker 2001, 88). Former POW Heino Erichsen wrote about his frustrations over the Americans' inability to identify the hardcore Nazis during their initial processing in the United States. "The Americans' idea of processing looked like the perfect place for a European criminal to create a new identity," Erichsen stated (2001, 56). "I worried that they would not try to sort the Nazis out from the rest of us. Heated political arguments I overheard on the ship convinced me that the Nazis still felt powerful, not only in Germany but in our midst. I could only hope the Americans understood that German POWs had major political differences. As I moved down the line, I got even more worried. I could tell that German/English interpreters were few and far between. The Americans didn't know whom they were dealing with. I saw that they left the German military branches intact: army, navy, and air force. They followed the rules of the Geneva Convention and segregated the officers from the enlisted men. Thus, rabid Nazis slipped by unnoticed." In another attempt to identify hardcore Nazis, the War Department published a pamphlet in November, 1944, entitled *What About the German Prisoner?* (War Department 1944c). It proved to be of limited use. The task of identifying and segregating ardent Nazis within the POW population proved to be exceedingly difficult for the U.S. Army.

To make matters worse, American commanders may have inadvertently allowed the Nazis to gain the upper hand in their camps. In order to maintain order in the POW camps and adhere to the Geneva Convention, the Germans in the camps maintained their rank structure and the privileges and respect they commanded. A strict code of military discipline was established and enforced by the highest-ranking prisoners within the camps. In a 1944 memorandum, Brig. Gen. Robert Dunlop noted that a majority of high-ranking German soldiers were most likely Nazis. "A majority of the German officers and noncommissioned officers with years of service in the regular German army," he stated, "are indoctrinated completely with the Nazi theory of discipline." Furthermore, the Geneva Convention permitted the POWs to choose compound and camp spokesmen to represent them to the American camp administrators. Generally, the highest-ranking individuals within the camp, who initially likely were men with Nazi leanings, occupied these positions. As former Camp Hearne POW Heino Erichsen (2001, 62) wrote: "Top military brass in Washington, D.C., were pleased to find that they were not faced with the chaos of hundreds of thousands of uncontrollable individuals, but rather with a tight obedient military unit in which each rank was responsible to its direct superior for its actions. This disciplinary tactic seemed sound to our captors, but it led to a disastrous strengthening of German militarism and Nazism inside the camps." This certainly was not the intent of the POW camp administrators. For the Americans, the entire POW program was new and unprecedented. It was largely operated on a trial-and-error basis (Krammer 1996).

Because of the army's inability to segregate ardent Nazis and because Nazis ascended to camp leadership positions, the stage was set for a confrontation between the Nazis and the anti-Nazis over the political control of the camps—including Camp Hearne.

Many guards and prisoners have vivid memories of the political turmoil at Camp Hearne in the summer of 1943. Former guard Tex Geyser stated: "When it [the camp] first opened up we had some problems with the prisoners. They had Nazis and anti-Nazis all mixed up, and they didn't get along with each other." Ken Johns remembered that soon after the prisoners arrived at Camp Hearne: "We had riots every couple of days. We had quite a few. They [the POWs] would go into the latrines and tear the boards apart and beat each other with the boards with the nails in the ends of the boards. They were rough." Matt Ware recalled: "We'd go in there with clubs, [of] course we weren't allowed to take guns in there, and they'd see us coming and stop." Johns said he thought the men were agitating over political issues: "Problems developed after they [the POWs] were in the compounds. They had the Social Democrats and the Nazis. They had their own two political parties in the camp . . . and that is why we had so many riots." He remembered that he often would have to interrupt his trips into town or to the movie theater when he heard the camp emergency siren requiring the return of all personnel to the camp: "There used to be a theater across the street here and [on] many nights my wife and I would go to the show, and [they would] stop the movie and turn on the lights. They would order everyone back to camp because there was a riot. The riots were always between the Social Democrats and the Nazis." When asked who had the biggest gang, Johns replied, "They were both really big, but the Nazis were stubborn and hard to get along with."

Leading the anti-Nazi effort at Camp Hearne were members of the Afrika Korps's 999th Probation Division, which was made up of court-martialed soldiers who had been convicted of offenses such as black marketeering and political crimes, but were not habitual criminals. These soldiers were authorized to perform combat duty for the purpose of rehabilitation (Bender and Law 1973; Forty 1997). On May 31, 1943, an American officer on the train bringing the first group of POWs to Camp Hearne reported that he had received a letter from a prisoner who was acting as the spokesman for members of "Africa Brigade 999." Because of their opposition to the Nazi government, they had been held in concentration camps. "They had to expiate their struggles for freedom and peace by the cruelty of Nazi terror—also directed against their families and relatives. Afterwards these men were forced to become soldiers." This letter contained a list of the names of about a hundred soldiers of the 999th Probation Division who were on the train and requested to be segregated from the other prisoners for fear of bodily harm (Pluth 1970, 306; Woods 1943b). Arno Einicke vividly recalled the members of the 999th Division. He described them as "political prisoners and criminals of enlisted rank. Some of them were communists. Some of the people of the Nine-Ninety-Ninth were professors and other highly intelligent people. These political prisoners were anti-Nazis." He remembers that they had been among the last Germans drafted into the army and had been placed in the most danger when sent into action. However, he added, their situation improved when they became prisoners: "They occupied a number of key positions in the camp. Such as being busy in the garbage disposal and in the kitchen and so on." This in turn provided them with more contacts outside the camp: "The noncommissioned officers were not expected to work. And from their [999th members] perspective these people [the other German NCOs] were just a bunch of Nazis. So they felt they had to fight them."

Evidence of the organization of anti-Nazis at Camp Hearne and the political tensions is found in a letter sent by a POW named Hans Hankner on August 21, 1943, to the American Friends of German Freedom on behalf of himself and other self-proclaimed anti-Nazis expressing support for that organization's goals. "Some of us have been bitter enemies of National Socialism for decades," wrote Hankner. "Many of us have felt the horrors of Adolf Hitler's concentration camps and prisons on our own bodies, because we chose to fight for the liberation of Germany from the barbarian yoke of Hitler fascism." He briefly described the political situation within Camp Hearne: "Here we have joined together in an anti-fascist company. Proof that we are going in the right direction, in case such proof is needed, has been supplied to us by the Nazis themselves, in that last week, goaded on by the minions of the Gestapo, who are especially well represented here as sergeants and staff sergeants [NCO ranks], especially in the Military Police, they attempted to assault one of our barracks and to set fire to another. Their plan was to kill us in order to intimidate the wavering people in their camp and keep them from coming over to us. This plan was foiled by our defense, even though many of our men were wounded." The Nazis "went on a rampage" during this attack, setting one barrack on fire, wrecking several others, and severely beating several anti-Nazis. Because of this riot, an American officer recommended that both the Nazis and the anti-Nazis be transferred to other camps. Four specific Nazis, who were seen as "arrogant and persistent

Nazi agitators," were sent to Camp Alva, Oklahoma (Edwards 1943c; Walker 2001, 96–97).

Einicke and Fritz Haus recalled a counterattack by the anti-Nazis, led by members of the 999th Probation Division, on November 9, 1943: "The anti-Nazis announced that would be the day of the revolution. They manufactured weapons out of pieces of wood, heavy wood." Haus said they were armed with "clubs attached to which were razor blades, short chains, and other things that you could hit with. . . . They had a plan in which certain people were identified for liquidation." Einicke agreed: Members of the 999th "planned who should die. They believed certain individuals had to be liquidated. They targeted those who they considered to be Nazis, including the Gestapo. In the afternoon of the ninth, the Nazis and other NCOs found out about their plan. The Americans did not know a thing about all of this. This was revealed to other Germans, the noncommissioned officers . . . apparently someone talked about it. So, the German NCOs positioned men, strong people at both ends of the barracks, ready for the attack by the Nine-Ninety-Ninth."

Einicke and Haus concurred that "shortly after lights out," members of the 999th Division attacked the suspected Nazi NCO barracks. "The members of the Division 999 were captured by the defenders," Einicke remembered. "They tried to get out, but they were kept in the barracks. They were boxing and fighting . . . screaming and howling. . . . An American guard shot into the barracks. Five bullets entered the barrack." Haus recalled that his barrack received machine-gun fire. He said that the Americans came in their jeeps, stopped the fighting, and "took the revolutionaries into [protective] custody." According to Einicke: "No one was wounded or killed. It was not long afterwards that the Nine-Ninety-Ninth members were removed from Camp Hearne entirely." When asked why they picked November 9 for the revolution, Einicke cited the years 1918 and 1923: "it was a special day. The ninth of November has special meaning in German history. Hitler's failed political putsch occurred on 9 November." Indeed, November 9 is an important day in German history. Germany's World War I revolution reached its climax on November 9, 1918, with the abdication of Kaiser Wilhelm II and the proclamation of a Republic from Berlin. In 1923, it was the day Hitler chose for his Munich "Beer Hall Putsch" in which he tried to take over the government. Later, in 1938, it was the date the Nazis called "Kristallnacht," the "night of broken glass," on which Jewish synagogues, businesses, and homes were vandalized throughout Germany. More recently, in 1989, it was the date the Berlin Wall was opened.

The attacks and counterattacks in 1943 clearly illustrate the intense struggle for internal control of the camp. With the removal of the members of the 999th Division from Camp Hearne, the Nazi element took control of the camp, the anti-Nazi sympathizers faded into the background, and an uneasy calm fell over the camp. Krammer (1996, 161) states, "The Nazis realized that an orderly and well-run camp would give them the continued backing of the American authorities and, therefore, the continued control over the camp." To consolidate their hold and rid the camp of anti-Nazi beliefs, a reign of terror was carried out in POW camps across the country as fanatical Nazis attacked suspected anti-Nazis in numerous violent incidents, including at least seven murders nation-wide, one of which occurred at Camp Hearne. The violence was widespread and followed a basic pattern: one or more prisoners suspected of being anti-Nazi, often on the flimsiest of grounds and evidence, would be "tried" and "found guilty" by a kangaroo court of Nazi prisoners and then sentenced to the appropriate punishment. This usually entailed a severe beating, but could mean death. Many suicides under questionable circumstances were probably either murders or forced suicides in which the victim was told to take his own life or others would do it for him (Krammer 1996, 169–74, 296; Pluth 1970, 311, 317–18, 323–24; Walker 2001, 90–91). This violence continued at Camp Hearne until early 1944.

Chaplain Gustave Zoch (1946, 7–9) provided detailed insights into the Nazis at Camp Hearne:

> The Nazis were exceedingly proud and arrogant in their general behavior. When you came in contact with them, they would not only make you feel inferior to them, but would even tell you so in a typical Nazi fashion. These boys cause[d] us all the trouble we experienced in our camp.
>
> [The Nazis were] especially so [hostile] toward the anti-Nazis in their own midst. Words fail me to properly describe the vicious and destructive attitude taken and shown by the Nazis toward the anti-Nazis. In their opinion there was not a more detestable creature in the world than a man in their own midst, who would say or do anything contrary to the wishes of Der Fuehrer and the Nazi party. Such a person, in their opinion, was not only a shameful betrayer of their beloved Fatherland, but was also worthy of the most cruel and ignominious death. And as soon as a fellow-German would act anti-Nazi or would say something unfavorable of Hitler and the Nazi party, he would immediately be reported to the Nazi Gestapo in the camp, placed on the black-list, and at the earliest opportune time, generally in the early morning hours when everybody was asleep, put to death in a most gruesome and merciless manner. For instance, one prisoner [Hugo Krauss] was overheard saying something somewhat favorable of things American, and by the next morning he was a dead corpse, having been mercilessly beaten to death with clubs. Another man made the statement: "I am afraid that Hitler made a mistake by having attacked Russia," and had it not been for the fast thinking and acting of our American guards, this man would have undoubtedly met with the same fate. As so we could go on showing the extreme hateful and destructive spirit of the true Nazis over against the anti-Nazis, as it existed in our camp.

Specific Germans in positions of influence were reported to be Nazis. For instance, the German medical officer at the camp was revealed to have been an "ardent Nazi" who intended to "incite unrest among prisoners of war in the compounds" (Pluth 1970, 313). Furthermore, according to Chaplain Zoch (1946, 14–15), some German clergymen "who should have upheld Christ and the cause of Christianity, denounced true Christianity and preached Nazism. They proclaimed Hitler as the Savior of Germany, and [whosoever] believes in him and works for him, shall not perish from the face of the earth, but have an abundant life in the future Germany."

Zoch also described the anti-Nazis at Camp Hearne (1946, 8):

> The anti-Nazis were an entirely different group of men. These were not trained and educated by Hitler and were, therefore, more democratic in spirit and friendly toward us. They were very coopera-tive and helpful to us, in fact so much so that at times it was difficult to realize that they were really our enemies in war. At the same time, however, they hated and were very fearful of their fellow-prisoners, the Nazis. So great was their hatred against the Nazi that they wished them forever destroyed, and their fear of them so great that they spent many sleepless nights while at the camp. Some in their fear and anxiety were even driven to commit suicide. . . . Since there was absolutely no way to telling who was a Nazi and who was not, it was very difficult to esti-mate the number of Nazi and the number of anti-Nazi at our camp. As closely as we could determine, however, we had approximately half and half—2000 Nazis and 2000 anti-Nazis.

According to Zoch, the more ardent Nazis tended to be younger because they had been brought up under Nazism and the older prisoners, enlisted men, were more inclined to be anti-Nazi or ambivalent because they had been brought up under the "Hindenburg regime." The former group were dominant, how-ever, as they had been promoted above others. These Nazis exercised consider-able influence within the camp through intimidation. For example, after a large number of prisoners began to attend Zoch's weekly religious services, atten-dance dropped dramatically because the Nazis took names and threatened those who went. Only a handful of POWs chose to defy the Nazis out of religious convictions. After Germany surrendered, they began to attend Zoch's services again and in larger numbers (Zoch 1946, 10, 15, 21–22).

Captain Oberwegner, the American commander of POW Company 3, re-lated another incident that took place in 1943 that illustrates the degree of Nazi intimidation at Camp Hearne. Oberwegner (Proceedings of a General Court-Martial 1946, 83) stated during the murder trial of Cpl. Hugo Krauss:

> The colonel was desirous to have volunteers to go out to work to help with the cotton. The colonel ordered me to question the com-pany as to how many would volunteer to work. So, at the next forma-tion, when I had the company lined up, I asked how many would volunteer to work and when that was translated to the prisoners the hands started to come up to volunteer for work and all at once went

back down. There were a few who still wanted to work and a short time after this formation Sergeant Boehmer [a POW] came into my office. Sergeant Boehmer stated that when I asked how many wanted to work, that the [POW] company leader who was standing directly in front of me gave a signal with his face to the members of the company ordering them not to volunteer to work.

The offending German company leader was removed from Camp Hearne and Boehmer, who appeared to be more cooperative, took over the position. Later, Boehmer would be convicted with others in the murder of Corporal Krauss.

"The Nazis gave us a lot of problems," said Paul Reinhold. "We always had trouble . . . [because] they beat up their own prisoners and they didn't want them to talk to the Americans." John Luparelli added, "They kept a close net on their troops, they didn't want them to get close to the American troops." Hans Lammersdorf's memory provides a personal account of this fact:

> I had problems because I was not a super Nazi. I was just a German. I obeyed the laws and accepted what I was told. But I had my own opinions and as a result I liked to read the *Houston Post,* which was available, and inform myself about what's going on in the world. My friends and comrades could not speak English or read English so they would ask me "What's the news?" And I said, "All I can do for you is translate literally without comment," because I knew better than being too open in my views [which could be dangerous]. So that got me in real trouble. They summoned me to the German leadership and gave me a warning. Never to divulge any information I had through the paper. So I knew there was a difference between my life under Hitler and the life in the American POW camp. Because there were leaders, I called them super Nazis, hard-boiled but I guess dedicated Nazis, they tolerated no dissent whatsoever. Anyway there was a terror I wasn't used to. And when I was transferred to Arizona [at his request], an ex-SS man who I happened to know [and who] was sort of a friend said, "Be glad you are leaving this camp." And I said, "What do you mean?" He said, "You were on the list to be eliminated by 'the Fehme.'" It's a secret organization they had in the Middle Ages, which would eliminate people who were in the way [and was revived by the Nazis]. [These were typical] Gestapo methods. So, that really [opened] my eyes to what I was, that I was almost a victim of those fanatics. I remember to this day that I was suppressed, really. . . . And that's one reason I came back [to America] as a free man, as an immigrant.

According to the *Webster's Dictionary,* there are two definitions for "Fehme": "(1) a late medieval German secret tribunal; (2) a unit of a secret Nazi organization intent upon seeking out and executing those considered enemies of National Socialism." *The Dictionary of Phrases and Fable* (1898) describes the Fehme as an organization that held "secret tribunals for the preservation of public peace [and] suppression of crime. The judges were enveloped in profound mystery; they had secret spies throughout all Germany; their judgments were certain, but no one could discover the executioner." Fehme courts (Fehmegerichte) operated in Germany during the 1920s and 1930s during the rise of the Nazi Party. These courts were composed of Nazis and rightist members of paramilitary organizations. The Fehmegerichte dispensed "brutal justice" (Snyder 1976, 91–92).

Former POW Arno Einicke also mentioned the Fehme in reference to the Nazi organization at Camp Hearne. Walter Werner recalled that "vengeance trials were held and prisoners felt in danger by other prisoners, I convinced many of these accused prisoners to transfer out. I brought several accused comrades to the gate of the camp during the night." They were then taken into protective custody and transferred to another camp.

Fritz Haus, an NCO in Compound 3, shared many memories of the Nazi shadow element at Camp Hearne: "you were walking on a knife's edge all the time. This feeling of being threatened was one of the things in Hearne." Everyone had to be very careful because "all the meetings [kangaroo courts], they were a reality in Hearne. If you weren't beaten, at least you lived under a threat, and you never knew whether you had taken it too far and who would be the next target. So you were very, very careful . . . politics and political atmosphere in Hearne was certainly there, pro- and anti-[Nazi]. And we all played [along] and tried to keep it from exploding and tried to make the best of it. You looked over your shoulder, even in church, you could never be absolutely frank. And if they [the Nazis] weren't listening inside then they were listening outside or passing by. The Nazi's were only a clique, a minority. A very, very small minority group. But very often they were the leaders, the Sergeants and Staff Sergeants and those who were in command and the leaders."

Former POW Erich Spix (1999), an enlisted man in Compound 1 who felt similar to Haus, said:

> The majority of POWs were not loyal to Hitler. There was a small group of fanatic Nazis which dominated in the camp and tried to get the others in their boat, but the silent majority did not care about it and let them live with their utopian hope. Naturally, every soldier on both sides wished the victory of their country, but it was clear to cool-headed men that the small country of Germany could not win the war against the whole world, surrounded by all other European nations with the massive help of the USA with their huge resources of war material and well-equipped army. Only the fanatic Nazis could ignore that, hoping for a miracle. The overwhelming part of the POWs were glad, that they did not have to fight anymore "for nothing." They were looking at the future; what would this damned war have left for the survivors in Germany? But, according to my experiences, this was the general attitude of the men in the working-camps, which were housing enlisted men and privates, who were required to work.

Haus went on to say that the biggest problem for the majority of German POWs was the same as for the Americans: identifying who were Nazis and who were not. There was always a core of ardent Nazis, but the number of followers varied. According to Haus:

> There weren't any definite lines. These groups were changing all the time. A Nazi [today] might become an anti-Nazi tomorrow, because he received a letter that his mother was killed and that his brother fell in Russia and so on. And the other way around, too. An anti-Nazi might get cold feet and got a warning and so he came over. You never knew. It was a hazy grey area and you never knew. You couldn't rise up because political fortunes [changed]. When Hitler [the army] took another 100 km [of territory] into Russia, then everybody became a Nazi again. And when [the attack on] Stalingrad [failed] and 300,000 or 200,000 [Germans] capitulated into Russian imprisonment, then suddenly they were all anti-Nazi. There were those who had very firm convictions, they were SS and a member of the Nazi Party. And there was a great majority who couldn't care less and they didn't want to but they had to be just running with the system because there was no other choice, but their heart wasn't in it. And they changed according to circumstances. And there were very, very few consistent Communists or anti-Nazis who let it be known that "I wish Hitler was dead" and so on. Because when they stood up for their convictions they were in trouble.

He added that all of the POWs knew that the Nazi faction in the camp kept tabs on their activities in an effort to identify any potential American sympathizers or spies.

As discussed in the previous section, the Nazis at Camp Hearne used the Postal Unit to expand their influence to other camps across the country. Nazis at Camp Hearne could correspond with Nazis in all the other camps across the United States. Anti-Nazi blacklists were compiled and the movements of these men were tracked through the Postal Unit.

There is some evidence of Gestapo activity inside Camp Hearne. Intelligence information indicated that members of the Gestapo (the German secret police agency) and the SS (the police arm of the Nazi Party), groups whose members tended to be fanatical Nazis, had established a means of transmitting messages from the United States to Germany, presumably from the POW camps. It was alleged that known Gestapo agents were residing in several Texas camps, including Camp Hearne (Walker 2001, 88). In October, 1943, a memorandum based on intelligence information from North Africa was sent to Brig. Gen. B. M. Bryan Jr., the assistant to the provost marshal general, whose office had oversight authority over the POW system in the United States. This memorandum identified three Gestapo agents named Menguen, Hey, and Dittmar. Menguen allegedly was a captain in the Gestapo "posing as a corporal in the army" (Jones 1943). Within a matter of days, Bryan's office had concluded that there were no prisoners named Menguen, but a man named Mengen was being held in a camp in Carson, Colorado. In addition, six prisoners named Hey had been identified and fifteen named Dittmar, including a Peter Hey and a Karl Dittmar, both residing at Camp Hearne. This information was too vague to act on, however, so more specific information was requested (Bryan 1943). Unfortunately this ambiguity prevents one from drawing any conclusions about Gestapo activity at Camp Hearne.

American officials received another indication of the severity of the problem a few months later. In March, 1944, an Austrian prisoner named Arnulf Krulla, while aboard a transport ship to the United States, told an American guard, Pvt. Israel Silberman, that the Nazi Party was well organized throughout the POW camps in North America. According to Silberman, Krulla claimed that these Nazis "are branching out and organizing so well that every shipment of P/W [POWs] to the States has a detachment of organizers who are to continue their efforts in the prisoner camps here." Krulla identified the leader aboard the vessel as a Gestapo officer named Klaus Toerpisch. This report eventually led to the recommendation that Toerpisch be transferred from Camp Greeley, Colorado, "to a camp for Nazi extremists" (Krammer 1996, 149; Roamer 1944; H. R. Rogers 1944b). While Toerpisch was not interned at Camp Hearne, Krulla's statements indirectly confirm the possibility of such activity at Hearne and every other camp in the United States. Reports like this, plus occurrences within the camps, fueled the conviction that there was a serious problem.

The Nazis at Camp Hearne were responsible for constructing and protecting the shortwave radios there. These men listened to the radio broadcasts from Germany and dispersed the news from Germany to the other POWs. They also published a secret underground newspaper, *Die Mahnung,* to spread Nazi propaganda (Bachmayer 1945; Hombeck 1945). To carry out some of their activities, they constructed a small network of tunnels and underground rooms to hold meetings and hide things from the Americans (Klughaupt 1945). A large portrait of Adolf Hitler hung in one room (Zoch 1946). The Nazis at Camp Hearne clearly were well organized and in control of the camp.

The Nazis also tried to keep National Socialism alive in the camp by organizing celebrations of Nazi holidays. According to Willi Nellessen: "holidays or events that had to do with the Nazi regime [resulted in] what they called a formation taking place where we would put on our uniforms and hats, and the leaders of each of these sections [compounds] would give speeches and we would sing the national anthem and other patriotic songs." He recalled such celebrations for the anniversary of the beginning of the war (September 1), Hitler's birthday (April 20), and November 9, the anniversary of Hitler's failed government takeover in 1923. "We were not allowed to forget these dates," recalled Fritz Haus. Some would say, "'Well today comrades, today is Adolf Hitler's birthday and long live the Fuehrer,' and so on. I think we sang on Hitler's birthday, we sang the German national anthem."

Chaplain Zoch (1946) also remembered that the Nazis in the camp "were very hostile towards us and everything American. They were so destructive and wasteful of our property and goods. Deliberately did they often damage and destroy our property, steal tools and other American goods, and shamefully waste our water and food." Civilian Annie Sweat said the German cooks in the American officers' mess deliberately threw away perfectly good food: "There was so much waste it was unbelievable. Of course, it was deliberate. The cooks were all German and they wanted America to go into debt. There would be whole hams and whole bunches of carrots and whole cabbages that were thrown away." Sweat saw some of this garbage herself on the way to work, but also learned about it from one of the camp's garbage haulers. This man told her that the local farmers bought the garbage for use as pig feed. They never reported this waste because they enjoyed getting quality feed at a low price.

Former guard Ben Mason said that about half of the prison population consisted of men who were just happy to be out of the line of fire, but the other half were belligerent individuals. "They could turn," said Mason. "They would get out inside an area [of the camp] and a bunch of them get to singing and yelling and they would try to storm the fence. A bunch of them would be singing and then all of a sudden they would all run toward the fence and start to jump it. If you didn't fire at them, I am sure that some of them would have gotten through." Mason estimated that between fifteen and twenty men were involved in these incidents. Ed Munson remembered an incident in which belligerent POWs deliberately pushed against a fence: "About fifty or one hundred prisoners were leaning against the fence and they would keep pushing and pushing until the fence was leaning at about a forty-five-degree angle. The camp commander decided it was getting out of hand and he opened up with a fifty-caliber machine gun and fired a couple of rounds down along the area between the fences, which is about twenty feet [wide], and that stopped it." As punishment, the prisoners were placed in solitary confinement. Paul Reinhold also remembered trouble along the fence lines: "They would tempt you and then you would put the machine gun towards them and they would back off. I think several of them were shot. I am not sure." While these incidents may not have been politically inspired, they clearly were more than pranks and exhibited a certain degree of belligerency on the part of some of the prisoners.

The hardcore Nazis at Camp Hearne appear to have been a small group, but these men occupied all the positions of power and rank. These individuals controlled the internal workings of the camp by intimidating the other POWs. This made life difficult for the average POW who just wanted to get home safely and carry on with his life.

THE MURDER OF CORPORAL HUGO KRAUSS

The most brutal example of Nazi activity at the camp was the murder of Cpl. Hugo Krauss, who was severely beaten on the night of December 17, 1943, and died six days later from the injuries he sustained in this attack (Porter 1945).

Born in Germany in 1919, Hugo Krauss came to the United States in 1928 with his parents, who became naturalized citizens. He grew up and went to school in New York City and returned to Germany in 1939, ironically, as a Nazi supporter. Krauss had become friends with a member of the German-American Bund (the U.S. Nazi Party) who arranged for that organization to pay part of his transportation expenses to Germany. Krauss lived with his grandfather while in Germany. When the war began, Krauss was drafted, but was released when he claimed to be an American citizen. Later, however, he voluntarily joined the German army and served in Russia and then North Africa, where he was captured in April, 1943 (Bryan 1944b; Porter 1945).

Around 11:45 in the evening on December 17, after lights out, six to ten men entered Krauss's barrack and beat him with clubs, nail-studded boards, and a lead pipe. He sustained serious wounds as a result: his skull was fractured, both arms were broken, and his entire body was battered. Medical records indicate that he had three skull fractures—one on the left side, one on the left front, and one on the right side near the front. These head wounds resulted in severe cerebral contusion, or bruising of the brain. In addition, Krauss's left ulna (forearm) was snapped in two; two bones in his left hand were broken, one completely; and his right arm was broken at the elbow. These wounds indicate that he was probably using his arms to protect his head, albeit unsuccessfully. Finally, he had multiple lacerations and bruises to his hands, feet, face, scalp, and torso (Hallaran 1943, photos 1–12). Krauss yelled for help during the attack, but no one intervened. The other prisoners in the barrack did nothing (*Hearne Democrat* 1946a; Porter 1945).

The motives for Krauss's murder are similar to those that prompted other assaults upon POWs at Hearne and other camps: other prisoners questioned his loyalty. In Krauss's case, the prisoners' suspicions may have been justified, but their chosen method for dealing with these suspicions certainly was not. For one thing, Krauss spoke English well and acted as an interpreter for the Americans. This immediately put him under suspicion. In addition, he frequently criticized the German government and military while publicly praising the United States and expressing the belief that America would win the war. Also, according to some witness statements, he told his fellow prisoners "he was going to get a Christmas furlough to visit his parents in New York and expected to arrange things so he could join the United States Army" (Porter 1945). Such pronouncements would be considered treasonous behavior in any army.

Additionally, Krauss's parents sent him a radio that, to the fury of the Nazi fanatics, he did not use to tune in to German music. Instead, he used it to listen to American news broadcasts, "which he interpreted with emphasis on American victories and derision of German claims." Krauss also refused to participate in German ceremonies and singing. His company customarily sang a German song after each meal, but Krauss always left immediately after eating and never took part in the singing. Moreover, he told the other prisoners that he was a German and an American. Because of these actions, "The Nazis charged him with making 'disloyal' statements about Germany and its Fuehrer." A more direct reason for his murder may have been the transfer of some German NCOs to another camp after they were accused of "inciting other prisoners not to cooperate in the POW work program on the score that it was helping the American war effort. Some of these NCOs had been suspected of complicity in other beatings." The ardent Nazis in the compound believed that Krauss had informed against these NCOs to the Americans. Another incident that took place on the day of the beating involved Krauss supposedly saying that German news bulletins being announced were untrue and that American news stories were more accurate (Dickson, Oliver, and Boyles 1946; Porter 1945). Most importantly, the pro-Nazi prisoners acted "on the belief that he [Krauss] had revealed to the camp authorities the fact that the other prisoners of war had a clandestine shortwave radio which they used to receive German news broadcasts. Apparently, It was generally understood about the camp that any prisoner of war who should reveal the shortwave radio would be put to death by his fellow prisoners of war" (Dickson, Oliver, and Boyles 1946). When the American authorities entered the camp and seized the radio, Hugo Krauss was labeled a traitor and his fate was sealed.

Several former prisoners had recollections of the murder. Hans Lammersdorf remembered: "All I know is one day they lined us up, all of us out of our barracks. And then the Americans looked at us to see, if there were some scratch marks maybe on the face on the hands or somewhere to give an indication of a struggle. But they couldn't catch anybody. We, of course, learned soon that a guy was killed. They had beat him so the guy was bleeding quite a bit. Of course the super Nazis spread the rumor that the man was a traitor."

"Krauss was a German who had migrated to America and returned to Germany, [and then] he was drafted," said Willi Nellessen. Over there, he became disillusioned with Nazi Germany, "And he wanted to get out of here [Camp Hearne] and therefore became relatively closely associated with Americans. The Nazis in the camp disapproved of Krauss's actions and they had a secret judgment against him and then he was murdered. The basic problem was that he was pro-American."

Heino Erichsen, who lived in the same barrack as Krauss, said of the attack: "There was a lot of noise and the lights went out and there was a scuffle and screaming and beating, and it didn't take that long and it was over. And then he was taken to the hospital and I think he died two days later. I didn't even know to what extent the injuries were because it was mum, and you didn't dare ask, 'What happened' . . . we were afraid. That was a no-no subject."

Krauss was a tailor by profession and one time when his parents visited him in camp, they presented him with a sewing machine. "My friend Hugo was thrilled with his gift and set himself up in business," Erichsen stated (2001, 64). "Word quickly got around that Hugo could custom tailor uniforms, shirts, and hats with his American sewing machine. Our barrack soon had a steady stream of visitors who wanted their baggy army cloths transformed into sleek fitted outfits." Erichsen remembered Krauss as a nice, congenial fellow: "I knew there was antagonism because he had American relatives who visited him in camp. He had numerous visitors, like in prison, and I think some people said, 'Oh you know, this guy is a spy, I mean he has people coming.' What the hell can you spy on in a prison?" Regarding the existence of spies in the camp, Fritz Haus concurred that the POWs had been warned about American plants amongst them. "I couldn't identify the spies, but we were warned," said Haus. "And there was a sort of notice going around, verbal notice, 'Be careful what you say and be careful to whom you speak, not all of them are genuine POWs. There are some who have been filtered into our camp and they pass on information to the Americans.' That's what we were told, I never knew a spy or identified one, but this was a general caution we were given."

Erichsen, in a 1997 interview, speculated that "a fanatic German paratrooper looked like the suspect to me, but it was dangerous to even poke my nose into such matters." He later wrote (2001, 65): "Hugo's murder made it clear that ardent Nazis were among us. It brought home the fact that I was in far more danger from my fellow Germans than from my American captors. Nights were the most dangerous, because the Americans did not guard our barracks. After Hugo's murder, I felt even more vulnerable, especially in bed. I would never relax. As if I were still in Africa, I slept lightly, alert to the faintest noise. So did my closest buddies. Since I had been a friend of Hugo's, I was terrified that the murderers would target me for that reason, or else because of my job as interpreter for the American military staff. I found Rolf the next morning and told him, 'I'm getting out of here.'" The next day, Erichsen requested a transfer to another camp and was first sent to Camp Mexia, Texas and then to Fort Knox, Kentucky.

Many of the American guards and civilian workers also had recollections of the murder. Typical of these stories was that of Ken Johns, who stated that Krauss's

> mother and sister came down to visit him. After he was captured then he started siding in with the American guards. He ended up being a so-called man without a country. His mother and sister brought him a radio and they found him a few days after that in the barracks and they had tortured him pretty bad. They had sharpened his fingers and toes like a pencil and they took the cord off the radio and that is what they used to tie him up with and they killed him. They took a razor blade or a very sharp knife and sharpened his toes and they did this slowly evidently because they said there was blood [that had] dripped all over that barracks . . . and no one reported, the rest of the prisoners just kept their mouths shut! That actually happened, that wasn't rumors . . . that actually happened . . . he was bloody from one end to the other when I saw him. He started siding with the Americans trying to buddy-buddy with the guards and the other prisoners would hear that, and he ended up a man without the country.

Paul Reinhold also remembered some of the gruesome details: "They beat up this prisoner and they cut his fingers to a point and tied him up and just beat him to death." Matt Ware also recalled that Krauss "worked and got eighty cents a day and if I understand it, the reason they killed him, was that he was buying U.S. war bonds with that eighty cents [a day] and there may be different stories to it but I don't know. My understanding of it, they tied him to the bed with bailing wire and beat him to death one night with pipes. There was a great commotion that night and I wasn't on guard duty that night. The story I heard was that he was beat[en] to death because he was buying U.S. war bonds with his eighty cents a day." Guard Francis Burdick related a similar story: "Well, the prisoner made the statement that he made a mistake in going back to Germany and so forth. I guess evidently he had made some derogatory remarks, something about the Nazis or something. But they got in that night and they stuffed his mouth with cotton or covered it with a bandage of some type and tied his hands and feet where he couldn't, you know, get released. And filed his uh, cut his ears and his fingers and his toes to a point to designate that he was a rat. And of course by the time we found out or he got loose and we got in there, well, we couldn't save him." Curiously, even though most of the American guards recollected that the murderers filed Krauss's fingers down and cut his ears to make him look like a rat and that he had been tied down during the attack, the medical report and autopsy photographs show that this did not actually happen—demonstrating the ability of rumors to distort the truth.

The former guards all noted that Krauss's sister visited him and was dating an American officer. Burdick said that while Krauss "was a prisoner in the camp his [Krauss's] sister came down to see him. And I know we went to a high school football game that night and it just so happened that she was an American citizen, of course, like he had been. And the football coach, I can't remember exactly the lieutenant's name, had a date with her that night." Matt Ware stated: "His sister came to see him while he was there. She was going out with American officers." Most of the guards characterized Krauss's sister as a "party girl."

After the beating, the American authorities at Hearne began a frustrating investigation that got nowhere because of "a complete lack of evidence until about mid-year 1945." One of the problems was that the POWs who had shared the barracks with Krauss claimed that they could not identify his attackers in the dark. To the Americans who investigated the murder, it was "apparent that many of these prisoners of war were deliberately withholding any knowledge which they might have had and that others openly stated that they would not tell or identify the assailants of Cpl. Krauss even if they knew. Many of them asserted that Krauss was a traitor to Germany; that he got what was coming to him; that it was the duty of all German soldiers to exterminate traitors and that they would gladly have participated had they known about it." The Americans concluded that they would not be able to discover who was responsible (Bryan 1944b; McMinn 1949).

Peter Spoden had a brother at Camp Hearne he says was in the same compound as Krauss. He stated that many people were questioned, including his brother, who he said was interrogated for fourteen days. Spoden stated that his brother was kept in jail with no mattress and no blankets. The questioning went on three or four times a day and sometimes during the night, so that Spoden's brother could not get any proper sleep. He said his brother got so mad that he decided not to say anything that would help the American investigation.

An interesting aspect of this case was the correspondence between Krauss's father and two American officers. When he first learned of his son's beating and death at the end of December, 1943, Henry Krauss of New York sent a letter inquiring about the incident and requesting more information: "As a citizen of the United States, I would like a further investigation made and all details sent to me." Understandably, Krauss's parents were distraught over their son's death (Krauss 1943). A few days later, Col. I. B. Summers, the director of the Prisoner of War Division, sent a response outlining the bare facts of the case. The letter stated that Krauss had been beaten in the night by unknown POWs and had died later. He added that "a full and complete investigation will be conducted into the facts surrounding the beating of your son. Every effort will be made to determine the identity of his assailants and prosecute them for their crime" (Summers 1944). However, this was not satisfactory to Krauss, who sent another letter at the end of February asking about his son's personal belongings, specifically mentioning the radio. Additionally, Krauss asked about the cause of the fight, why his son had been unable to defend himself, and, most importantly he asked, "Through your investigation, have you found the ones responsible for this crime?" (Krauss 1944).

This resulted in a more detailed response from the assistant provost marshal general's executive officer, who reported on the "exhaustive investigation" that had taken place in which "forty-nine witnesses were examined, five being American personnel and the remainder German prisoners of war." The investigation revealed "that Hugo Krauss was often antagonistic toward the German prisoners of war and in many ways indicated his favoritism of America over Germany." Furthermore, "your son's attitude and conduct, praiseworthy from an American viewpoint, incurred for him the enmity of other German prisoners of war and was undoubtedly the underlying basis for the attack on him." The letter stated that the attackers remained "unidentified" and included a note about the disposition of the deceased's personal effects (Rogers 1944c).

The assistant provost marshal general himself wrote to the State Department about the case, presumably in response to inquiries from the Swiss Legation, representing Germany's interests. His letter reiterated most of the details outlined in the second letter sent to Henry Krauss in New York, and added a few pertinent details such as Krauss's acting as an interpreter at Camp Hearne, his use of the radio, the views he expressed about the German and American armies, and so on. For these reasons, the letter said, "it is reported that he [Krauss] was very much disliked and was considered a traitor to Germany, especially by the younger prisoners of war who were devout Hitlerites." Interestingly, the letter also confirmed what the German POWs had long suspected: that Krauss had informed on the German NCOs who were behind the work stoppages. "The evidence," wrote General Bryan (1944b), "developed the fact that they suspected that Cpl. Krauss had told about them and had caused their transfer, and there was evidence that they had threatened him."

In 1945, one of Krauss's assailants, Guenther Meisel (fig. 30), had an attack of conscience and came forward to describe in detail what had happened that fateful night. The result was another investigation that led to much more

Fig. 30. Photograph of Guenther Meisel, one of the POWs responsible for the death of Cpl. Hugo Krauss. Meisel came forward in 1945 and provided key testimony that enabled American authorities to solve the Krauss murder. Camp Hearne Collection, Texas A&M University.

substantial evidence being uncovered against seven POWs: Unteroffizier (NCO) Anton Boehmer, Obergefreiter (Cpl.) Heinrich Braun, Gefreiter (Cpl.) Werner Hossann, Obergefreiter Erich Von der Heydt, Obergefreiter Werner Jaschko, Unteroffizier Helmut Meyer, and Obergefreiter Guenther Meisel. These men were charged with Krauss's murder and a court-martial was convened at nearby Camp Swift, a POW camp in Bastrop, Texas, January 22–30, 1946. The forthrightness of Meisel, the prisoner who first confessed, and of Hossann, was particularly significant. The prosecution went so far as to praise them in the closing arguments for their honesty regarding the murder: "There are two of the accused who have been of assistance to me in the breaking of this case. Particularly, was I assisted by the accused, Meisel. So much was his contribution to the investigation of this case that I feel that I would be derelict in my legal duty if I said less than that the complete picture of this case might never have been ferreted out and known . . . except for [his] cooperation." Not only did they admit their own culpability, they also helped identify other participants in the crime (Massey 1946; McMinn 1949; Prosecution Closing Arguments 1946; Tollefson 1946).

Fritz Haus recalled his conversations with Meisel, the man who came forward with the facts in the case. They both had been at Camp Hearne and later were together in nearby Camp Swift. In early March, 1946, Haus was called to the camp stockade by an American officer at Camp Swift. Meisel wanted to meet with Haus because he had listened to Haus's weekly sermons broadcast over the camp public address system. "I was not prepared for, and could hardly believe, in the story I was told," Haus recalled. "For the next two months, until I left Camp Swift for Europe, I visited Guenther [Meisel] three or four times a week; somehow both of us sensed that our time was short." During these visits, Meisel told Haus about his participation in the murder of Hugo Krauss and how a woman with whom he had fallen in love had convinced him to come forward and confess to the crime.

According to Meisel, Haus elaborated, Krauss "was supposed to be a collaborator. That's the story we got. We were told, 'Be careful. He has to pay with his life. Now don't you do the same. Watch your steps.'" Haus said that Guenther Meisel had an American girlfriend who encouraged him to turn himself in for murdering Krauss. According to Haus, the woman still loved Meisel with a "superhuman strength." Meisel showed Haus the letters she had written him, in which she encouraged him to confess to the authorities.

Meisel said he had been an ardent member of the Hitler Youth who blindly followed the Fuehrer's philosophies. When he was interned at Camp Hearne, Meisel worked in the truck workshops and regularly drove a truck between the camp and other army posts. During one of these trips he met the woman who was to profoundly affect his life. Haus recalled Meisel's words:

> One late afternoon, on my way home, I noticed a young girl on the side of the road; the bonnet [hood] of her car was open and she was obviously in trouble. I stopped and offered help; the fault was located and fixed within ten minutes. She was very grateful and we talked for a little while. Before we pulled off in different directions I asked for her address and whether she would allow me to write. She would be pleased, was her reply. Naturally, in my first letter I had to confess that I was in fact a German prisoner of war, as she would see from the postal address, and not a long distance hauler. She can't explain why she did not drop the whole matter and forget the mechanic who helped her with the car; but she wrote back and a regular correspondence ensued. She was a Christian and she hoped that I, dearest Guenther, loved Jesus too. Jesus Christ meant all the world to her and was more important than anything else in her life. Did I have a Bible? She would be happy to send me one.

Meisel told Haus that Hitler was his god at the time. He said he was wary of religious types, but the appeal of fraternizing with an American, and a woman no less, was sweet forbidden fruit. Once or twice he managed to meet the woman outside the camp. Meisel arranged to have his work detail switched to cotton picking so that she could visit him on the farm. He was increasingly drawn to the woman, but was at the same time racked with conflicting feelings. "The girl held a fascination for me but also stirred my conscience, thereby creating agony and conflict in my soul," Meisel told Haus. "It must have been her prayers and religious letters which unsettled me completely. 'Unless you repent and believe in Jesus Christ as your Savior you cannot be forgiven for your sins,' she wrote. The irony of it was she did not have the faintest clue of how grave and serious my sins were!"

One day, while working in the cotton fields, Meisel confessed to the woman that he had killed a fellow prisoner by beating him with a big stick. The crime had been committed eighteen months earlier, and as of yet the authorities did not know the identity of the murderers. Meisel told the young woman to leave immediately and have no further contact with him. To his surprise, she instead prayed with him and for him. She also told him that he must confess. Meisel told Haus: "I asked for some days of reflection, which was restless and hurting, until the peace of God came over me as we prayed together several days later. I was full of remorse for my past but the burden of guilt had rolled from off my shoulders; I was forgiven and a child of God. We both smiled from under tears. Some days later I made a full statement to the officer in charge of the labor camp. He shook his head in disbelief. He asked, did I realize what I was saying and doing to myself? [And I responded that,] Yes, I knew."

Meisel made a full voluntary confession, pled guilty at his trial, and was sentenced to life in prison. In his prison cell at Camp Swift, Meisel had a large filing cabinet filled with paperwork related to his trial and many, many letters from the young woman. He encouraged Haus to read the letters. This, as well as his conversations with Meisel, is undoubtedly how Haus learned so much about the case.

Curiously, however, during the trial the affidavits of Meisel and Hossann—the two that were the most revealing—were admitted into evidence only to the extent that they implicated themselves. The American legal officer of the court ruled that any evidence they provided against other accused prisoners was inadmissible. The statements have handwritten brackets indicating those parts that were to be read in court and those that were to be omitted and the trial record indicates the gaps where such evidence was left out (Dickson, Oliver, Boyles 1946; Hossann 1945; Meisel 1945; Prosecution Closing Arguments 1946).

In July, 1945, several other German POWs who were being held in four different camps in four different states along the eastern seaboard, were mentioned in a memorandum related to the second investigation of the crime. The additional eight men were: Kurt Gintzel, Franz Hagl, Johann Kreutzer, Wilhelm Hinzdorf, Werner Schrepel, Alfred Grohe, Josef Warenitsch, and Josef Hausmann. For unknown reasons, probably a lack of evidence, the American officials decided not to call any of these prisoners as witnesses in the case (Coyne 1945b; Tollefson 1945b).

The affidavits from the renewed investigation are startling in their revelations concerning the murder. Meisel's was the most incredible in this way. He said Boehmer, the leader of Company 3, Compound 1, announced on December 17, 1943, "that Hugo Krauss should be waited upon." Meisel understood this to mean that "we should get the job done." Boehmer provided the "spark" for the beating later that night: "All of Company 3 was waiting for the word. There were approximately four hundred in Company 3 and not one person in the company said one word against the action. Everybody was for the beating, but many of them were too clever to join in. They encouraged us by talking for it. Everybody in the company disliked Krauss." After the evening meal, Meyer went to all of the barracks to urge their participation. Similar discussions occurred elsewhere: "Everybody in the whole company was talking about it. Group meetings were formed by prisoners in every barracks in Compound 1 to discuss the beating that everybody knew what was to take place. Practically everybody joined in these groups" (Meisel 1945).

Meisel went to Barrack 1 (where Hugo Krauss lived) to discuss the beating with Boehmer. Von der Heydt joined them and Meisel suggested that men from a different company be used to attack Krauss because "Company 3 would naturally be suspected, since this was Krauss's company." The three decided that Von der Heydt would select men from Company 4. He had no difficulty finding volunteers for the action "because he showed up in Barracks 4 right away with five or seven men." A meeting was held in Barrack 4 at about 10:00 P.M., "At the meeting we figured out what everybody was going to do [and] the best way to beat Krauss. . . . six or eight of us were to beat Krauss." Meisel and the others decided to post lookouts outside the building to keep an eye on the American tower guards and to look for other dangers. They also agreed that Boehmer should remain in his bed during the attack to divert suspicion away from him. "Someone was to turn off the light switch in Barracks 1 [Krauss's barrack]," said Meisel. "Everyone was instructed to bury their sticks at any place they could, immediately after the beating was finished. Nobody said how Krauss should be beaten." Whether or not murder was their intention, each man "at the meeting had brought sticks of wood with them. I [Meisel] had a piece of pipe about 9 inches long and about ½ inch or ¾ inch in diameter. I sharpened a piece of wood and drove it into the pipe" as a handle. Several of the others had two-by-fours about three feet long "with one end whittled down so they could hold them. Spikes about 4½ inches long had been driven through the sticks and the points of the spikes stuck out about 2½ inches from the boards" (Meisel 1945). Meisel recalled that one fellow, Heinrich Braun, did not have a club. When another POW asked him why he did not have one, "Braun made the statement that 'he was strong enough; he could do it with his fists.' [Later] Braun did have a club. After another prisoner of war had declined to go along, Heinrich Braun called him a 'coward-dog." Without any firearms or knives, the POWs had managed to assemble a formidable—and deadly—arsenal.

The other men in Barrack 4 heard the discussion. They were all awake and some added their input with comments such as "That is a good idea" and "The best thing is to kill him right now." Von der Heydt was there with Meisel and the others (whom Meisel did not know), but Boehmer was not present. "It was too early to attack Krauss because he was still awake. He [Krauss] spent the evening playing cards until around 10:30 P.M." The victim knew something was going to happen. While in Barrack 1, Meisel heard Krauss loudly exclaim, "Let them come. I am not afraid." He was strong and apparently believed he could take care of himself (Meisel 1945). According to another affidavit, Meyer knew that Krauss "was one of the strongest men in his Company" (Schiller 1945). However, his considerable strength proved an insufficient defense against an attack by several armed assailants.

Meisel (1945) stated: "While we were gathered in Barrack 4, someone reported that Krauss was asleep. This was about 23:45 hours [11:45 P.M.]. We all carried our sticks and went to Barracks 1. All members of Barrack 1 had instructions to stay in bed and be quiet." Lookouts were on duty outside Barrack 1 and someone guarded the light switch. "As soon as we entered Barrack 1," Meisel continued, "we started beating Krauss. [Krauss was in the top bunk at the end of Barrack 1 near the doorway]. We were supposed to hit him at certain places, but we got nervous and hit him anywhere we could. All six or eight joined in the beating." The attack on Krauss lasted less than a minute. During the attack, Meisel recalled that Krauss cried out something like, "Meyer, cut it out, I am bleeding"; or "Meyer, no"; or "Meyer, Meyer!" but he did not know why because Meyer was not present. "All Meyer did was to support the idea by making a speech in the barracks, urging that the job be done." At first Meisel said he was at the victim's feet. "I then went up toward his shoulders. I don't think I hit him on the head. I just hit him. My stick broke and I lost the pipe." Meisel also smashed Krauss's radio that he "hated" so much. "The sounds of the beating could be heard all over the compound." POW Heypeter, in Barrack 4, was 35 meters from the scene of the murder in Barrack 1. According to the trial records (Dickson, Oliver, and Boyles 1946), Pvt. Peter Heypeter, a prosecution witness, "opened a window in that [his] barrack [number four] and listened. Heypeter heard the beating and the deceased [Krauss] screaming; the blows could be heard distinctly and lasted about half a minute." Meisel recalled that the beating stopped when "Krauss got out of bed and everybody was nervous and ran out of the barracks." The assailants scattered (Meisel 1945).

As the beating was taking place, prisoner Merkel, in the bunk below Krauss, went to the other end of the barrack and awakened Boehmer. Merkel (Dickson, Oliver, and Boyles1946) shouted to Boehmer: "Anton, wake up; they are beating Krauss." According to the trial records (1946), Boehmer got up and started putting on his trousers, trying to button them and running at the same time. He turned on the lights and went to Krauss's bunk. The victim was sitting in bed, covered with blood, and screaming loudly. Boehmer went after a first-aid man and a litter. Krauss got up and went to the latrine.

Immediately after the attack, Meisel walked past Barrack 2 on his way back to his barrack and noticed that all of the occupants were looking out the windows. "I shall never forget those faces," he recalled. "Someone asked if Krauss was dead. I knew then the affair was serious. I had not intended to kill Krauss or to help the others kill him. I just wanted to beat him. I had tried not to hit him on the head because I did not want him to die." Meisel walked through Barrack 4 and told the occupants, "It's all over." He then went to the latrine to clean up. His hands had been bandaged from work in the woods and now the bandages were splattered with Krauss's blood. "When I approached the latrine, I saw Krauss, Merkel and someone else standing on the steps of the first Barracks. I knew then he was not dead. Immediately after I entered the latrine, Krauss came in. He was bleeding all over. He said nothing, except he continued to cry and yell. He had been yelling since the beating started." Meisel unwrapped the bandages on his hands, washed the blood from his hands, and rewrapped the bandages so that the bloodstains would be on the inside (Meisel 1945). While in the latrine, Meisel noticed that one of the sticks used in the beating was in the trashcan. Someone obviously had forgotten to bury it in the confusion following the attack.

Nervously, Meisel left the latrine "while Krauss was still there" and went to Barrack 7. According to the trial records (Dickson, Oliver, and Boyles 1946), Boehmer went to the latrine, helped Krauss return to his bed, and then put him on the litter. Boehmer, Zehrer, and others then took Krauss to the camp hospital. On the operating table Krauss "was given first aid by an American doctor; his eyes were closed and thick and bloody; his head was bleeding from several places; his hands and arms were beaten."

After returning to Barrack 7, Meisel got into his bed. All of the other prisoners were also in their beds. Meisel recalled that while he was smoking a cigarette in his bunk, two American officers walked through the barracks with flashlights "to check the beds" about fifteen minutes after the assault on Krauss. Meisel remembered that he had left his club in Barrack 1, so he went there in his bedclothes to look for it, but was unsuccessful. He noted that the lights were out and that Krauss had been taken away. He went back to his own bed for the night.

In the morning "the American company commander found [Krauss's] bed was torn up and splattered with blood, his radio was smashed, and the walls and ceiling were also splattered with blood." The American authorities subsequently inspected the whole compound and all prisoners were "checked for blood stains" (Meisel 1945). It seems they had no immediate success in finding the assailants and the investigation foundered. Krauss was transferred to McCloskey General Hospital in Temple, Texas, on December 18, 1943, and died there on the twenty-third, thirty days short of his twenty-fifth birthday.

Meisel claimed that he had not been questioned during the original investigation and that he might have told the whole story if he had been asked: "From the time of the beating until now I have had a bad conscience. I felt afraid. I wanted to tell someone to get it 'off my chest.' I have wondered why someone didn't ask me about it." Lastly, Meisel revealed the following about the camp spokesman: "It was generally understood about the camp that Karl Osterhorn [the spokesman] had decreed that anyone who should betray the shortwave radio set should be put to death. It was believed that Krauss had reported the radio." At Krauss's funeral, Meisel heard Osterhorn say, "This is the home he's been looking for" or some statement to that effect (Meisel 1945).

Meisel's affidavit provides a remarkable, albeit gruesome, account of the attack on Krauss. While not as thorough or detailed, Hossann also provided an informative statement. Like Meisel, he described Boehmer reading the German news reports after which Krauss "came in and shouted around in the barracks, that those reports were false reports, the American reports were true" and that Krauss had supposedly "betrayed the shortwave radio set." Afterward, Boehmer "told the company, that Krauss had again done something swinish, and that it was time, to give him the Holy Ghost" (Hossann 1945).

"Holy Ghost" was a phrase used by the Germans in the military to describe a nighttime surprise beating to modify a soldier's behavior. Some of the prisoners interviewed referred to this practice as giving someone the "Heilige Geist" which translates into "Holy Ghost" or "Holy Spirit." Walter Fricke described this practice as a sort of punishment for a soldier who makes continual mistakes and gets the group in trouble. For example, if a POW did something that caused his comrades to be punished, they might later physically beat him. "I remember in boot camp," Heino Erichsen said, "if you had a guy that didn't measure up to the rest of them, then it was encouraged by NCOs in Germany, in training, to give them what they call 'the Holy Spirit.'. . . They came in at night and put shoe polish on his ass or things like that. And . . . you didn't get involved."

Hossann went on to describe the meeting in Barrack 4. He said that soon after someone reported that Krauss was asleep, about ten men, including Meisel and Braun, went to Barrack 1. He briefly corroborated Meisel's description of the weapons they had and then added: "Jaschko and I went to Barrack 1. My task was, to stand on the main light switch, which was pulled, together with Jaschko; I fulfilled this task." Although he did not describe the actual beating, he did admit to his own participation, corroborated some of the facts presented by Meisel, and implicated others in the murder (Hossann 1945). Of course, as with Meisel's affidavit, these accusations were not used in the trial.

Von der Heydt also provided a statement that was somewhat useful to the prosecution. He vaguely described Boehmer's announcement about Krauss's betrayal of the shortwave radio and the general antipathy toward Krauss: "As a result of the statement, everyone in general was talking about Krauss: saying it was not right for him to use his job as interpreter to report everything to the American authorities. All the compound was for the idea [the beating]. Boehmer was the main instigator when he said to the Company, 'You know what to do about it.'" Von der Heydt also described Krauss's refutation of Boehmer delivering the German news reports: "Krauss was listening from the outside. Krauss returned to the barrack and said the news Boehmer was giving out was false—that the Russians were making progress" (Von der Heydt 1945). While Krauss was undoubtedly correct, his actions were not very wise and ultimately proved fatal.

"After Boehmer's announcement," Von der Heydt continued, "Meisel and I went to Boehmer's bed and talked about the beating. It is possible it was decided I should go to Company 1 for volunteers to help." He then went to another barrack. "When I arrived, they were all talking about the Krauss affair." He only knew one of those present whose name was Paul—but he did not know the man's last name. "Naturally, Paul and everyone else were enthused about it [the planned attack]." Van der Heydt attended the meeting in Barrack 4 with several others but remained for only a few minutes. "I told the prisoners to leave it alone. I remember something about the talk of where each man should hit Krauss, and I said, 'Stop it. Don't do it that way—do it half way!' I then left the meeting, and have had nothing to do with it since" (Von der Heydt 1945).

When Von der Heydt entered another barrack, he told the men inside to stay quiet if they heard anything. He then went to bed. He stressed his lack of participation in the attack: "I did not get up at any time during the night. I did not join in the beating, or see it done." He talked to Paul about the beating the next day and they were "both disturbed about it." They were both "easy going" men who "did not want anything bad to happen." Clearly, Von der Heydt had not wanted to have anything to do with a murder. That was not his intention. However, he recognized his own guilt: "I realized the men came from Company 1 on my request—I am guilty in this respect." That was enough for the prosecution to include him among the accused. His statement concluded with his signature attesting to the accuracy of the German translation, but not knowing anything about the English text (Von der Heydt 1945).

The affidavit of another German prisoner, not one of the accused, added some pertinent information. Hans Schiller described the attitudes of the POWs toward Krauss: "There had been talk against Krauss for days and weeks before he actually was beaten." Meyer, specifically, "did not think well of Krauss." While Schiller did not accuse Meyer of participation in the murder, he did implicate Boehmer in the crime. "On the date of the beating, Boehmer announced to the more than 400 men of the Company: 'We have a man in our ranks who is disloyal to the cause,' and urged the Company not to do anything about it, because, he added, 'this thing is in good hands,' or 'with the proper people.' We understood it to mean that we should leave the action alone, because the proper action would be taken." Finally, Schiller described the close friendship between Meisel and Boehmer: "If Meisel is guilty, so is Boehmer" (Schiller 1945).

Lastly, Jaschko gave a statement, but it was noncommittal and provided nothing of substance. According to a handwritten note by the investigating officer, Jaschko, when asked to sign his statement, refused on the grounds that he could not understand the English text (Jaschko 1945). It is reasonable to assume that he was provided a German translation as was done for Von der Heydt, so it is likely that his actions were the result of a stubborn lack of cooperation. It is also possible, however, that he doubted the accuracy of the translation for some reason. Other Germans provided testimony in the trial—some of which was useful to the prosecution in that it corroborated the affidavits and provided additional evidence against the accused. In addition, several of the accused testified, some providing sworn testimony and others unsworn statements. In short, the court found enough evidence to find each of the accused guilty of participating in the murder of Hugo Krauss. After deliberating for more than two hours, the judges presiding over the court-martial ruled that all seven were guilty. They were each sentenced to life imprisonment at hard labor (Dickson, Oliver, Boyle 1946; *Hearne Democrat* 1946b).

On March 14, 1946, the reviewing authority confirmed the sentences and it was decided to hold the prisoners at the federal penitentiary in Leavenworth, Kansas (Tollefson 1946b; Walker 1946; Weller and McElroy 1946). In December, 1946, a review board thoroughly examined the trial records. The board's detailed report provides an excellent summary of the case. In brief, this report describes the basic facts of Krauss's reception by his fellow prisoners, the events surrounding his murder, and the evidence against each of the accused. The review board concluded that Meisel and Braun had been present during Krauss's beating, that Hossann and Von der Heydt had been present in the Barrack 4 meeting when the attack was plotted and that each had contributed to the outcome, and that Boehmer was the main instigator of the attack. With regards to Jaschko and Meyer, they found the record more difficult to interpret. Jaschko's job was to guard the light switch, but the trial did not provide adequate evidence that he had done so. Likewise, the trial did not present enough evidence to demonstrate that Meyer had played an active role in the affair. The review board also had difficulty with the evidence against Boehmer. After a lengthy analysis of the trial record, the board members decided: "The record as a whole leads to the inescapable conclusion" that Boehmer knew about the beating that was being planned and that his announcements to the company, "clearly and indubitably constituted the most effective type of abetting, counseling, inducing and encouraging that could have been indulged by any member of that company." The fact that he was a leader only gave his words more force: "His action in rendering assistance to the deceased pales into insignificance." In sum, the review board concluded that the evidence was "legally sufficient to sustain the findings of guilty" for each of the accused except Jaschko and Meyer (Dickson, Oliver, and Boyles 1946). As a result, the findings against Jaschko and Meyer were disapproved, Meisel's sentence was reduced to fifteen years, and the sentences of Boehmer, Braun, Hossann, and Von der Heydt were reduced to ten years (Hoover 1946; Wainright 1947).

Soon after the verdict was issued, the defense counsel felt compelled to send a memorandum to a higher authority recommending clemency for Meyer and Jaschko (Fagan 1946). It did not work immediately, however, since the Review Board did not report its findings until several months later. The question of the other prisoners' confinement did not end with the sentencing. From Leavenworth, each prisoner's case was reviewed annually and requests for clemency were denied for all five men in 1947 and again in 1948 (Witsell 1947a, 1947b, 1947c, 1947d, 1947e, 1948a, 1948b, 1948c, 1948d, 1949a, 1949b, 1949c, 1949d, 1949e). Meisel's case received considerable attention in 1948, making its way to Pres. Harry S. Truman, on whose orders Meisel's sentence was reduced to ten years (Secretary of the Army 1948). Finally, in 1949, all five were paroled and returned to Germany after only three years in prison (Adjutant General 1949a, 1949b, 1949c, 1949d, 1949e).

Hugo Krauss was initially buried in the Camp Hearne cemetery in 1943. After the war, his remains were moved to the National Cemetery at Fort Sam Houston in San Antonio. He still rests there in a separate section of the cemetery with other German POWs.

CHAPTER 4

The Final Months

From V-E Day to the Camp's Closing

IN THE EARLY YEARS OF THE WAR, most of the POWs could not fathom the idea of a German defeat. Their confidence in a German victory was based on their complete trust in the Fuehrer and in the fighting ability of the German military. In some but not all cases, the soldiers' faith also stemmed from the belief that they were fighting for a just cause.

THE MOOD OF THE POWs

Guards and other employees of Camp Hearne were aware that the POWs, despite being imprisoned, continued to maintain hope for a German victory. Some of the POWs thought that the German army would invade America and rescue them from imprisonment. Guard Bobby Sullivan recalled, "They thought when Hitler came over here he would laugh at the fatigues with 'PW' written on them, when he came to liberate them."

"We were proud and we didn't really feel we were defeated," said POW Willi Nellessen. Nellessen remembered that when they were initially imprisoned in 1943, the soldiers thought that a German victory was imminent. "There was a lot of betting taking place. One person said, 'I bet in one-half year the war will be over.' In fact, he was so convinced of it that he said, 'I will shave my head now.' He believed that if he shaved his head and the sun shone on it that it would encourage the growth of new hair. He said, 'So when I return to Germany in one-half year, I will have a beautiful, full head of hair on my head and everyone will be impressed by me, especially the girls.' This soldier convinced the others in his barrack to shave their heads as well and one day, to the amusement of everyone, when it was time for lunch, they all appeared . . . a group of people who had all these white heads glistening in the sun."

Hugo Wannemacher remembered the same optimism: "You know, we had these sayings. For instance, we're going to return in half a year. And there was a time when everybody thought in half a year, we're going to return to Germany." Werner Kritzler agreed: "First we didn't doubt, we couldn't conceive of the possibility that we would lose the war. In the beginning, we never had any doubt of this."

Wannemacher related an incident that reflects the POWs' willingness to believe a German victory was possible even toward the end of the war. When the men in his barrack heard a radio report that the fighting between the Russians and the Germans had stopped, they mistakenly interpreted it to mean that the Germans had won and that the two countries were now entering into peace negotiations. "So we got very, very happy," he explained. He said they were thinking, "If we only had to fight the British and the Americans, we might not outright win, but there will be a peace settlement." The surge of joy caused some of the POWs to smash furniture in the barracks. Apparently the men figured they would be leaving the camp soon and therefore would no longer need their furniture. They also ripped boards off the lavatory walls.

Willi Nellessen told another story involving a false rumor. The American newspapers had reported on the brutalities of Russian soldiers toward the Germans as the Russians reclaimed portions of their territory. Nellessen said the word around the camp was that the Americans were now siding with the Germans against the Russians, "that the United States established some sort of alliance with the democratic movement in Germany . . . 'We're the United States against the Russians' and therefore the German prisoners in the United States would be immediately repatriated to Germany to join the forces of that alliance."

Even when it should have been obvious that the Germans were losing the war, some of the POWs could not reconcile themselves to the facts. Hans Lammersdorf commented: "It didn't look good. The air war was very perturbing, to see our cities leveled one after the other. But there still was not total defeatism, we still hoped somehow we could make it. [We believed what was] against common sense." As the war progressed, it was increasingly hard to remain optimistic. "The majority hoped [for a German victory], though they had serious doubts," Lammersdorf recalled. "Of course, those fanatics never would concede that there was a possibility of losing the war." Lammersdorf himself could not believe, given all the bombings, that Germany had any hope of winning. Instead of hoping for a victory, he focused on praying that his family remained alive. "We thought that we would win the war," added Walter Fricke, "but then we changed. Particularly the day after the landings in Normandy."

Clerk-typist Annie Sweat noted the POWs' reactions to the arrival of a new shipment of prisoners. "Not too long before I quit working there," she said, "they brought in a lot of prisoners. They were old men and boys, people who should not be soldiering, and the German prisoners knew from then on that they were losing the war. [Earlier in the war if] they would see a headline of something wonderful the Americans had done [and] they would say it was propaganda. When they saw the old men and boys arrive, they never mentioned that again. So I know that they knew they were losing the war after that. You could just tell by their appearance, the downcast look on their faces where there had been smiles before."

Fritz Pferdekämper-Geissel and Alfred Jasper agreed that the POWs at first had been convinced that Germany would win the war. However, as the war progressed, they came to understand that defeat was inevitable. They remembered that men who had identified themselves as Nazis shifted their positions at the end and claimed they had never been party members. Ernst Froembsdorf stated that the POWs who maintained hope for a German victory tended to spend time together. Froembsdorf said that he himself was pessimistic about Germany's chances of being able to pull off a victory.

In a diary entry dated April 15, 1945, Fritz Haus wrote: "The Generals are expecting a miracle, but Germany is being crushed. Everything is collapsing and they are hoping of building all their secret weapons and that the Fuehrer and the generals will still pull it off and do the miracle now. But isn't that far too late? Isn't that the last thing of wanting, of idolatry, and of insanity?"

Nevertheless, some prisoners still clung to the possibility of a German victory. They circulated rumors among the men in the camp about secret German weapons that would change the war's outcome. After the war in Europe ended, the camp newspaper included an editorial about such false hopes, but this time regarding the existence of a secret weapon in the hands of the Japanese. Apparently, Dr. Hidecki Yukawa from the University of Kyoto was said to have announced in January, 1945, that the Japanese had a "death ray" capable of destroying all of Washington, D.C., and other targets. The editorialist related a conversation he had with one of the German rumormongers at Camp Hearne. He had asked, in jest, about the progress of the secret weapon to which the man had responded, in all seriousness, "Oh, once again we have invented a new highly explosive flak ammunition shooting down all the machines within a certain sphere of activity." When he asked about the significance of such a weapon at the end of the war, the other man responded with disappointment, "Well, you better read the 'MAHNUNG' [Camp Hearne's underground Nazi newspaper]; you will find every explanation of it." He argued that the Germans had been fooled in the past by the Nazi regime's lies regarding miracle weapons that would enable them to win the war and that these rumors had been proved false. "Unfortunately," he added, "there are still some people who try to agitate their comrades with latrine rumors that the plans of the secret weapon have been shipped to Japan in time." His point was that this was just more of the same rhetoric, an effort by fanatics to boost false hopes. He implied that those who believed such rumors were gullible and emphasized the need for the Germans to reject their Nazi past and help to rebuild a democratic Germany (Hombeck 1945).

Some of the POWs felt uneasy about Germany's chances of winning the war from the moment they arrived in the United States. Apparently some of the Germans had been told that the Axis powers had bombed cities in the United States and that New York City had been completely destroyed. Fritz Haus, who was processed in New York City, realized he had been lied to when he saw the city intact. He lamented the fact that so many German cities had been destroyed whereas in America it seemed as if there was no war at all. The enormous size of the country surprised Haus and the number of ships in the harbor impressed him. Guards Bobby Sullivan and John Shugers confirmed that the POWs were surprised to discover that the United States had not been bombed and were aware that the Germans were upset about being misled. "They had been told that New York had been bombed and when they got there, they saw that it wasn't . . . that helped with their arrogance," Sullivan said.

After his capture, Joseph Pohl was surprised by the vast inventory of supplies he saw, "Even at the beginning, when we went across the ocean, twenty-seven ships and two warships protecting us and looking at the resources of the United States as we traveled to the camp. It was just amazing, we thought God this is a big, big, rich country. How are we ever going to defeat them?" Hugo Wannemacher became depressed when he saw America's enormous resources. Upon seeing all the oil wells and storage tanks in Texas, he remembered thinking there was "no way that Germany's going to take the U.S." He recalled that people in Germany made gasoline out of potatoes and that rationing in the United States was not nearly as severe as it was in Germany. Wannemacher was convinced that continuing the war was futile.

Heino Erichsen (2001) wrote in his memoir:

> The majority of Germans held captive were battle-hardened veterans of the Africa Campaign. Although Germany was taking heavy losses on the Eastern front and the air war over Germany had intensified, there was still a strong allegiance toward our homeland and our government, and a belief in victory.
>
> I had quietly discarded my belief in a German victory after seeing the overwhelming amount of war material owned by the Allies in North Africa. My observations on our train ride from New York to Texas, as we passed cities industrious by day and fully lit at night, added to my skepticism. No blackouts here. The Americans didn't worry about getting bombed. In Germany, they worried about it day and night. If the abundance of supplies in a small camp like Hearne was typical, Germany was doomed.

As the war progressed, it became increasingly obvious that Germany would lose. Local farmer John Nigliazzo remembered that the POWs were sad because they were losing the war. He said one of the Germans had a three-year-old daughter, the same age as Nigliazzo's own daughter, and that the man did not know if his wife and child were still alive. Hans Goebeler described the POWs' moods at the late stages of the war: "It was kind of depress[ing], because those fellows from Normandy, they knew that everything was lost . . . so we had to learn the whole thing over and realize that we lost the war." However, some of the German prisoners gained a false sense of renewed hope for victory when they heard about the 1944 German winter offensive known as the Battle of the Bulge. Willi Nellessen recalled that "some fellows had maps in our barrack and they recorded the changing lines of the German army." However, Nellessen pointed out that many "thought, essentially, that this was a waste of energy." The battle lasted for only a few weeks and the Allies quickly recovered. "We were longing for good news from the front," said Nellessen. But it was not to come.

Peter Spoden remembered reacting with anger when he heard that an attempt had been made on Hitler's life on July 20, 1944. A nephew of Lt. Col. Claus von Stauffenberg, the would-be assassin, was a POW at Camp Hearne. Spoden recalled that Stauffenberg's nephew was placed in protective custody at the camp for his own safety. Had he stayed in the compound, he might have been harmed or even killed by the ardent Nazis in the camp. Arno Einicke recalled that the younger Stauffenberg refused a transfer to another camp and returned to his compound. There he denounced his uncle's actions and told his comrades that he was a faithful German soldier who had taken an oath to fight for the Fatherland. Stauffenberg remained at Camp Hearne and was not bothered by the other POWs. However, in 1945 he was struck by a guard for "taking an arrogant attitude apparently endeavoring to prove his loyalty to the Nazi way of thinking" (Fischer 1945). Lieutenant Colonel Rainbolt, the camp commander at the time, realized that the prisoner's behavior did not justify the attack and transferred the guard.

Fritz Haus wrote in his diary on April 28, 1945, just ten days before the collapse of the Third Reich: "It is now terrible, untold misery comes down over Germany. Everything has collapsed. And we here behind barbed wire, there is a sadness and a worry and indifference . . . the life has gone out. And this whole machinery and this whole ideology of Hitler and all this, it was now finally finished." Upon hearing of the German surrender on May 8, Nellessen commented that the men were "Sad, very sad." Arno Einicke remembered that while the prisoners were eating breakfast, the Americans posted the news of Germany's surrender on the camp bulletin board. "The first one who read the news went into the barrack and upon the question, 'What has happened?' The answer was, 'Why don't you look yourself?' So everybody in turn wandered out of the barrack and when he would come back, he would throw himself on the bed. And then there was someone who sort of broke this mood, this tension. While he was lying on his bed, he started to sing and the lyrics to the song were something like, 'and we carry ourselves with patience since we are to blame.' And pretty soon the rest of the barracks joined in and sang the song as well."

Haus, a devout man who eventually became a Baptist minister, had never really believed in the Nazi Party because its philosophies were so decidedly un-Christian. In the early years of the war, while he was still in Germany, his family had secretly housed a Jewish woman in order to protect her. Haus also mentioned during his lengthy interview that he and several other ministers he knew secretly prayed for a German defeat so that all of the killing would come to an end. When Germany was finally defeated, Haus described it as a sort of divine retribution:

> The fighting and all the bloodshed was useless and absolutely senseless and Germany is just absolutely destroyed. And all the plans and the

great speeches of Hitler and all the party machinery, they are lying buried under the rubble and rubbish of the big cities in Germany. It's all the judgment of God and we have, as a nation, we have deserved it. And all the weapons, the secret weapon as a last hope, this also has come to nothing. Political ideas, politics became religion. And nationalism, socialism [National Socialism or Nazism], was raised and put on a pedestal as a god, and above the Bible. All human propaganda was useless and had no substance and the whole nation danced around the golden calf. And I wished that people would beat their own breast and would repent and say, "Well, it serves us right, but let's make a new start."

Chaplain Gustave Zoch (1946) noted that after the news of Germany's defeat sank in there was a greater demand for Bibles and other religious literature. "Germany was beaten," he explained, "the dream of Nazism crushed, the spirit of the Nazis broken. Anti-Nazis rejoiced and regained the upper hand and a great deal of the boys, both Nazi and anti-Nazi, again began to think of God and the Christian religion." According to Max Weiss (1945c), the prisoners at Camp Hearne wanted to help their comrades and families in less fortunate circumstances in Europe, so they solicited donations from each other for "the P.W.'s in France and Africa, for the children in Germany, Austria and in all the former German territories." Individual gifts ranged from $2.68 to $10.50, and a total of $14,624.20 was raised. "I hope that this sum will contribute to relieve the need in our country and of our comrades," wrote Weiss. "The above mentioned amount is to be distributed as follows through the International and Swedish Red Cross: For the P.W.'s in France and Africa $6,624.20, For the children in Germany and all the former German territories $6,000.00, and for the children in Austria $2,000.00."

When the war in Europe ended, most of the prisoners sensed that Japan's defeat was inevitable. Most recalled hearing on the radio that the Americans had dropped an atomic bomb on Japan. Shortly thereafter, the war in the Pacific ended and the German POWs prepared to return home.

American Propaganda Efforts

During the last year of the war, American officials initiated an education program to instill in the prisoners negative attitudes about the Nazi ideology and regime and to encourage them to think in more democratic ways. The POWs were shown films and provided with newspapers, literature, music, art, and formal education that emphasized American and democratic ideologies as a positive alternative to Nazism. For justification, the U.S. government used a clause in the Geneva Convention that charged the detaining power with the responsibility for providing educational opportunities to prisoners. Yet from the beginning, the program was operated in utmost secrecy out of fear of retaliation against American POWs, including possible Nazi propaganda efforts of their own. The program was staffed by both American and German prisoner personnel, the latter being former professors, linguists, and writers who were dedicated anti-Nazis (Krammer 1996, 196–98, 201).

One of the early results of these efforts was the establishment of *Der Ruf* (*The Call*), a national POW newspaper. *Der Ruf* was an "enormously sophisticated German-language publication" published bimonthly on quality paper with numerous illustrations. The Americans also encouraged the printing of newspapers at individual camps (Krammer 1996, 202). The prisoners at Camp Hearne published a paper entitled *Der Spiegel* (*The Mirror*).

Although the prisoners expressed interest in publishing a newspaper at Camp Hearne in 1943 (Fischer 1943b), the first issue was not released until June, 1945. In all, ten issues of *Der Spiegel* were published from June 1 through December 15, 1945. The paper was printed monthly until September, 1945, after which issues came out twice a month. *Der Spiegel,* like newspapers in many other POW camps across the country, was intended to promote the benefits of free speech and democracy.

The first edition of *Der Spiegel* was entirely in German, nine pages long, and had five articles on topics such as camp sports, news from Germany, and film reviews. Subsequent issues provided a line-by-line English translation. Not only did this increase the length of the paper twofold, it also made monitoring the paper's content easier for the Americans. Later editions also included letters to the editor, crossword puzzles, and a regular section on music theory.

All issues of *Der Spiegel* demonstrate that Nazism was no longer as powerful a force in the camp as it had been before V-E Day (May 8, 1945). Camp spokesman Max Weiss, in an article in *Der Spiegel,* described a meeting among the POWs in which a group of Nazis revealed themselves. "I was glad that some men of Companies 3 and 5, left the mess hall in order to protest," Weiss (1945d) wrote, "for by doing so the black sheep of our camp who up to now had only moved around behind the scenery, separated themselves from the rest." Although Weiss did not specify what the men were protesting, it was probably some public expression of anti-Nazi or pro-American sentiment. Weiss clearly indicated that the Nazis were a shadow element in the camp whose identities were unknown to the other prisoners. He even referred his readers to an article in *Der Ruf* to emphasize his point. "Today it is necessary for us to form our own opinion," he added. "Please let me tell you as an older comrade that we must finally cease to wait for orders from higher authorities in every situation of life. We must recognize soberly that the Nazi terror is at an end, and that all the decisions in Germany must be made and solved by ourselves." In another issue of *Der Spiegel,* an open letter to the editor by Hans Bachmayer (1945) expressed relief that the underground Nazi paper was no longer in operation: "Who does not, with a cold shuddering, remember the former secret newspaper of the obscure [sic] men 'Die Mahnung,' the supreme task of which was the despotic political and personal tutelage. Created for the political instigation and for keeping the P.W.'s under control by awakening fright and terror, this slovenly paper (to use a word of 'Der Spiegel') had been created out of nothing with the fanatical zeal of the small anonymous clique. This paper has bereft many comrades of the last bit of reasoning faculty. They became mental slaves, weak-minded instruments doing slave-labor for those obscure men."

Walter Karg (1945a) echoed this sentiment in another open letter in the same issue of *Der Spiegel:* "We are involved in a process of transformation of an immense extent. Every one who is not total[ly] blind, should be able to recognize that he as been deceived and cheated. Even those who were faithful adherents of the Nazi ideas up to the last minute gradually abandoned them, so much were they influenced by the defeat and the atrocities discovered. He who has psychological knowledge that nothing disturbs such a process of transformation more than the permanent reference to committed mistakes. These men will pretty soon recognize that they have been duped by 'Die Mahnung'." Quite likely, these men expressed the sentiments of many prisoners who were no longer under Nazi influence and who looked forward to a post-Nazi Germany. Of course, such statements were sanctioned in the official newspaper and more than likely actively promoted by the Americans, who wanted to encourage such thinking among the prisoners.

The American reeducation program also included a variety of other activities. The American government published and distributed classic literary works that had been banned by the Nazis, as well as translations of popular American books. In addition, books and pamphlets about American history and political institutions written especially for the POWs were provided in bilingual texts. Hugo Wannemacher still retains a copy of a paperback book on America entitled *Kleiner Führer durch Amerika* (*Small Guide through America*) that he received at Camp Hearne. Another medium used in the education effort was film. In addition to the steady flow of standard Hollywood fare of limited educational value, the Americans showed the prisoners documentaries on American history and government.

Toward the end of the war, the Americans showed the German POWs films of Nazi atrocities perpetrated in concentration camps. Many of the prisoners, including the Nazis, were horrified. Most had no previous knowledge of what had occurred in the death camps and many Nazi supporters turned against the Nazi Party after viewing the films (Zoch 1946, 23). But not all of them were so credulous. Nationwide, the majority of German POWs viewed these films with great skepticism (Krammer 1996, 210). The Americans showed the POWs films by Nazi filmmakers that documented horrible human rights abuses and included footage shot inside concentration camps. At first most of the prisoners, even those who did not consider themselves Nazis, refused to believe what they saw in the films. It was too horrible to be true; it was unthinkable that they had fought in a war for a Fuehrer who would be responsible for such crimes. The men were in denial. Hugo Wannemacher remembered that each POW was given a slip of paper on which to anonymously record his reaction to the films. He said he wrote, "I cannot believe this." He was one of many who simply refused to believe the Holocaust films were genuine. According to Fritz Haus: "After April of 1945 we had to see films of concentration camps twice. Our reaction was that it was all propaganda. It was the Russians doing it, not the Germans." Willi Nellessen said he believed what he read in the American newspapers, but that he did not believe the Holocaust films because "We could not believe that our own people, the Germans, would do something like that, because during and after the First World War it was pointed out that supposedly the German soldiers cut off the hands of children of Belgium, which turned out to be total propaganda." Because the Allies had lied about the Germans in the past, it seemed reasonable to assume that the concentration camp footage was also a lie. Walter Fricke recalled hearing of a concentration camp in Poland before the war, but said a man he met who worked there told him that it was only a labor camp. Fricke added that he did not hear about the concentration camp at Auschwitz for the first time until he was at Camp Hearne: "And that's the truth. That was the first time we have heard it, [when we were] in Texas." Ernst Froembsdorf, recalling his feelings when the concentration camps were discovered, said: "I was devastated. The nation was devastated." As the truth sank in, most of the POWs began to feel that way.

Through these various efforts, the Americans hoped to instill positive political attitudes in the prisoners by demonstrating the evils of Nazism in stark contrast to democracy. These educational efforts were successful, especially in conjunction with the destruction of the Nazi regime in Germany. From various POW camps across the country, even a pro-Nazi camp, petitions rejecting Nazism and supporting Western-style ideologies were circulated and presented to American authorities. Several thousand POWs even "volunteered to enlist in the American Army, unbelievably, to fight against the Japanese!" (Krammer 1996, 217). Although the idea of using German soldiers had been given serious consideration, the Americans decided that English-speaking Germans who accepted American ideals would be needed to help administer a postwar occupied Germany. Select POWs underwent a special training program established for that purpose. Later evaluations of the program by both Germans and Americans were mixed, but most Americans thought it had been a qualified success. The Germans were decidedly less enthusiastic. Considering the nature of the task and the timetable for reeducation, any success would be fairly remarkable (Krammer 1996, 217–19, 225–26).

The Fate of the POWs after the War

Over 371,000 German prisoners were being held in the United States on V-E Day, May 8, 1945—3,855 of them at Camp Hearne. In November, two months after the Japanese surrender on September 2, the War Department announced a plan to return all of the German POWs to Europe by April, 1946. However, because most American servicemen were still overseas and time was needed for their demobilization and discharge, POW labor was still needed for agriculture and other sectors of the economy that were still feeling the effects of wartime labor shortages. Pressure from groups that still needed POW labor convinced President Truman to delay the prisoners' return for another sixty days. By the end of June, 1946, only a few hundred POWs remained in the United States.

Over time, the German prisoners at Camp Hearne were slowly removed and sent to other camps in Texas and elsewhere in the United States to help with agricultural work. On August 16, 1945, there were 2,648 German prisoners at Hearne, 2,154 on October 1, and 1,279 on October 16. The last prisoners were finally shipped out during the last two weeks of December, 1945. The branch camps administered by Camp Hearne were also closed at about this time. Camp Huntsville closed at the end of October, 1945, Camp Navasota in November, and Camp Mexia in early December. German prisoners held at the small Chance Farm camp worked there until the middle of January, 1946, when it was finally closed. After nearly three years—sometime between December 15, 1945, and January 1, 1946—Camp Hearne and its branch camps were once again empty.

"I was kind of amazed how quickly the [prisoners in the] camp disappeared," said civilian Jim Stegall. "They repatriated those people back to Germany pretty fast." He described the closure of the camp as a mass exodus: "They dropped the bomb, oh, I can't remember those dates, but seems like in the summer of '45, World War II came to an end, and the camp [population] almost disappeared overnight, it seems." The POWs disappeared so quickly that some wondered if the prisoners were being shipped out at night. Many people in town had seen the POWs arrive, but few saw them leave.

The prisoners at Camp Hearne were transferred to camps where labor, especially agricultural labor, was needed. Arno Einicke left Hearne in the spring of 1945 and went to El Campo and Camp Swift in Texas, and then on to Camp Shanks in New York before being sent to Europe. Willi Nellessen, another long-time Hearne resident, was transferred to Camp Rosenberg, Texas, when the war ended to help with harvesting in that area. He recalled that many of the barracks were cleared out at the same time because there was a high demand for labor. Peter Spoden went to Camp Swift, then to a camp in Baton Rouge, Louisiana, before returning to Europe. Werner Kritzler left Hearne on July 3, 1945, and went to Fort Sill, Oklahoma. From there he went to Camp Florence, Arizona, on August 30 and then was transferred to Stockton, California, on September 4. He left for Europe on April 15, 1946.

The Camp Hearne POWs were anxious to return home when the war ended. This is evident from the final issue of *Der Spiegel,* dated December 15, 1945. Nearly all of the articles dealt with repatriation, rebuilding, and continuation of life in a free Germany. Helen Palmos said the prisoners "were excited about going home. But they were reluctant to go because they did not know what they had left over there. They wanted to get over there to see who they had left, and what they had left." Some of the prisoners, however, did not want to return to Germany. Ernst Froembsdorf said he longed to stay in America. He worked in a tin factory outside a camp in West Virginia after his transfer from Camp Hearne. When the war ended, his employer wanted to retain him as an employee. The man appealed to Washington on Froembsdorf's behalf, but his request was denied. Robert Goede, who had been transferred from Camp Hearne to Camp Wallace, Texas, also wanted to remain in the United States. He wrote to a cousin who lived in Los Angeles and asked for his help. Goede said his cousin hired a lawyer who contacted the authorities in Washington, D.C., "and six weeks later I got a letter from Washington that they would have to send me back to Germany. I couldn't stay here because of the Geneva Convention. Well, according to the Geneva Convention they had to send every prisoner of war home."

When the day arrived for the former prisoners held at Camp Hearne and other camps in the United States to return to Europe, they were transferred to embarkation points along the East Coast. Each man was allowed to take one duffel bag of possessions weighing no more than thirty pounds. Hugo Wannemacher recalled that they threw away their old canteens and "tried to fill it [the bag] up as much as possible, to a particular weight, the maximum weight that you could get." Ernst Froembsdorf said if a POW's baggage weighed too much, an inspector would randomly discard items until the proper weight was reached.

At some camps, however, the restrictions were less well enforced. Werner Kritzler found a clever way to bring home as much as possible. Apparently the rules stated that each POW could only bring home one bag. Kritzler said he got around the rule by sewing two bags together. There was one problem, however: "I couldn't carry it because it was so heavy, so I put an axle and wheels on it and I was able to push and pull my bag."

Most of the prisoners assumed that they would be returning directly to Germany as they got onto ships docked at various East Coast harbors. Much to their dismay, they soon discovered that they first would have to provide additional service to countries such as France, Great Britain, Belgium, and Holland. There the POWs were required to work on farms, in coal mines, and to assist with the general cleanup of the debris created by the war. All of the men were severely disappointed that they were not returning directly to Germany. Hans Lammersdorf, Hans Goebeler, Arno Einicke, Peter Spoden, and Fritz Haus all ended up in either England or Scotland. There the POWs had a generally favorable experience. They were allowed to roam the countryside and some, like Walter Fricke, acquired an English girlfriend.

Alfred Jasper spent some time working on a farm in France. Ernst Froembsdorf also ended up in France. He said his belongings were confiscated there and that the French guards stole all his cigarettes. Unfortunately, there was no one to complain to when such abuses occurred. Froembsdorf stated that in France the POWs were forced to work in either the mines or in the agricultural fields. Agricultural work was by far the better choice, but the men did not have any say in where they would work. The decision instead was based on a doctor's exam: The most physically fit prisoners were sent to the mines. Those who wore glasses were among those disqualified from performing this strenuous work. On the day Froembsdorf had to undergo his exam, a crafty Frenchman was positioned outside the doctor's office. For the price of a pack of cigarettes, the man would loan his glasses to POWs to wear during their examination. Froembsdorf took advantage of this offer and thus was able to avoid the dreaded mines.

Very few prisoners returned directly to Germany. Joseph Pohl was able to carry out a scheme that enabled him to be repatriated directly to Germany when the war ended. He knew that all of the prisoners in his group were going to be sent to work in England—except for those who were too ill to work. Pohl feigned having a medical condition characterized by numbness in the legs. He said the doctor who examined him "took a pin and stuck it in my leg. With the condition I told them I had you couldn't feel pain. I controlled myself, I didn't move and so the doctor was convinced that I was really sick. And so I got a discharge and I went to Germany right away." Most of the prisoners labored an average of one year before they eventually returned home. Upon repatriation they began to rebuild their lives.

JAPANESE PRISONERS OF WAR AT CAMP HEARNE

The number of Japanese prisoners captured by American forces and detained in American camps (n = 5424) was relatively low compared to the number of German or Italian prisoners. This disparity was a consequence of a number of factors. First, the Japanese soldiers were taught to "prefer death to surrender" (Krammer 1983b); therefore, most fought to the death in battle or committed suicide rather than be captured. Capture at the hands of the enemy was seen as an irredeemable shame. Many of those taken prisoner were unable to protest because they were either wounded or unconscious at the time of capture (Krammer 1983b). Second, most prisoners captured in the Pacific were sent to camps in Australia and to a lesser extent New Zealand. The only Japanese prisoners sent to the United States were those slated for "special interrogation" because of their potential knowledge of important military matters or because they had been captured geographically closer to the U.S. mainland than to either Australia or New Zealand.

Japanese prisoners were processed at Fort McDowell at Angel Island, California, after which they were interrogated at a center in Tracy, California. They were then transferred back to a POW camp at Angel Island or to the camps in McCoy, Wisconsin, or Clarinda, Iowa. Later in 1945, some Japanese prisoners were transferred to Camp Hearne and two other camps in Texas for a special re-education program.

The earliest available official military correspondence regarding Japanese POWs at Camp Hearne is a memo dated August 8, 1945, sent by Col. A. M. Tollefson, director of the Prisoner of War Operations Division of the Provost Marshal General's Office (Tollefson 1945c). This memo confirmed a conversation between Col. Alexander Adair of the Eighth Service Command in Dallas and Lieutenant Ferris of the Provost Marshal General's Office. The men discussed the impending transfer of Japanese prisoners from the POW processing station at Fort McDowell to Camp Hearne. It confirmed that the commanding general of the Ninth Service Command, Gen. Brehon B. Somervell, was requested to transfer a total of 254 Japanese prisoners to Camp Hearne. These prisoners were to be transferred under guard on August 11, 1945, according to the memo. The roster of prisoners included four medical patients (four enlisted men) and 250 "able-bodied" prisoners. The list of healthy prisoners included

Table 6. Japanese POW Population at Camp Hearne

Date	Officers	NCO	Enlisted	Total
Sept. 1, 1945	2	40	212	254
Sept. 16, 1945	5	87	386	478
Oct. 1, 1945	5	78	315	398
Oct. 16, 1945	7	63	234	304
Nov. 1, 1945	14	65	244	323
Nov. 16, 1945	11	53	256	320

Source: Census data 1945.

202 enlisted men, forty-five noncommissioned officers, and three officers. It was noted that three of the enlisted men were under age eighteen.

Further correspondence on September 5, 1945, documented the impending transfer of additional Japanese prisoners from California to Camp Hearne. Specifically, Colonel Urwiller (1945), then the acting director of the Prisoner of War Operations Division of the Provost Marshal General's Office, wrote a memo to confirm a conversation between Lieutenant Ferris of the Provost Marshal General's Office and Major Coyne and Captain King of the Eighth Service Command in Dallas regarding the impending transfer of an additional 324 Japanese prisoners to Camp Hearne. No date for this transfer was given; however, it was again noted that the prisoners would be transferred under guard from the Angel Island POW processing station. The prisoner roster included four officers, fifty-two NCOs, 254 enlisted men, five Korean civilians, and nine medical patients (one NCO and eight enlisted men). Some of these prisoners remained at Hearne, while the others were transferred to the branch camp at Huntsville. The number of Japanese prisoners at Camp Hearne fluctuated during their brief stay, but never exceeded five hundred men (Table 6; Census data 1945).

At least two trainloads of Japanese prisoners arrived at Hearne in 1945. The train ride from California required more guards than typically used for the German prisoners because there were reports of fighting among the Japanese. The prisoners were unloaded from the Union Pacific Railroad line at the intersection of Alamo Street and marched north through town under heavy guard. Civilians were told to stay home and cover their windows and not watch the arrival of the Japanese prisoners. Johnoween Mathis recalled that the Japanese "arrived early in the morning, I would say around 8 o'clock. I wanted to see what they looked like. They came off the train and they were the littlest people I've ever seen, I mean some of them looked like kids. They marched them out there by foot to the POW camp. Then I thought, how did those people ever decide that they was going to get into a war with anybody when they were just midgets?" Once the prisoners arrived at the camp they were deloused and given burr haircuts, which they resisted. They then were placed in Compound 3.

The Japanese prisoners were transferred to Camp Hearne to participate in a secret reeducation project approved by the secretary of war on July 18, 1945. In this program, three POW camps in Texas—Huntsville, Kenedy, and Hearne—were chosen as "re-orientation centers" where cooperative Japanese prisoners were to be educated in the ways of democracy. The purpose of the program was "to impress on the minds of the Japanese prisoners of war what the attitude of a citizen of the United States is toward life and government and to create an application of American principles and traditions" (Krammer 1983b). These "reconstructed" POWs could be useful "in the indoctrination of the remaining POWs and of the Japanese people," and they would be "useful to the military government authorities" assisting in America's postwar occupation of Japan.

Lieutenant Colonel B. C. Moore and Dr. C. W. Hepner, both of whom had extensive expertise with Asian affairs, authored the program. John K. Emerson was also instrumental in developing it (Walker 1980, 2001). The reeducation included lectures put together by Sam Houston State Teachers College faculty members, as well as studies in English language and literature, and general comparisons of American and Japanese printed media (Krammer 1983b). In addition, American-style leisure pursuits were also encouraged. These included listening to American music, looking at American newspapers and movies, and playing baseball. The prisoners were also urged to attend Christian church services (Krammer 1983b). Chaplain Zoch expressed concern for the spiritual welfare of these men. He described them as "spiritually blind" because the majority of them were Shintoists or Buddhists rather than Lutherans like himself (Zoch 1946). "Monthly services conducted by Chaplain McIlwaine of Huntsville (a Presbyterian) were very well attended," Zoch added. "Out of the 500 Japanese prisoners, we had an average attendance of about 300. However, that does not mean that they were all interested in religion. In my opinion it was mostly curiosity that brought them to the service." It is also possible that they were influenced by the fact that they were prisoners of the nation that had defeated Japan.

Camp Huntsville was designated as the main center for the Japanese reeducation project (Walker 2001). Lieutenant Colonel Moore was appointed as the camp's commander and an education director and Japanese-speaking chaplain were assigned to him. Approximately two hundred receptive prisoners were chosen to participate, selected from the Japanese prisoners at Camp Hearne and Camp Kenedy. The Japanese prisoners at both camps had already been screened at Angel Island before being transferred to Texas. At Hearne, the prospective students were screened again to determine who would be the most receptive to reeducation. Lieutenant Colonel Moore spent much time interviewing the candidates at Camps Hearne and Kenedy as well as preparing Camp Huntsville for receiving its first students. Eventually, about two hundred candidates were chosen and moved to Huntsville. Transfer of the prisoners began in early October, 1945. At about this time the decision was made to begin repatriating the Japanese prisoners. This affected the reeducation project by limiting the potential number of participants to the two hundred already selected and a crash course in democracy was initiated only at Camp Huntsville. Some indoctrination also took place at Camp Hearne. Chaplain Zoch (1946) mentioned that the Japanese prisoners were shown "appropriate and instructive movies several times a week." He felt that even though the Japanese were only at Camp Hearne for a short period, "many of the Japanese were quite favorably impressed with our democratic form of government, our freedom of speech, our system of education, and in things American in general" (Zoch 1946, 21).

Jack Kuttruff, who came to Camp Hearne in the fall of 1945 to guard the Japanese prisoners after a tour of duty in Europe, described the Japanese prisoners as being "docile" during the day while Americans were in the compound, but added that they "had some pretty rough fights" among themselves "especially at night." He claimed that the word amongst the Japanese was that there were some informants in the compound and "when they were found out, then they would beat the hell out of them." These fights tended to occur between the Japanese military personnel and Korean prisoners, who were civilians in Japanese work battalions and whom the Japanese prisoners accused of being informants. This may have been because of the longstanding history of mistrust and animosity between the two peoples. There were also bitter rivalries between Japanese soldiers and sailors. Some of these were just traditional attitudes, but each branch of the military also blamed the other for their country's military failures (Krammer 1983b). Those prisoners engaging in fights were kept in the guardhouse and given reduced rations.

The Japanese prisoners also created problems for the Americans. German prisoner Peter Spoden said that while he was being jailed (for some unmentioned reason) he had a brief conversation in English with a Japanese lieutenant who was also being detained. The lieutenant told him that the Japanese had attached electric lines to the lock on the compound gate and that when the American guard inserted his key into the lock, "he got a nice shock."

The Japanese prisoners at Camp Hearne were housed separately in Compound 3, away from the German prisoners, and the two groups were never allowed to mingle (Zoch 1946). Even though the Japanese and Germans were allies, they disliked each other because of "their respective racist ideologies" and their history as enemies in World War I (Krammer 1983b). Many of the Germans at Camp Hearne considered the Japanese to be a "shadowy" element and they did not like the Japanese because their cooking "smelled bad" (Blanchett 1989). Jim Potts noted that at Camp Rosenburg, pro-Nazis asked for permission to beat up the Japanese POWs and later help the Americans fight the Japanese. Potts claimed the Germans said, "Hell, we'll whip those Japs. Just give us permission to go. We wasn't trained to bail hay and pick cotton, we were trained to fight." Needless to say, the Nazis were denied permission.

According to former guard Jack Kuttruff, the Japanese prisoners were left to themselves after the morning headcount. "I remember that they never did very much," he said. "They didn't really do anything except sit around, and they did not even participate in crafts." Kuttruff did not remember the Japanese reading, celebrating holidays, seeing movies, gardening, sending out mail, or even attempting to escape, "they were just there." There was one exception to this laxity: he recalled that they enjoyed baseball. They would "play baseball, lots and lots of baseball. That was the thing for them." Zoch (1946) agreed stating, "The life of the Japanese prisoners of war was a very simple and uneventful one the short while they were in our camp. Their leisure time was spent chiefly in sleeping, talking, and in the playing of baseball." Additionally, "Since the majority of them could not read nor [could they] write, there naturally was very little reading and writing done to occupy their spare time."

The Japanese soldiers were allowed to prepare their own style of food. This consisted of lots of rice, fish, and some kind of cooked greens that may have been spinach. Their meals were cooked in a large wok that Kuttruff stated was about three feet across. The food looked quite tasty to Kuttruff, who also recalled that buzzards drawn by the scent would circle over the roof of the mess hall. Former POW Kurt Schulz reported that the Japanese liked to eat "fresh green grasshoppers" that were present in the grass around the camp (*Hearne Democrat* 1988).

Kuttruff found the Japanese to be quiet and polite. When they passed him, he said they either saluted or bowed. "Their relationship towards us Americans was exceptionally good," added Chaplain Zoch (1946, 6). "It seemed that they were in constant fear of possible reprisals for their sneaky attack upon Pearl Harbor on December 7, 1941." Helen Palmos noted that the Japanese seemed very skittish. Palmos described them as usually "clustered up together" hanging out by the fence line talking among themselves until a vehicle would pass by at which point they would "scatter like a covey of quail."

The American guards also had some fun with the Japanese prisoners. Carl Maisen recalled that some of the guards taught the prisoners obscene gestures and phrases that the prisoners then used, without knowing their true meaning, when they spoke to American officers. This resulted in unknown consequences for the prisoners. The offending guards were never discovered, however, and as a consequence the entire guard contingent was transferred to Camp Mexia (Blanchett 1989).

Unlike the Germans, Japanese prisoners never engaged in work outside the camp. There was a general attitude among those associated with Camp Hearne that the Japanese prisoners did not make good workers and consequently they were not asked to work. Chaplain Zoch confirmed that the Japanese prisoners did not have to work except for taking care of their barracks and the grounds of their compound. He claimed that the reason for this inactivity was their "utter ignorance of American labor and their slowness in learning it." Only a small number of Japanese prisoners worked in the compound canteen (Zoch 1946).

Security of the Japanese prisoners was very tight. Kuttruff said that compared to the Germans, who were free to move around the camp, "the Japanese were always in that cage . . . there was a lot of security . . . they just never got out. They were there, period." Johnoween Mathis, who lived close to the camp, recalled that "this old lady asked me one day, she said, 'well honey, since they are so little,' she said, 'can they crawl through that fence down there.' I said, 'I don't think so,' I said, 'they may try to crawl through but they'll never make it, that'll be the end of them.'"

Mathis also remembered that "the service personnel out there told me that they really didn't like to go in there [the Japanese compound] and the reason they didn't was because they didn't know what they [the Japanese prisoners] were thinking, they did not know what they were talking about because they were talking Japanese. One of those guys in particular said, 'In fact, they [the Japanese prisoners] were pretty damn scary.'" She says that unlike the Germans, who were "pretty trustworthy for prisoners," the Japanese were not allowed out of their compound. "I never saw one of them out, never."

Chaplain Zoch described the Japanese POWs as individuals of small stature who appeared to be poorly nourished and unhealthy (Zoch 1946). They were clothed in the smallest American uniforms available and even those were noticeably baggy. Zoch described them as being "very simple and ignorant." This was probably because one of the Japanese officers had told him that education beyond six years was not encouraged in Japan.

Jim Steiger related that the Americans "had a different feeling for the Japanese than we did for the Germans. We felt like, in that day and time, we felt like the Japanese were the most terrible thing there was." Much of this antagonism was directly related to the surprise attack on Pearl Harbor, the Bataan Death March, and other reports of war atrocities, he added. "Japan had their way pretty much like they wanted it in the early part of that war in places like Wake Island and the Philippines, horrible stories came out of there."

The Japanese left Camp Hearne as quickly as they came. Population data (Census Data 1945) and labor reports (War Department 1945) indicate that the Japanese prisoners were removed from Camp Hearne sometime during the first two weeks of December, 1945, and transferred to holding camps in Lamont, California, from which they were repatriated to Japan (Krammer 1983b).

The Camp's Closure

Even before the end of the war, city officials were anxious to know the potential fate of the property and facilities that made up Camp Hearne. As early as September, 1944, Burt Collins, president of the Hearne Chamber of Commerce, contacted Rep. Luther Johnson about the camp's eventual fate (Collins 1944). Johnson contacted War Department officials regarding the possible disposition of the property after the war and was informed that while they could not furnish any specific information, they expected that the camp would become surplus property and sold when it was no longer needed by the War Department (Howard 1944c; Johnson 1944).

The first portion of the camp to be sold was the undeveloped property around the perimeter of the main camp. In late 1945, even before the prisoners had left Camp Hearne, the federal government placed an official notice in the *Hearne Democrat* and other Texas newspapers announcing that the property (about 438 acres) was for sale. The original notice divided the land into six tracts that were similar to the parcels purchased from the original landowners in 1943. The land was for sale according to the following priorities: (1) government agencies, (2) state and local governments, (3) former owners of the property, (4) tenants of the former owners, (5) World War II veterans, (6) owner-operators, (7) non-profit institutions, and (8) private citizens. Bids were to be accepted for ninety days and were due on February 20, 1946 (*Hearne Democrat* 1945b).

The land was sold along with many items from the camp, which by then was vacant, in February, 1946. The equipment from the Camp Hearne theater was sold to the Gascondale Theater Corporation of Rolla, Missouri (*Hearne Democrat* 1946c). Helen Palmos remembered purchasing cookware for her cafe. She bid $75.01 on what she thought would be a supply of utensils. To her delight, the price included tables and cabinets as well. She recalled that some of the furniture came from the officers' quarters and was of high quality—not regular army issue furniture. Palmos's lot included so many supplies and pieces of furniture that she needed a truck to haul it all away. Remaining supplies such as blankets, mess hall trays, and other items were burned or buried. After this initial sale all that remained was the developed camp property, including all buildings and associated materials (for example, fencing, lighting fixtures, poles, gas meters, and other odds and ends). Because the War Department no longer needed the camp, it was assigned to the Federal Public Housing Administration for disposal. Hearne city officials campaigned vigorously to obtain this property and its associated structures from the federal government. In January, 1946, Hearne's mayor and city manager, as well as three other local officials, met with Federal Public Housing Administration officials in Washington, D.C., to discuss their plans to acquire the camp property for the city. The government planned to give the city a five-year lease on the property for one dollar per year. The lease included 160 acres of improved land (the American compound, warehouse area, administration area, and hospital) and its facilities: buildings, a water treatment plant, sewage treatment plant, the fire department, and two trucks. That amounted to the entire camp, except for the POW compounds. According to the plan, the hospital area was to be used by the Hearne Independent School District for temporary use as a school for African-American children whose school had been destroyed by fire in 1945. The camp headquarters buildings and the officers' club were to be used by the American Legion post and possibly by the Boy Scouts and Girl Scouts. The remaining American barracks were to be used as emergency housing for veterans and their families. The Hearne Chamber of Commerce already had a list of fifty veterans' families who were requesting housing at Camp Hearne. Near the end of the month it was announced that the city's lease on the property was expected to begin on the last day of January (*Hearne Democrat* 1946d). Moreover, the city planned that once it had been granted the five-year lease, it would begin negotiations to acquire title to the 160 acres and associated buildings (*Hearne Democrat* 1946e). Once the property was purchased, the city planned to move the buildings used for the segregated school from the camp and relocate them to a different location. The vacant property would then be used as part of a proposed municipal airport.

These actions were supported in a town meeting held the week before (*Hearne Democrat* 1946f). After an unexplained delay, a meeting was held between the Federal Public Housing Administration and Hearne's mayor pro-tem in March, 1946, regarding the approval of plans to convert the barracks in the American compound into emergency housing (*Hearne Democrat* 1946g). That same month, an official from the U.S. Public Health Service inspected the camp to evaluate potential threats to public health and the suitability of converting the barracks into civilian housing. He observed that the buildings were in good condition, but could only be considered to be of fair quality and were generally below the standards usually considered for living quarters. The health inspector recommended that the property be converted back to agricultural pursuits. He further recommended that all camp property, with the exception of the sewage system, be removed as scrap or salvage (Shirck and Moore 1946). Shortly thereafter, on April 22, Camp Hearne was officially declared surplus property (*Hearne Democrat* 1946h).

In May, the process of negotiating for the former Camp Hearne property became more complicated. At the beginning of the month, the city council rejected the lease offered by the Federal Public Housing Administration. Provisions within the lease required that the city upgrade the barracks before they could be inhabited, which would cost about $3,000 per unit. In addition, some of the buildings could not be modified. Finally, there were no assurances that the city could purchase the land after the lease terminated. Subsequently, the city appointed a committee to endeavor to purchase the land (*Hearne Democrat* 1946i) and gave it power to act on the city's behalf to that end. Later in the month, the authority to sell the property and buildings was transferred from the Federal Public Housing Administration to the Federal Land Bank in Houston. In July, the Federal Land Bank, which had previously been designated to dispose of the entire camp facility, transferred the authority to sell the buildings and material assets at the camp to the War Assets Administration in Dallas. Thus, the purchase of the land was to be negotiated with the Federal Land Bank in Houston and the purchase of the buildings and other assets of the camp were to be negotiated with the War Assets Administration in Dallas (*Hearne Democrat* 1946j). An editorial entitled "The Run Around" appeared on the front page of the *Hearne Democrat* on July 12. The editorial writer complained about the disorganized administration of the property and expressed the frustration of city officials in their attempts to acquire the land (*Hearne Democrat* 1946k). "With a serious shortage of housing in Hearne," the author wrote, "with a shortage of many materials and much equipment and with a definite need for much of the property now owned but not being used by the government at the ex-prisoner of war site near Hearne, the federal government continues to play football with this property—kicking it from one agency to another and, so far, successfully evading every effort by the City of Hearne to purchase the property."

In June, appraisers for the Federal Land Bank in Houston spent three days at Camp Hearne determining the property's value. Later in the summer, appraisers for the War Assets Administration arrived at the site and evaluated the value of the buildings and remaining hardware (for example, fencing, gates, light poles, and so forth) (*Hearne Democrat* 1946l). The War Assets Administration estimated that the total salvage value of the building materials, if scrapped, was about $220,532. The salvage (scrap) value of an individual barrack building was estimated at $939. The appraisers estimated the value of the structures, unaltered and used where they were, at approximately $717,300 (Priestly 1946).

In September, the regional supervisor of the surplus property disposal department of the Federal Land Bank of Houston met with Hearne city officials and other local officials. The meeting was held to discuss the procedure for acquiring facilities at Camp Hearne. The city officials wanted to obtain all land, the sewer treatment system, the water treatment system, four warehouses, one truck and trailer, one jeep, two fire trucks, one tractor, and one bulldozer. The Hearne Independent School District wanted all of the buildings in the hospital area. Other communities expressed interest in many of the other buildings (*Hearne Democrat* 1946m). At the end of November, a representative of the War Assets Administration in Dallas came to Hearne to receive applications for the purchase of the camp buildings (*Hearne Democrat* 1946n).

In January, 1947, the city council approved the application for the purchase of the land (290.34 acres—the entire acreage of the developed camp), the water and sewage processing plants, and one warehouse (*Hearne Democrat* 1947a). The following month, the War Assets Administration offered for sale all of Camp Hearne's buildings and remaining assets, including fencing, flagpoles, gates, wire, gasoline pumps, and plumbing fixtures (*Hearne Democrat* 1947b). The same priority was given to bidders as in the original auction held in 1946. The War Assets Administration placed advertisements in the *Hearne Democrat, Houston Chronicle,* and other Texas newspapers to draw attention to the upcoming auction. Bids were mailed to and opened in Dallas. Successful bidders were subsequently notified and had sixty days to remove any items purchased from the camp.

As a result of the auction, three buildings were sold to the city. These included a cold-storage warehouse, the officers' club, and the administration building at a cost of $1,830. Johnoween Mathis recalled that the officers' club became the American Legion Hall. The American Legion Hall, which stood where the Robertson County Fair is currently held, burned down in 1992. The county school board was also awarded four buildings: three barracks and a sentry post. Their net cost was reported to be $125 after discounts given by the federal government (*Hearne Democrat* 1947c). All of the hospital area buildings were awarded to the Hearne Independent School District. Twelve of the buildings were designated for the new segregated school and two were designated for the Hearne High School, one for a classroom and one for a cafeteria. These buildings, valued at $64,919, were received free from the federal government. Other school districts received the following number of buildings: Cameron School District, 20; Falls County Vocational School in Marlin, 11; Robertson County School District, 4; Rosebud School District, 3; Caldwell School District, 4; and Thrall School District, 1. These buildings were transferred after "generous discounts" from the federal government (*Hearne Democrat* 1947d). Mildred Payne worked for four years at Eastside Junior High School in Hearne. The faculty lunchroom was a former Camp Hearne barrack building. Today, two buildings originally used in the Camp Hearne hospital area are still in use by the Blackshire School in Hearne.

The remaining buildings were sold to private citizens. These were taken away and converted into homes, barns, and warehouses. E. R. Mason bid on the chapel, but did not bid high enough. Former POW Fritz Haus maintained contact with his American friends after the war and learned from them that his beloved chapel had been sold to the local Methodist congregation. He heard that it was moved to either Huntsville or Hearne. Mason was successful in purchasing the theater building in Compound 3 for $170.30. He cut the hundred-foot-long building into four pieces so that it could be transported on the highway to nearby Franklin. There, the pieces were reassembled into two separate buildings; a sixty-foot-long section became The Assembly of God Church and a forty-foot section became the church's parsonage. The rectory later burned down, but the church building still stands. It is currently covered with siding and is located near the old Franklin High School. Mike Jones grew up in a house that was originally a clinic building in the hospital area. This building is still located at 206 East Second Street in Hearne. The barbed wire surrounding the camp was purchased by local ranchers and used to fence their fields. Buildings that did not sell were demolished and removed in order to make room for an airfield. Some of the buildings that were demolished had beautiful frescoes painted by the POWs. Mason, who was present when buildings were demolished at the camp, asked the bulldozer operator if he could gather up some of the pieces, but the operator would not allow him to take anything.

Finally, in May, 1947, it was reported that a substantial amount of camp property had been sold to the city of Hearne. Specifically, the city purchased 290 acres of land (the entire camp), the water and sewage treatment plants, and one frame warehouse. City officials planned to use the water treatment system to service the northwestern portion of Hearne. The water treatment system sold for the discounted price of $5,700. The sewage treatment system was sold for a "nominal" price. The land, which sold for $14,500 cash, was intended for future industrial expansion and a proposed airport. The warehouse sold for $4,000 and was intended for uses associated with the water and sewage treatment systems. Local congressman Olin E. Teague notified city officials of the sale (*Hearne Democrat* 1947e).

By the summer of 1947, all that remained of Camp Hearne was a vacant lot. Local children used the land as a playground, teenagers had parties and danced on the old cement foundations, and local farmers grazed their cattle and goats there. Units of the army's 82d Airborne Division bivouacked on the site for two or three days in February, 1952, during a training exercise. Mildred Payne recalled that people continued to play on the grounds for years after the camp was abandoned. A fire hydrant was occasionally turned on as a test and children would run in the stream of water—until the city permanently shut off the water supply. People also dug things up from the site, scavenging items of interest. "I got enough rocks to go around the flowerbed," said Mrs. Payne.

Many modifications have occurred to the old camp since its deactivation. Several businesses are now located along the edges of the old camp. The Hearne Steel Company now occupies the area where the guardhouse once stood, as well as parts of Compounds 2 and 3. The Robertson County Fair Grounds parking lot is located where the administration building and camp commander's house were once located. A bulldozer destroyed some of the fountains the prisoners constructed, for example the "Devil Fountain," during a period of land clearing. The mess hall foundations of Companies 5 and 6 in Compound 2 were connected by an extra concrete slab, which served as a foundation for an aircraft painting company that was later destroyed by a tornado. However, much of the camp remains undisturbed and obscured under a dense growth of vegetation.

CHAPTER 5

Camp Hearne Artifacts

OVER FOURTEEN HUNDRED ARTIFACTS were recovered from Camp Hearne as a result of archaeological survey and excavation. This study represents the first intensive archaeological investigation of a German POW camp and is among the first at a World War II–era archaeological site. Camp Hearne's grounds have been given the official Texas archaeological site designation 41RT517.

The first phase of the investigation included a preliminary archaeological survey and excavation of parts of Compounds 2 and 3 in 1996. Mowers, provided by the city of Hearne, cleared the vegetation so the ground surface could be examined. The mowing revealed building foundations and cement fountains built by the POWs. Metal detectors were then used to locate isolated artifacts and artifact concentrations. Initial test excavations undertaken around two barracks and several small fountains were recorded. A much more extensive survey was conducted in the summer of 1997 when the city of Hearne burned the vegetation from a large segment of the camp. All the burned areas—the southeast quarter of Compound 1, southern half of Compound 2, and southwest quarter of Compound 3—were surveyed utilizing metal detectors. Artifacts were located, plotted onto maps, and collected.

This survey and initial excavations conducted in 1996 indicated that most artifacts were located in high traffic areas such as walkways and the entrances to the barracks and other buildings. Many artifacts also were found behind the lavatories where clothes were washed. Otherwise, artifacts were scattered throughout the camp, with the lowest densities occurring in the recreation areas. The only exceptions were the deliberate dumps of field equipment and the purposeful burial of individual canteens and mess kits at various places in the camp. Based on this knowledge of artifact spatial distribution, extensive excavations were undertaken in the fall semester of 1997 near the entrances of several barracks in Compounds 2 and 3 (the NCO compounds). The entrances and backsides of two lavatories in Compounds 2 and 3 also were investigated. Limited testing was conducted in Compound 1 (the enlisted men's compound) due to logistical problems and extensive ground disturbance.

Sixteen graduate students and more than three hundred undergraduate students from introductory anthropology classes at Texas A&M University were involved in the surveys and excavations at Camp Hearne. They excavated more than five hundred three-foot-by-three-foot excavation units. All units were excavated to a depth of ten centimeters and the sediment screened through quarter-inch mesh. All artifacts recovered during the survey and excavation were carefully cleaned, conserved, cataloged, and subsequently analyzed. More than twenty POW-built features—including fountains, remnants of formal flower gardens, a theater, and a spectacular fountain with a miniature castle complete with cement figurines—were recorded during the survey and excavations.

The artifacts from Camp Hearne included items made of metal, glass, plastic, rubber, leather, paper, and cloth. All artifacts described here were found within the three POW compounds, but most came from Compounds 2 and 3. The POWs brought many of these items to the camp from battlefields in North Africa and Europe, whereas they were issued, purchased, or made other items while they were in the United States. Many of these artifacts were unintentionally lost, whereas others were intentionally discarded. The Camp Hearne artifacts are discussed under six major headings: German uniforms, American uniforms, military and political insignia and identification tags, military equipment, POW-made items, and personal items. Where possible, insights into the use of artifacts recovered from Camp Hearne are provided by former POWs and guards. Other materials, primarily construction debris, were also encountered at the site. Nails, tacks, tarpaper from the building walls, broken window glass, bricks, and metal fittings occur in great quantity. These materials from the construction and dismantling of the camp are not discussed.

The following discussion provides a good representation of the types of artifacts that can be found at a German POW camp and provides more insights into life as a POW at Camp Hearne.

It should be noted that the German POWs and their American guards left all of the artifacts found on the camp's grounds. No archaeological evidence of the brief presence of Japanese POWs was found at the site.

German Uniforms

The photographic record and the recollections of former POWs and guards show that the prisoners wore a variety of German uniforms. Metal and Bakelite (a hard, heat-treated plastic) artifacts such as buttons, cinches, hooks, buckles, and shoe fragments found in the POW compounds have confirmed this.

All of the former POWs recalled that they were encouraged to discard their German uniforms when they arrived in the United States. They were told they would receive new and better clothes once they were processed. Joseph Pohl and Hans Lammersdorf stated that their German uniforms were immediately replaced when they arrived in this country. Peter Spoden and Fritz Haus remembered wearing their German army uniforms to Camp Hearne. Later, Spoden traded his uniform for two American uniforms. Local citizens and guards recalled seeing the German soldiers depart from the trains arriving at Hearne wearing overcoats, as well as their tropical and field gray continental uniforms.

According to regulations, a prisoner was allowed to retain his national uniform and insignia (Dorwart 1945). Many of the men at Camp Hearne chose to keep their uniforms and wore them on Sundays and holidays, while attending theater productions and special concerts, and at other events, such as funerals.

Prisoners who did not have a national uniform but desired one modified American uniforms to look like their own. Many American uniform pieces, especially the cotton and canvas jackets, were bleached white by the camp tailors to imitate the appearance of German tropical tunics. The fading was accomplished with antigas tablets brought to the camp or with bleach used for cleaning clothing. German tailors also made complete new uniforms (fig. 11). One tailor even made imitations of the distinctive billed cap worn by members of the Africa Korps. Prisoners also embroidered the insignia sewn on these uniforms and replaced the American buttons with pebbled German buttons from worn-out tunics. Walter Fricke, for instance, hand embroidered a small circular patch indicating that he was a qualified glider pilot.

A variety of buttons and other items from German uniform tunics and trousers were found in the POW compounds. The individual artifacts derived from these uniforms are described in the following section.

German Military Buttons

A variety of metal and Bakelite buttons from German military shirts, tunics, and trousers were recovered from the POW compounds. One of the most common is a metal button with a pebbled surface. These are three-piece buttons (n = 48) consisting of a domed faceplate, concave back plate, and riveted loop shank (fig. 31, item f). The faceplate is stamped with a fine to coarse pebbling that is crimped onto the back plate and rolled along the edge. The pebbled buttons from Camp Hearne are made from a light metal alloy (87 percent) or aluminum (13 percent). The faceplates were originally painted field gray for army continental combat tunics, blue-gray for Luftwaffe (air force) field uniforms, or olive to tan for tropical combat tunics worn by members of both the army and the Luftwaffe. During use, these buttons typically lost their paint and the metal or aluminum surface became exposed. Many buttons recovered from Camp Hearne retain traces of their original paint.

Forty-seven of the metal buttons found at Camp Hearne have a diameter of nineteen millimeters, while one button had a diameter of twenty-one millimeters. The nineteen-millimeter buttons were used on the fronts and pockets of army and Luftwaffe combat tunics (Angolia and Schlicht 1984, 73–74; 1996, 223–25). The larger button could be from either a tunic or greatcoat. Buttons were sewn directly onto continental uniforms. However, buttons on tropical uniforms were not sewn onto the uniforms, but were attached to the tropical tunic with a devise known as a "split ring." The split ring is a piece of sturdy wire that was bent into a circular shape with a raised crossbar (fig. 31, item h). The shank of the button was secured to the crossbar of the split ring through the

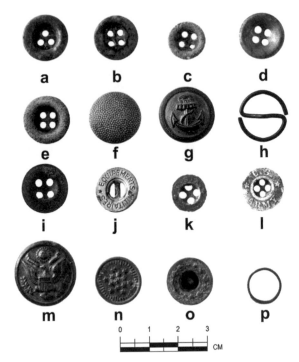

Fig. 31. Metal buttons recovered at Camp Hearne: a. three-hole deep-dish button; b. four-hole, two-piece dish button; c. small four-hole shallow-dish button; d. large four-hole shallow-dish button; e. four-hole deep-dish button; f. pebbled tunic button; g. navy button; h. split ring; i. British four-hole button; j. French "Equipements Militaires" button; k. U.S.A. button; l. U.S. Army button; m. general service button; n. star button; o. wreath button; and p. metal ring. Camp Hearne Collection, Texas A&M University.

buttonhole. One button found at Camp Hearne still retained the split-ring attaching device. Twenty-four buttons are stamped with manufacturer's markings, representing seventeen different makers.

Three tunic buttons used by the German navy (Kreigsmarine) on the field gray continental tunics and tropical tunics (front and pockets) of members of coastal artillery and naval units were found in Compound 1 (Angolia and Schlicht, 1991a, 197–99). These buttons are of one-piece construction, having a stamped faceplate with a loop shank attached to the back (fig. 31, item g). The front of the button is domed and shows a fouled anchor entwined with rope on a pebbled background. Surrounding the anchor is a slightly raised, pebbled border. These buttons are twenty millimeters in diameter and made of a light metal alloy. No maker marks are present. These buttons were originally painted matte gray, however no paint remains on these specimens.

Thirty-five four-holed buttons of one-piece construction made from aluminum or a light metal alloy were also found in the compounds (fig. 31, items c and d). The front of the buttons have a shallow concavity surrounded by a rim that varies from flat to slightly beveled. The backs are convex and slope directly from the edges or from the slight bevel. These buttons are seventeen millimeters (n = 22) and fourteen millimeters (n = 13) in diameter. Slight variations in size, rim treatment, hole diameter, and hole placement reflect different manufacturers. These buttons were used on the sleeves of combat tunics and some shirts, but most commonly appeared on trousers (Angolia and Schlicht 1984, 74; 1996, 226).

Five four-hole buttons of two-piece construction with a stamped faceplate crimped over a back plate (fig. 31, item b) were recovered. The face is slightly concave in the center, with a smooth beveled rim. They are 16.5 to seventeen millimeters in diameter and appear to be made of a light metal alloy or steel. These buttons are similar to their single-piece counterparts described above and were probably used on the waist, pockets, and flies of trousers (Angolia and Schlicht 1984, 73–74; 1996, 223–25).

Twenty-one Bakelite buttons of German origin were recovered. These buttons all have four holes for attachment and are brown, gray, white, or green in color. Most buttons range from 14 to 17 millimeters in diameter (n = 19), while two buttons are 10 and 12 millimeters in diameter.

The larger buttons were used on the sleeves, inside pockets, and collars of tunics; the fronts and pockets of shirts; and on the pockets, flies, waists, and legs of shorts and trousers. The smaller buttons were used to button down the collar on some shirts (Angolia and Schlicht 1996, 225–26; De Lagarde 1994, 47, 51; Scipion and Bastien 1996, 91).

British and French Military Buttons

A number of British and French buttons were found in the POW compounds. British buttons are four-hole buttons with a flat rim and deep-dish center (fig. 31, item i). They are of one-piece construction and made of a light metal alloy. Two sizes are present: 14.5 millimeters in diameter (n = 9) and 17.5 millimeters in diameter (n = 17). Most of these buttons have maker's marks on the reverse side of the rims representing eight different companies. They were used on British military shirts, trousers, and jackets (Bouchery 1998; Brayley and Ingram 1998). Undoubtedly, German soldiers in North Africa either used British shirts or the buttons were found on the battlefields and used to make field repairs to German uniforms.

French buttons are metal alloy buttons (n = 51) measuring sixteen millimeters in diameter (fig. 31, item j). These buttons are of single-piece construction with two large holes and a bar-type shank raised above the back of the buttons. On the front of the buttons is a wide flat rim on which is stamped the words "EQUIPEMENTS MILITAIRES" with a star.

These buttons are of a size and style consistent with use on the fronts and pockets of shirts, or on the waists and pockets of trousers. McGuirk (1993) reports that the Germans captured large numbers of French tropical field shirts in 1940 and modified them for use by the Afrika Korps. Many of the buttons from Camp Hearne are undoubtedly from this source (Bender and Law 1973, 144). These buttons were also used on some field equipment bags.

German Clothing Buckles and Hooks

Two hooks (Seitenhaken) made of thin aluminum rod were found. The hooks, which were inserted through eyelets in the midriff area of combat tunics, served to support and keep the belt in place on enlisted and NCO tunics (Angolia and Schlicht 1984; 1996, 226; 1997; Krawczyk 1996, 78). These particular tunic hooks have traces of brown paint, which clearly indicates their use on tropical uniforms.

Two metal buckles measuring twenty-four by forty-three millimeters and having an adjustable slide fitted across the center were found during the excavations. The buckles served as cinches around the waist of trousers and tropical shorts, or were used to cinch cloth belts on trousers and shorts (De Lagarde 1994, 47).

German Boots

Former POWs Fritz Haus and Arno Einicke both remembered that all the men wore their German army boots when they first arrived at Camp Hearne. Both recalled that the men had to make do with what they had upon arrival and were later issued U.S. Army footwear. The recollections are confirmed by the recovery of German boot hardware from the POW compounds.

Three U-shaped pieces of steel that attached to the outside of a boot heel (De Lagarde 1994, 27, 78; Scipion and Bastien 1996, 38) and one half-circle, tap-style cleat used on both the toe and heel of boots (De Lagarde 1994, 30; Scipion and Bastien 1996, 38) were found. Most German boots were constructed with leather soles and heels, and many combinations of metal studs and cleats were employed to prolong the life of the leather. The metal cleats found at Camp Hearne represent the two types used on German footwear and are typical of the variations found on tropical-issue boots.

AMERICAN UNIFORMS

Documentary and photographic evidence indicates that the German POWs wore a variety of American uniforms while at Camp Hearne. These included surplus World War I uniforms, other older stock items, and some new army-issue clothing. This is confirmed by archaeological investigations that recovered many metal and plastic items from these uniforms.

The prisoners were issued American military clothing upon their arrival in the United States and could buy extra items at the camp PX. Ernst Froembsdorf, one of the first prisoners to arrive at Camp Hearne, remarked that although he was glad to finally receive a clean, new uniform, he was disappointed that it was marred by the letters "PW" painted on the back and sleeves of the shirt and on the seat and legs of the trousers.

Artifacts from American uniforms recovered in the POW compounds are discussed in the following section. Most of these items were lost by the German prisoners, but some may have been lost by American guards during inspections and while they were patrolling the compounds.

American Military Buttons

A variety of metal and plastic buttons from American uniforms were recovered at the camp. One of the most distinctive is the general service button. These buttons are constructed of three pieces: an upper domed face crimped around a flat back plate, to which a looped shank was attached (fig. 31, item m). These buttons exhibit the raised Great Seal, which features an eagle with outstretched wings clutching an olive branch in one claw and arrows in the other. From its beak hangs a banner with the words "E Pluribus Unum" and above its head are stars enclosed with a circle of stars. Fine horizontal lines mark the background. These buttons have a diameter of 28 millimeters (n = 1), 23 millimeters (n = 11), and 16 millimeters (n = 9). All of the buttons are bronze with some having traces of black paint. One 16-millimeter-diameter button had a gilt finish. Nineteen of the buttons recovered contained manufacturer's markings, representing eleven different makers. These bronze buttons were used on a number of styles of jackets and coats (Lewis 1993, 83). The 28-millimeter-diameter button was most commonly used on overcoats, the 23-millimeter-diameter button for uniform front buttons and pockets, and the small 16-millimeter buttons on cuffs and to secure shoulder boards. The gilt buttons were used on dress uniforms (Albert 1976, 41–42).

Thirty-two dished, four-hole metal buttons with a prominent rim were also recovered from the POW compounds (fig. 31, item k). They are of one–piece construction, made of a light metal alloy, and are fourteen millimeters in diameter. The front rim is marked with the abbreviation "U.S.A." and flanked on both sides by a star. The remainder of the rim is stippled. No maker marks are present. These buttons were used as fly buttons on surplus World War I blue denim, dungaree, and wool trousers (Lewis 1993, 116).

Another type of dished, four-hole metal button (n = 13) with a distinct rim was also found (fig. 31, item l). These are of one-piece construction, are made from a light metal alloy, and measure seventeen millimeters in diameter. The front rim is marked "U.S. ARMY." A star flanks the words on each side. No manufacturer markings are present. These buttons were used as waist buttons on surplus World War I wool, blue denim, and dungaree trousers. They were also used on the fronts and pockets of the 1940 pattern blue denim work jumper and dungarees (Lewis 1993, 70).

Nine buttons with a stud-type shank were recovered. These were not sewn to clothing items, but rather were riveted to the cloth. The fronts of these buttons measure seventeen millimeters in diameter and are decorated with thirteen stars and short radiating lines along the edge (fig. 31, item n). The back portion of the buttons is made of either aluminum or steel and the fronts are a bronze alloy. No manufacturing marks are present. These buttons were used on herringbone-twill shirts (front and pockets), trousers, and jumpsuits (Lewis 1993, 71–73, 117–18).

Another type of button (n = 2) with a stud-type shank was found in the compounds (fig. 31, item o). These were fastened to clothing as described above for the "star" button. The front of these buttons measures eighteen millimeters in diameter and is decorated with a wreath of leaves around the edge. The centers are hollowed for the rivet attachment. These buttons were used on the herringbone-twill shirts, trousers, and jumpsuits (Lewis 1993, 71–73, 117–18).

A variety of plastic buttons (n = 27) from American uniforms was found within the prison compounds at Camp Hearne. All have either four holes or two holes for attachment. These buttons range from twelve to thirty-two millimeters in diameter and are mostly black and brown or white in color. These buttons were used on the fronts, pockets, collars, and cuffs of wool and cotton shirts, overcoats, jackets, mackinaws, raincoats, waist and fly areas of wool trousers, sweaters, underwear (long johns), and shorts (Lewis 1993, 64, 83–85, 88–89, 104, 110, 111, 131–36, 138–39).

Two double-coil steel rings of stiff fine wire measuring thirteen millimeters in diameter (fig. 31, item p) were recovered from the prisoner compounds. These rings were used to secure the general service buttons to obsolete World War I American canvas tunics. One was found attached to a German pebbled button, obviously used to secure the button to a German tunic.

American Belts and Buckles

A single large, metal buckle made of a heavy-gauge, bronzelike material was found in the POW compounds. It is rectangular in shape and contains a fixed bar across its center. A single prong fitted to its base served to hold and tighten the belt. The buckle, which measures fifty-two by fifty-seven millimeters, was part of the enlisted man's leather belt worn with the four-pocket tunic and was no longer issued after 1942 (Lewis 1993, 183).

Five pieces from a standard-issue U.S. Army service web belt were recovered (Lewis 1993, 183). One end of the belt had a brass buckle of two-piece design consisting of a frame measuring 41 by 32 millimeters upon which a smaller, flat rectangular plate is attached to one end. This piece pivots upward slightly and is toothed at one end to secure the belt. One frame and two pivoting pieces were recovered. Two brass belt tips measuring 13 by 32 millimeters also were found. These kept the opposite end of the web belt from fraying.

Three rectangular buckles that are rounded at one end were also found. They are made of metal and come in two sizes: three by 2.4 centimeters and 2.8 by two centimeters. Two bars span the rectangular portion of the buckle through which passed a cloth belt. These buckles, which were sewn on the waist of army-issue shorts, were used to secure and cinch a cloth belt attached to the other side of the waist (Lewis 1993, 110).

One rectangular steel slide buckle with a flattened metal frame was excavated. It measures 4.2 by 7.1 centimeters and has a central bar that bisects the short segment of the buckle. Fragments of cloth belt were found attached to the buckle when it was excavated. This slide buckle was used to secure the cloth waist belt attached to the M1938-style mackinaw jacket (Lewis 1993, 136).

Also found at the site was a rectangular, pronged, nickel-plated, steel cinch of two-piece construction measuring twenty-two by thirty millimeters. This buckle served as a cinch on trousers and compared favorably with cinches on the waist of World War I army-issue wool trousers.

American Boots and Shoes

German military boots were slowly replaced with American military boots and shoes. A number of American boot fragments were recovered from the POW compounds. Fritz Haus recalled that a rumor circulated among the POWs that before the Americans issued boots to them, the letters "PW" would be carved into the heels so the prisoners could be tracked in the event that they escaped. Haus's reaction to the rumor was that he not only had not heard of such a thing, but that it was nonsense. He was correct.

Six hard, black, rubber boot soles with a central crosshatch design were found in the POW compounds. The bottom of each sole is marked "U.S. Army." A series of small circles and the shoe size are present at the base of the sole. Manufacturer's marks are found on the back of the sole. These soles, referred to as an outside tap, were used on the Type II U.S. service shoe (Lewis 1993, 151). The use of the rubber outside tap over a leather sole served as a transition between the earlier leather-soled Type I U.S. service shoe and the later rubber-soled Type III U.S. service shoe. Five identifiable rubber heels were recovered, three from military boots and two from dress shoes. None of the boots had the letters "PW" carved in them.

Forty-four eyelets were found. The eyelets are 4.7 millimeters in diameter and are painted brown (n = 16), black (n = 27), or olive drab (n = 1). Twenty-six are still attached to fragments of leather. These eyelets and associated leather are probably from American boots of the Type II variety. However, there is a possibility that some may be from German boots. A fragment of a woven cotton shoestring was found. It is the type commonly associated with the Type II U.S. service shoe and other U.S. Army–issue footwear. Finally, two small, rectangular buckles made of brass were found at the site. These buckles were used on leggings to secure the webbed strap that passed under the boot (Lewis 1993, 149–50, 151).

Many fragments of boot leather and heel rubber were found scattered around the compound. These leather and rubber heel fragments may have been the result of shoe repairs. Camp Hearne housed many skilled craftsmen, including men who had been trained as cobblers in Germany. Guard Edwin Munson recalled that Americans would trade pies in exchange for shoe repairs. Fritz Pferdekämper-Geissel said that he repaired shoes for local farmers in order to earn a little cash under the table. He also recycled leather salvaged from boots for art projects. Thus, some of the leather and rubber shoe fragments found at the camp may have come from these repair and artistic activities.

Military and Government Insignia, Medals, Identification Tags, and Seals

Both German and American military insignia, medals, and identification tags were found at Camp Hearne. In addition, insignia representing affiliation with the N.S.D.A.P. (Nazi Party) were also found.

German Military Decorations and Insignia

Two German military medals were found in the POW compounds. The first is the Italo-German Campaign Medal given to German troops serving in North Africa (fig. 32, item g; Angolia 1976; Bender and Law 1973). The Italian government used this De Marchis–designed medal to commemorate the work done by the Afrika Korps and its mutual cooperation with the Italian forces.

Fig. 32. German and American military insignia, decorations, and identity tags recovered at Camp Hearne: a. German rank "pip"; b. German political insignia; c. Italian collar star; d. Italian pith helmet insignia; e. German identification disk; f. American identification "dog tag"; g. Italo-German campaign medal for service in North Africa; h. Spanish Cross awarded to members of the German "Condor Legion" for service in the Spanish Civil War in 1936. i. ring from Tunisia. Camp Hearne Collection, Texas A&M University.

The medal is three centimeters in diameter and has a five-millimeter loop at the top for attaching a ribbon. The medal has a maximum thickness of five millimeters. It was cast in bronze and decorated on both sides. On the reverse side, a scene surrounded by a four-millimeter border depicts two gladiators representing Italy and Germany working together to force shut the jaws of a crocodile, which represents Great Britain. The maker's mark, "LORIOLI MILANO," appears above the crocodile's left arm. The Italian Felini Arch dominates the front side. A fasces (a stylized sheaf of wheat with an axe), the symbol for Italy, appears to the left of the arch and a swastika, the symbol for Nazi Germany, appears to the right. The Royal Knot of Savoy appears below the arch. Surrounding the figure along the border is the phrase "Italo-German Campaign in Africa" in both Italian and German.

The second German medal found was the Spanish Cross (fig. 32, item h). This particular piece is the silver level award with swords, of which only 8,304 were issued (Angolia, 1976). A Maltese cross measuring 5.5 centimeters across dominates the medal. In its center is a swastika surrounded by a circle. Behind the Maltese cross are two crossed swords. Attached to the blade of each sword, between each section of the Maltese cross, are four Luftwaffe eagles. Each eagle has its wings outstretched and is clutching a small swastika in its claws. No maker's marks appear on the badge. The Spanish Cross was presented to members of the Luftwaffe for specific acts of bravery while serving in the "Legion Condor" during the Spanish Civil War (Angolia, 1976).

The final piece of German military insignia found at Camp Hearne was a rank "pip." Pips were worn on the epaulets of German uniform tunics to designate different NCO ranks (fig. 10; Bender and Law 1993; Davis 1992, 1991). This insignia is made of a metal alloy and is a four-sided star measuring 1.3 by 1.3 centimeters with rays originating from the center (fig. 32, item a). Each side has four rays exclusive of those comprising the four points of the star for a total of twenty rays. The center is composed of two concentric circles (De Lagarde 1994).

German Political Insignia

One item of German political insignia was recovered (fig. 32, item b). This is a small, 1.1-centimeter-square insignia made of aluminum. On the front is a raised circle with small "tick" marks around the edge. Raised in the middle of the circle is the German national emblem with an eagle facing to its right and holding a swastika. The letters "RfS" are inscribed in a half-circle over the top edge. The circle's design was pressed from the back, forming a small hollow. Within this hollow the letters "LL" appear above the number "167." It appears to have been attached to two small cords by crimping the sides over the back and around each strand of cord.

This insignia appears to be associated with the "Reichsführerschule" or National Leadership School, where future Nazi Party political leaders were trained (Angolia 1992; Littlejohn 1988). This small insignia, which was intended for attachment, may have been used to identify soldiers who had been through this political training.

American Military Insignia

Two examples of U.S. military insignia were found. The first is a parachutist's badge of the type worn by members of American airborne units (Lewis 1993; Rentz 1999). The design consists of a parachute bounded by a pair of outstretched wings. The piece is made of sterling silver and measures 3.8 centimeters wide by two centimeters tall.

The second example is a marksman's cross or American sharpshooter badge (second class gunner; n = 2). The medal is a cross measuring 2.2 centimeters across composed of four triangles joined at their apices by a circle. The design is black with a one-millimeter-wide metal border. In addition, a rectangular "rifle" qualification bar that would have hung from the attachment at the base of the badge was found (Du Bois 1943). Personnel from the 82d Airborne Division probably lost the badges when they bivouacked in the area in 1952.

Italian Military Insignia

Two examples of Italian insignia were found at Camp Hearne. The first is a five-pointed silver star of the type worn on the collar of Italian uniforms (fig. 32, item c; Jowett and Andrew 2000, 2001; Trye, 1995). The second is an insignia stamped from a single piece of brass (fig. 32, item d). The design is of an eagle with folded wings that is bounded by a wreath with the Royal Knot of Savoy at the base. The royal crown has been broken away from the top of the eagle's head. This insignia was used on the front of Italian hats and pith helmets (Jowett and Andrew 2000, 2001; Trye, 1995).

American Identification Tags

American identification tags, commonly known as "dog tags," are flat pieces of stainless steel stamped with a soldier's personal information (fig. 32 item f; Lewis 1993, 237). They are rectangular in shape, measuring about three by five centimeters, and have rounded edges and a single hole near one of the short ends. At the other short end is a small indentation. Two such tags were recovered at Camp Hearne: One belonged to Martin Ehrlich and is dated 1944; the other belonged to Harold E. Kelley and is dated 1947. Ehrlich's tag dates to the period when the camp was active, whereas Kelley's postdates the camp. Kelley probably lost his tag when the 82d Airborne Division bivouacked on the grounds in 1952.

German Identity Discs

German identity discs are flat pieces of metal that have been cut into an oval, typically measuring 5.5 centimeters long and two centimeters wide, and perforated along the long axis (fig. 32, item e). Personal information was stamped onto each half of the disc. There were two holes perforated in the top of the disc so that it could be kept on a string about the neck. One hole was perforated into the bottom half of the disc. If a soldier was killed in combat, half of the disc remained with the corpse for identification purposes and the other half was separated for record keeping. The discs were made from various materials. Zinc and light metal alloys gradually replaced aluminum, which was used early in the war (Angolia and Schlicht 1987, 136–38; 1998, 88–91; Burroughs and Burroughs 1995).

Eight complete and ten fragmentary discs were found. Most discs belonged to members of the army (panzer reconnaissance, mountain troop, artillery, and infantry units), a few are from Luftwaffe units (antiaircraft units and the Hermann Göring Regiment), and one was from a Waffen SS Panzer unit.

While many of the German identity discs were discarded intact, many were intentionally broken. One specimen was cut into five fragments that were discarded together. The former POWs interviewed offered little insight as to why so many identity discs were found at Camp Hearne. Hugo Wannemacher speculated that perhaps Austrian soldiers threw them away at the end of the war in order to separate themselves from the Germans. Fritz Haus said that the men would simply have had no need to retain them. The war was over, so they no longer had to fear being wounded in battle. Men carried identity papers and therefore had little need for the identification tags. Furthermore, the tags carried negative connotations of a lost war and the hardships of battle.

Mailbag Seals

Four round and seven square seals used to secure mailbags, most likely bags brought to the camp post office for processing, were recovered at Camp Hearne.

All of the seals are made of lead. The round seals are twenty millimeters in diameter and approximately five millimeters thick. The seals were cast with two parallel holes or slots running transversely through the center of the disks. Strings for cinching the mailbags were passed through each hole, the bags closed, and the seal secured. Partial raised text appears in a circle around the edge of the seal on three of the four seals. The most complete sequence reads, "GÖTEBO . . ." with three flowers. It is likely that these seals were derived from German or Swiss mailbags, based on the German text appearing on the seals.

The square seals came from U.S. Postal Service bags. Only one of the seven had any text. One side has raised lettering that reads "U.S. MAIL" and the other side reads "__OL VA." These seals measure sixteen by eighteen millimeters, and are five millimeters thick. Four parallel holes traverse the long axis of each seal. The seals are crimped in two places perpendicular to the holes, folding them into an S-shape. These lead seals were found in Compounds 2 and 3, where others like them may have been the source of lead used to make German badges and insignia as described in a later section.

Military Field Equipment

Photographic evidence and the recollections of former guards and POWs indicate that captured German soldiers were allowed to keep some of their combat equipment (fig. 33). Guard Edwin Munson said POWs were allowed to keep canteens and other pieces of equipment if they desired. Ben Mason remembered that the prisoners "still had their mess kits, canteens, and uniforms that were issued from Germany." However, all of the former POWs interviewed said they were encouraged to discard their gear, either upon capture, upon arrival in the United States, or at Camp Hearne. Heino Erichsen remarked that the men in his troop were stripped of their canteens, utensils, and all other metal objects before boarding a Liberty ship bound for the United States. "If you had a nail file or anything, they took it," said Erichsen. "Anything they thought you could make signals with." Some prisoners saw no reason to keep canteens and utensils because they would henceforth be eating in mess halls. Willi Nellessen, Fritz Pferdekämper-Geissel, and Alfred Jasper said they simply did not need their canteens any longer. Peter Spoden, on the other hand, had no interest in keeping his mess kit: "If you were served on equipment like that for two years, why would you keep it?"

Former POW Werner Kritzler recalled how some prisoners smuggled contraband into Camp Hearne inside their field equipment. Prior to capture or during their time of temporary internment in North Africa, some German soldiers concealed pistols and ammunition in their canteens. "They cut open the canteen on its side," explained Kritzler. "The pistol was wrapped in the cleaning cloth used for your gun and put inside the canteen. Then the felt cover was closed. If you shook the canteen, it didn't make any noise." The prisoners then were allowed to carry their field equipment onto the ships that took them to the United States. Upon arrival in New York, Kritzler remembers that they were

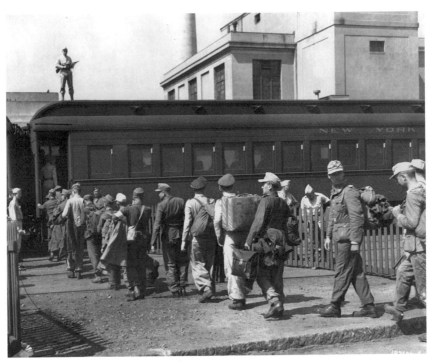

Fig. 33. Captured German soldiers board a train in New York bound for POW camps across the United States. Note that all wear their German uniforms and most are carrying various military bags and other field equipment. Photo courtesy the National Archives and Records Administration, College Park, Maryland.

stripped of all their equipment, including canteens. However, about three months after Kritzler arrived at Hearne, a shipment of confiscated materials came in and belongings were returned to the prisoners. The shipment included all their field equipment. The Americans saw no harm in returning these belongings because it was considered to be merely "soldier stuff." One guard commented on the extraordinary weight of some of the field equipment as he tossed gear onto men's bunks. Little did he realize what was hidden inside some of the items. A prisoner in Kritzler's barrack opened his canteen and revealed a small pistol. He kept it hidden in the canteen, which hung from the wall in the barrack, and would take the pistol out once a week and clean it. Everyone thought this was quite amusing. "The soldier with the gun sold it to an American officer," Kritzler recalled. "He just kept the pistol hidden, he never used it. You see, it was in the canteen, so nobody was looking for it."

Guard Edwin Munson recalled that prisoners who retained their equipment did not opt to keep it after the war. When the POWs left the camp, they discarded most of their equipment because of the limited weight and space allowed for personal items on the return trip to Europe.

Metal hardware items from bags and rucksacks, as well as canteens and mess kits, were the most common artifacts recovered from the POW compounds. Most of this equipment was German; however some pieces of Italian, French, Russian, and American field equipment were also recovered. In this section, the pieces of equipment found at Camp Hearne are described, followed by a discussion of the types of equipment represented.

German Field Equipment

The basic equipment issued to individual German soldiers during the Second World War was designed as an integrated collection of items that would meet the minimum functional requirements of field life and at the same time be relatively easy to carry. The prisoners at Camp Hearne retained a smaller subset of the total equipment issued to German soldiers. The particular circumstances of a soldier's capture or surrender would determine the equipment he might choose to keep or be allowed to keep. While a soldier captured in battle might have only a bare minimum of items, a surrendering soldier might carry all his possessions with him. Furthermore, the items a German soldier might be allowed to retain were at the discretion of his captors once he became a prisoner.

For both practical and precautionary reasons, equipment items such as entrenching tools, cartridge pouches, helmets, and gas masks would not have made the journey to Texas. Other equipment—such as belts, belt support straps, mess kits, canteens, bread bags, shelter quarters, and rucksacks—that still had utilitarian value made its way to the United States.

The following section provides a description of the types of German field equipment brought to Camp Hearne. While some pieces of equipment are obvious and well preserved, such as canteens and mess kits, much of the equipment taken to the camp was made of cloth and leather that deteriorated over the years. Thus, only the metal hardware remains, such as a variety of metal rings, clips, hooks, and buttons (table 7). From these hardware pieces it is possible to determine the types of field equipment that were brought to the camp. Identifications were made by matching hardware recovered in excavations at the camp with descriptions, photographs, and actual pieces of German-issued equipment.

Belts and Buckles
The belt worn by enlisted men and NCOs was 4.5 centimeters wide and made of smooth, black leather. Belts issued to troops in tropical climates were made of tan webbed cloth. A removable buckle was attached to the belt by either a leather or cloth tongue that had several holes for making adjustments. The other end of the belt was fitted with a metal catch. In the field, the belt was used to carry equipment (Angolia and Schlicht 1987, 49–55; 1998, 163–67; Angolia 2001, 131–45).

Three Luftwaffe belt buckles were recovered at Camp Hearne. These are rectangular buckles (sixty-five by forty-eight millimeters) made of stamped aluminum. Each buckle has two movable prongs and a slotted bar on the reverse for the belt attachment (fig. 34, item h). The fronts feature an oval wreath surrounding an eagle with outstretched wings and holding a swastika in its claws.

Table 7. Field Equipment and Hardware Found at Camp Hearne

Field Equipment Item	Number Recovered
Belt buckle	3
Catch	1
Eyelets	2
Complete mess kit (pot with lid)	7
Mess kit pot	12
Mess kit lid	5
Mess kit handle	5
Mess kit bail attachment	3
Canteen flask	63
Canteen screw cap	45
Canteen cup	9
Spoon	2
Can opener	1
Folding fork and spoon combination	2
Fat container	1
O-ring (3.5 cm diameter)	6
O-ring (4.5 cm diameter)	1
D-ring (2 cm)	14
D-ring (3 cm)	49
D-ring (4 cm)	13
D-ring (5.5 cm)	4
D-ring (6 cm)	15
Elongated D-ring (3 cm)	12
Elongated D-ring (3.5 cm)	4
D-ring with hook	21
Triangle ring	6
Canteen clip	21
Rucksack clip	2
Bread bag clip	11
Strong hook (sewn type)	3
Strong hook (riveted type)	15
Front belt hook	13
Rucksack front belt support hook	8
T-hook	4
Friction buckle	9
Single-prong buckle (1.7 cm long by 1.4 cm wide)	1
Single-prong buckle (2.3 cm long by 1.7 cm wide)	24
Single-prong buckle (2.5 cm long by 1.9 cm wide)	9
Single-prong buckle (2.8 cm long by 2.1 cm wide)	4
Single-prong buckle with center bar	4

Table 7. *continued*

Field Equipment Item	Number Recovered
Rectangular open slide	4
Rectangular bar slide	18
Rectangular bar slide with nipple	3
Square bar slide	15
Three-hole deep dish buttons	177
Four-hole deep dish buttons	63
Canteen cover strap stud	20
Utility strap stud	4
Rivet	23
Double button	7
Steel rivets	7
Press snaps	81
Drawstring tip	6
Strap tip	9
Smaller grommets (2 cm diameter)	236
Larger grommets (3 cm diameter)	38
Gas tablet container	1
Total Items	1,146

The area within the oval wreath is domed and the entire background is finely pebbled. Two styles of Luftwaffe buckles are present. The first style (n = 1), pre-dating 1938, has down-turned tail feathers. The second style (n = 2), introduced in 1938, has flared tail feathers (fig. 34, item h; Angolia 2001, 131–45; Angolia and Schlicht 1998, 163–67; Davis 1991, 215–16). Luftwaffe enlisted men and non-commissioned officers wore both styles of buckle (Angolia 2001; Davis 1991).

Also found at the site was an aluminum belt catch (fig. 34, item b). This piece was attached to the end of the belt and hooked to the buckle (Angolia 2001, 131–45; Bender and Law 1973, 183; Scipion and Bastien 1994, 10). Two eyelets from a tropical web belt were found in close proximity to one of the belt buckles. These eyelets are one centimeter in diameter and are made of a light metal alloy. Traces of the cotton web material are still attached to the eyelets. These pieces are from the adjustment holes on the belt and accommodated the prongs on the back of the buckle.

Belt Supports with Auxiliary Straps
Belt supports with auxiliary straps, commonly referred to as "Y-straps," were first introduced in April, 1939. Belt supports with auxiliary straps were designed as a platform on which equipment loads appropriate to various missions could

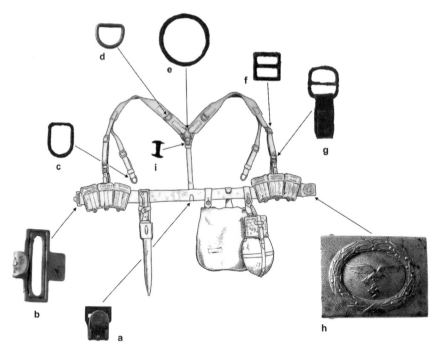

Fig. 34. *Typical combat field equipment carried by German soldiers in North Africa. Two cartridge cases were carried on the belt along with a bayonet and frog, bread bag, and canteen. Supporting the heavy equipment on the belt was the belt support with auxiliary straps (Y-straps). Shown here is the hardware from a belt and Y-straps found at Camp Hearne: a. strong hook (sewn type); b. belt catch; c. elongated D-ring; d. D-ring; e. O-ring; f. rectangular bar slides; g. front belt hooks; h. belt buckle; and i. double button. The cloth and leather portions of the belt and straps rotted away and the bayonet, frog, and cartridge pouches were discarded in the field (modified from Rottman and Volstad 1995).*

be accommodated (fig. 34; Angolia and Schlicht 1987, 66–70; Bender and Law 1973, 211–15; Scipion and Bastien 1996, 11).

Two varieties of belt support straps with auxiliary straps were made: one of black leather and the other of reed green or olive drab webbing. The leather supports were issued to troops in Europe. The webbed supports were first issued in 1940 to troops fighting in North Africa and, as the war progressed, to all troops due to shortages of leather.

The leather belt supports with auxiliary straps were composed of a vertical back strap and two front straps attached to a 4.5-centimeter-diameter O-ring that rode high on the back. An O-ring is a circular ring made of tubular aluminum or steel (fig. 34, item e). The vertical back strap was attached to the O-ring by a steel double button with two rounded heads (one head smaller than the other) attached to the ends of a thin steel rod (fig. 34, item i). The distance between the heads ranges from 1.5 to 1.7 centimeters. These were inserted in one of six buttonholes to adjust the length of the strap. Riveted on the end of this strap was a strong hook (fig. 34, item a) that attached beneath the center of the enlisted man's belt. A strong hook is made of thin aluminum or steel bent into a U-shape. These hooks have one or two rivets and are typically 3.5 centimeters high and 2 to 2.5 centimeters wide. The two front straps ran over the shoulders and had adjustable front belt hooks with pronged buckles on their ends, which hooked to D-rings on the cartridge pouch or support loops at the infantryman's waist belt. Two D-rings (3 centimeters long on the straight edge) were sewn on the front straps a short distance above the O-ring. D-rings are pieces of solid tubular aluminum or steel that were fashioned into a D-shaped ring. Two auxiliary straps were attached to the front straps with a rivet 28 centimeters from the O-ring. These rivets, made of either aluminum or steel, have a round and slightly domed head from which extends a metal rod onto which was pressed a corresponding round head. They are typically one centimeter thick and the heads are 1.4 centimeters in diameter. The auxiliary straps were adjusted through the use of a double button or rectangular bar slide with nipple and eight buttonholes on each strap. On the end of the auxiliary straps were D-rings (3 centimeters long on the straight edge) that could be attached to a pack, the combat pack frame of the assault pack, or some wartime rucksacks. If none of these were being used, the auxiliary straps were tucked under the infantryman's belt.

The webbed supports were of the same design and construction as their leather counterparts, but with some differences in hardware. Four rectangular bar slides were used to adjust the front and auxiliary straps (fig. 34, item f). Rectangular bar slides are made of flat, 2-millimeter-thick aluminum or steel. They are rectangular, slightly convex, and have a central bar. The frame is 5 millimeters wide and the edges are slightly rounded. These slides ranged from 3.3 to 3.5 centimeters long and 2.7 to 2.85 centimeters wide. Two front belt hooks (without prongs) were used on the ends of the front straps (fig. 34, item g). Front belt hooks are of two-piece construction with an upper fixed bar-type buckle made of flat steel attached to a lower piece of flat steel that is bent into a U shape. The loose fit allows the two pieces to pivot. The two-piece front belt hook has an overall length of 7.5 centimeters. The upper buckle is 3.5 centimeters wide and the lower hook is two centimeters wide. A 3.5-centimeter-diameter O-ring was used on the back to connect the three main straps. A strong hook was sewn onto the back strap. These strong hooks are made of a thin sheet of steel that was bent into a U shape (fig. 34, item a). One end is rectangular and wider (28.6 millimeters), than the other end (18.2 millimeters), which is rounded and approximately 5 millimeters shorter. There is a narrow slit near the top of the wider end that served to attach the hook to a cloth strap. Elongated D-rings were used on the auxiliary straps. Elongated D-rings are D-shaped rings made of solid tubular aluminum or steel that have a more elongated loop (fig. 34, item c). The straight bar of the elongated D-ring measures 3 centimeters. Two regular D-rings were used on the back straps (fig. 34, item d).

Utility "Greatcoat" Straps
Greatcoat straps were black leather straps used to secure the greatcoat roll, which consisted of a blanket and tent quarter in summer with the addition of a great-

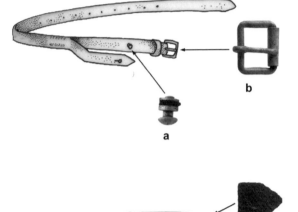

Fig. 35. At the top is a great-coat utility strap (leather issue) and the hardware (a. strap stud; b. single-prong buckle) from this type of strap found at Camp Hearne. At the bottom is a greatcoat utility strap (tropical issue) and associated hardware (c. strap stud; d. strap tip; e. friction buckle) found at Camp Hearne (modified from Rottman and Volstad 1995).

b

a

d

c

e

coat in autumn and winter (fig. 35; Angolia and Schlicht 1987, 91; 1998, 182; Scipion and Bastien 1996, 11). The greatcoat strap secured these items using a single-prong buckle (fig. 35, item b). These buckles have a rectangular frame (2.5 by 1.9 centimeters) made of tubular aluminum or steel. The edges of the frame are rounded and a single pivoting prong is attached to the bottom of one of the long edges. On the other long edge of most buckles is a lightweight piece of metal that is crimped loosely around the frame that rolls. Some buckles do not have this roller. A buttoning strap was sewn to the main strap and secured by a utility strap stud. These studs are made of steel or aluminum. They are 1.3 centimeters long with a prominent dome at one end and a 0.9-centimeter-diameter rivet on the other end (fig. 35, items a and c). The buttoning strap was used to attach the greatcoat strap to the loops on packs, rucksacks, and combat pack frames. Additionally, the strap was used to secure a wide variety of other equipment.

A tropical version of the greatcoat strap for use in North Africa was manufactured of an olive green or reed green webbing (fig. 35). The web greatcoat strap had a friction buckle in place of the single-prong buckle and had a metal strap tip at the end of the strap to keep it from fraying during use. Friction buckles are made of steel and are rectangular (2.7 by 3.3 centimeters) with a fixed central bar (fig. 35, item e). Attached to the central bar is a thin, flat piece of metal, serrated at one end and squared at the other, that pivots. Strap tips are small (2.7 by 2.2 centimeter) steel fittings that are squared at one end and pointed at the other (fig. 35, item d). Later in the war, the webbed version became the general-issue greatcoat strap for the entire German army (Rottman and Volstad 1995, 19).

Bread Bags

The bread bag was a canvas single- or double-compartment haversack (fig. 36). The bag was constructed of a single front/back piece, sewed to two wedge-shaped sidepieces and a front flap. The flap covered the entire outside of the bag, providing added protection from the elements. The bottom corners of the bag and flap were rounded. The army bags were made of a field gray to olive green canvas. Luftwaffe bags were blue (Angolia and Schlicht 1987, 98–102; 1998, 182–85; Bender and Law 1973, 208–209; Rottman and Volstad 1995, 12; Scipion and Bastien 1996, 13).

At the top of the bag were cloth straps for attaching the bag to the infantryman's belt. These cloth straps were folded over the belt and secured by two metal three-hole deep-dish buttons (figs. 31, item a, and 36, item a) sewn onto the base of the strap. The three-hole deep-dish buttons are stamped from a single piece of aluminum or a light metal alloy. They are seventeen millimeters in diameter and have a deep straight-walled dish with a beveled rim. At the top and center of the bag was a short strap with a strong hook (fig. 36, item b) riveted to it that secured the bag to the infantryman's belt. Located on the bag just below the cloth loops were two D-rings with a three-centimeter-long straight edge (fig. 36, item f). These were used for attaching the canteen and mess kit. Two leather or web tabs sewn near the base of the flap on either side served as additional points for securing the canteen and mess kit.

On the back of the bag near the top corners were two D-rings with a 2-centimeter-long straight edge used for attaching the shoulder strap. The shoul-

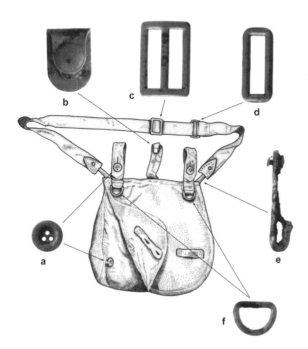

Fig. 36. Shown here is a bread bag and its carrying strap. The following hardware from a bread bag and its associated strap was found at Camp Hearne: a. three-hole deep-dish button; b. strong hook (riveted type); c. rectangular bar slide; d. rectangular open slide; e. bread-bag clip; and f. D-ring (modified from Rottman and Volstad 1995).

der strap was used to carry the bread bag when it was not attached to the belt. The shoulder strap had a bread bag clip riveted on either end. These clips are slender, spring-loaded clips that measure 5.7 by 0.7 centimeters and are made of aluminum or steel (fig. 36, item e). A stiff steel tang is riveted to the top of the hook. A rectangular open slide (fig. 36, item d) connected the two separate portions of the cloth shoulder strap, allowing the longer portion to be looped back through a rectangular bar slide (fig. 36, item c) measuring 3.9 by 2.7 centimeters used for adjustment purposes. Rectangular open slides have a flattened aluminum or steel rectangular frame. Most are 1.6 by 3.9 centimeters.

Two leather straps with two buttonholes were sewn on the underside of the flap in the lower corners. These straps were secured to two metal three-hole deep-dish buttons (fig. 36, item a) that were sewn to the lower corner of the bag. A longer leather strap was sewn to the back of the bag and attached to another metal three-hole deep-dish button sewn to the front edge of the bag. The Afrika Korps used a tropical version of the bread bag that had web rather than leather straps.

Mess Kits
A complete mess kit consists of a lower pot body and an upper lid with handle. The shallow lid is slightly larger than the pot and fits over a slightly recessed lip on the body of the pot. A folding handle attached to the lid locks the lid onto the pot. Eyes on the top and base of the handle allow a strap to pass through to hold the lid and pot together, allowing them to be affixed for carrying. A black leather or web mess kit strap fitted with a single-prong roller buckle (1.9 by 2.5 centimeters) or a friction buckle was used to secure the mess kit to the bread bag or Y-straps. A metal strap end was also present when a web strap was used to secure the mess kit. The pot is fitted with a wire bail attached with two oval-shaped aluminum fixtures with eyes. The pot has a 1.7-liter capacity with gradient marks for each half-liter impressed on the front side. The kit is kidney-shaped in cross section with an overall height of fifteen centimeters, 13.8 centimeters of which is the pot. The pot measures sixteen centimeters wide and nine centimeters deep (Angolia and Schlicht 1987, 92; 1998, 186; Bender and Law 1973, 211; Fisch 1989, 116; Rottman and Volstad 1995, 13).

Mess kits were initially constructed entirely of aluminum. As the war progressed, however, bails and handles were made of steel. Near the end of the war, the entire kit was being produced in steel. The manufacturer markings and production dates are found on both the handle hinge and on the left bail attachment. Early production kits were painted dark gray until a new production order in 1941 stipulated that they be painted olive green. Some kits for use in North Africa were painted sand color (Rottman and Volstad 1995, 13).

Seven complete mess kits with both pot and lid were recovered at Camp Hearne (fig. 37). Of these, five were painted olive green, one was painted black, and one had an olive green body with a black top. All seven of the kits had personalized markings on either the pot or lid, or both. The following names appear: Müller, Rilkes, Paul Keinallg, Lammel, Kuhl, G. Plass. One mess kit lid

Fig. 37. An open German mess kit is depicted here. At left is the inside of the mess-kit lid with handle extended; at right is the reverse side of the mess-kit pot. Camp Hearne Collection, Texas A&M University.

had the initials "GR" inscribed over a skull and crossbones (probably representing a soldier in a panzer unit). Dates on mess kits recovered from Camp Hearne range from 1937 to 1942. Twelve mess kit pots without lids, five mess kit lids without handles, one aluminum and four steel mess kit handles, and three individual bail attachments were also recovered.

Other Mess Equipment

A number of complete and fragmentary eating utensils were recovered. These include spoon and fork combinations, single spoons, a can opener, and a fat container.

One complete spoon (fig. 38, item c) and one handle of a German-issue spoon were recovered. They are made of stainless steel. Both of the handles are marked with the German army eagle holding a swastika. The complete specimen has the manufacturer's code and date ("T.W.S. 41") marked near the spoon end. The owner's name ("Asch") is inscribed on the end of the handle.

One large can opener made of stainless steel was found (fig. 38, item b). The sides of the handle are bent up and slightly over at the top of the edge forming a small ridge. The result is a "hollow" track channel into which a knife, spoon, and fork were inserted for compact storage (Angolia and Schlicht 1987, 95–96; De Lagarde 1994, 33; Lee 1992, 101). This utensil combination is called an Essbesteck. The spoon described above is part of this set. The handle of the opener is marked with the German army eagle and swastika, the manufacturer's code

Fig. 38. German eating uten-sils: a. folding fork and spoon combination; b. can opener; and c. spoon. Note the eagle and swastika symbol on b and c, and the date. Camp Hearne Collection, Texas A&M University.

and date "H.& K. H. 42 ROSTFREI," and personalized with the initials "HW" scratched into the metal surface.

Two examples of a fork-and-spoon combination made of lightweight aluminum were recovered (fig. 38, item a). Each piece was made separately and attached near the ends of their handles by a rivet. On one set, the maker's mark "W.J.S." and date of manufacture "40" (1940) are present on the back of the fork. The personal initials "LA" also are inscribed on the fork. The other set is stamped with an army eagle proof mark and the date "WaA45." Both are described as the soldier's folding fork and spoon set (Lee 1992, 101) and are a carryover from a similar model used during World War I (Angolia and Schlicht 1987, 95).

Three fragments of a small plastic container known as a Fettbüchse were recovered. The fragments are orange colored and include two bottom pieces and one lid piece. The Fettbüsche is a round, flat container measuring four centimeters deep and having a diameter of ten centimeters that was used to store fat and butter while in the field. It had a screw lid made of white, yellow-white, orange, or brownish Bakelite (Angolia and Schlicht 1987, 98; 1998, 189).

Canteens with Drinking Cups
The standard-issue water field flask (canteen) is oval in shape and has a 0.8-liter capacity. It is twenty-five centimeters tall, 15.8 centimeters wide, and seven cen-

timeters deep. Canteens were originally made of aluminum, with wartime variations including flasks made of steel, enameled steel, as well as some bottles covered with a dark brown plastic-impregnated wood. Both aluminum and Bakelite caps were screwed on to the threaded necks of the field flask (Angolia and Schlicht 1987, 102; 1998, 189–92; Rottman and Volstad 1995, 12).

A drinking cup was carried inverted over the neck of the flask. Typically, this was a three-eighths-liter, oval-shaped drinking cup made of aluminum painted black or olive green. A folding aluminum or steel handle made of two wire loops was riveted to the back of the cup. On the front was riveted a one-centimeter-wide metal eye used to accommodate the securing strap. Later variations of the drinking cup included smaller, round tapered Bakelite and aluminum cups (Angolia and Schlicht 1987, 102; Bender and Law 1973, 210; Rottman and Volstad 1995, 13).

Sixty-two aluminum canteens (fig. 39, item f), one steel canteen, and one resin composition canteen were recovered at Camp Hearne. All but two were of the standard 0.8-liter size. Manufacturer's marks and dates are found stamped on the neck of the bottles and on the tops of both aluminum and Bakelite screw caps. Twenty-three flask manufacturers were identified, with manufacturing dates ranging from 1937 to 1943. In addition to manufacturer's markings, some

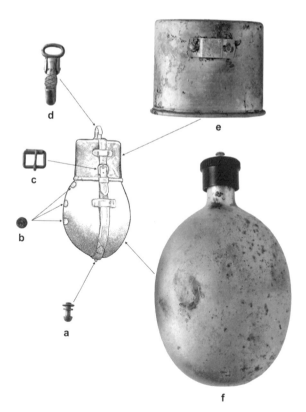

Fig. 39. A canteen with cover, drinking cup, and carrying strap are shown here. The following items depicted above were found at Camp Hearne: a. canteen cover strap stud; b. press snap; c. single-prong buckle; d. canteen clip; e. cup; and f. flask (modified from Rottman and Volstad 1995).

of the flasks and caps have personal identification markings. Four flasks and two caps were marked. Flask markings include the names, "C Eidjen Müller" and "WEIZEN MÜLLER," and the initials "H" and "P.W."

Also recovered was a World War I German-issue water bottle dated "4/14." This is similar in appearance and size to the World War II–issue canteens. Also found was a 1.5-liter German medical canteen. This again is similar in appearance to the other canteens, only larger in size.

A total of twenty-nine screw caps were found with flasks: ten made of aluminum and nineteen of black Bakelite. Sixteen additional whole and fragmentary black Bakelite screw caps were recovered. The caps represent seventeen manufacturers and the production dates stamped on them range from 1937 to 1942.

Nine cups (seven aluminum and two Bakelite) were recovered. Six of the aluminum cups are of the typical World War II–issue oval shape (fig. 39, item e). Five of the aluminum cups are painted black and one is unpainted aluminum. Four separate manufacturers are represented, with dates ranging between 1936 and 1940. Two of the cups have personalized markings, including a specimen etched with a swastika, and another marked with the initial "G" on the front. The last aluminum cup is of the smaller, rounded and tapered variety and is painted black. One World War I German-issue aluminum cup also was recovered. It is similar in appearance and size to the World War II–issue cups, but is more narrow and elongated (Fisch 1989, 117).

Twelve black fragments and three brown fragments represent the remains of two Bakelite round and tapered cups. Of the black fragments, eight were refitted to form part of one cup. The other four black fragments were found in close proximity to those units containing the eight refitted pieces, suggesting that they are probably from the same cup. The three brown fragments are also from three closely grouped excavation blocks and probably represent pieces of a single cup.

To carry the canteen, a brown, gray, or olive felt insulating cover was issued with aluminum and steel flasks. The flask could be removed from the cover via a slit on the upper left side secured by three to five press snaps (fig. 39, item b). These are round, 1.2-centimeter-diameter snaps made of bronze, aluminum, or steel. The plain aluminum and steel snaps have smooth domed faces that were painted black. The faceplates of the bronze snaps were engraved with four diamonds that point in the cardinal directions. A dot was engraved between each of the diamonds and dots also ring the edge of the faceplate. These decorated snaps were also painted black. Leather loops were sewn to the front and back of the cover to anchor a vertical, black leather securing strap secured by a metal canteen cover strap stud riveted to the bottom of the cover. The canteen cover strap studs are 2-centimeter-long aluminum or steel studs with a prominent domed head (fig. 39, item a). The stud has one flange at the base of the post and a second flange six millimeters from the base. Between these flanges is a free-moving washer. To the other end of this strap was sewn a single-prong buckle (1.7 by 1.4 centimeters or 2.3 by 1.7 centimeters) with roller (fig. 39, item c).

The second half of the securing strap was sewn to the back of the cover with the lower end also fastening to the flask cover strap button. The upper portion of this strap secured the cup by threading through the wire handles and metal eye of the cup, and was then buckled to the front strap. A canteen clip sewn to the rear strap was used to attach the flask to a bread bag D-ring. The basic canteen clip is a 6.5-centimeter-long aluminum or steel hook with an oval ring attached to one end (fig. 39, item d). A broad tang is hinged below the oval ring and butts against the hook. By pushing down on the tang and compressing the spring, the tang separates from the hook, allowing it to be attached to a D-ring.

Wartime variations included the use of web securing straps with friction buckles and ends reinforced by metal strap tips. Webbed securing straps were initially fitted to tropical covers and were used with the resin composition bottles. These resin flasks were fitted with an additional horizontal webbed strap, as were some of the later aluminum and steel flasks.

Shelter Quarters/Ponchos

The shelter quarter was a versatile piece of field equipment that was used for shelter, as a ground cover, or as a foul weather cape (fig. 40). The shelter quarter was made of a triangular piece of water-repellent cotton gabardine twill measuring 203 centimeters long at the sides and 250 centimeters long at the base. The material was printed with a dark camouflage pattern with greens and browns on one side and with a light camouflage pattern on the reverse. A limited number of all green or all tan shelter quarters were issued to troops serving in North Africa (Angolia and Schlicht 1987, 106–11; 1998, 193–98; Rottman and Volstad 1995, 18; Scipion and Bastien 1996, 12).

On each of the sides of the shelter quarter were twelve buttonholes and twelve metal four-hole deep-dish buttons (figs. 31, item e, and 40, item a). These are identical in construction to the three-hole deep-dish buttons described earlier, but with four instead of three holes. Along the base were an additional six buttonholes and six metal four-hole deep-dish buttons. The buttons and buttonholes along the sides were used for attaching multiple shelter quarters together to make larger tents. The buttons and buttonholes along the base were used to attach the shelter quarters around the legs when it was being worn as a foul weather cape. In the center of the shelter quarter was a slit closed by double, overlapping flaps for the wearer's head when worn as a poncho.

One large grommet was attached in each of the three corners and two small grommets were affixed in each corner and in the center of the base. The grommets are of two-piece construction consisting of the main ring body and a free moving washer held on by a flange. The washer served to keep the ring from pulling through the material to which it was affixed. The small grommets have an outside diameter of 2 centimeters and the metal ring is about 0.5 centimeters wide (fig. 40, item b). These grommets are made of aluminum, a light metal alloy, or bronze. The large grommets have an outside diameter of 3 centimeters, with the metal ring ranging from 0.7 to 0.8 centimeters wide (fig. 40, item c). These large grommets are made of aluminum, a light metal alloy, or bronze. The grommets were used to secure tent stakes and poles (Rottman and Volstad 1995, 18).

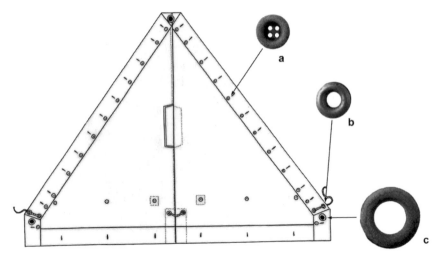

Fig. 40. Depicted here is a shelter quarter/poncho and related hardware. Buttons and grommets from several shelter quarters were recovered at Camp Hearne: a. four-hole deep-dish button; b. small grommet; c. large grommet (modified from Davis 1992).

Rucksacks

The rucksack was standard issue for all mountain troops throughout the duration of the war (figs. 41 and 42). A directive issued in late 1941 mandated the issue of rucksacks to troops serving on the eastern front and in North Africa, where conditions required the carrying of additional clothing and rations (Angolia and Schlicht 1987, 84–89; 1998, 179–81; Bender and Law 1973, 215; Rottman and Volstad 1995, 39).

The rucksack was made of water-repellent canvas. Army-issue rucksacks were olive green, reed green, gray, brown, and tan colored and Luftwaffe rucksacks were typically blue to gray-blue. Rucksacks had a single large compartment that was closed by a drawstring. This compartment was 50 centimeters high, 54 centimeters wide, and 10 centimeters deep at the bottom. It was closed with a drawstring threaded through sixteen small grommets measuring 2 centimeters in diameter (fig. 41, item c). The ends of the drawstring cord in prewar rucksacks were reinforced with drawstring tips to prevent fraying. Drawstring tips are small, 2-centimeter-long pieces of aluminum that were crimped around the ends of cloth cords (fig. 41, item b). A flap was sewn onto the back of the rucksack and secured by one to three leather straps that attached to corresponding (2.3 by 1.7 and 2.8 by 2.1 centimeters) single-prong buckles (fig. 41, item m)—with and without rollers—sewn to the front of the rucksack. Also sewn to the front of the rucksack was either a small, single compartment secured by two straps with single-prong buckles (2.3 by 1.7 and 2.8 by 2.1 centimeters) or two separate compartments, each with one strap. Single-prong buckles with a center bar were also used in place of the single-prong buckles. The single-prong buckles with a center bar have a rectangular frame with an upraised central bar

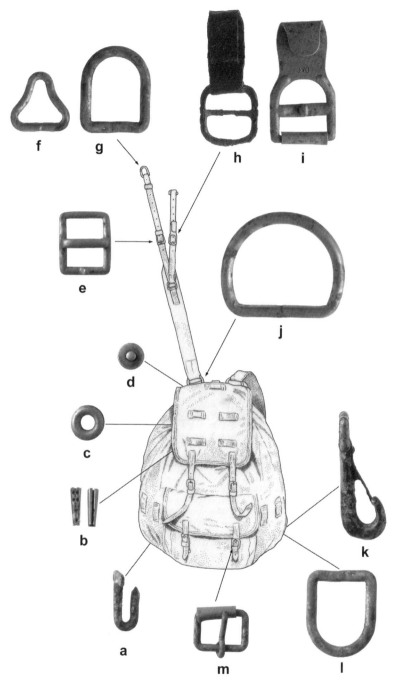

Fig. 41. Shown here is a typical rucksack and associated hardware found at Camp Hearne: a. T-hook; b. drawstring tips; c. small grommet; d. rivet; e. rectangular bar slide with nipple; f. triangle ring; g. elongated D-ring; h. front belt support hook; i. rucksack front belt support hook; j. D-ring; k. rucksack clip; l. elongated D-ring; and m. single-prong buckle (modified from Rottman and Volstad 1995).

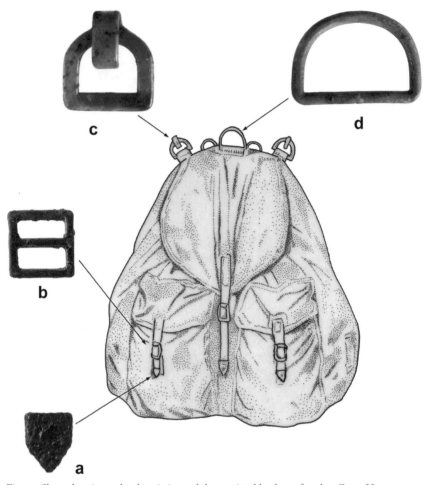

Fig. 42. Shown here is a rucksack variation and the associated hardware found at Camp Hearne: a. strap tip; b. square bar slide; c. D-ring with hook; and d. D-ring (modified from Rottman and Volstad 1995).

and a pivoting prong. Loosely crimped around one of the short outside frame edges is a piece of metal that rolls. These buckles are made of both aluminum and steel and occurred in two sizes: 3.1 by 2.9 and 3.7 by 2.8 centimeters. Inside, a pouch was sewn to the back of the bag and secured by two or three straps that fastened to metal four-hole deep-dish buttons.

Leather carrying straps were attached to two large D-rings (measuring 6, 5.5, or 4 centimeters along the flat edge) fastened to a leather tab on the upper center portion of the bag (fig. 41, item j). This tab was fastened by means of two metal rivets (fig. 41, item d) to an identical tab on the inside of the bag. Straps were made of two pieces of leather held together by a metal rivet similar in design to the combat belt support straps with auxiliary straps. Some bags had metal reinforcement plates between the leather. The two short straps on each side ended in front belt hooks as used on combat belt support straps (fig. 41, item h) or rucksack front belt support hooks (fig. 41, item i) specifically designed for the rucksack for attachment to ammunition pouches on the infantryman's belt. Rucksack front belt support hooks are made of aluminum or steel. The upper half of the hook is a molded buckle with a center bar. Riveted to the center bar is a small hook that points downward. On the upper bar of the aluminum buckle is an aluminum roller. Below the buckle is a wide, rounded hook made by folding the metal back onto itself toward the top of the buckle. The aluminum buckles are 3.8 centimeters wide at the buckle, 2.8 centimeters wide at the hook, and 6 centimeters long. The steel buckles are the same width as the aluminum specimens, but are one centimeter longer. The long straps were attached to the bottom of the rucksack. One strap had a rucksack clip (fig. 41, item k) that attached to an elongated D-ring (3.5 centimeters along its length) sewn to the lower corner (fig. 41, item l), while the other strap had a triangle ring (fig. 41, item f) or elongated D-ring (fig. 41, item g) that attached to a T-hook (fig. 41, item a) sewn into the corner of the bag. These straps were adjusted with a rectangular bar slide with nipple (fig. 41, item e). Rucksack clips are spring-loaded clips made of aluminum that have a rectangular attachment at its upper end (fig. 41, item k). A stiff steel tang riveted below the rectangular attachment closes at the hook. This clip is seven centimeters long. T-hooks are 3.3 centimeters long and extend from a 1.7-centimeter-wide tab (fig. 41, item a). The hook is T-shaped in appearance when viewed straight on, with the hook extending perpendicular to the flat face of the tab. Triangle rings are made of rounded aluminum or steel bar stock, bent into a triangular shape with one straight and two in-curving sides (fig. 41, item f). These rings measure 3 centimeters on each side. Rectangular bar sides with nipples are rectangular slides made of solid tubular aluminum or steel that measure 3.2 by 2.7 centimeters (fig. 41, item e). They have a raised center bar and a small nipple that extends from the center of one of the outside bars.

There were many wartime variations in rucksack design and construction. One type did not have built-in straps, but instead had four D-rings with hooks that attached directly to the combat belt support straps. D-Rings with hooks are D-shaped rings made of flat aluminum or steel that have a wide hook attached to the rounded end of the loop (fig. 42, item c). This hook protrudes from the flat metal of the D-ring and is bent back toward the straight portion of the ring. The straight bar of the ring measures four centimeters. Another variation had one large D-ring (5.5 or 6 centimeters along its flat edge) at the top middle and straps with adjustment buckles that ended in D-rings (3 centimeters along its flat edge). These attached to two D-rings with hooks at the base of the sack. Some tropical-issue rucksacks had webbed shoulder straps and securing straps. The shoulder straps had either square bar slides or friction buckles to adjust the length of the strap and both had metal strap tips. Square bar slides (fig. 42, item b) are made of flat, two-millimeter-thick steel or four-millimeter-thick aluminum. They are slightly convex and have a 3-centimeter-square frame that is bisected by a central bar. The frame is five millimeters wide and the edges are slightly rounded.

Early prewar rucksacks were issued with four linen bags and two shoe bags. They were made of muslin and had either a sewn-in drawstring or six large grommets measuring three centimeters in diameter for closure. These bags were discontinued during the war because of shortages of cloth.

Clothing Bags

The clothing bag was a field gray to olive green single compartment satchel with a flap made from a piece of canvas (fig. 43). The flap was secured to the body of the bag by two leather straps fastened to single-prong buckles (2.3 by 1.7 and 2.8 by 2.1 centimeters) with rollers. All seams and the edge of the flap were finished with black leather. A leather carrying strap was sewn onto the bag's top edge. Every soldier in combat was issued a clothing bag. Those in rear areas who were not issued a pack were issued two clothing bags (Angolia and Schlicht 1987, 105).

Other Field Equipment

A single gas tablet container was found at Camp Hearne. It is a rectangular plastic container made of brown Bakelite and measures 7.7 centimeters long, 2.5 millimeters wide, and 1.5 centimeters thick. There is a white powder substance (probably the remains of Losantine tablets) in the bottom of the container. These tablets were to be used to decontaminate the skin after a gas attack (Angolia and Schlicht 1987, 129).

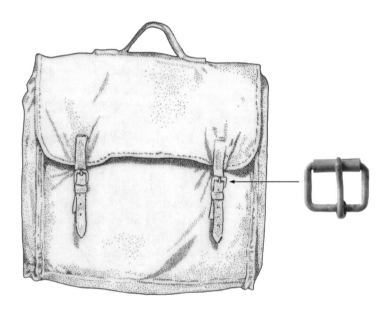

Fig. 43. Depicted here is a clothing bag and associated hardware (single-prong buckle) found at Camp Hearne (modified from Rottman and Volstad 1995).

Italian Military Equipment

Several pieces of equipment and equipment hardware identified as being of Italian origin were recovered. These items include a large capacity canteen, two mess kits, and hardware associated with rucksacks and packs. These pieces of equipment were picked up and used by German troops in North Africa.

The canteen is a two-liter water bottle constructed of aluminum and has rounded shoulders and a flat base. Welded to the top of the bottle is a fixture with aluminum lugs onto which a webbed shoulder strap was attached.

The mess kits are kidney-shaped and measure 13.5 centimeters long, 15.5 centimeters wide, and ten centimeters deep. They are made of aluminum and consist of two parts: the lower pot, which has a wire bail, and an upper lid (Fisch 1989, 120–21: Trye 1995, 132).

The hardware from Italian-made rucksacks and packs found in the POW compound included seven metal slides, five with a square frame and two with a rectangular frame and a middle cross bar. These slides were used to secure and adjust canvas straps on the haversack, infantry knapsack, and rucksack used by Italian troops. Two clips were also found. The clips consist of a rectangular piece of metal from which a clip is suspended. The rectangular ring was sewn to one side of a shoulder strap and the hook attached to a D-ring that was sewn to a cloth bag. Two steel studs measuring 1.5 centimeters tall and having a domed head and flat base were found. They were attached to round (three centimeter diameter) pieces of leather that were sewn to rucksacks, knapsacks, and haversacks. They were used to secure leather straps to close the main compartment of these bags (Fisch 1989, 54–57, 78–79; Trye 1995, 130–31).

French Military Equipment

German troops sometimes used French field equipment, so it is not surprising that a two-piece French mess kit including a pot with bail and lid with wire loop handle was found in the POW compound. The wire bail is attached to an aluminum post riveted to the sides of the pot (Fisch 1989, 114–15). The wire-loop handle, attached by a hinge riveted to the front of the lid, has a bend that slips onto the bottom of the pot to secure the lid to the pot. The aluminum mess kit's overall shape is rectangular. Assembled, it measures thirteen centimeters tall, sixteen centimeters wide, and ten centimeters deep. The kit is stamped on the bottom with a cartouche showing two bears and an inscription reading "MARQUE DEL 1939." The mess kit described here could have been procured in either France or North Africa.

Russian Military Equipment

One Russian mess kit pot was recovered from the prisoner compounds. This mess kit is of the same construction and size as German mess kit pots. The only difference between the two is the bail attachments. Russian mess kit bail attachments were secured to the pot by rivets driven from the inside rather than from the outside, in contrast to German bail attachments. The kit is unmarked

(Russian kits are only marked on the handles). The pot is pea green in color, typical of Russian manufacture (Fisch 1989, 124–25). The pot has the name "Adler" inscribed in it. A German soldier who served in Russia could have picked this mess kit there and then carried it with him to North Africa.

American Military Equipment

Little American field equipment was found in the POW compounds. All items that were recovered were army-issue eating utensils. Part of one fork, with most of the handle missing, was found. Four partial and one complete spoon also were recovered. The four partial specimens are all missing their handles. All of the spoons are of different sizes and vary in the form of their handles. One is marked "U.S." on the end of the handle. Three utensil handles were also found. Two of these handles belong to the U.S. M1926-type knife, fork, and spoon set. This type is identified by a prominent oval hole in the handle with "U.S." stamped below the hole. Both handles have been cut above the hole and thus the exact utensil cannot be determined (Lewis 1993, 208).

Equipment Dumps

A number of concentrations of German and Italian field equipment were found at Camp Hearne. These represent small dumps where field equipment was intentionally discarded and buried in shallow pits. Twelve buried equipment concentrations were discovered during the course of the fieldwork. The dumps were found in both Compounds 1 and 2, next to barracks, in front of barracks, under barracks, or adjacent to foundations. None were found in Compound 3. Paul Russell reports that he found at least ten other dumps within the POW compounds that were filled with canteens and mess kits.

In all cases, field equipment was placed in small pits about ten to thirty centimeters deep. The size of the pits in which the equipment was buried depended on the size and amount of equipment to be buried. The most commonly buried items were canteens, mess kits, rucksacks, bread bags, and straps. Equipment was then either placed directly into the hole or, in several cases, placed in a burlap sack and then buried. The canteens and mess kits were crushed before burial in many of the dumps. It is not clear at this time who buried this equipment or when and why it was buried.

The Germans interviewed during the course of this project had no recollection of field equipment being buried by their fellow prisoners. It seems more likely that burying equipment was an expedient means of disposal used by American personnel charged with cleaning up the camp as the buildings were sold and relocated in 1946. This speculation is supported by the fact that four of the dumps were found in areas that would have been beneath barracks. Although prisoners did have access to the areas beneath their barracks, the limited clearance would seem to preclude the digging of holes for burying equipment. In contrast, the prisoners may have made the dumps located outside the barracks. In one hole, a Luftwaffe belt buckle was carefully placed at the bottom and covered with a burlap sack filled with field equipment (Dump 5). The German

POWs most likely created this particular dump, because an American probably would have kept the buckle as a souvenir.

The artifacts in each dump were examined and the type of equipment identified by the hardware associated with it. Most of the metal items were specific to a particular piece of equipment. For example, small grommets were used only on rucksacks or shelter quarters; O-rings were used only on belt support straps; snaps, domed studs, and a specific clip type were used only on canteens; and distinctive hooks and rings were used exclusively on either bread bag or rucksack straps. Equipment hardware is identified for each dump. By comparing the list of recovered hardware to the known makeup of pieces of equipment described in the previous section, we were able to determine the approximate number of equipment items that were buried and whether they were complete or fragmentary at the time of burial. It is interesting to note that canteen covers and carrying straps, straps and buckles from rucksacks, and straps from the belt support straps were often missing. Because recovery at the dumps was complete, this indicates that the prisoners were salvaging straps, material, and hardware from these equipment pieces for other needs at Camp Hearne. A list of the items buried at each dump is provided in Table 8.

In addition to the twelve dumps with multiple pieces of field equipment, eighteen individual canteens were intentionally buried within the POW compounds. Some were buried without caps, others with caps, and some were buried with all the canteen carrying hardware (clip, snaps, and stud). Most ap-

---

Table 8. Contents of Dumps at Camp Hearne

	Dump Number										
Item	*1*	*2*	*3*	*4*	*5*	*6*	*7*	*8*	*9*	*10*	*11*
German canteen flask	5	8	1	1	—	1	5	1	7	7	6
German canteen cover	1	4–6	1	2	1	2	1	1	1–2	2	6
German canteen cup	—	—	—	1	—	—	—	—	—	—	—
German mess kit	3	2	—	1	—	—	—	—	—	2	3
German belt and buckle	—	—	—	—	1	—	—	—	—	—	—
German rucksack	—	3	1	2	2	—	—	—	—	—	3–4
German belt support strap	1	—	—	2	1	—	—	—	—	—	2
German utility strap	—	—	—	—	2	—	—	—	—	—	6
German bread bag	—	—	—	—	—	—	—	—	—	—	5
German bread bag strap	—	—	—	—	1	—	—	—	—	—	3
Italian canteen	—	—	—	—	—	1	—	—	—	—	—
Italian rucksack	—	—	—	—	1	—	—	—	—	—	2
Italian strap	—	—	—	—	—	1	—	—	—	—	—
American beer bottle	—	—	—	—	—	—	—	1	—	—	—

pear to have been buried as a means of discarding them. One canteen, however, was intentionally stashed. It was found standing upright next to the brick footer at the entrance to the barrack in Compound 1.

One Italian and eight German mess kits were also intentionally buried within the POW compounds. Some were just pots without lids and others were complete. One German mess kit was stashed next to the brick footer of a barrack in Compound 3. It was buried upright and immediately adjacent to a brick support.

The reason for the isolated and intentional burial of pieces of field equipment is unknown. Perhaps these items were buried when the Germans attempted to thwart American efforts to find the hidden broadcast station with their metal detectors as described in Chapter 2.

POW-Made Items

Although the POWs at Camp Hearne brought a variety of military equipment and personal effects with them and could purchase many items at the camp PX, they also manufactured many of the things they needed or desired (fig. 44). This was possible because of the wide variety of skills and previous training these men had received before they were captured. As already pointed out, the prisoners made shortwave radios, a broadcasting station, Nazi flags, a pipe organ for the church, furniture, military uniforms and caps, orchestra and

Fig. 44. Drawing done by Werner Kritzler of a POW undertaking an art project in the recreation room, perhaps making military insignia. Camp Hearne Collection, Texas A&M University.

sports uniforms, theatrical stage supplies and clothing, and many other items. Many of these things are seen in the photographs and remembered by the POWs. However, a number of other POW-made items were found at the site. These include military badges and insignia, national emblems, stamps, identification tags, rings, and a number of other items.

Many of the POWs remembered fellow prisoners making insignia from lead and aluminum. Tin cans, mess kits, and canteens were cut and shaped, and lead was melted and cast. Hugo Wannemacher recalled that there were men in the camp who were goldsmiths, jewelers, and watch repairmen by trade, and that these men sometimes made decorative items from scrap metal. Because they all had a wealth of free time on their hands, some POWs dabbled in jewelry making while at Camp Hearne. Peter Spoden explained that it was relatively easy to do this because even a candle generated enough heat to melt lead. He recalled that various arts and crafts courses were taught and that several workshops were open to the prisoners. Camp life provided ample opportunities for the prisoners to experiment with making insignia. Some soldiers made them to replace lost insignia, as in the case of Willi Nellessen, who had traded his flak badge to an American soldier for cigarettes while on the ship to America. Heino Erichsen recalled that men made national emblems from the aluminum of their canteens and used them to embellish their hats. Fritz Pferdekämper-Geissel remembered items cast from lead being sold to guards for cigarettes and beer. Hugo Wannemacher concurred: "Much of it was really produced not for the Germans so much as for the guards in exchange for cigarettes or something."

Military Insignia and Badges

The POWs at Camp Hearne reproduced a variety of German military insignia and combat awards. In addition, the prisoners also manufactured American campaign ribbons for the guards.

National Emblems and Reich Cockade
Two insignia, the national emblem and the Reich Cockade, appeared on all German army, air force, and navy uniforms and hats. The national emblem was required to be worn over the right breast pocket (most commonly made of cloth) and a smaller version on all headgear (on caps both cloth and metal insignia were worn). The national emblem of the army and navy consisted of an eagle facing left with outstretched wings (the emblem of Germany) grasping a swastika encircled by a wreath (the emblem of the Nazi Party; Davis 1992, 10). The Luftwaffe design is of an eagle with outstretched wings (in a flying position) with its head facing left and tail feathers fanned outward (Davis 1991, 10–13). It grasps a swastika in its claws. The Reich Cockade was a circular "bull's-eye" type of insignia that displayed Germany's national colors (Davis 1991, 10–13; 1992, 10). It had a red center, white middle circle, and black outer ring.

Nine POW-manufactured national emblems (army, n = 6; figs. 45, items a and b, and 46, items a and b; Luftwaffe, n = 3; figs. 45, item d, and 46, items c and d) and one Reich Cockade (fig. 46, item f) were recovered in the POW

Fig. 45. Depicted here are items of POW insignia made of aluminum found at Camp Hearne: a and b. German army eagles; c. German Panzer skull; d. German Luftwaffe eagle; e, f, and g. miniature shields. Camp Hearne Collection, Texas A&M University.

compounds. Five are made of aluminum cut and shaped from canteens and mess kits, and four are molded from lead.

The detail on the aluminum pieces is excellent (fig. 45). Rows of incised parallel, crosshatched, and zigzag lines, and indented punctuation marks were used on the wings and chest to simulate feathers. The eagle's beak is often pronounced and well defined. The army specimens were created with the eagle clutching in its claws a circular disk into which has been punched zigzag lines along its edge to simulate a wreath and inside the wreath a swastika. In one specimen, the swastika is cut out of the wreath. These insignia were attached by thread (as indicated by small holes drilled at the ends of the wings), by adhesives, or prongs.

The specimens cast from lead (fig. 46) are less detailed than their aluminum counterparts. The heads are indistinct and long horizontal grooves and ridges shape most of the specimens' wing feathers. One specimen, however, has distinct simulated feathers on the wing, body, and tail. The wreath held in the eagle's talons of the army insignia has either a narrow smooth border around its rim or detailed leaves, and the swastika is raised. These insignia were mounted or attached onto something as indicated by prongs on the reverse side of the wings or holes that were drilled through the wings. Both Luftwaffe insignia were cast with the eagle facing to the right, opposite to that prescribed by air force regulations.

The swastika is found on all army insignia and on only one item of Luftwaffe insignia. It is interesting to note that the swastika is missing from the claws of two of the Luftwaffe specimens. It appears that these emblems were produced without a swastika. This is unusual and may represent a POW who wanted to show his affiliation with the German air force but not the Nazi Party.

A single Reich Cockade made of lead (Davis 1991, 10–13; 1992, 10) was found (fig. 46, item f). It is of circular design, composed of two rings having a ropelike wreath design with a plain circular center. Remnants of paint indicate that the center was painted red and the outer rings were black and white. This specimen was attached to a cap by prongs on the reverse side.

Panzer Death's Head

The Totenkopf or "death's head" insignia consists of a skull and crossbones. It was initially designed for use by Prussian cavalry regiments (Angolia and Schlicht 1984, 191–94; Feist and McGuirl 1996; Krawczyk 1999, 3; Pruett and Edwards 1993, 1) before the First World War. During the Second World War, it was adopted as the symbol of the German army's Panzer (tank) corps. These

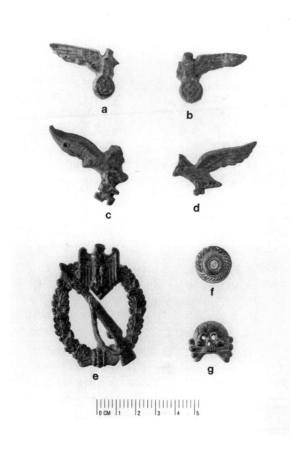

Fig. 46. The following lead POW insignia items were found at Camp Hearne: a and b. German army eagles; c, d. German Luftwaffe eagles; e. German Infantry Assault Badge; f. German Reich Cockade; g. German Panzer skull. Camp Hearne Collection, Texas A&M University.

"death's heads" were originally attached to cloth tabs sewn on the collars of the black wool tunics worn by tank crewmen. They were also affixed to the lapels of tropical tunics worn by panzer troops serving in North Africa. Three Panzer Totenkopf insignia were found in the POW compounds. Two are finished and the other is in an initial stage of manufacture. Two are made of lead and one of aluminum.

The first specimen is complete and made of lead (fig. 46, item g). It is a skull superimposed over a set of crossed leg bones. The skull displays excellent detail: the bones, eye sockets, teeth, and skull sutures are well defined. Holes have been carefully punched for the eyes and nose. There are two places on the back that contain remnants of soldering (probably for the attachment of a clasp). The second specimen is unfinished and is made of lead. The death's head occurs at the center of a lead disk that is 3.5 centimeters in diameter.

The third specimen is made of aluminum (fig. 45, item c). It is crudely cut out and asymmetrical. Vertical lines were engraved to imitate the teeth of the skull and circular indentations were punched for the eyes and nose. Otherwise, the specimen is smooth. There are no provisions for attachment and this particular piece may have been intended for an adhesive type of attachment.

Military Badges

Both the Infantry Assault Badge and Army Artillery Badge were replicated at Camp Hearne. The Infantry Assault Badge, created in December, 1939, was awarded to officers and enlisted men of the infantry and motorized infantry (Angolia 1976, 81). The badge consists of an oval wreath of oak leaves with the Wehrmacht eagle (an eagle with semioutstretched wings holding a swastika) at its top and a Mauser K98 rifle with bayonet affixed at an angle across the wreath. This badge was awarded to soldiers who participated in infantry assaults (including counterattacks), armed reconnaissance operations, hand-to-hand combat, or participated in the restoration of the combat line on three different days. It was worn on the left breast pocket of all uniform tunics (Angolia 1976, 80–83).

Two POW-made Infantry Assault Badges were found in the prison compounds (fig. 46, item e). Both badges are finished and made of lead. Both specimens are well executed with fine detail on the eagle, wreath, and rifle. For example, on the rifle, the bayonet, sling, and breach are clear and distinct. On the reverse side of both badges are areas at the top and bottom for the attachment of pin assemblies that are missing. One badge is 60.6 millimeters long, 46.9 millimeters wide, and 3 to 3.6 millimeters thick. The other specimen is slightly larger than the first, being 61 by 48 millimeters.

The Army Flak Badge was created in July, 1941, and awarded to members of gun crews. This badge consisted of an 88-mm gun surrounded by an oak-leaf wreath. Attached to the top of the wreath is the German Wehrmacht eagle and swastika. Award of the badge was based on an accumulated point basis, with sixteen points needed. For example, four points were awarded for the downing of an enemy aircraft without support. The badge could also be bestowed for any act of bravery in the conduct of performing an antiaircraft mission. This badge was worn on the lower left breast pocket of the tunic (Angolia 1976, 97–98).

Former POW Willi Nellessen retained a single specimen of this badge. It is made of lead and has a pin on the back for attachment to the tunic. The badge shows exceptional detail, almost of similar quality to an original badge. This specimen is similar in size to the Infantry Assault Badge.

Miniature Shields

Three miniature shields made by the POWs were found in the compounds. All were made of aluminum and one was painted. The use and meaning of these shields is not known. They may represent military, city, or family crests and could have been affixed to anything.

Shield 1 is made of aluminum and measures nineteen millimeters wide, twenty-six millimeters high, and one millimeter thick (fig. 45, item e). The shield has a rounded base, a flat top, and beveled edges. Around the shield's perimeter is a narrow border with an incised fine zigzag design. An incised stripe runs diagonally across the shield and roughly divides it into three parts. The central stripe has been painted a red/maroon color, the lower third a yellow/green color, and the upper portion a greenish yellow color. There is no means of attachment present other than by an adhesive. Shield 2 is very similar to the first shield, but is unpainted and slightly larger (fig. 45, item f).

Shield 3 is made of aluminum and has a pointed base, sharp corners, and a flat top (fig. 45, item g). It measures 22 millimeters wide, 25 millimeters tall, and 1 millimeter thick. The only design on this specimen is a 2-millimeter-wide incised zigzag design around its border. There are three holes for attachment, two at the upper corners and one at the base.

Manufacturing Debris

Ninety-eight pieces of cut aluminum were recovered at Camp Hearne (fig. 47). The majority of these are irregular fragments having no definable shape or design. Shapes vary from linear, square, triangular, and partly rounded to irregular. Sizes vary with shape, but most are two to twenty millimeters in length. The majority of these were cut with tin snips or a similar metal cutter, but six have been sawed. The cut marks were created from the cutting of large areas that did not require detailed workmanship. Sawing would have been performed on areas requiring more detailed cutting. Perhaps the fragments having saw marks are part of a cutaway design that is not definable. There are indications that other items besides national emblems were being produced and that some of the indefinable fragments could be part of that production effort.

One piece of cut aluminum contains a cutout of a complete Luftwaffe-style eagle. The remaining definable cutouts include two with upper wing and head fragments, two lower wing fragments, two upper wing fragments, one possible head fragment, and one possible swastika cutout. The latter two fragments probably represent a roughened cutout that would be detailed later. All of these fragments contain saw marks and several contain both saw and cut marks.

Fig. 47. Shown here is debris from the manufacture of aluminum insignia. Note the cut mess-kit pot and lid toward the back and the cut canteen bottle and spouts in the foreground.

American Campaign Ribbons from Toothbrush Handle Fragments

Four toothbrush handle fragments were found at the camp. These were short segments twelve to thirty-two millimeters long that had been cut from the base of the handles near the hole. Two of the fragments are orange, one is red, and the other is light blue. A former guard, John Luparelli, provided insight into the meaning of these fragments.

Luparelli recalled that some of the POWs quite skillfully cut the plastic handles of different colored toothbrushes into small little rectangular pieces and crafted American uniform campaign ribbons from them. "The toothbrush parts were the same colors as the ribbon itself," he explained. "We would give them toothbrushes and they would cut them up to match the colors of the ribbon. They would paste it all together and put a rod through it and it was the most beautiful thing. The guys wanted ones that were custom made." The guards were especially pleased with the plastic ribbon bars because they found they did not get as dirty as the standard cloth ribbons did with day-to-day use. The POWs gave, traded, or sold these ribbons to the guards.

Underground Nazi Newspaper Metal Stamp

A large rectangular stamp with raised lettering made on an 18.3 by 3.6 centimeter piece of lead (fig. 48) was found in the northern part of Compound 3. The thickness of the stamp is 5.2 millimeters and the area with the raised letters is six millimeters thick. The lettering is well executed and is a German font. Prisoners made the letters by chiseling and carving out the lead. Carved backward, the letters spell the words "DIE MAHNUNG." On the back of the stamp are two iron prongs that were probably used for attaching a wooden backing or handle.

This stamp was used to print the banner of Camp Hearne's underground Nazi newspaper, *Die Mahnung*. In an open letter to the editor of the official camp newspaper, *Der Spiegel*, POW Hans Bachmayer (1945) described the underground newspaper as follows: "Who does not, with a cold shuddering, remember the former secret newspaper of the obscure (*dunkelmaenner*) men '*Die Mahnung*,' the supreme task of which was the despotic political and personal tutelage, created for the political instigation and for keeping the P.W.'s under control by awakening fright and terror." Nazi elements in the camp used *Die Mahnung* as a propaganda tool to promote the German war effort, improve morale, and foster false hopes of victory in the minds of the POWs. Rudolf Hombeck (1945) ridiculed the absurd nature of some of this propaganda in a letter published in *Der Spiegel*. In it, he tells the following story: "At the beginning of this year (1945), I asked one of the comrades jestingly how the secret weapon [the Nazi's were supposedly developing] was proceeding. 'Oh,' he answered assiduously, 'once again, we have invented a new highly explosive flak ammunition that will destroy all the machines within a certain sphere of activity;' whereupon, I asked humbly, if such a thing was of decisive importance in the final stage of the war. Thereupon, this comrade replied somewhat disappointed: 'Well, you better read 'The Mahnung'; you will find every explanation in it.'"

The literal translation of *Die Mahnung* is "The Admonition" (or reminder or warning). While none of the former POWs interviewed recalled the name of the underground paper, they did offer some insight into the meaning of *Die Mah-*

Fig. 48. A metal stamp made by the POWs is shown here. The name of the underground Nazi newsletter, Die Mahnung, *is carved into this piece. Camp Hearne Collection, Texas A&M University.*

nung. Fritz Pferdekämper-Geissel suggested it might have served as a reminder not to dishonor or betray the Fatherland. Fritz Haus thought the phrase was a reminder and warning to carefully evaluate, think, and be cautious. He believed that in this context the phrase on the stamp was intended to remind the reader of his responsibilities as a German soldier. Like Haus, Ernst Froembsdorf thought the phrase was meant to reinforce a soldier's sense of duty. Former POW Hans Lammersdorf said that the phrase was a caution or threat: "If you get a Mahnung from your superior, it means you better straighten out. It's a kind of warning without drastic action yet. Action takes place if you don't listen—it's a warning."

Rubber Company Stamp

This is a small square stamp, measuring twenty by 17.1 millimeters and 6.4 millimeters thick. It was cut and carved from the rubber heal of an American boot. The stamp has a raised rim around its perimeter, the lower half contains a series of angled lines, and the upper half is inscribed "7 KP," the German abbreviation for 7th Company. This stamp was probably used on correspondence originating from the POW company's office.

Rings

Two homemade rings made from coins were recovered. These were made by cutting out the center of a large coin and then pounding or filing the edge to smooth and size the ring. One of the rings is in an early stage of manufacture, having only the center cut out. The second ring is a finished specimen. Its finish is smooth, but some markings left on its surface identify the coin as a French franc from the 1920s. The first ring is small enough to be worn. The second is much larger than the first and clearly too large for a finger. The use of this large diameter ring is unknown. Perhaps it was in its initial stages and had yet to be cut down to a smaller size.

Knives

A thin knife made from aluminum cut from a German mess kit was found at the Camp Hearne site. It measures 12.8 centimeters long, 0.7 millimeters wide (near the distal tip), and is 1.1 millimeters thick. The upper edge has been sawed from a wider piece of aluminum and the lower edge has been ground into a sharp cutting blade. This knife was probably made as a boot knife or hideaway knife often called a "shiv." Pieces of flatware were also modified into sharp knives. Several U.S. Army utensil handles found in the equipment section had been deliberately cut at an angle. This is debris from the manufacture of some unknown item. Perhaps the prisoners were making knives from these utensils.

Identification Tag and Wire Letter

A single diamond-shaped tag was found. It is made of aluminum and contains a small iron ring for suspension at its top. Three lines of numbers and letters were made by punching small holes into the metal. The top line reads "5600," the name "Steiner" is on the second line, and the third line contains two numbers. This object was probably used as an identification tag on a personal possession.

Also found was a wire letter made by loosely coiling two wires together and then shaping them into a circle approximately sixty-two millimeters in diameter. One end was bent in a straight line across the circle's center and the other end forms a short curl at the juncture, forming a large letter "G." Its exact function is not known. It may have been used to adorn a piece of POW art or some personal item.

Engraved Canteens and Mess Kits

A mess kit top and canteen, both of which had been engraved, were among the items recovered at Camp Hearne. Tony Painter has another example of an engraved canteen in his personal collection.

Engraved Mess Kit Top
This German mess kit top was found next to one of the recreation buildings in Compound 2. A design was engraved by carving smooth lines and by punching a series of nested curved lines into the top and side of the mess kit top. The owner's name, "RATH," framed by two palm trees is on the side of the mess kit top (fig. 49). Adjacent to the palm trees on either side are the dates "42" and "43." The following inscription is engraved across the top of the lid:

VON
20. X. 42

Fig. 49. Pictured here is a side view of an engraved German mess-kit top showing the owner's name and palm trees. Camp Hearne Collection, Texas A&M University.

AFRIKA
nach
AMERIKA
22. VIII. 43

This translates to read: "From Africa (October 20, 1942) to America (August 22, 1943)," clearly recording the journey of this German soldier from his arrival in Africa to his capture and subsequent transport to the United States.

Engraved Canteens

Two engraved German canteens are known to have come from Camp Hearne. Paul Russell found one of them in a canteen and mess kit dump in Compound 1. A crude carving of a German armored half-track with a German identification cross on its side is engraved on the convex side of this canteen.

Tony Painter of Houston purchased the other specimen at an auction many years ago. Both faces and the sides of the canteen were elaborately engraved to illustrate the journey of a German soldier from Africa to Camp Hearne. The

Fig. 50. This is a front view of an engraved German canteen showing a scene from a North African village. Camp Hearne Collection, Texas A&M University.

canteen itself is German with the manufacturer's code and date, "CFL41," stamped on the neck. A scene from an African city is depicted on the canteen's convex side (fig. 50). In this scene, a Muslim woman carries a jar on her head and a bag in her hand. She is clad in traditional garb: a long dress, hood, and veil over her face. A bearded man wearing a short, turban-style hat and long robe walks behind her. In the background is a city wall with a tower at the corner. The wall has two elaborately designed arches built into it and through one of the arches; other buildings and a mosque are also visible. A palm tree grows behind the man. Traces of red and green paint occur on the palm tree and buildings, indicating that the scene was painted at one time.

The canteen's concave side has a view of Camp Hearne (fig. 51) with text above and below reading "HEARNE TEXAS, U.S.A." and "PRISONER OF WAR CAMP." Depicted is a view from slightly above the camp, looking down on one of the guard towers. The camp's double perimeter fence and the edge of a barrack can be seen. The soldier recorded the history of his military career by carving around the edge of the canteen the names of cities and geographic locales he passed through on his way to Camp Hearne. The names start at the canteen's mouth and run all the way around to the other side of the mouth. They read in order: "NEAPEL, PALERMO, TUNIS, ORAN, FEZ, CASABLANCA, ATLANTIK, PITTSBURGH, NEW YORK, PHILADELPHIA, ST. LOUIS, HEARNE TEXAS." This soldier's journey began in Italy, where he was probably stationed before being transferred to Sicily and then to Tunis. His stationing in Tunis suggests he entered North Africa late in the campaign. After arriving in North Africa he was captured and spent time in temporary internment camps in Oran, Fez, and Casablanca. He subsequently crossed the Atlantic, arriving in New York. He then traveled through Philadelphia, Pittsburgh, and St. Louis before arriving at Camp Hearne.

Personal Items

A number of items belonging to individual POWs were found within the compounds. These included a variety of things related to health and hygiene, jewelry, coins, smoking paraphernalia, art and writing supplies, and other possessions.

Wash Gear, Hygiene, and Health

A number of artifacts recovered in Camp Hearne's POW compounds are related to the prisoners' personal hygiene and health. These included everyday items used for grooming and cleaning. Also found were several items related to the prisoners' medical needs.

Some of the artifacts (for example, British toothbrushes and German toothpaste tubes) clearly represent items brought by the POWs from North Africa or items that arrived in Red Cross parcels or other packages from home. Once in the United States, the POWs were initially issued some items. Ernst Froembsdorf recalled being issued towels and Palmolive brand shaving cream while in New York. Willi Nellessen said that he was given soap, a razor and razor blades, and a toothbrush. The POWs were also given bar soap for the purposes of cleaning both themselves and their uniforms. After that, however, the prisoners were required to purchase their own toiletries from the camp PX. The list of items available there correlates with many of the hygiene-related items found at Camp Hearne.

Toothbrushes and Toothpaste Tubes

Four complete toothbrushes (one with bristles) and six fragments of toothbrushes were recovered. Three of the complete brushes are similar in shape, having long bristle areas (4.5 to 5.2 centimeters in length), and a recurved-style handle. The fourth specimen differs by having a shorter bristle area (3.4 centimeters) and a flat handle. Colors include red, peach, tan/brown, and other colors that have faded. The fragmented specimens include five ends, complete with hole, and one head. All of the fragments have been deliberately cut from the rest of the handle.

Manufacturer's markings are found on three of the four complete specimens.

These markings indicate that one toothbrush is American, two are foreign, and one is of unknown origin. The American specimen is marked "Dr. West's 25," a popular and well-advertised brand of the time. Of the two foreign tooth-brushes, one is English and is marked in two lines, "Warranted All Bristle, M. N. & L. Ltd., London 1940." The other foreign brush is Italian and is marked "Non-Plus-Ultra Marca Depositata" in two lines. The unknown specimen has no markings.

Fifty-four toothpaste tubes were found. These are all typical squeeze-type tubes made of soft, pliable metal alloys. Most were recovered in a rolled or folded state. Some of the tubes were complete with caps, but most were fragmentary. Six American brands are represented: Colgate (n = 25), Forham's (n = 3), Ipana (n = 3), Pepsodent (n = 3), Listerine (n = 10), and Milk of Magnesia Dental Creame (n = 1). One German brand is represented: Doramad "Radioactive Zahn-creme" (n = 8).

Twenty screw-on caps from toothpaste tubes were recovered. Ten black and red plastic caps were identified by monograms on top of the cap or by compar-ing their shape with known tubes that have caps. Those identified include: Col-gate (n = 4), Forham's (n = 2), Ipana (n = 2), and Pepsodent (n = 2).

Shaving Paraphernalia
The remains of a shaving brush, several razors and mirrors, and numerous shav-ing cream tubes were recovered from the POW compounds. The items included white plastic fragments from the handle of a shaving brush and portions of four double-edge razors—three heads and one base. One is of German manufacture and the rest are American.

Eighteen squeeze-type shaving cream tubes made of soft, pliable metal were found scattered in all of the POW compounds, many in a rolled or folded state. Conditions varied from complete to fragmentary, with most missing some por-tion (usually the top and cap). Six American brands in a variety of sizes are rep-resented: Barbasol (n = 5), Mennen (n = 3), Old Spice (n = 1), Palmolive (n = 4), and Woodbury (n = 5). One cap to a Woodbury shaving cream tube was also found.

The fragments of three glass mirrors and one polished metal mirror were found. One glass mirror was a small, round, pocket-sized mirror of unknown manufacture. The second glass mirror is rectangular and of German manufacture. Lettering on paper on the back of the mirror appears to be an advertisement.

One metal mirror was found. It is round, approximately five centimeters in diameter, and has a small hole at the top for suspension. One side is highly pol-ished and reflective.

Combs
Twenty-one fragments of a number of combs were recovered. These fragments consist of individual teeth, as well as back portions with and without teeth. Seven specimens have finely spaced teeth (15–22 teeth per inch), while seven other specimens have more widely spaced teeth (10–13 teeth per inch). All are

made of plastic and are black, translucent mottled brown, translucent orange, or translucent yellow in color. Manufacturer's markings include "Made in USA" and "Lord Nelson," the latter probably being a British product. One comb is etched with the letters "GR," likely the owner's initials.

Hair Tonic, Shampoo, and Lotion Bottles

Thirteen shampoo, lotion, and hair-tonic bottles were collected. Three of the bottles are embossed with a specific manufacturer's name and ten have diagnostic characteristics (morphology) or markings particular to these types of products. Three of the specimens are complete bottles and the other ten are fragmentary.

The shampoo and hair-tonic bottles are typically rectangular with a square base. They have a distinctive long, tapered neck with a constricted opening. Some bottles still retain their black plastic screw caps. Other screw caps mentioned earlier probably came from these or other similar bottles. Three bottles are embossed with the brand names, "Fitch's" (n = 2) and "Kerml" (n = 1), both makers of hair tonics and shampoos. A skin-lotion bottle from Germany was also recovered. It is made of amber-colored glass with arched panels, flat sides, and a flat elliptical base. A fragmentary and illegible paper label is still attached. Embossed on the base of the bottle are the German words "HAUT OL" (skin oil) and the metric volume, "Ca 55 cm^2."

It is known that prisoners had access to grooming items from the PX. A "Price List for Canteen Store" dated July 18, 1945, provides information on the types of goods that the prisoners could buy (see table 3 in chapter 2). Of these items, all goods that were packaged in glass bottles, with the exception of ink, are related to grooming and hygiene. Included in this list are seventeen hair tonics, shampoos, and lotions. These products include: Kreml Shampoo; Fitch's Hair Tonic, Dandruff Remover Shampoo, and Coconut Oil Shampoo; Wildroot and Wildroot White Oil; Wilder Cream Oil; Vaseline Hair Tonic; Lucky Tiger Hair Tonic and Lucky Tiger Combination; G. P. Coldcream; Noxema Skin Cream; London Lotion; Green Shampoo; Mennen Skin Balm; Jergens Lotion; and Cramer's Lotion.

Twelve black plastic caps of various size and style were recovered. These appear to have been used on small bottles and are similar to a cap found on a broken hair-tonic bottle. Many of the caps fit on one or more of the complete shampoo, aftershave, and hair-tonic bottles recovered and likely came from bottles that held these products.

Prescription Bottles and Health-Related Items

Three examples of prescription bottles were recovered. These include two complete bottles and one fragmentary bottle. The complete bottles are clear glass and one retains a black screw cap. These bottles are rectangular in shape with concave shoulders. One panel of the bottle is rounded, while the other is flat. Both bottles have size and manufacturer markings. One bottle holds two ounces and is dated 1942 and the other is a one-ounce bottle dated 1943. The fragmentary specimen is a round, 2.5-ounce, clear glass bottle, with the distinctive flattened finish of a cork-stopped medicinal bottle. In addition to the bottles, two clear glass eyedroppers and a fragment of a glass thermometer were found.

One .75-ounce squeeze-type tube of "Squibb Cream" was recovered. It is made of a soft, pliable metal and has a tan and black label. The label indicates that it was a sunburn cream manufactured by E. Squibb and Sons of New York.

Rings

Two men's rings with flat, signet-shaped centerpieces were found. One ring is made of brass and has a translucent red stone set flush in the center of the setting. A stylized palm tree is incised into both sides of the band.

The second ring is also a signet-style man's ring made of silver (fig. 32, item i). The ring was cast as a single, solid piece. The ring's central panel is flat and roughly rectangular (eleven by fourteen millimeters). Incised into this surface is a scene depicting two people crossing the desert. One figure is riding a camel, while a second walks behind it holding a riding crop. In the left foreground is a palm tree and in the upper right corner are a crescent moon and star (Islamic symbols). The sun is just visible above the horizon in the background. "Tunis" and "1943" are engraved on the left and right sides of the band. This style of ring was a popular souvenir among all ranks and was made by Arab silversmiths especially for the Afrika Korps. Rings of this type often included the initials DAK (for Deutsches Afrika Korps) as part of the design (McGuirk 1993).

Pendants

Six pendants, two secular and four religious, were excavated from the POW compounds. Of the two secular pendants, one is an American penny minted in 1941. The penny is perforated above Lincoln's head in order to accommodate a chain. The second secular pendant is a four-leaf clover made of brass.

The first religious pendant is a silver Saint Christopher medal that is decorated on both sides. The second religious medal, devoted to Saint Guiseppe, is a circular medallion made of light metal alloy. This medal has Italian text on the outer border that reads: "S. GUISEPPE PREGATE PER NOI" ("Saint Joseph Pray for us"). The third religious medal depicts Christ as an adult with the inscription "CHRIST THE KING." The medal is made of metal plated with gold. The fourth religious medal is a corroded two-centimeter-diameter disk, with the figure of a man with a halo encircling his bowed head. The following German text appears to the right of the figure: "KONRAD BIII F F. U." The four religious medals recovered represent Christian religious iconography.

Coins

A total of 118 coins were found in the compounds. The majority of these coins are American (fig. 52, items a and b; n = 72) and German (fig. 52, items c and d; n= 30). The next most commonly represented countries are France (fig. 52, items e and f; n = 15), Tunisia (fig. 52, items g and h; n = 14), and Italy (fig. 52, items j and k; n = 11). Only a few coins are from Austria (n = 2), China (n = 1), and Great Britain (fig. 52i; n = 1). Table 9 lists each coin by its country of ori-

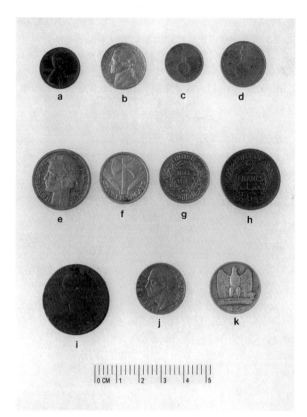

gin, denomination, and date. All of the coins—with the exception of post-1945 American coins (n = 4) and perhaps the Chinese coin (which may have come from a sewing basket)—date from the time the camp was in operation. Heino Erichsen recalled that the prisoners saved coins obtained during their travels as souvenirs. The coins record where a soldier fought and vacationed. The former POWs suggested that their comrades and the guards accidentally lost the coins.

The British coin is a large one-pence coin dated 1894. It may have been a lucky charm carried by a British soldier in North Africa that was later found by a German soldier.

Even though POWs were not allowed to have American currency, almost all those interviewed recalled having some. Werner Kritzler, an artist in the camp, "sold pictures to the American guards for approximately three dollars per picture." Fritz Pferdekämper-Geissel stated that he found much American money when cleaning the theater in the American compound. "We took a rest while cleaning the cinema," he recalled. "I sat down and said to myself 'What's that between the seat? A dime!' I went from seat to seat and looked for dimes. The other guys asked 'What are you doing?' One by one, they started looking, too." Pferdekämper-Geissel gave most of the money to the guards and asked them to buy him some cigarettes and cigars. The guards kept some of the money as a fee.

Table 9. Coins Found at Camp Hearne

Nationality	Denomination	Number	Remarks
United States	One Cent	56	1917–45 (n = 53)
			1948–51 (n = 3)
	Nickel	11	1937–45 (n = 10)
			1947 (n = 1)
	Dime	4	1917–45
France	10 Centimes	2	1920, 1941
	25 Centimes	1	1932
	50 Centimes	3	1927, 1941 (n = 2)
	1 Franc	1	1942
	2 Francs	3	1933, 1934, 1936
Italy	5 Centesimi	1	1941
	10 Centesimi	8	1921–40
	20 Centesimi	1	1921
	5 Lira	1	1927
Tunisia	10 Centimes	4	1941 (n = 4)
	25 Centimes	1	1920
	50 Centimes	2	1921
	1 Franc	6	1926, 1941 (n = 5)
	2 Francs	1	1941
Austria	1 Groschen	1	1926
	2 Groschen	1	1924
Germany	1 Pfennig	14	1930–43
	2 Pfennig	2	1923, 1939
	5 Pfennig	6	1924–39
	10 Pfennig	7	1924–40
	5 Marks	1	1936
Great Britain	1 Pence	1	1894
China	Cast of coin	1	ca. 1860–80 from sewing basket

Thus, through work details and illegal purchases, American money made its way into the POW compounds. Pferdekämper-Geissel said he kept American money hidden in a hollowed-out bar of soap and would loan it to a friendly guard when he was short of cash at the end of the month. He said the guard always paid him back what he owed and would later return the favor.

Smoking Paraphernalia

Among the items recovered was a partial cigarette lighter case made of a metal alloy. The case is decorated on both sides with alternating thick and thin lines coming together at one corner in a herringbone pattern. A brown plastic cigarette holder measuring 3.5 centimeters long was also found. Two metal matchbook covers were recovered. These artifacts are made of a metal alloy and are designed to be a protective cover for the wooden matchboxes issued to German soldiers (De Lagarde 1994, 33). The covers are three by 4.5 centimeters and form the top part of the cover, which was formed of a single piece of metal with a side and corresponding back plate. The center of the cover is embossed with a three-centimeter-diameter circle that has an upraised profile of a German soldier wearing a helmet.

Art and Writing Materials

A hexagonal-shaped ink bottle made of clear glass with a maximum width of 6.7 centimeters was found on the camp's grounds. The bottle has a rectangular base with truncated corners and measures 4.7 by 3.7 centimeters. The text, "WATERMANS, 2 OZ, PAT 098958, 18," appears on the base of the bottle. On the side, near the bottle's base, is the date "1943."

Three fragments of mechanical pencils were recovered. The first is a cone-shaped metal part from the writing end of the pencil. Two fragments of the metallic case or body of a pencil were also recovered. The fragments are of a hexagonal-shaped body painted with red metallic paint.

Three pen fragments were recovered. The first is a Bakelite outer casing with a mixed black and mother-of-pearl pattern. The second fragment is the metallic, possibly brass, body of a pen. The piece has fine parallel lines along its body. The final artifact is metallic, possibly brass, and is the base or closed end of a pen.

All that remains of two small paintbrushes recovered at the camp are the metallic cones used to secure the bristles to the handles. One is five millimeters in diameter and the other seven millimeters. Portions of the bristles are still present and both fragments are crushed. In addition, several oil paint tubes and caps were found.

Other Items

A single luggage tag made of metal was found. The piece is stamped from the back with the following name, address, and dates in standard typeset: "TH. C. W. JUHREND, MEIENDAAL 87, R-DAM. Z., 1940, 1941." A brown, triangular, plastic guitar pick and one clear, circular shot glass were recovered. Two paper artifacts associated with censored letters from Germany were found in Compound 1. These are strips of tape with the word "EXAMINED" printed on them in bold block letters. American censors used the tapes to reseal envelopes once they had examined the contents. Military censors examined all mail coming from Germany to the POWs.

Several complete or nearly complete glass containers and a number of fragmentary portions of bottles and jars were recovered. An intact one-gallon jug was recovered under a POW barrack in Compound 2. The one-gallon jug is marked as such and is made of clear glass, has a finger-hole grip at the neck, and is marked "Duraglas" near the bottom. The former POWs said that gallon jars such as this one were used to ferment fruit rinds into alcoholic beverages. A glass shot glass was recovered from the same barrack. Beverage containers recovered at the site included one beer bottle dated 1944 and two soda pop bottles. Fragments from three canning jars, a porcelain insert from a canning jar lid, and several condiment jars were discovered. Additionally, a single shard from a serving dish and several fragments of an ashtray were found.

CONCLUSIONS AND FUTURE STUDIES

The archaeological studies added much to our knowledge of life at Camp Hearne. Clearly, the camp's archaeological record verified many of the stories told by the former POWs and guards. Their comments also provided a way of interpreting the artifacts recovered from the site. While this chapter on the archaeological materials from Camp Hearne is primarily descriptive, it does provide a baseline for future studies. Most of the artifacts described in this chapter came from Compounds 2 and 3, the NCO compounds. Little work was conducted in the enlisted men's compound. This was due to a lack of knowledge, until later in the project, about the rank distribution of the prisoners at Camp Hearne as well as problems of disturbance and equal accessibility to all of the compounds. In the future, the junior enlisted men's compounds should be examined in more detail to determine if different or similar activities took place there (such as the manufacturing of insignia and other items) and if they had more material possessions compared to the other compounds because the junior enlisted men worked and thus had more money to spend than the nonworking NCOs. It would also be interesting to examine the American compound. The American soldiers were not confined to their compound and thus experienced a different lifestyle than the POWs.

In addition to these studies, additional work is needed at other POW camps. Preliminary studies have been done at Fort Carson, Colorado (Connor et. al. 1999), and Camp Swift, Texas (Nightengale and Moncure 1996). These studies have primarily documented surface features with minimal excavation. More intensive investigations are needed at an officers' camp (such as the one at Mexia, Texas), a camp made up entirely of junior enlisted men, and a small agricultural branch camp. Such studies would provide an interesting comparison and contrast to Camp Hearne, a mostly nonworking NCO camp. Furthermore, it is hoped that research similar to that done at Camp Hearne will be conducted at other camps in other states. It would be interesting to see if similar artifacts are found there. It also would be interesting to compare and contrast Camp Hearne with a camp that held Italian POWs, a camp for Nazis (such as the one at Alva, Oklahoma), and a camp for anti-Nazis.

The study of POW camps and other World War II–era sites holds many possibilities. The Camp Hearne studies, besides adding new knowledge about the camp, also provide a basis for comparison for future studies conducted elsewhere.

CHAPTER 6

Fountains, Statues, and Buildings

THE FIRST PART OF THIS CHAPTER describes the fountains, basins, statues, gardens, and other features built by the POWs during their internment at Camp Hearne (fig. 53). Many of these fountains were found during the survey and subsequently excavated and recorded. Others, however, are known only from period photographs. The latter were either destroyed by later land use at the site or lie undiscovered in the extensive vegetation covering it. The second part of this chapter describes the buildings and remaining foundations at the camp.

FOUNTAINS

Three large fountains were found during the archaeological investigation of Camp Hearne. These fountains were a communal effort and required concrete, piping, access to water and electricity, and pumps. They were located in common areas of the camp for everyone to enjoy.

The Kneeling Woman

This fountain is located in the southwest portion of Compound 1, in Company 1's area, just outside the southwest corner of the mess hall (fig. 53). It has a 4.6-meter-diameter circular concrete basin (figs. 54 and 55). The edge of the basin is raised approximately fifteen centimeters above the ground surface. The maximum depth of the fountain basin is eighty-four centimeters. A square, beveled-edge, tapered pedestal extends upward from the central base of the fountain. The pedestal is hollow and is capped by a removable beveled concrete lid. The sides of the pedestal are oriented with the cardinal directions.

The pedestal cap was decorated with a concrete statue of a nude woman with shoulder-length hair. The woman held a platter and was kneeling and leaning back on her heels. The statue is no longer associated with the fountain and its whereabouts is unknown. Only concrete scars remain on the pedestal top to indicate where her knees and feet were attached to the pedestal surface.

Three concrete frogs, seated on semicircular pedestals, are located at equal

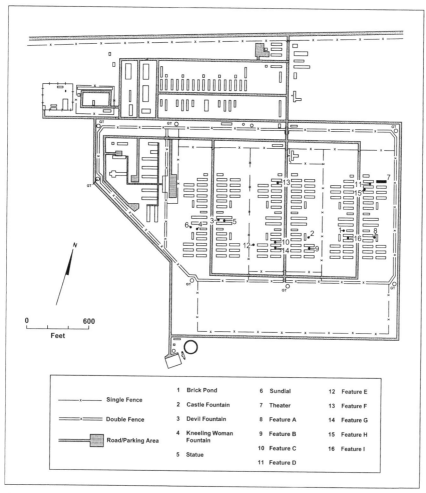

Fig. 53. Map showing the location of fountains, basins, statue platforms, and other features built by the POWs at Camp Hearne. Camp Hearne Collection, Texas A&M University.

intervals around the perimeter of the fountain (figs. 54 and 55). The frogs faced inward toward the center pedestal. Each concrete frog was formed around a ta-pered, nineteen-centimeter-long iron pipe that was angled toward the center of the feature. Water shot out of their mouths and collected in the statue's platter and cascaded into the fountain's basin. The frogs were broken away from their pedestals after the camp was abandoned and two were later recovered. The frogs are constructed of the same high-quality concrete as that of the pedestal and the surface layer of the basin. Pipes extending from the feature to its water source were not found during excavation; however, it is thought that water was routed from the nearby mess hall.

The fountain's basin was constructed in three layers. After the pit had been

Fig. 54. The kneeling woman fountain in Compound 1. Camp Hearne Collection, Texas A&M University.

Fig. 55. The kneeling woman fountain today. Camp Hearne Collection, Texas A&M University.

dug into the ground and shaped, large rocks and river cobbles were laid on the ground surface to serve as a foundation. This layer was then covered with a relatively poor-quality concrete that had many inclusions. Finally, a surface layer of high-quality concrete measuring about 1.3 centimeters thick was smoothed over the base layer.

The feature basin's basal concrete layer is divided into sixteen sections that vary in size between sixty and eighty centimeters at the perimeter of the feature. Prominent seams divide each section, which appear to have been poured individually. After all the sections were poured and set, a thin layer of high-quality concrete was smoothed over each seam and the entire basin to make a continuous, watertight surface. The majority of the dividing lines extend toward the center of the feature but do not meet.

Photographs taken during the camp's operation show that the fountain was able to hold water at a level close to its ground surface level. A three-centimeter-diameter drainpipe that extends five centimeters above the concrete near the edge of the basin maintained a maximum water level in the feature basin.

The Devil Fountain

This fountain was constructed between two mess hall buildings in Company 3's area, Compound 1 (fig. 53). The feature was demolished and the debris dumped nearby after the camp was abandoned.

Fig. 56. The devil fountain outside the mess hall in Compound 1. Camp Hearne Collection, Texas A&M University.

A vertical wall in the rear made up of three adjoining alcoves bounded by arches at their uppermost points dominated the feature (fig. 56). The feature was constructed of locally made "Groesbeck Red" bricks, faced with concrete, and then whitewashed.

The face of a devil adorned each alcove directly below its arch. The center devil and parts of the two adjacent devils were recovered in the field. The center devil appears to have the face of an adult man, with small horns protruding from its hairline and pointed ears. The center face is thirty-nine centimeters tall and thirty-two centimeters wide. The two adjacent devils appear to have youthful, cherublike faces. They also have horns supported by iron wires sprouting from their hairlines. The lips of all three faces were pursed around pipes that spouted water into the collecting pools below. Each of the faces was constructed from relatively high-quality concrete containing few inclusions.

Photographs show a large rectangular collecting pool constructed directly below the arched alcoves. A small, semicircular collecting pool was constructed at the center of the anterior wall of the main pool. A notch was located in the center of this wall to allow water to overflow into the smaller pool.

The Castle

This fountain was located in the southeast quadrant of Compound 2, Company 8, behind the lavatory in the open area facing Compound 3 (fig. 53). Because most of this fountain was damaged through years of neglect, livestock trampling, and vandalism, only fragments of the miniature castle that once adorned a small mound and the fountain's rough structure remain. The following description of this feature is derived from the investigation of these remains and a period photograph.

The fountain had an irregular oval shape measuring almost thirteen meters at the long axis and about seven meters along the short axis. It consisted of a large mound and small island surrounded by a moat (figs. 57, 58, and 59). The moat was dug twenty centimeters below the ground surface and lined with a thin layer of fine-grained white concrete. In some places this concrete appears to have been originally painted blue. An irregularly formed concrete lip extended all of the way around the edge of the moat, which averaged one meter in width. A small, low-lying island was situated in the moat's southeastern quadrant and may have been built to accommodate miniature buildings or perhaps flowers. At the south end is a concrete box that could have served as a pump housing or as a drain.

In the center of the fountain was a large mound measuring 7.2 meters long and 4.6 meters wide. The fountain stood a meter above the ground surface and 1.2 meters above the moat floor. The mound was constructed by piling dirt and rocks above the ground surface. Part of the mound was covered with a layer of fine-grained concrete and part was protected by concrete retaining walls embellished with rounded pebbles. A pond and a miniature replica of a German walled village were situated on the mound.

The miniature buildings of the village were built on multiple platforms at

Fig. 57. The castle fountain behind the lavatory in Compound 2. This photograph was taken before the moat was added, probably in 1943 or early 1944. Camp Hearne Collection, Texas A&M University.

Fig. 58. The castle fountain as it looks today. Note the broad cement-lined moat surrounding the central island that contained the castle. Camp Hearne Collection, Texas A&M University.

FOUNTAINS, STATUES, AND BUILDINGS

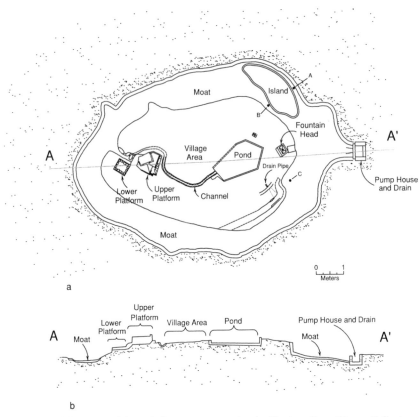

Fig. 59. Detailed drawing of the castle fountain: a. map view, b. side view. Camp Hearne Collection, Texas A&M University.

different heights. Two buildings were situated on the lower and upper platforms (fig. 59). At the top of the mound, a wall surrounds a concentration of several miniature buildings. Each building was made of concrete and showed considerable detail, including multipaned windows, chimneys, walls embellished with stones, and red roofs. A wide roadway paved with fine gravel connected the various platforms.

The pond, which is not shown in the photograph, was located at the south end of the mound (fig. 59). It had an irregular shape measuring 1.5 by 1.0 meters and was constructed with coarse concrete capped by a two-millimeter-thick layer of fine-grained white concrete. The pond has two outlets. The main outlet fed a three-meter-wide, concrete-lined channel that ran along the edge of the village. Water from the pond flowed around the west side of the village, around the east side of the large building on the upper platform, and into the moat. The second outlet consisted of a short length of pipe. The water from this outlet drained along a short but wide channel before entering the moat. Because the pond was located above the moat, a pump was needed to convey the water upward. At the south end of the moat was an intake for water that was pumped through a metal pipe into a small concrete box at the top of the mound. This water then cascaded over a concrete staircase into the pond.

A plaque placed at the front of the feature read "Burg Schwanstein." The village in the photograph is reminiscent of both the castles and villages at Neuschwanstein and Hohenschwangau in Germany. Fragments of this sign were found during excavation and are made of concrete. The letters were raised and cast with the sign. The letters were painted black and the background white.

Two small figures, both made of concrete, were found during excavation. One is of a man sitting with his legs crossed and arms down along his sides (fig. 60). A small hole present in his right hand may have held a miniature fishing pole. The man is dressed in trousers and a shirt and is wearing a cowboy hat. The figure, which was found in three parts, measured about thirty centimeters tall when reconstructed. The man is pursing his lips as though whistling.

The second figure, measuring about fifteen centimeters tall, is of a long-haired woman. The shape of the lower half of the woman's body suggests that she may have been a mermaid. The woman is not clothed and her left arm is held at her side and her right arm is folded over her head.

Fig. 60. Shown here is a figurine made of cement that was recovered from the castle fountain. It is of a man sitting with his legs crossed. He is fishing, and a hole is located in his left hand for the attachment of a fishing rod. He was probably sitting on the moat or island as a decoration. Camp Hearne Collection, Texas A&M University.

By comparing the photograph of the fountain with the feature as it was excavated, it is obvious that it was changed after the photograph was taken. The small channel around the miniature village is present in the photograph, but not the moat. The photograph also does not include the area where the pond was located, so it cannot be determined whether the pond was present at the time it was taken. However, if one assumes that all water-related structures were added at the same time, as seems likely, it thus appears the fountain was constructed in two phases: the mound and village were completed first and the moat and pond were added later.

Immediately west of the fountain is an eight-by-ten-meter concrete slab. This slab abuts the back of the lavatory in Company 8 and extends to within 2.4 meters of the castle moat. The concrete is of poor quality, stretched by the addition of a large amount of small pebbles. This slab was added by the prisoners and probably served as a sitting area adjacent to the fountain.

Basin Features

Nine small features made of concrete were recorded in Compounds 2 and 3 (fig. 53, features a–i). Each of these features is a shallow basin set into the ground (fig. 61). Feature d deviates slightly from this pattern in that it is set into an artificial mound of earth that rises forty centimeters above the ground surface. These basins were designed to retain water and drains made of pipe and glass bottles were incorporated into each of them. All of the basins are fairly uniform in size, with lengths ranging from 160 to 290 centimeters and widths varying from 140 to 290 centimeters. All are a single basin, except for features h and i.

Fig. 61. Photograph of one of the basin features (feature c). Camp Hearne Collection, Texas A&M University.

Fig. 62. Shown here is a 1945 photograph of one of the basin features between the barracks. This may be the feature shown in Fig. 61. Note the walkways and the grass and shrubs planted by the POWs. Camp Hearne Collection, Texas A&M University.

The basin of feature h is divided in half by a concrete dam, whereas the basin in feature i is more of a moat surrounding an upraised concrete-walled island. The interior of this feature was probably used as a planter.

Despite their common aspects, many characteristics of these features are variable. These traits include shape, quality of concrete, and degree of decoration. The basins are categorized into four shapes: ovals (features a, b, h, and i); circles (features c, d, and e); a rectangle (feature g); and a hexagon (feature f). Most of the basins are symmetrical, but some of the oval features are slightly irregular.

Features a, b, and d were constructed of relatively high-quality concrete with a small amount of filler material (little pebbles) mixed into it. The concrete at the core of the remaining features (features c, e, f, g, h, and i) was of relatively poor quality and included coarse sand, small pebbles, and in one case bricks (feature h) in order to extend the cement used to construct the basins. The thickness of the basin walls ranges from one to three centimeters. All features were surfaced with a thin layer, usually about one centimeter thick, of higher-quality concrete and then smoothed in order to cover the core material of the feature. This technique was devised to conserve the amount of cement used in construction. Three of the features had rounded gravel embedded in their surfaces as a decoration. Small pebbles were pressed into the floor of feature g. Rounded gravels were arranged in a random manner in the moat and raised area of feature i, and gravels also decorated the inside divider and outer rim of feature h. A sandstone boulder measuring approximately eight centimeters wide makes up the center portion of the divider of feature h.

These features were all located at the entrance or between barracks (figs. 53 and 62), except feature d, which was associated with the PX in Compound 3. In all cases, water to fill the ponds was hauled in buckets from the latrine.

The Hexagonal Brick Pond

This was a hexagonal concrete pond with a brick veneer. The concrete pond was inset thirty-three centimeters into the ground and the walls extended thirty-nine centimeters above the ground surface. High-quality concrete was used. The aboveground portion of the concrete pond was veneered on the exterior with four layers of bricks (Groesbeck Reds) and a layer of bricks capped the concrete basin. The latter bricks lay on their sides flush with the interior pond wall and slightly overhang the exterior brick wall to provide a decorative ledge. At the corners of the hexagon were small seats made of brick, which are incorporated as part of the ledge.

The bricks were mortared together with relatively poor-quality concrete and sand was used as filler. The mortared surfaces were faced with a higher-quality concrete in an effort to conserve concrete during the pond's construction. The hexagon measured 206 centimeters on the inside and 244 centimeters on the outside.

A small pedestal of bricks arranged in two tiers and stacked to mirror its shape was located in the center of the feature. Additional courses of bricks appear to have been present at one time and something (perhaps a statue or flowerpot) sat on the bricks. A drain hole occurs at the base of the pond, and a large sandstone block lies next to it. This pond was located in Compound 3 in the common area between Company 10's mess hall, company office, and lavatory (fig. 53).

The Pet Enclosure

A small pet enclosure was located on the west edge of Compound 1 (fig. 53). Although it was never found, a photograph and the recollections of POW Peter Spoden attest to its existence. The enclosure measured about three meters on each side and was about thirty centimeters deep (fig. 63). Wood lined the sides of the hole and a concrete or tile cap topped the wooden wall. Cages covered with screen doors were located in the walls for the containment of the animals. In the middle of the feature is a small hill. A miniature castle and another structure are visible on the hill, as are some boulders and winding pathways. The castle consisted of one square building, no more than thirty centimeters long, with small cylindrical turrets on the corners and a cylindrical tower in the middle. A short wall with an arched gateway surrounded the castle and there was a pathway for animals to run underneath it. The other structure appeared to be a domestic building that may have been constructed as a home for the animals. Two types of animals can be seen in the photograph: a family of opossums and a snapping turtle. It is possible that other animals were on display

Fig. 63. The pet enclosure built by the POWs is shown here. It was probably located in Compound 1. Note the miniature castle, the snapping turtle, opossum with babies, and cages for the animals to the right. Camp Hearne Collection, Texas A&M University.

there during the camp's occupation. A gravel pathway surrounded the enclosure and there was a bench along one side of the enclosure from which one could observe the animals.

MINIATURE CASTLES

Two miniature castles are primarily known from photographs. Fragments of each of these creations were found in the compounds, but their exact location was never determined.

The first miniature castle was built upon a large concrete foundation (fig. 64). The castle was also constructed of concrete and small stones were embedded in it to give the castle a realistic look. The castle consisted of a central rectangular building surrounded by other buildings, towers, and a wall. Each of the buildings shows considerable detail: windows with panes, chimneys, and a wooden door at the gate. The highest tower is topped with a conical roof on which sits a flagpole that flies the Nazi flag. Outside, a curving road leads around a small pond that surrounds the castle. A miniature statue of a man can be seen at the edge of the pond.

The second miniature castle is also constructed of concrete. High walls studded with gravel surround several rectangular buildings and a tower. Several frag-

Fig. 64. Shown here is a miniature castle and moat built by the POWs. Note the small Nazi flag flying from the turret. Camp Hearne Collection, Texas A&M University.

ments of this castle's roof were recovered. They were painted orange, the color of roofs in a typical German town. A moat surrounds the walls and a wooden bridge extends from the arched entry.

STATUARY

Although some statuary was created at Camp Hearne, there is only one photograph of a statue made there: that of a nude woman located in Company 4 of Compound 1 (figs. 53 and 65). Today, only the base, which measured fifty by sixty centimeters, remains. The statue was made of concrete and was less than two meters tall. The woman is depicted standing with her right hand resting on her right thigh. Her left arm is bent up so that her left hand is grasping her hair, which is braided and hanging over her left shoulder. The woman's head is tilted slightly down and to the left, as if in a contemplative pose.

According to Ida Blanchette (1989), other statues were present at the camp. She reports that an eight-foot-tall statue of Jesus Christ was situated in a twenty-foot-square sunken monument. Former guards also recalled seeing other statues at the camp, but they did not remember much about them.

Fig. 65. Statue of nude woman sculptured by the POWs and displayed in Compound 1. Camp Hearne Collection, Texas A&M University.

The Sundial

According to photographic evidence, a sundial was located in Compound 1 about four to five meters west of the Kneeling Woman Fountain (fig. 53). It had a circular concrete lip around the edge that rose from the ground at about a forty-five-degree angle. Gravels of different colors were laid down to create a patterned mosaic with numerals at the sundial's base. A thin pole rose out from the center of the sundial at about a thirty-degree angle in order to cast a shadow to indicate the time. The sundial appears to have been about 1.0 to 1.5 meters in diameter. A circular gravel path and some landscaping surrounded this feature.

Remembering the Fountains and Features

Numerous American soldiers, civilians, and German POWs remember the construction of the various fountains, ponds, and statuary at Camp Hearne. Materials used to build these features were obtained in several ways. Some of the prisoners who worked outside the camp were able to bring back bricks and other materials left over or discarded from work projects. On other occasions, the Germans asked for and received cement from the American officer in charge of the compound. The Americans thought that fulfilling requests for building materials would keep the prisoners busy and they thus would experience fewer behavior problems. If the Americans denied the prisoners' requests for building materials, the POWs would purchase them with "canteen funds."

Former POW Hugo Wannemacher said he thought the construction of the fountains, miniature castles, and statues had a very important "positive psychological" effect on the prisoners by reminding them of Germany. Construction of these features began as soon as the POWs arrived and settled in at the camp. In an article appearing December 31, 1943—just six months after the arrival of the first prisoners—the *Hearne Democrat* reported that there were "neat, formal gardens between the barracks, some of which contain miniature reproductions of German castles done in pebbles and cement; concrete water fountain, and sundial."

Peter Spoden remembered one fountain in particular that was adorned with impressions of three heads, the fountain previously described here as the "Devil Fountain" (fig. 56). Although the Americans often speculated as to who the heads, which sprouted devil-like horns, represented, Spoden said they were the likenesses of one of the guards, a fellow named Obermeyer, and his two children. "When someone was angry at Obermeyer," said Spoden, "they would say that he was going to be buried there." Needless to say, Spoden recalled that the images were not a very flattering portrait. It was an insiders' joke about which the Americans never learned.

Fritz Pferdekämper-Geissel, who considered himself a naturalist, collected various animals such as turtles, lizards, and rabbits that he kept in a small enclosure he built. Arno Einicke built a tub-shaped concrete basin that he covered with wire screen in which he kept a collection of bullfrogs and turtles (fig. 53, feature a).

Guard Matt Ware remembered the POWs constructing the sundial. "It was made out of pea gravel," he recalled. "It was three and a half foot in diameter and they made their own metal dial to go up and at each change of the season they'd change it, it kept good time." There were also a number of decorative mosaics at the camp. Walter Fricke recalled seeing mosaics located at "the entrance of the barracks on the left and right sides. Sometimes it would be the sign of a particular town, coat of arms, or eagle in different colors."

Many of the POWs recalled that there were several statues at Camp Hearne. Guard John Luparelli said he watched the POWs make one of these statues, using "one of the prisoners for the model. What they did was stripped him and then they used newspapers and they wet them and put the paper around him. They molded the paper around him and when the paper dried they had a mold. That is what they used for the concrete. That was how they got the mold for the statue."

Often associated with the fountains were flowerbeds in which irises, lilies, and other flowers were planted. These bulb plants still emerge and flower every year exactly where the POWs planted them.

LARGE POW-BUILT FEATURES

The Band Shell

Only remnants of the foundation of the large band shell that was located in Compound 2 remain (fig. 53). This band shell was about three to four meters high and about six meters long and had a raised stage and a cleared area for the audience (fig. 66). Landscaping that included trellises covered with ivy surrounded the band shell. The band shell itself was constructed mainly of wood, however the stairs leading up to the stage were made of bricks. The stage was semicircular and had nine panels along the back that formed a rounded wall measuring about 2.5 to three meters tall. Ivy was trained to grow up wire guides positioned along the back of this wall. A latticework of boards was placed along the bottom of the structure in order to close off the empty space beneath the stage.

A small, circular pond constructed mainly of bricks was at one corner of the audience area. There was a raised cube of bricks in the center of the pond. The structure was no more than two meters in diameter and rose about ten centimeters above the ground. The raised cube in the middle of the pond was used to hold decorative plants.

Fig. 66. Shown here are a band shell, fountain, and garden built by the POWs in Compound 2. Camp Hearne Collection, Texas A&M University.

The Theater (Die Deutsche Bühne)

The theater (Die Deutsche Bühne) located in the northeastern end of Compound 3, Company 11 (fig. 53), was created by modifying a wooden-floored recreation building that measured one hundred feet long by twenty feet wide (fig. 67).

The theater was separated into four main areas (fig. 67): the stage (figs. 68 and 69), orchestra pit, seating area (figs. 70 and 71), and lobby. The concrete stage was located at the western end of the structure and was nine meters long. During its use, a wooden floor covered the concrete. A one-meter-wide tunnel was present below the surface of the stage and extended from the edge of the stage and orchestra pit for 3.7 meters into the body of the stage. The wooden floor would have covered this open walkway while the theater was in use. The tunnel, which perhaps allowed actors to enter center stage through a trapdoor, was used for storing theater equipment.

The stage area appears to have been divided into two parts: the front and backstage areas. The backstage area is not structurally separated from the stage itself, but the separation clearly shows in photographs. Three shallow square holes were found on the stage floor. These may have held supports for the partition separating the two stage areas. In the backstage area, a 3.7-meter-long pipe extends from the rear doorway to the center of the backstage floor that was inset into the concrete stage floor. Both ends of the pipe extend at an angle above the backstage floor. This pipe would have been covered by the wooden floor and may have been a conduit for wires.

From the doorway leading into the backstage area is a nine-meter-long and one-meter-wide concrete walkway that leads to the PX. This was built by the POWs to connect the two buildings. Perhaps the east end of the PX (which was

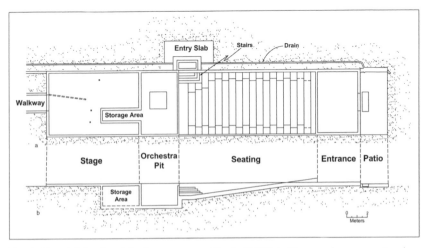

Fig. 67. Detailed drawing of the theater constructed by the POWs in Compound 3: a. map view; b. side view. Camp Hearne Collection, Texas A&M University.

Fig. 68. This photograph of the inside of the theater was taken in 1944 facing from the seating area toward the stage. Note the wall sconces. Camp Hearne Collection, Texas A&M University.

Fig. 69. This is a similar view of the theater taken recently facing from the seating area toward the stage. Camp Hearne Collection, Texas A&M University.

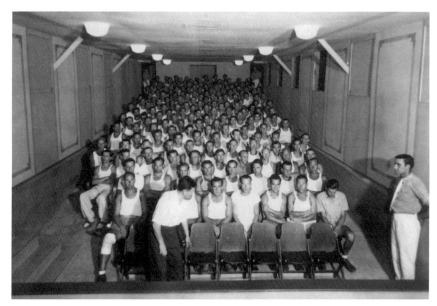

Fig. 70. Shown here is a 1944 photograph taken from the stage looking over the orchestra pit wall to the seating area. German prisoners are seated and the front rows remain empty, probably awaiting the entry of the American officers and guards down the steps to the left. Camp Hearne Collection, Texas A&M University.

Fig. 71. This is a similar view taken recently facing from the stage looking over the orchestra pit to the seating area. Camp Hearne Collection, Texas A&M University.

also likely the barbershop) was used as a dressing room and for costume changes during the show.

Although not preserved today, two wall sconces were located on either side of the stage walls (fig. 68). The sconces were presumably made of concrete or plaster and were in the shape of an eagle with outstretched wings that was bounded by a flowing ribbon border. Located directly below each eagle were two electric light bulbs set atop simulated candlesticks. Both a white and a dark fabric curtain were hung directly behind the wooden border of the stage. The archival photos also indicate that the orchestra pit was sometimes covered with a cloth tarp when not in use.

The orchestra pit was immediately east of the stage and separated the audience area from the stage. A ten-centimeter-thick wall of ceramic brick covered with concrete separated the orchestra pit from the seating area. The pit was approximately 1.8 meters deep and 3.5 meters wide. The tunnel mentioned previously extended from the rear wall of the pit.

The seating area was the largest section of the structure, extending back 13.5 meters. It was located directly east of the orchestra pit. The seating was tiered upward toward the back in order to provide the audience with a good view of the stage. The rows for the seats were organized in a stair-step fashion and were bounded by smooth ramps on either side. The seating area contained about twenty rows and seated about two hundred people.

The lobby, located at the easternmost end of the structure, was about 4.2 meters long. A wooden wall separated it from the seating area. Theater patrons were able to enter the seating area by one of two curtained entryways on either side of the lobby's western wall or by a door near the front rows that led directly outside. The lobby may also have been used as a projection room for showing movies in the theater. Archival photos indicate that a rectangular hole was present in the upper half of the wall.

A second entry was located on the north end of the building, next to the orchestra pit. A flight of stairs descended from the doorway to the floor of the seating area. The former POWs indicated that the American officers entered through that doorway and occupied the front-row seats during performances.

A patio measuring 2.7 meters long was constructed just outside the lobby entrance. A cistern measuring sixty by 185 centimeters was constructed directly below the entrance to the building. A metal grate covered the cistern so that the theater patrons could wipe their feet before entering the theater. A similar patio and cistern/grate system was constructed just outside the northern entrance to the seating area. A concrete drain was constructed along the northern edge of the building. This was probably designed to facilitate drainage around the theater and keep the orchestra pit and seating area from filling with water during and after storms.

Remembering the Theater

Construction of the theater, which began in late 1943 and was completed in early 1944, took six months. Hugo Wannemacher recalled: "we had all kinds of talented guys, including actors, musicians, and so on, and they asked the American officer if they could build a theater. The American officer told us to wait. Suddenly, within days or so, material was arriving to build the theater."

The POWs modified a barrack to create the theater. First, the wooden floor was removed. Then the stage was leveled, the orchestra pit and seating area dug out, the dirt hauled away, and those areas paved with cement. The POWs made everything. According to Otto Schulz: "Clothing [was] made from flour-bags from the kitchen, electric-wire for spotlights was made from the metal bands from boxes (insolating tape out of paper), the spotlights were made of metal-containers, and so on." Former POW Robert Goede recalled: "We made electrical wire by taking barbed wire apart, wrapping it with toilet paper, and using some flour paste to make it stick. The electrical sockets for the light bulbs were made out of cardboard and pieces of tin cans." Light bulbs were temporarily removed from the barracks and used to light the theater since there were no spare bulbs. It was not all that difficult when one considers that, as Hugo Wannemacher put it, "with three thousand men in the camp you could find a man for everything."

Buildings at Camp Hearne

All of the structures at Camp Hearne were easy and inexpensive to build temporary war mobilization buildings designed to provide service for no more than twenty years. Private contractors built them according to military specifications. This section describes the four basic types of structures found in a POW company area: barracks, lavatories, mess halls, and company offices (Garner 1993; Kriv 1993; Kruse 1946).

The barracks were a hundred feet long and twenty feet wide (Garner 1993; Kriv 1993; Kruse 1946; U.S. Engineers Office 1943). At each end of the building was a six-foot by one-foot concrete slab. These slabs were placed at the base of a short flight of stairs that led to an open porch that measured five by six feet. Entry to the building was gained through a set of double doors.

The building itself was constructed of a wooden frame supported by piers made of brick blocks. In the blueprints, the piers are spaced every eight feet along the length of the building. A pier was placed at each edge and in the middle of the building along the width. The frame was tied to these piers with metal straps.

The exterior wooden frame was covered with tar paper, which minimized the cost and time needed to construct the buildings. The photographs and blueprints show that the walls of the buildings had two-by-four-inch studs placed every two feet. The tar paper was nailed to the studs and then another two-by-four was nailed over the tar paper at the place of the existing stud to hold the paper securely. Former guard Bobby Sullivan noted that the black-walled buildings earned the nickname "Black Beauties."

Twelve windows were present on the long walls of each barrack. They were placed every four feet and were themselves four feet wide. Judging from the photographs and blueprints, the roofing material seems to have been a prefab-ricated shingle. At the peak of the roof were three exhaust pipes for the furnaces, as well as roof vents that ran along the length of the building. At each end of the building there were also wooden louvers for venting it.

Robert Goede recalled that the buildings were not finished inside: studs were exposed and there was no plaster on the walls or insulation. The floors consisted of tightly fitted wooden floorboards. Three furnaces are present in the blueprints, spaced evenly throughout the building. Inside the building there was room for thirty-four double bunks that could accommodate sixty-eight men. The blueprint shows eight light fixtures controlled by a single switch near one of the doors. The electrical notes on the blueprint call for the fixtures to be bare-bulb porcelain sockets. "There was bunk beds to the left and right with a cen-tral walkway in between, sort of in the center," recalled POW Arno Einicke. "But every few meters there was a heating fire-stove and you had a thermostat that was located at the window which automatically shut the thing off and on . . . there was nothing that you could desire for there [at Camp Hearne], as far as the quarters were concerned . . . they were as good as German apartments."

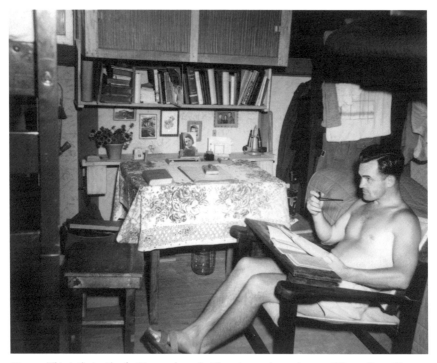

Fig. 72. This is the inside of a German barrack. The prisoners knew they would be at Camp Hearne for a long time, so they decided to make it as comfortable as possible. Shown here is a POW sitting in a chair made with a writing desk that was made at the carpentry shop. Against the wall are cabinets, bookshelves, and a table that have been added. Note the flowers, pictures, and other items. Camp Hearne Collection, Texas A&M University.

Alfred Jasper described them as "comfy." The barracks were comfortable in the winter because they had gas stoves. However, frequent reference was made to the fact that the barracks were hot during warmer weather. Walter Fricke said that after lunch he would try to sleep because it was just too hot to do anything. Willi Nellessen adopted the same strategy, sometimes even sleeping under the barracks on the ground. Between the bunks, the prisoners tried to make their new home as comfortable as possible (fig. 72). They built shelves to keep their toiletries and personal belongings, and rods to hang clothes. They also built writing desks, chairs, and other furniture. Fritz Haus recalls that some of the POWs even decorated the exterior of the barracks with white picket fences.

During the excavations around the barracks, nails, tacks, window glass, porcelain light fixtures, wire, and tar paper from the roofs and walls were found. In addition, the concrete doorsteps and many of the brick piers were still present.

The lavatories were constructed to be more durable because these buildings would receive heavy use. Thus, lavatory buildings had concrete foundations. Even so, the walls were the same as the barracks, wood frames covered with tar paper, and the roof was covered with roofing felt. The interior of the lavatory was divided into four rooms. The largest room was the toilet room, which housed twenty-four sinks, fourteen urinals, twenty toilets, and a heater. The toilet room was 34 by 20 feet. Immediately adjacent to the toilet room was the dressing room, which measured 12 by 8 feet. It was bounded by benches along three walls with a walkway along the interior wall that led into the shower room. The shower room was 14 by 8 feet. Its walls were constructed of treated fiberboard,

Fig. 73. The inside of one of Camp Hearne's mess halls is shown here. Camp Hearne Collection, Texas A&M University.

LONE STAR STALAG

presumably to make the walls waterproof. There were nine partitioned shower stalls and a recessed drain ran around the periphery of the room. The last room was the heater room, which measured 8 by 22 feet. This room contained a water storage tank and two water heaters and could not be accessed from the other rooms. The lavatory had only one entrance near the center of the building. In some company areas, the POWs expanded the concrete slab at the entrance with cement and stone. Another doorway entered the heater room. Each long wall had six windows and the short wall had one or two windows.

Mess halls measured 156 feet long by twenty feet wide (fig. 73). All mess halls had a concrete slab foundation on which a wooden frame was constructed and, as with the other buildings, covered with tar paper. The mess halls were divided into two parts: the kitchen at one end and the dining room. The dining room occupied almost two-thirds of the structure and had at least twenty-five wooden tables arranged it. There were three entrances to each mess hall: two double-door entrances in the middle and one at the far end. Each mess hall was large enough to accommodate four hundred men at a time (Fischer 1943b).

The kitchen was separated from the dining area by a partition. The kitchen was equipped with ranges, ovens, stoves, tables, pan racks, refrigerators, and sinks. It could be entered either through the partition or from the outside. Small concrete entrance slabs were placed at all entrances. In some company areas, the POWs expanded these entrance slabs with additional concrete and stone.

The company office and storeroom was sixty feet long and twenty feet wide. This structure had a concrete foundation on which a wooden-framed, tar-paper-covered structure was built. There was one entrance into these buildings and a small concrete slab was present outside the entrance.

CHAPTER 7

Legacy

IN THE FINAL ISSUE OF *Der Spiegel,* dated December 15, 1945, POW Max Weiss (the camp spokesman) and POW Walter Karg (the German Kulturwart or "Head of Cultural Activities") wrote the following editorial entitled "Farewell Words."

Since a few days the whole camp has been seized by the traveling fever, and when this last edition of our newspaper appears, many will not be able to read it, many who inspected every edition with close attention; and others will overlook it in the haste of the moment. Nevertheless we want it to speak to you again in this moment when we have to part.

Soon the camp in which we felt and grew together, will lie waste. Certainly we were not of the same opinion in many respects, and we are not today. And yet we form a unity of Germans. One thing we have in common: The love of our mother country. All of us have the longing wish that it may grow up again out of the ruins of the present time, that it may become worthy of a human being again. An enormous task is waiting for us. Infinitely much misery and distress must be overcome, old hatred be buried, charity be rendered, wounds be healed, ruins be removed, new morals be found or re-established. He is well off who is armed internally when the disappointments rush down on him. Let us not lose courage then. During the time of our imprisonment we have had less to suffer than our beloved at home. We have bodily and spiritual resources of power which we can use for the benefit of our people. Let us not become relapsed in that we nourish an idea of revenge. We ourselves should not be able to take revenge, and the more we are leering at allies we think strong enough to "liberate" us through another war, the more irresponsible we should act. Another war will lead to a definite destruction of Germany. Let us not thrust the hand away which is stretched out towards us. But let us do one thing: work on ourselves; let us prove by deeds that we have learned from the events of the present time. If the other peoples realize that, they will not deny us their recognition. In practice that means that we shall have to build a wall—not of concrete and barbed wire, but an inner wall—against all dictatorial inclinations of single persons or groups. Western Europe has become small. Let us cling to this piece of earth that is left to us, and let us seek what we love in common with the peoples of the west, what is based on the common historical, political and religious facts. During the recent past, the word German which was a respected name, has been made cruel sport of. It is our task and that of our children to acquire for it the respect it deserves.

We should have liked to spend Christmas here in common. Now it has been decided otherwise. Let us not be sad about it. Every day less we spend here, brings us nearer to our home. Celebrating without our families would have made many a man's heart sad by the remembrance of better times. During the coming holidays, many a man will direct his look from the exterior to the interior. That is the very intention of this holiday. Not the loudness, but the quietude brings forth great deeds. So we shall probably spend these holidays much better in other surroundings than at this accustomed place with glittering lights. Let us light candles in our hearts and be filled with the power from a world from which Christmas gets its true consecration. This power will help us in the new year, too.

We say farewell to you wishing that all of you find the right way that will prove to be the most beneficial for our country, so that at the end of your lives you can testify to yourselves that you have recognized your duty and acted accordingly. Let us hope that the coming generations will not have to say that the present time found a miserable generation.

It has now been nearly sixty years since those words were written at the end of the Second World War. The German POWs of Camp Hearne and other camps eventually returned to Germany and rebuilt their lives and reconstructed a shattered nation. The former POWs interviewed for this book were all repatriated to Germany by 1947, one and a half years after leaving Camp Hearne. Upon his return, Willi Nellessen was able to get back his former job at a bank. He married, had three children, and eventually became the chairman of a German bank. Fritz Pferdekämper-Geissel became a successful businessman, married, and had three children. Erich Spix returned to his hometown of Cologne, married, had four children, and was a representative for a wine and confectionary import company. Carl Bruns went back to school, finished his university studies, and became a high school teacher and eventually headmaster of the school. He, too, is married and has two sons. Alfred Jasper returned to the engineering college at Hagen and became a mechanical engineer, married, and had one child. Walter Koch became a graphics designer, married, and had one child. Walter Werner married, had three children, and became a partner in an import company. Walter Fricke finally returned to Germany in 1947 after 1,469 days in captivity. He married, raised a family, and was a successful businessman. Werner Kritzler also married and raised a family. He owned and operated his own factory. Hugo Wannemacher went to school upon his return and went into the construction industry. He married and had children. Peter Spoden, Arno Einicke, and all the rest followed a similar pattern.

Some former POWs found their way back to the United States and became American citizens. Heino Erichsen was repatriated to Germany in 1947 and emigrated to the United States in 1953. After holding a number of different positions, he eventually founded the Los Niños International Adoption Center in Houston in 1981 and served as its executive director until 2001.

Some former prisoners went to other nations. Fritz Haus was repatriated to Germany in November, 1946. He returned to a Baptist theological college in Hamburg and graduated in 1948. In 1950, Fritz and his wife went to South Africa as missionaries and had oversight of the German Baptist churches there. He had three children and still lives with his wife in South Africa.

Clearly, the challenge Max Weiss and Walter Karg issued to their peers in the final issue of *Der Spiegel* has been met. No, this was not a "miserable generation"; it instead was one that survived terrible times and found the strength to deal with the challenges of reconstructing its country and moving forward. Camp Hearne's grounds may be obscured by vegetation and forgotten, but the legacy of those times and the people who were there is not.

Works Cited

Adair, Alexander. 1944. Memorandum to Headquarters, Eighth Service Command, December 22, 1944, Record Group (hereafter RG) 389, Provost Marshal General's Office (hereafter PMGO), Enemy POW Information Bureau, Reporting Branch, Subject File, Modern Military Records Branch, National Archives, College Park, Md. (Hereafter MMRB, NA.)

———. 1945. Memorandum to commanding officer, Camp Hearne, Texas, February 19, 1945, RG 389, PMGO, Enemy POW Information Bureau, Reporting Branch, Subject File, MMRB, NA.

Adjutant General. 1949a. Parole of Anton Boehmer, July 13, 1949, *U.S. v German POWs Boehmer et al.* (CM 312330), Court-Martial Records, Archives of the Clerk of Court, U.S. Army Judiciary, Arlington, Va.

———. 1949b. Parole of Heinrich Braun, July 13, 1949, *U.S. v German POWs Boehmer et al.* (CM 312330), Court-Martial Records, Archives of the Clerk of Court, U.S. Army Judiciary, Arlington, Va.

———. 1949c. Parole of Werner Hossann, July 13, 1949, *U.S. v German POWs Boehmer et al.* (CM 312330), Court-Martial Records, Archives of the Clerk of Court, U.S. Army Judiciary, Arlington, Va.

———. 1949d. Parole of Gunther Meisel, July 13, 1949, *U.S. v German POWs Boehmer et al.* (CM 312330), Court-Martial Records, Archives of the Clerk of Court, U.S. Army Judiciary, Arlington, Va.

———. 1949e. Parole of Erich Von der Heydt, July 12, 1949, *U.S. v German POWs Boehmer et al.* (CM 312330), Court-Martial Records, Archives of the Clerk of Court, U.S. Army Judiciary, Arlington, Va.

Albert, A. H. 1976. *Record of American Uniform and Historical Buttons.* Boyertown, Pa.: Boyertown.

Angolia, John R. 1976. *For the Fuhrer and Fatherland: Military Awards of the Third Reich.* San Jose, Calif.: R. James Bender.

———. 1992. *The HJ.* Vol. 2. San Jose, Calif.: R. James Bender.

————. 2001. *Belt Buckles and Brocades of the Third Reich.* San Jose, Calif.:
R. James Bender.

————, and Adolf Schlicht. 1984. *Uniforms and Traditions of the German Army,*
1933–1945. Vol. 1. San Jose, Calif.: R. James Bender.

————. 1986. *Uniforms and Traditions of the German Army, 1933–1945.* Vol. 2.
San Jose, Calif.: R. James Bender.

————. 1987. *Uniforms and Traditions of the German Army, 1933–1945.* Vol. 3.
San Jose, Calif.: R. James Bender.

————. 1991a. *Die Kriegsmarine: Uniforms and Traditions.* Vol. 1. San Jose,
Calif.: R. James Bender.

————. 1996. *Uniforms and Traditions of the Luftwaffe.* Vol. 1. San Jose, Calif.:
R. James Bender.

————. 1997. *Uniforms and Traditions of the Luftwaffe.* Vol. 2. San Jose, Calif.:
R. James Bender.

————. 1998. *Uniforms and Traditions of the Luftwaffe.* Vol. 3. San Jose, Calif.:
R. James Bender.

Axberg, Ole. 1945. Report on Camp Hearne inspection conducted August 4–
5, 1945, RG 389, PMGO, Enemy POW Information Bureau, Reporting
Branch, Subject File, MMRB, NA.

Bachmayer, Hans. 1945. "Open Letter to the Editor." *Der Spiegel,* August 10.

Bailey, Ronald H. 1981. *Prisoners of War.* Alexandria, Va.: Time-Life.

Bender, Roger J., and Richard D. Law. 1973. *Uniforms, Organizations and His-*
tory of the Afrikakorps. San Jose, Calif.: R. James Bender.

Billinger, Robert D., Jr. 2000. *Hitler's Soldiers in the Sunshine State: German*
POWs in Florida. Gainesville: University Press of Florida.

Blanchette, Ida M. 1989. "Axis POWs in Texas." Unpublished document in
author's collection, Texas A&M University, College Station.

Bouchery, Jean. 1998. *From D-Day to VE-Day: The British Soldier.* Vol. 1, *Uni-*
forms, Insignia, Equipments. Paris: Histoire and Collections.

Brayley, Martin, and Richard Ingram. 1998. *The World War II Tommy: British*
Army Uniforms, European Theatre, 1939–45, in Colour Photographs. Ram-
bury, U.K.: Crowood Press.

Bruns, Carl. 1999. POW 8WG41649, Enlisted Man, Afrika Korps (Heer),
Compound 1, Camp Hearne, Texas, August, 1943, to November, 1945.
Correspondence and memoir, October.

Bryan, B. M. 1942a. To Rep. Luther Johnson, March 14, 1942, RG 389,
PMGO, POW Operations Division, Operations Branch, Subject Correspondence File, MMRB, NA.

————. 1942b. To Chief of Engineers, September 26, 1942, RG 389, PMGO,
POW Operations Division, Operations Branch, Subject Correspondence
File, MMRB, NA.

————. 1943. Memorandum to Assistant Chief of Staff, October 25, 1943,
RG 389, PMGO, POW Operations Division, Operations Branch, Classified Decimal File, MMRB, NA.

————. 1944a. Memorandum to Commanding General, Eighth Service

Command, January 19, 1944, RG 389, PMGO, POW Operations Division, Operations Branch, Classified Decimal File, MMRB, NA.

———. 1944b. To Special Division, Department of State, Washington D.C., January 12, 1944, RG 389, PMGO, POW Operations Division, Operations Branch, Classified Decimal File, MMRB, NA.

———. 1945a. Memorandum to Army Service Forces, June 27, 1945, RG 389, PMGO, Records of the Legal Branch, General Correspondence File, MMRB, NA.

Bryan (Texas) Daily Eagle. 1944a. "Prisoner of War Commits Suicide; Gets Under Train." June 29.

———. 1944b. "Three Prisoners of War Flee From George Chance Farm." December 26.

———. 1945. "Unnamed Civilian Captures POW in Bryan on Sunday." December 3.

Burdick, Francis. 1997. Private, 420th Military Police Escort Guard Unit, guard at Camp Hearne. Interview, April.

Burdick, Wanda. 1997. Local resident, married Francis Burdick. Interview, April.

Burroughs, Michael, and Ian Burroughs. 1995. German Identity Discs of World War Two. N.p.

Bussell, Tom. 1997. Private, Military Police Escort Guard Unit, guard at Camp Hearne from ca. summer, 1943, to spring, 1944. Interview, March.

Byrd, Daniel B. 1943. Memorandum to Provost Marshal General, Washington, D.C., dated 24 December 1943, RG 389, PMGO, Enemy POW Information Bureau, Reporting Branch, Subject File, MMRB, NA.

———. 1944a. Memorandum to Provost Marshal General, Washington, D.C., dated 26 April 1944, RG 389, PMGO, Enemy POW Information Bureau, Reporting Branch, Subject File, MMRB, NA.

———. 1944b. Memorandum to Provost Marshal General, Washington, D.C., dated 3 May 1944, RG 389, PMGO, POW Operations Division, Operations Branch, Unclassified Decimal File, MMRB, NA.

Cameron (Texas) Herald. 1944a. "3 German Prisoners Captured Near Bryan." August 17.

———. 1944b. "Many See Flag Dishonored by American Army Officer as he Orders it Down to Please German Musicians at Hearne Prison Camp on July 4th." August 10.

———. 1944c. "German Prisoners at Hearne Camp Cause U.S. Flag to be Removed From Officers Club While Playing Music for Entertainment on July 4th." August 3.

———. 1944d. "'When We Come Home They Won't Need Prison Camps,' Says Cpl. Krenek Writing From France After Flag is Lowered at Hearne to Please Nazi." September 21.

———. 1944e. "Pfc. Alfred Dusek Says Flag Incident Shocked Soldiers Now Fighting." September 21.

Cardinaux, A. L. 1943. Report on Camp Hearne Inspection conducted August 17, 1943, RG 389, PMGO, Enemy POW Information Bureau, Reporting Branch, Subject File, MMRB, NA.

———. 1944. Report on Camp Hearne. Inspection conducted February 17, 1944, RG 389, PMGO, Enemy POW Information Bureau, Reporting Branch, Subject File, MMRB, NA.

Carlson, Lewis H. 1997. *We Were Each Other's Prisoners.* New York: Basic Books.

Carnahan, Hugh L. 1944. Memorandum to Commanding General, Eighth Service Command, March 7, 1944, RG 389, PMGO, POW Operations Division, Operations Branch, Classified Decimal File, MMRB, NA.

Carpenter, Edwin J. 1945. Memorandum to B. M. Bryan, March 10, 1945, RG 389, Records of the Legal Branch, General Correspondence File, MMRB, NA.

Census Data. 1943. Census data for Camp Hearne, Texas, RG 407, PMGO, Military Reference Microfilm, POW Population Lists, National Archives, College Park, Md.

———. 1944. Census data for Camp Hearne, Texas, RG 407, PMGO, Military Reference Microfilm, POW Population Lists, National Archives, College Park, Md.

———. 1945. Census data for Camp Hearne, Texas, RG 407, PMGO, Military Reference Microfilm, POW Population Lists, National Archives, College Park, Md.

Choate, Mark. 1989. *Nazis in the Pineywoods.* Lufkin: Best of East Texas.

Connor, Melissa A., Julie S. Field, and Karin Roberts. 1999. *Archeological Testing of the World War II Prisoner-of-War Camp (5EP1211) at Fort Carson, El Paso, County, Colorado.* Report prepared for Midwest Archeological Center. Lincoln, Nebr.: National Park Service.

Cowley, Betty. 2002. *Stalag Wisconsin: Inside WWII Prisoner-of-War Camp.* Oregon, Wisc: Badger Books.

Coyne, E. J. 1945a. Memorandum to Commanding General, Eighth Service Command, October 5, 1945, RG 389, PMGO, Enemy POW Information Bureau, Reporting Branch, Subject File, MMRB, NA.

———. 1945b. Memorandum to Commanding General, Army Service Forces, Director Prisoner of War Operations Division, Washington, D.C., July 19, 1945, with corrections dated July 26, 1945, RG 389, PMGO, Enemy POW Information Bureau, Reporting Branch, Subject File, MMRB, NA.

Davis, Brian L. 1991. *Uniforms and Insignia of the Luftwaffe.* Vol. 1, 1933–1940. London: Arms and Armour Press.

———. 1992. *German Army Uniforms and Insignia, 1933–1945.* London: Arms and Armour Press.

Dawson, L. T., and D. L. Schwieger. 1944. Report on October 7–11, 1944, inspection of Camp Hearne, Texas, December 20, 1944, RG 389, PMGO, Enemy POW Information Bureau, Reporting Branch, Subject File, MMRB, NA.

De Lagarde, Jean. 1994. *German Soldiers of World War Two.* Paris: Histoire and Collections.

Department of State. 1944. Note to the War Department, January 13, 1944, RG 389, PMGO, POW Operations Division, Operations Branch, Classified Decimal File, MMRB, NA.

————. 1945. To Secretary of War concerning death of POW Hans Lukowski, February 8, 1945, RG 389, PMGO, POW Operations Division, Operations Branch, Unclassified Decimal File, MMRB, NA.

Der Spiegel. 1945a. "Our Camp, Soccer." June 27.

————. 1945b. "Our Camp, Sports, Soccer." September 1.

Dickson, Charles M., W. Wayne Oliver, and Francis I. Boyles. 1946. Board of Review, *U.S. v. Boehmer et al.,* December 19, 1946, *U.S. v German POWs Boehmer et al.* (CM 312330), Court-Martial Records, Archives of the Clerk of Court, U.S. Army Judiciary, Arlington, Va.

Dorsey, Mary. 1996. Brazos Valley resident. Interview, November.

Dorwart, John E. 1944. Standard Operating Procedures for Camp Hearne, Texas, August 10, 1944, RG 389, PMGO, Enemy POW Information Bureau, Reporting Branch, Subject File, Enemy POW Information Bureau, Reporting Branch, Subject File, MMRB, NA.

————. 1945. Memorandum no. 11: Property Permitted to be Retained by Prisoner of War, June 15, 1945, RG 59, General Records of the Department of State, Special War Problems Division, Inspection Reports on POW Camps, 1942–46, MMRB, NA.

Du Bois, Arthur E. 1943. "The Heraldry of Heroism." *National Geographic* 83, no. 6 (June): 409–44.

Dunlop, Robert H. 1944. Memorandum to Commanding Generals of all Nine Service Commands, March 24, 1944, RG 389, PMGO, POW Operations Division, Operations Branch, Classified Decimal File, MMRB, NA.

Dunn, John L. 1944a. Memorandum to the Commanding General, Eighth Service Command, February 16, 1944, RG 389, PMGO, Enemy POW Information Bureau, Reporting Branch, Subject File, MMRB, NA.

————. 1944b. Memorandum to Commanding General, Eighth Service Command, April 21, 1944, RG 389, PMGO, Enemy POW Information Bureau, Reporting Branch, Subject File, MMRB, NA.

————. 1944c. Memorandum to Commanding General, Eighth Service Command, June 21, 1944, RG 389, PMGO, POW Operations Division, Operations Branch, Unclassified Decimal File, MMRB, NA.

————. 1944d. Memorandum to Office of Provost Marshal General, May 2, 1944, RG 389, PMGO, POW Operations Division, Operations Branch, Subject Correspondence File, MMRB, NA.

Dvorovy, John. 1945. Addendum to memorandum by Paul A. Neuland, February 9, 1945, RG 389, PMGO, Internal Security Division, Coordination Branch, Subject File, MMRB, NA.

Edwards, Earl L. 1943a. Memorandum to Commanding General, Eighth Service Command, October 28, 1943, RG 389, PMGO, Enemy POW Information Bureau, Reporting Branch, Subject File, MMRB, NA.

———. 1943b. Memorandum to Commanding General, Eighth Service Command, October 9, 1943, RG 389, PMGO, Enemy POW Information Bureau, Reporting Branch, Subject File, MMRB, NA.

———. 1943c. Memorandum to Commanding General, Eighth Service Command, October 8, 1943, with attached trans. of letter by Hans Hankner, August 21, 1943, RG 389, PMGO, Enemy POW Information Bureau, Reporting Branch, Subject File, MMRB, NA.

———. 1944a. Memorandum to Commanding General, Eighth Service Command, March 21, 1944, RG 389, PMGO, Enemy POW Information Bureau, Reporting Branch, Subject File, MMRB, NA.

———. 1944b. Memorandum to Commanding General, Eighth Service Command, February 25, 1944, RG 389, PMGO, Enemy POW Information Bureau, Reporting Branch, Subject File, MMRB, NA.

———. 1944c. Memorandum to Commanding General, Eighth Service Command, February 26, 1944, RG 389, PMGO, Enemy POW Information Bureau, Reporting Branch, Subject File, MMRB, NA.

———. 1944d. Memorandum to Commanding General, Eighth Service Command, January 4, 1944, RG 389, PMGO, Enemy POW Information Bureau, Reporting Branch, Subject File, MMRB, NA.

———. 1944e. Memorandum to Commanding General, Eighth Service Command, March 1, 1944, RG 389, PMGO, Enemy POW Information Bureau, Reporting Branch, Subject File, MMRB, NA.

Eighth Service Command. 1945. PMG list 101, German Roster PW Camp Hearne, Texas, November 5, 1945, RG 389, PMGO, Enemy POW Information Bureau, Detention Roster, Subject File, MMRB, NA.

Einicke, Arno. 1997. POW 8WG36848, NCO (Unteroffizier), Afrika Korps (Luftwaffe, antiaircraft gunner), Camp Hearne, Texas, August, 1943, to May, 1945. Interview, July.

Elfenbein, Harold L. 1944. Investigation Report of Internal Security Office, Staten Island Terminal, War Department, January 31, 1944, RG 389, PMGO, POW Operations Division, Operations Branch, Classified Decimal File, MMRB, NA.

Emshoff, Dori. 1998. Local resident, visited camp as a child and interacted with the POWs. Interview, February.

Erichsen, Heino R. 1997. POW 81G26500, Enlisted Man, Afrika Korps (Heer, antitank), Compound 1, Camp Hearne, Texas, June, 1943, to February, 1944. Interview, December.

———. 2001. *The Reluctant Warrior: Former German POW Finds Peace in Texas.* Austin, Tex.: Eakin Press.

Fagan, Edgar J. 1946. Memorandum to Commanding General, Eighth Service Command, January 31, 1946, *U.S. v German POWs Boehmer et al.* (CM 312330), Court-Martial Records, Archives of the Clerk of Court, U.S. Army Judiciary, Arlington, Va.

Farrand, Stephen M. 1945. Memorandum to Major Chandler, February 26, 1945, RG 389, PMGO, POW Operations Division, Operations Branch, Classified Decimal File, MMRB, NA.

Feist, Uwe, and Thomas McGuirl. 1996. *Panzertruppe.* Bellingham, Wash.: Ryton.

Fisch, Robert. 1989. *Field Equipment of the Infantry, 1914–1945.* Sykesville, Md.: Greenberg.

Fischer, Rudolph. 1943a. Report on Camp Hearne inspection conducted June 24–25, 1943, Archives of the World Alliance of Young Men's Christian Associations, Geneva, Switzerland.

———. 1943b. Report on September 25–27, 1943, inspection of Camp Hearne, Texas, RG 389, PMGO, Enemy POW Information Bureau, Reporting Branch, Subject File, MMRB, NA.

———. 1944. Report on August 10–11, 1944, inspection of Camp Hearne, Texas, RG 389, PMGO, Enemy POW Information Bureau, Reporting Branch, Subject File, MMRB, NA.

———. 1945. Report on Camp Hearne inspection conducted January 19–20, 1945, RG 389, PMGO, Enemy POW Information Bureau, Reporting Branch, Subject File, MMRB, NA.

Forty, George. 1997. *The Armies of Rommel.* London: Arms and Armour Press.

Fricke, Walter. 1997. POW 8WG12517, NCO (Unteroffizier), Afrika Korps (Luftwaffe, glider pilot), Compound 3, Camp Hearne, Texas, August, 1943, to June, 1945. Interview and correspondence, June.

Froembsdorf, Ernst-Otto. 1997. POW, Afrika Korps (Luftwaffe), Compound 2, Camp Hearne, Texas, June, 1943, to June, 1944. Interview, June.

Garner, John S. 1993. *World War II Temporary Military Buildings.* Technical Report no. CRC-93/01. Champlain, Ill.: U.S. Army Corps of Engineers Research Laboratories.

Geiger, Jeffrey E. 1996. *German Prisoners of War at Camp Cooke, California: Personal Accounts, 1944–1946.* Jefferson, N.C: McFarland.

German Embassy. 1956. Letter to U.S. Department of State, August 17, 1956, *U.S. v German POWs Boehmer et al.* (CM 312330), Court-Martial Records, Archives of the Clerk of Court, U.S. Army Judiciary, Arlington, Va.

Geyser, John "Tex." 1998. Private, 346th Military Police Escort Guard Unit, guard at Camp Hearne from ca. summer, 1943, to 1944. Interview, February.

Glaser, F. R. 1944. Addendum to a note by P. L. Sullivan, April 26, 1944, RG 389, PMGO, POW Operations Division, Operations Branch, Classified Decimal File, MMRB, NA.

Goebeler, Hans. 1998. POW, Enlisted Man, Kriegesmarine (U-boat crewman), Compound 1, Camp Hearne, Texas, summer, 1943. Interview, February.

Goede, Robert. 1997. POW, Enlisted Man, Afrika Korps (Heer), Camp Hearne, Texas, summer, 1943. Interview, March.

Greuter, Emil. 1944. Report on February 4–5, 1944, inspection of Camp Hearne, Texas, RG 389, PMGO, Enemy POW Information Bureau, Reporting Branch, Subject File, MMRB, NA.

Guerre, L. F. 1944. Memorandum to Provost Marshal General, February 17, 1944, RG 389, PMGO, Enemy POW Information Bureau, Reporting Branch, Subject File, MMRB, NA.

Haddock, John N. 1945. Report on investigation of POW shooting at Camp Hearne, Texas, with Exhibits A–H attached, July 18, 1945, RG 389, PMGO, POW Operations Division, Operations Branch, Unclassified Decimal File, MMRB, NA.

Hallaran, W. R. 1943. Death Certificate, McCloskey General Hospital, Temple, Texas, December 23, 1943, *U.S. v German POWs Boehmer et al.* (CM 312330), Court-Martial Records, Archives of the Clerk of Court, U.S. Army Judiciary, Arlington, Va.

Hambuch, Rudolf. 1944. To Albert Sieger, RG 389, PMGO, POW Operations Division, Classified Decimal File, MMRB, NA.

Hanker, Hans. 1943. Translation of letter dated August 21, 1943. RG 389, PMGO, POW Operations Division, Classified Decimal File, MMRB, NA.

Haus, Fritz. 1997. POW 8WG36765, NCO (Unteroffizier), Afrika Korps (Luftwaffe, antiaircraft gunner), Compound 3, Camp Hearne, Texas, October 14, 1943, to May 22, 1945. Unpublished correspondence and memoir. Interview, October.

Hearne (Texas) Democrat. 1942a. "No News of Alien Camp Available." September 11.

———. 1942b. "Business Good in Hearne at Present." November 6.

———. 1942c. "Rooms Available for Newcomers." October 30.

———. 1942d. "Commanding Officer of Camp Arrives." December 4.

———. 1943. "Christmas at Hearne Prisoner of War Camp." December 31.

———. 1944a. "Man at P W Camp is Visited by Brother." May 12.

———. 1944b. "Two Men Taken into Custody: Suspected of Being Escaped German Prisoners." March, 17.

———. 1944c. "Prisoner of War Back in Camp." August 18.

———. 1944d. "'When we Come Home They Won't Need Prison Camps' Says Cpl. Krenet Writing From France After Flag is Lowered at Hearne to Please Nazi." October, 6.

———. 1945a. "Reception Honors Lt. Colonel Rainbolt." January, 19.

———. 1945b. "Notice of Sale-Surplus Government Real Estate." November 23.

———. 1946a. "German Prisoners on Trial for Death at Camp Hearne." January 25.

———. 1946b. "German POWs Get Life for Killing at Hearne." February 1.

———. 1946c. "Equipment of Camp Sold." February 8.

———. 1946d. "City Expects Camp Lease." January 31.

———. 1946e. "Plans Are Near Complete for City to Acquire Camp Site." January 18.

———. 1946f. "A Big Step." March 8.

———. 1946g. "To Obtain Plan for Converting Camp." March 15.

———. 1946h. "Federal Land Bank to Sell Hearne Camp." May 24.

———. 1946i. "Committee is Appointed to Secure Camp." May 10.

———. 1946j. "POW Camp Matters Assume New Status." July 5.

———. 1946k. "The 'Run Around'." July 12.

———. 1946l. "Appraise P.W. Camp for Federal Land Bank." June 14.

———. 1946m. "Hearne Plans to Purchase Part of Camp." September 13.

———. 1946n. "Disposing of Camp Property." November 29.

———. 1947a. "Hearne to Bid on Camp Site and Utilities." January 10.

———. 1947b. "Announce Another Sale at Hearne." February 14.

———. 1947c. "City Awarded 3 Buildings in Camp Sale." February 28.

———. 1947d. "14 Buildings Awarded to Local Schools." March 28.

———. 1947e. "City Awarded POW Camp Site and Utilities." May 2.

———. 1988. "Former WWII Prisoner Visits Site of Hearne POW Camp." June 2.

———. 1993. "Former German Prisoner of War at Hearne POW Camp Visits Democrat Office." September 2.

Henry, Roy H. 1943. To Rep. Luther Johnson, March 13, 1943, RG 389, PMGO, POW Operations Division, Operations Branch, Subject Correspondence File, MMRB, NA.

Henry, Roy. 1998. Local teenager who was friends with camp commander's son and made deliveries to the camp. Interview, February.

Hermann, Peter. 1998. POW 31G203298, Enlisted Man, Waffen SS (panzer artillery), Camp Hearne, Texas, July 26, 1944, to September 17, 1945. Interview and correspondence, April.

Hertwig, Antonius. 1944. Memorandum to Commanding Officer, Camp Fannin, Texas, requesting transfer, July 18, 1944, RG 389, PMGO, POW Operations Division, Operations Division, Subject Correspondence File, MMRB, NA.

Holmes, Don N. 1943. Memorandum to Commanding Officer, Camp Hearne, Texas, December 24, 1943, RG 389, PMGO, POW Operations Division, Operations Branch, Classified Decimal File, MMRB, NA.

Hombeck, Rudolf. 1945. "Secret Weapons." *Der Spiegel,* August 10.

Hoover, Hubert D. 1946. Memorandum to Commanding General, Fourth Army, Fort Sam Houston, Texas, December 27, 1946, *U.S. v German POWs Boehmer et al.* (CM 312330), Court-Martial Records, Archives of the Clerk of Court, U.S. Army Judiciary, Arlington, Va.

Hossann, Werner. 1945. Sworn affidavit on Krauss murder to Summary Court, 1st Lt. Ralph J. Lyle, June 18, 1945, *U.S. v German POWs Boehmer et al.* (CM 312330), Court-Martial Records, Archives of the Clerk of Court, U.S. Army Judiciary, Arlington, Va.

Howard, Francis E. 1944a. To Special War Problems Division, Department of State, August 11, 1944, RG 389, PMGO, POW Operations Division, Operations Branch, Unclassified Decimal File, MMRB, NA.

———. 1944b. To Bernard Gufler, Special War Problems Division, Department of State, August 2, 1944, RG 389, PMGO, POW Operations Division, Operations Branch, Unclassified Decimal File, MMRB, NA.

————. 1944c. To Luther Johnson, September 27, 1944, RG 389, PMGO, POW Operations Division, Operations Division, Subject Correspondence File, MMRB, NA.

Hoza, Steve. 1995. *PW: First-Person Accounts of German Prisoners of War in Arizona.* Phoenix: n.p.

Hughes, Patrick. 1999. Sergeant, 1805th Service Unit, guard at Camp Hearne, Texas, 1943–44. Interview, November.

Inventory, Compound 1, Company 3. 1944. Entertainments and presentations for Company 3, including an inventory of sporting equipment, books, furniture, and musical equipment, RG 389, PMGO, Enemy POW Information Bureau, Reporting Branch, Subject File, MMRB, NA.

Inventory, Compound 2. 1944. Inventory of furniture, books, musical and sporting equipment, and educational courses with their enrollments, RG 389, PMGO, Enemy POW Information Bureau, Reporting Branch, Subject File, MMRB, NA.

Inventory, Compound 3. 1944. Inventory of furniture, books, musical and sporting equipment, and educational courses with their enrollments, RG 389, PMGO, Enemy POW Information Bureau, Reporting Branch, Subject File, MMRB, NA.

Irlenborn, Henry N. 1944. To E. J. Carpenter, March 22, 1944, RG 389, Records of the Legal Branch, General Correspondence File, MMRB, NA.

Jaffe, Sidney. 1943. Extract of Clinical Record of Hans Palmmeire, Station Hospital, Camp Hulen, Texas, December 28, 1943, RG 389, PMGO, POW Operations Division, Operations Branch, Classified Decimal File, MMRB, NA.

Jaschko, Werner. 1945. Unsworn affidavit on Krauss murder to Asst. Judge Advocate Capt. William V. M. Lemens with handwritten note by Captain Lemens, July 12, 1945, *U.S. v German POWs Boehmer et al.* (CM 312330), Court-Martial Records, Archives of the Clerk of Court, U.S. Army Judiciary, Arlington, Va.

Jasper, Alfred. 1997. POW 8WG16929, NCO (Unteroffizier), Afrika Korps (Heer, infantry), Compound 3, Company 10, Camp Hearne, Texas, July 2, 1943, to June 7, 1945. Interview and correspondence, June.

Johns, Kenneth. 1996. Sergeant, 346th Military Police Escort Guard Unit, guard at Camp Hearne from ca. summer, 1943, to spring, 1944. Interview, November.

Johnson, Luther A. 1942. To Brig. Gen. B. M. Bryan, April 6, 1942, RG 389, PMGO, POW Operations Division, Operations Division, Subject Correspondence File, MMRB, NA.

————. 1944. To General Lerch, September 22, 1944, RG 389, PMGO, POW Operations Division, Operations Branch, Subject Correspondence File, MMRB, NA.

Jones, Catesby C. 1943. Memorandum to Brig. Gen. B. M. Bryan, October 21, 1943, RG 389, PMGO, POW Operations Division, Operations Branch, Classified Decimal File, MMRB, NA.

———. 1944. Memorandum to Provost Marshal General, War Department, February 24, 1944, PMGO, Enemy POW Information Bureau, Reporting Branch, Subject File 1942–46, MMRB, NA.

Jowett, Philip S., and Stephen Andrew. 2000. *The Italian Army, 1940–45.* Vol. 1, *Europe, 1940–43.* Men-at-Arms Series, no. 340. Elms Court, UK: Osprey.

———. 2001. *The Italian Army, 1940–45.* Vol. 2, *Africa, 1940–43.* Men-at-Arms Series, no. 349. Elms Court, UK: Osprey.

Karg, Walter. 1945a. "Also an Open Letter." *Der Spiegel,* August 10.

———. 1945b. "From Our Camp." *Der Spiegel,* September 16.

Klughaupt, Martin. 1945. Memorandum to H. N. Kirkman, May 30, 1945, RG 389, Records of the Legal Branch, General Correspondence File, MMRB, NA.

Koch, Walter. 2000. POW, NCO (Unteroffizier), Afrika Korps (Luftwaffe, paratrooper), Compound 2, Company 10, Camp Hearne, Texas, September, 1943, to December, 1945. Correspondence, August.

Koop, Allen V. 1988. *Stark Decency: German Prisoners of War in a New England Village.* Hanover, N.H.: University Press of New England.

Krammer, Arnold. 1977. "When the Afrika Korps Came to Texas." *Southwest Historical Quarterly* 80, no. 3 (January): 247–82.

———. 1983a. "Hitler's Legions in America." *American History Illustrated* 18, no. 4 (July–August): 55–64.

———. 1983b. "Japanese Prisoners of War in America." *Pacific Historical Review* 52 (February): 67–91.

———. 1994. "Members of Vaunted Afrika Korps Made Hearne Home." *Bryan-College Station Eagle,* June 5.

———. 1996. *Nazi Prisoners of War in America.* Lanham, Md.: Scarborough House.

Krauss, Henry. 1943. To Office of Provost Marshal General, Washington, D.C., December 28, 1943, RG 389, PMGO, POW Operations Division, Operations Branch, Classified Decimal File, MMRB, NA.

———. 1944. To Office of Provost Marshal General, Washington, D.C., February 27, 1944, RG 389, PMGO, POW Operations Division, Operations Branch, Classified Decimal File, MMRB, NA.

Krawczyk, Wade. 1996. *German Army Uniforms of World War II in Color Photographs.* Osceola, Wisc.: Motorbooks International.

———. 1999. *Army Panzer Uniforms in Colour Photographs.* Ramburg, UK: Crowood Press.

Kritzler, Werner. 1997. POW 8WG16954, NCO (Unteroffizier), Afrika Korps (Luftwaffe), Compound 2, Company 5, Camp Hearne, Texas, July 2, 1943, to July 3, 1945. Interview and correspondence, June.

Kriv, Arlene R., ed. 1993. *World War II and the U.S. Army Mobilization Program: A History of* 700 and 800 Series Cantonment Construction. Washington, D.C.: U.S. Department of the Interior, National Park Service.

Kruse, Arthur M. 1946. "Custody of Prisoners of War in the United States." *Military Engineer* 38 (February): 70–74.

Kuttruff, Jack. 1998. Guard at Camp Hearne for one month after VE-Day in 1945. Interview, February.

Lakes, A. 1945. Field Service Camp Survey conducted January 19–20, 1945, RG 389, PMGO, POW Special Projects Division, Administrative Branch, Decimal File, MMRB, NA.

Lammersdorf, Hans. 1998. POW, Enlisted Man, Kriegsmarine (coastal artillery), Camp Hearne, Texas, August 15, 1943, to February 22, 1944. Interview, March.

Langford, Thomas B. 1944. Investigation report of attempted escape from Camp Hearne, Texas, by prisoner of war Hans Lukowski, June 21, 1944, RG 389, PMGO, POW Operations Division, Operations Branch, Unclassified Decimal File, MMRB, NA.

Lee, Cyrus. 1992. *Soldat: The World War II German Army Combat Uniform Collector's Handbook, Equipping the German Army Foot Soldier in Europe, 1939–1942.* Vol. 1. Missoula, Mont.: Pictorial Histories.

Leonhardt, Hermann. 2000. POW 8WG44416, NCO (Unteroffizier), Afrika Korps (Heer), Camp Hearne, Texas, October 20, 1943, to May 4, 1945. Correspondence, June.

Lerch, Archer L. 1945. Memorandum to Commanding General, Army Service Forces, March 12, 1945, RG 389, PMGO, POW Operations Division, Operations Branch, Classified Decimal File, MMRB, NA.

Lewis, Kenneth. 1993. *Doughboy to GI: US Army Clothing and Equipment, 1900–1945.* Warley, UK: Norman D. Landing.

Littlejohn, David. 1988. *The Hitler Youth.* Somerset, Ky.: Agincourt.

Lukowski, Hans. 1944. Death certificate of Hans Lukowski, McCloskey General Hospital, Temple, Texas, July 16, 1944, *U.S. v German POWs Boehmer et al.* (CM 312330), Court-Martial Records, Archives of the Clerk of Court, U.S. Army Judiciary, Arlington, Va.

Luparelli, A. John. 1998. 1805th Service Unit, guard at Camp Hearne, Texas, from ca. summer, 1943, to 1944. Interview and correspondence, May.

Mail Dispatch and Strength Report. 1945. Mail dispatch and strength report for Camp Hearne, Texas, June 2, 1945, RG 389, PMGO, Records of the Legal Branch, General Correspondence File, MMRB, NA.

Mason, Ben. 1998. Private, Military Police Escort Guard Unit, guard at Camp Hearne, Texas, from ca. summer, 1943, to summer, 1944. Interview, March.

Mason, E. R. 1998. Local resident who bought buildings after the war. Interview, February.

Massey, O. M. 1946. Memorandum to Provost Marshal General, January 2, 1946, RG 389, PMGO, POW Operations Division, Operations Branch, Classified Decimal File, MMRB, NA.

Mathis, Johnoween. 1996. Local resident and civilian employee at the Camp Hearne administration building. Interview, November.

Matthews, Raymond A. 1944. Memorandum to Commanding General, Eighth Service Command, August 3, 1944, RG 389, PMGO, Operations Division, Operations Branch, Subject Correspondence File, MMRB, NA.

May, Lowell A. 1995. *Camp Concordia: German POWs in the Midwest.* Manhattan, Kans.: Sunflower University Press.

McCarver, Norman L. 1958. *Hearne on the Brazos.* San Antonio: Century Press.

McGuirk, Dale. 1993. *Rommel's Army in Africa.* Shrewsburg, UK: Airlife.

McMinn, Walter P. 1949. Memo routing slip to Chief, PW Office, ATTN: Miss Smith, February 17, 1949, RG 389, PMGO, POW Operations Division, Operations Branch, Classified Decimal File, MMRB, NA.

Meisel, Gunther. 1945. Sworn affidavit on Krauss murder to Asst. Judge Advocate Capt. William V. M. Lemens, October 19, 1945, *U.S. v German POWs Boehmer et al.* (CM 312330), Court-Martial Records, Archives of the Clerk of Court, U.S. Army Judiciary, Arlington, Va.

Metraux, Guy S. 1945. Report on July 17–19, 1945, inspection of Camp Hearne, Texas, RG 59, General Records of the Department of State, Special War Problems Division, Inspection Reports on Prisoner of War Camps, 1942–46, MMRB, NA.

Miley, Porter T. 1944. Memorandum to T. B. Birdsong, April 18, 1944, RG 389, PMGO, POW Operations Division, Operations Branch, Classified Decimal File, MMRB, NA.

Military Intelligence Service. 1943. *German Military Abbreviations.* Special Series no. 12. Washington, D.C.: United States War Department.

Morgan, Jack. 1942. To Tom Connelly, September 5, 1942, RG 389, PMGO, POW Operations Division, Operations Division, Subject Correspondence File, MMRB, NA.

Munson, Edwin. 1998. Private, 1805th Service Unit, guard at Camp Hearne, Texas, from ca. summer, 1943, to 1944. Interview, February.

Nellessen, Willi. 1997. POW, NCO (Unteroffizier), Afrika Korps (Luftwaffe, antiaircraft gunner), Compound 3, Camp Hearne, Texas, July, 1943, to June, 1945. Interview and correspondence, June.

Neuland, Paul. 1945a. Memorandum, Subject: Description of problems reported during January 19–20, 1945, inspection of the German Postal Unit, February 22, 1945, RG 389, PMGO, POW Special Projects Division, Administrative Branch, Decimal File, MMRB, NA.

———. 1945b. Memorandum to Director, POW Special Projects Division, Subject: Field Service Report on Visit to Prisoner of War Camp, Hearne, Texas, January 19–20, 1945, by Capt. Alexander Lakes, February 22, 1945, RG 389, PMGO, POW Special Projects Division, Administrative Branch, Decimal File, MMRB, NA.

———. 1945c. Memorandum to Director, POW Special Projects Division, February 8, 1945, RG 389, PMGO, POW Special Projects Division, Administrative Branch, Decimal File, MMRB, NA.

Nightengale, Bruce A., and Henry B. Moncure. 1996. *Intensive Cultural Resource Survey and Monitoring at the LCRA Camp Swift Regional Wastewater Project, Bastrop County, Texas.* Cultural Resources Report no. 3. N.p.: Lower Colorado River Authority, Texas.

Nigliazzo, John. 1996. Local farmer, Brazos Valley. Interview, November.

O'Brien, John G. 1956. To Secretary of State, October 16, 1956, *U.S. v German POWs Boehmer et al.* (CM 312330), Court-Martial Records, Archives of the Clerk of Court, U.S. Army Judiciary, Arlington, Va.

Office of the Chief of Engineers. 1942. Memorandum on Engineering Features of Proposed Site for 3000-Man Alien Internment Camp at Hearne, Texas, June 9, 1942, RG 389, PMGO, Operations Division, Operations Branch, Correspondence File, MMRB, NA.

Organizational Chart. 1945. Organizational chart for Camp Hearne, Texas, January 11, 1945, RG 389, PMGO, POW Special Projects Division, Administrative Branch, Decimal File, MMRB, NA.

Osmond, J. R. 1944. Memorandum to Security and Intelligence Division, First Service Command, April 14, 1944, RG 389, PMGO, POW Operations Division, Operations Branch, Classified Decimal File, MMRB, NA.

Palmos, Helen. 1996. Owner of the City Cafe, Hearne, Texas. Interview, June.

Payne, Mildred. 1996. Local citizen who lived adjacent to Camp Hearne. Interview, October.

Peabody, P. E. 1945. Report form Captured Personnel and Material Branch, August 10, 1945, RG 389, PMGO, Records of the Legal Branch, Miscellaneous Records, 1942–57, MMRB, NA.

Perret, M. 1945. Report on April 4–5, 1945, inspection of Camp Hearne, Texas, RG 389, PMGO, Enemy POW Information Bureau, Reporting Branch, Subject File, MMRB, NA.

Pferdekämper-Geissel, Fritz. 1997. POW 8WG16929, NCO (Unteroffizier), Afrika Korps (Heer, infantry), Compound 3, Company 11, Camp Hearne, Texas, October 17, 1944, to May 22, 1945. Diary and correspondence. Interview, June.

Pluth, Edward J. 1970. "The Administration and Operation of German Prisoner of War Camps in the United States During World War II." Ph.D. diss. Department of History, Ball State University, Muncie, Ind.

Pohl, Joseph. 1997. POW, NCO (Unteroffizier), Afrika Korps (Heer, assault engineers), Compound 3, Company 12, Camp Hearne, Texas, ca. 1943–44. Interview, June.

Porter, Russell. 1945. "Ex-Yorksville Man Slain as Prisoner." *New York Times,* January 17.

Potts, Jim. 1996. Former director, Agricultural Extension's Emergency War Service. Interview, November.

Powell, Allan K. 1989. *Splinters of a Nation: German Prisoners of War in Utah.* Salt Lake City: University of Utah.

Priestly, H. B. 1946. Appraisal of buildings and installation at Hearne POW camp, September 5, 1946, Farm Credit Administration, Real Property Disposal Case Files, Hearne POW Camp, National Archives, Southwest Region, Fort Worth, Tex. (Hereafter NA-SWR.)

Proceedings of a General Court-Martial. 1946. *U.S. v German POWs Boehmer et al.* (CM 312330), Court-Martial Records, Archives of the Clerk of the Court, U.S. Army Judiciary, Arlington, Va.

Prosecution Closing Arguments. 1946. Closing Arguments, *U.S. v Boehmer et al.* (Krauss Murder Trial), January 22–30, 1946, *U.S. v German POWs Boehmer et al.* (CM 312330), Court-Martial Records, Archives of the Clerk of Court, U.S. Army Judiciary, Arlington, Va.

Pruett, Michael H., and Edward, Robert J. 1993. *Field Uniforms of German Army Panzer Forces in World War II.* Winnipeg: J. J. Fedovowicz.

Rapp, Walter H. 1945. Memorandum to Commanding Officer, Prisoner of War Camp, Hearne, Texas, Report of Field Service Visit, September 13, 1945, RG 389, PMGO, Special Projects Division, Administrative Branch, Decimal File, MMRB, NA.

Record of Mail Received. 1945. Record of mail received at the German Postal Unit, Camp Hearne, Texas, July 31, 1945, RG 389, PMGO, Records of the Legal Branch, Miscellaneous Records, 1942–57, MMRB, NA.

Reinhold, Paul. 1998. Private, 346th Military Police Escort Guard Unit, guard at Camp Hearne in 1944. Interview, February.

Rentz, Bill. 1999. *Geronimo! U.S. Airborne Uniform, Insignia, and Equipment in World War II.* Atglen, Pa.: Schiffer.

Richardson, Harold H. 1944. Memorandum to Provost Marshal General, August 11, 1944, RG 389, PMGO, POW Operations Division, Operations Branch, Unclassified Decimal File, MMRB, NA.

Richter, Berthold. 1944. Trans. of note surreptitiously inserted in letter for Heinz Lebender, RG 389, PMGO, POW Operations Division, Operations Branch, Classified Decimal File, MMRB, NA.

Roamer, J. M. 1944. Memorandum with extracts of intelligence report, March 17, 1944, RG 389, PMGO, POW Operations Division, Operations Branch, Classified Decimal File, MMRB, NA.

Robins, Thomas M. 1942. Memorandum to Provost Marshal General on proposed site for 3,000-man alien internment camp at Hearne, Texas, June 9, 1942, RG 389, PMGO, Operations Division, Operations Branch, Correspondence File, MMRB, NA.

Rogers, Clarence B. 1944. Investigation of Attempted Escape of Prisoner of War Hans Lukowski, June 21, 1944, RG 389, PMGO, POW Operations Division, Operations Branch, Unclassified Decimal File, MMRB, NA.

Rogers, Horatio R. 1944a. To Special War Problems Division, Department of State, March 10, 1944, RG 389, PMGO, POW Operations Division, Operations Branch, Classified Decimal File, MMRB, NA.

———. 1944b. Memorandum to Commanding General, Seventh Service Command, March 28, 1944, RG 389, PMGO, POW Operations Division, Operations Branch, Classified Decimal File, MMRB, NA.

———. 1944c. To Mr. Henry Krauss, New York, March 6, 1944, RG 389, PMGO, POW Operations Division, Operations Branch, Classified Decimal File, MMRB, NA.

Rottman, Gordon, and Ron Volstad. 1995. *German Combat Equipment, 1939–45.* Men-at-Arms Series no. 234. Elms Court, UK: Osprey.

Ryan, Tommy. 1998. Local citizen who as a child lived close to Camp Hearne, Texas. Interview, December.

Schiller, Hans. 1945. Sworn Affidavit on Krauss murder to Asst. Judge Advocate Capt. William V. M. Lemens, November 10, 1945, *U.S. v German POWs Boehmer et al.* (CM 312330), Court-Martial Records, Archives of the Clerk of Court, U.S. Army Judiciary, Arlington, Va.

Schulz, Otto. 2001. POW, NCO (Unteroffizier), Afrika Korps (Luftwaffe, flak), Compound 3, Camp Hearne, Texas, October, 1943, to October, 1945. Correspondence, January.

Schwieger, D. L., and E. C. Shannahan. 1945. Memorandum to Col. Clifford S. Urwiller, chief, Labor and Liaison Branch, POW Division, PMGO, March 8, 1945, RG 389, PMGO, Enemy POW Information Bureau, Reporting Branch, Subject File, MMRB, NA.

Scipion, Jacques, and Yves Bastien. 1996. *Afrikakorps: Tropical Uniforms of the German Army, 1940–1945.* Paris: Histoire and Collections.

Secretary of the Army. 1948. Note on Gunther Meisel, April 27, 1948, *U.S. v German POWs Boehmer et al.* (CM 312330), Court-Martial Records, Archives of the Clerk of Court, U.S. Army Judiciary, Arlington, Va.

Shaw, Halbert C. 1943. Memorandum to Commanding General, Eighth Service Command, December 23, 1943, RG 389, PMGO, Enemy POW Information Bureau, Reporting Branch, Subject File, MMRB, NA.

———. 1944. Standard Operating Procedure for Prisoner of War Companies, March 1, 1944, RG 389, PMGO, Enemy POW Information Bureau, Reporting Branch, Subject File, MMRB, NA.

Shirck, E. D., and Adriel Moore. 1946. Report of field investigation to Camp Hearne on the possibility of using surplus property for local community, March, 1946, Farm Credit Administration, Real Property Disposal Case Files, Hearne POW Camp, NA-SWR.

Shugars, John. 1998. Private, 346th Military Police Escort Guard Unit, guard at Camp Hearne, Texas, from ca. summer, 1943, to summer, 1944. Interview, March.

Simmons, Dean B. 2000. *Swords into Plowshares: Minnesota's POW Camps during World War II.* St. Paul: Cathedral Hill Books.

Smith, Howard W. 1944a. Memorandum to the Commanding General, Eighth Service Command, dated 29 December 1944, RG 389, PMGO, Enemy POW Information Bureau, Reporting Branch, Subject File, MMRB, NA.

———. 1944b. Memorandum to Commanding General, Eighth Service Command, November 20, 1944, RG 389, PMGO, Enemy POW Information Bureau, Reporting Branch, Subject File, MMRB, NA.

———. 1944c. Memorandum to Commanding Officer, German Postal Unit, Prisoner of War Camp, Hearne, Texas, August 28, 1944, RG 389, PMGO,

Enemy POW Information Bureau, Reporting Branch, Subject File, MMRB, NA.

———. 1944d. Memorandum to Commanding General, Eighth Service Command, August 9, 1944, RG 389, PMGO, POW Operations Division, Operations Branch, Subject Correspondence File, MMRB, NA.

———. 1945a. Memorandum to Commanding General, Eighth Service Command, January 4, 1945, RG 389, PMGO, Enemy POW Information Bureau, Reporting Branch, Subject File, MMRB, NA.

———. 1945b. Memorandum to Provost Marshal General, February 8, 1945, RG 389, PMGO, POW Operations Division, Operations Branch, Unclassified Decimal File, MMRB, NA.

Snyder, Louis. 1976. *Encyclopedia of the Third Reich*. New York: Paragon House.

Spix, Erich. 1999. POW 8WG17086, Enlisted Man, Afrika Korps (Luftwaffe, flak), Compound 2, Company 5, Camp Hearne, Texas, July 1, 1943, to January 29, 1944. Interview and correspondence, November.

Spoden, Peter. 1997. POW 8WG51097, Enlisted Man, Afrika Korps (Luftwaffe, paratrooper), Compound 1, Camp Hearne, Texas, August 26, 1943, to December 13, 1945. Interview, June.

Stegall, Jim. 1998. Local citizen who as a teenager lived in Franklin, Tex. Interview, December.

Stiles, Cecil E. 1943a. Memorandum to Commanding Officer, Prisoner of War Camp, Hearne, Texas, December 22, 1943, RG 389, PMGO, Enemy POW Information Bureau, Reporting Branch, Subject File, MMRB, NA.

———. 1943b. Memorandum to Commanding Officer, Prisoner of War Camp, Hearne, Texas, December 20, 1943, RG 389, PMGO, POW Operations Division, Operations Branch, Classified Decimal File, MMRB, NA.

———. 1944a. Memorandum to Commanding General, Eighth Service Command, December 18, 1944, RG 389, PMGO, Enemy POW Information Bureau, Reporting Branch, Subject File, MMRB, NA.

———. 1944b. Memorandum to Commanding Officer, Prisoner of War Camp, Hearne, Texas, February 14, 1944, RG 389, PMGO, Enemy POW Information Bureau, Reporting Branch, Subject File, MMRB, NA.

———. 1944c. Memorandum to Commanding Officer, Prisoner of War Camp, Hearne, Texas, January 19, 1944, RG 389, PMGO, POW Operations Division, Operations Branch, Classified Decimal File, MMRB, NA.

———. 1944d. Report of Investigation into the death of POW Hans Lukowski, July 25, 1944, RG 389, PMGO, POW Operations Division, Operations Branch, Unclassified Decimal File, MMRB, NA.

———. 1944e. Memorandum to Commanding General, Eighth Service Command, July 17, 1944, RG 389, PMGO, POW Operations Division, Operations Branch, Unclassified Decimal File, MMRB, NA.

———. 1944f. Prisoner of War escape report, August 11, 1944, RG 389, PMGO, POW Operations Division, Operations Branch, Unclassified Decimal File, MMRB, NA.

————. 1944g. Memorandum to Commanding General, Eighth Service Command, September 20, 1944, RG 389, PMGO, Enemy POW Information Bureau, Reporting Branch, Subject File, MMRB, NA.

Sullivan, Bobby. 1996. Private, 420th Military Police Escort Guard Unit, guard at Camp Hearne, Texas, from ca. summer, 1943, to January, 1944. Interview, November.

Summers, I. B. 1943a. Memorandum to Commanding General, Eighth Service Command, July 6, 1943, RG 389, PMGO, Enemy POW Information Bureau, Reporting Branch, Subject File, MMRB, NA.

————. 1943b. Memorandum to Director, Prisoner of War Information Bureau, December 11, 1943, RG 389, PMGO, Enemy POW Information Bureau, Reporting Branch, Subject File, MMRB, NA.

————. 1944. To Henry Krauss, New York, January 3, 1944, RG 389, PMGO, POW Operations Division, Operations Branch, Classified Decimal File, MMRB, NA.

Sweat, Annie. 1998. Local resident and civilian employee at Camp Hearne, Texas. Interview, May.

Swiss Legation. 1943. Memorandum to Department of State, December 29, 1943, RG 389, PMGO, POW Operations Division, Operations Branch, Classified Decimal File, MMRB, NA.

————. 1945. Memorandum to Department of State, January 2, 1945, RG 389, PMGO, POW Operations Division, Operations Branch, Unclassified Decimal File, MMRB, NA.

Szilagyi, N. 1944. Memorandum to Provost Marshal General, December 23, 1944, RG 389, PMGO, Internal Security Division, Coordinating Branch, Subject File, MMRB, NA.

Thompson, Glenn. 1993. *Prisoners on the Plains: German POWs in America.* Holdrege, Nebr.: Phelps County Historical Society.

Tissing, Robert W. 1976. "Stalag-Texas 1943–1945." *Military History of Texas and the Southwest* 13, no. 1 (fall): 24–34.

Tollefson, A. M. 1944a. Memorandum to Special Division, Department of State, January 19, 1944, RG 389, PMGO, POW Operations Division, Operations Branch, Classified Decimal File, MMRB, NA.

————. 1945a. To Special War Problems Division, Department of State, February 15, 1945, RG 389, PMGO, POW Operations Division, Operations Branch, Unclassified Decimal File, MMRB, NA.

————. 1945b. Memorandum to Commanding General, Eighth Service Command, July 30, 1945, *U.S. v German POWs Boehmer et al.* (CM 312330), Court-Martial Records, Archives of the Clerk of Court, U.S. Army Judiciary, Arlington, Va.

————. 1945c. Memorandum, Subject: Transfer of Japanese Prisoners of War, August 8, 1945, RG 389, PMGO, Enemy POW Information Bureau, Reporting Branch, Subject File, MMRB, NA.

————. 1946. Memo to Special Projects Division, Department of State, April 4,

1946, RG 389, PMGO, POW Operations Division, Operations Branch, Classified Decimal File, MMRB, NA.

Traue, Rudi. 1944. To Commanding Officer, Prisoner of War Camp, Hearne, Texas, September 14, 1944, RG 389, PMGO, Enemy POW Information Bureau, Reporting Branch, Subject File, MMRB, NA.

Trye, Rex. 1995. *Mussolini's Soldiers.* Shrewsbury, UK: Airlife.

Tulatz, Herbert A. 1944. Memorandum to Lt. Kubertanz, April 10, 1944, RG 389, PMGO, POW Operations Division, Operations Branch, Classified Decimal File, MMRB, NA.

Turner, Harmon M.1944. Standard Operating Procedure, German Postal Unit, October 10, 1944, RG 389, PMGO, Enemy POW Information Bureau, Reporting Branch, Subject File, MMRB, NA.

———. 1945. Standard Operating Procedure, German Postal Unit, May 26, 1945, RG 389, Records of the Legal Branch, General Correspondence File, MMRB, NA.

Tyler, Harry W. 1944. Memorandum to Provost Marshal General, Army Services Forces, February 7, 1944, RG 389, PMGO, POW Operations Division, Operations Branch, Classified Decimal File, MMRB, NA.

Ulio, J. A. 1943. Outgoing message to Commanding Officer, Eighth Service Command, December 10, 1943, RG 389, PMGO, Enemy POW Information Bureau, Reporting Branch, Subject File, MMRB, NA.

———. 1945. Memorandum to Commanding General, Army Service Forces, February 12, 1945, RG 389, PMGO, POW Operations Division, Operations Branch, Classified Decimal File, MMRB, NA.

U.S. Engineers Office. 1943. Alien Internment Camp Hearne, Texas, Building Layout Post Numbering System, December, 1943, RG 270, War Assets Administration, and RG 77, Chief Engineers Office, Real Property Disposal Case Files, Hearne POW Camp, NA-SWR.

Urwiller, Clifford S. 1945. Memorandum, Subject: Transfer of Japanese Prisoners of War, September 5, 1945. RG 389, PMGO, Enemy POW Information Bureau, Reporting Branch, Subject File, MMRB, NA.

Venable, Marvin C. 1944. Memorandum to Commanding Officer, Prisoner of War Camp, Hearne, Texas, February 15, 1945, RG 389, PMGO, Enemy POW Information Bureau, Reporting Branch, Subject File, MMRB, NA.

Von der Heydt, Erich. 1945. Sworn Affidavit on Krauss murder to Asst. Judge Advocate Capt. William V. M. Lemens, November 10, 1945, *U.S. v German POWs Boehmer et al.* (CM 312330), Court-Martial Records, Archives of the Clerk of Court, U.S. Army Judiciary, Arlington, Va.

Wainright, J. M. 1947. Note on *U.S. v Boehmer et al.,* January 8, 1947, *U.S. v German POWs Boehmer et al.* (CM 312330), Court-Martial Records, Archives of the Clerk of Court, U.S. Army Judiciary, Arlington, Va.

Walker, Richard P. 1980. "Prisoners of War in Texas During World War II." Ph.D. diss. Department of History, North Texas State University, Denton.

———. 1989. "The Swastika and the Lone Star: Nazi Activity in Texas POW Camps." *Military History of the Southwest* 19, no. 1 (Spring): 39–70.

———. 2001. *The Lone Star and the Swastika: Prisoners of War in Texas.* Austin, Tex.: Eakin Press.

Walker, Walton H. 1946. Note on *U.S. v Boehmer et al.,* March 25, 1946, *U.S. v German POWs Boehmer et al.* (CM 312330), Court-Martial Records, Archives of the Clerk of Court, U.S. Army Judiciary, Arlington, Va.

Wannemacher, Hugo. 1997. POW ISN346339MI, NCO (Unteroffizier), Afrika Korps (Heer, infantry), Compound 2, Camp Hearne, Texas, January 31, 1944, to June 24, 1945. Interview, June.

War Department. 1944a. Prisoner of War Camp Labor Report: PW Camp Hearne, Texas. RG 389, PMGO, Enemy POW Information Bureau, Reporting Branch, Subject File, MMRB, NA.

———. 1944b. *War Department Technical Manual: Enemy Prisoners of War.* TM 19-500. Washington, D.C.: GPO, October 5, 1944.

———. 1944c. *What About the German Prisoner?* Confidential War Department Pamphlet no. 19-1. Washington, D.C.: GPO, November 20, 1944.

———. 1945. Prisoner of War Camp Labor Report: PW Camp Hearne, Texas. RG 389, PMGO, Enemy POW Information Bureau, Reporting Branch, Subject File, MMRB, NA.

Ware, Matt. 1997. Private, 420th Military Police Escort Guard Unit, guard at Camp Hearne, Texas, from ca. summer, 1943, to summer, 1944. Interview, April.

Weiss, Max. 1945a. Canteen Price List, July 18, 1945, RG 59, General Records of the Department of State, Special War Problems Division, Inspection Reports on Prisoner of War Camps, 1942–46, MMRB, NA.

———. 1945b. To Swiss Legation, April 19, 1945, RG 59, General Records of the Department of State, Special War Problems Division, Inspection Reports on Prisoner of War Camps, 1942–46, MMRB, NA.

———. 1945c. "The Collection in Our Camp." *Der Spiegel,* November 4.

———. 1945d. "Once More the National Insignia." *Der Spiegel,* November 4.

Weller, Morris, and Thomas K. McElroy. 1946. Review of Krauss Murder Trial, March 14, 1946, *U.S. v German POWs Boehmer et al.* (CM 312330), Court-Martial Records, Archives of the Clerk of Court, U.S. Army Judiciary, Arlington, Va.

Weller, Robert. 1945. Trans. of memorandum to Commanding Officer, Prisoner of War Camp, Hearne, Texas, August 10, 1945, RG 389, PMGO, Enemy POW Information Bureau, Reporting Branch, Subject File, MMRB, NA.

Werner, Walter. 2000. POW 81G45402, NCO (Unteroffizier), Afrika Korps (Heer, infantry), Compound 2, Company 6, Camp Hearne, Texas, June 8, 1944, to December, 1945. Unpublished memoir and correspondence, January.

Whitson, Robert K. 1943. Memorandum to Commanding General, Eighth

Service Command, October 19, 1943, RG 389, PMGO, Enemy POW Information Bureau, Reporting Branch, Subject File, MMRB, NA.

Williamson, Gordon, and Ron Volstad. 1991. *Afrikakorps, 1941–43.* Osprey Military Elite Series no. 34. London: Reed International Books.

Witsell, Edward F. 1947a. To Warden, U.S. Penitentiary, Leavenworth, Kansas, May 6, 1947, *U.S. v German POWs Boehmer et al.* (CM 312330), Court-Martial Records, Archives of the Clerk of Court, U.S. Army Judiciary, Arlington, Va.

———. 1947b. To Warden, U.S. Penitentiary, Leavenworth, Kansas, May 7, 1947, *U.S. v German POWs Boehmer et al.* (CM 312330), Court-Martial Records, Archives of the Clerk of Court, U.S. Army Judiciary, Arlington, Va.

———. 1947c. To Warden, U.S. Penitentiary, Leavenworth, Kansas, May 7, 1947, *U.S. v German POWs Boehmer et al.* (CM 312330), Court-Martial Records, Archives of the Clerk of Court, U.S. Army Judiciary, Arlington, Va.

———. 1947d. To Warden, U.S. Penitentiary, Leavenworth, Kansas, May 8, 1947, *U.S. v German POWs Boehmer et al.* (CM 312330), Court-Martial Records, Archives of the Clerk of Court, U.S. Army Judiciary, Arlington, Va.

———. 1947e. To Warden, U.S. Penitentiary, Leavenworth, Kansas, May 12, 1947, *U.S. v German POWs Boehmer et al.* (CM 312330), Court-Martial Records, Archives of the Clerk of Court, U.S. Army Judiciary, Arlington, Va.

———. 1948a. To Warden, U.S. Penitentiary, Leavenworth, Kansas, April 22, 1948, *U.S. v German POWs Boehmer et al.* (CM 312330), Court-Martial Records, Archives of the Clerk of Court, U.S. Army Judiciary, Arlington, Va.

———. 1948b. To Warden, U.S. Penitentiary, Leavenworth, Kansas, April 22, 1948, *U.S. v German POWs Boehmer et al.* (CM 312330), Court-Martial Records, Archives of the Clerk of Court, U.S. Army Judiciary, Arlington, Va.

———. 1948c. To Warden, U.S. Penitentiary, Leavenworth, Kansas, April 22, 1948, *U.S. v German POWs Boehmer et al.* (CM 312330), Court-Martial Records, Archives of the Clerk of Court, U.S. Army Judiciary, Arlington, Va.

———. 1948d. To Warden, U.S. Penitentiary, Leavenworth, Kansas, April 23, 1948, *U.S. v German POWs Boehmer et al.* (CM 312330), Court-Martial Records, Archives of the Clerk of Court, U.S. Army Judiciary, Arlington, Va.

———. 1949a. To Warden, U.S. Penitentiary, Leavenworth, Kansas, May 24, 1949, *U.S. v German POWs Boehmer et al.* (CM 312330), Court-Martial Records, Archives of the Clerk of Court, U.S. Army Judiciary, Arlington, Va.

———. 1949b. To Warden, U.S. Penitentiary, Leavenworth, Kansas, May 24,

1949, *U.S. v German POWs Boehmer et al.* (CM 312330), Court-Martial
Records, Archives of the Clerk of Court, U.S. Army Judiciary, Arlington, Va.

———. 1949c. To Warden, U.S. Penitentiary, Leavenworth, Kansas, May 24,
1949, *U.S. v German POWs Boehmer et al.* (CM 312330), Court-Martial
Records, Archives of the Clerk of Court, U.S. Army Judiciary, Arlington, Va.

———. 1949d. To Warden, U.S. Penitentiary, Leavenworth, Kansas, May 24,
1949, *U.S. v German POWs Boehmer et al.* (CM 312330), Court-Martial
Records, Archives of the Clerk of Court, U.S. Army Judiciary, Arlington, Va.

———. 1949e. To Warden, U.S. Penitentiary, Leavenworth, Kansas, May 27,
1949, *U.S. v German POWs Boehmer et al.* (CM 312330), Court-Martial
Records, Archives of the Clerk of Court, U.S. Army Judiciary, Arlington, Va.

Woods, William J. 1943a. Memorandum to Commanding General, Second
Service Command, June 6, 1943, RG 389, PMGO, Enemy POW Information Bureau, Reporting Branch, Subject File, MMRB, NA.

———. 1943b. Prisoner of War document with attached list of names, May
31, 1943, RG 389, PMGO, Enemy POW Information Bureau, Reporting
Branch, Subject File, MMRB, NA.

Zaetsch, Theodore N. 1945a. Memorandum to Commanding General,
Eighth Service Command, September 1, 1945, RG 389, PMGO, Enemy
POW Information Bureau, Reporting Branch, Subject File, MMRB, NA.

———. 1945b. Memorandum to Commanding General, Eighth Service
Command, with attached roster of POWs, October 4, 1945, RG 389,
PMGO, Enemy POW Information Bureau, Reporting Branch, Subject
File, MMRB, NA.

Zoch, Glenn. 1998. Son of Chaplain Gustave Zoch, interacted with POWs at
Camp Hearne, Texas. Interview, May.

Zoch, Gustave A. 1946. "A Chaplain's Work in a Prisoner of War Camp."
Unpublished MS in author's collection, Texas A&M University, College
Station.

Index

Photos and illustrations are indicated with *italic* type.

ISBN 1-58544-318-2